A HISTORICAL COMMENTARY ON
TACITUS' *HISTORIES* I AND II

A HISTORICAL COMMENTARY ON TACITUS' *HISTORIES* I AND II

BY

G.E.F. CHILVER

CLARENDON PRESS · OXFORD

1979

Oxford University Press, Walton Street, Oxford OX2 6DP

OXFORD LONDON GLASGOW

NEW YORK TORONTO MELBOURNE WELLINGTON

KUALA LUMPUR SINGAPORE JAKARTA HONG KONG TOKYO

DELHI BOMBAY CALCUTTA MADRAS KARACHI

NAIROBI DAR ES SALAAM CAPE TOWN

British Libraries Cataloguing Data

Chilver, G. E. F.
  A historical commentary on Tacitus' 'Histories'
  I and II.
    1. Tacitus, Cornelius. Historiae. I–II
    2. Rome—Politics and government—30 B.C.–284 A.D.
  I. Title
  937'.07   DG286   79-40593

ISBN 0-19-814830-5

Typeset by CCC and printed and bound at William Clowes & Sons Limited
Beccles and London

CONTENTS

MAPS

BIBLIOGRAPHY OF SHORT TITLES

(To the great bibliography of work on Tacitus provided by Syme in 1958 H. W. Benario has added three valuable articles in *Classical Weekly*, 1964, 1970, and 1977. My list below does not include citations from ancient authors, which I have given in recognized form.)

(A) EDITIONS AND COMMENTARIES

Fisher	C. D. Fisher, Tacitus' *Historiae* (Oxford, 1911).
H.	W. Heraeus, *Tacitus, Die Historien* i⁶ (Leipzig and Berlin, 1929). based on the edition by his father, C. Heraeus (Leipzig, 1864).
G.	C. Giarratano (Rome, 1939). Text only.
Heubner	H. Heubner, *Tacitus, Die Historien*, Band i. (Heidelberg, 1963), ii (1968), iii (1972), iv (1976). Commentary only.
K.	E. Koestermann (Teubner, 7th edn., 1950, with further revision 1961). Text only.
Sp.	W. A. Spooner (Macmillan, London, 1891), the last complete commentary in English, other than school editions.
Till	R. Till (Heidelberg, 1963). Text only.
V.	L. Valmaggi, *Il libro Primo delle Storie* (Turin, 1891), *Secondo* (1897), *Terzo* (1906).
Wolff	E. Wolff and G. Andresen (Berlin, 1926). Commentary only.

To which add two valuable English 'school' editions:

Alford	M. Alford (London, 1912). Book I only.
Irvine	A. L. Irvine (London, 1952).

(B) TRANSLATIONS

CB	A. J. Church and W. J. Brodribb² (London, 1882).

Fyfe   W. H. Fyfe (Oxford, 1912).
Goelzer   H. Goelzer (Budé, Paris, 1946–9), into French.
Ramsay   G. G. Ramsay (London, 1915).
Wellesley   K. Wellesley (Penguin Books, London, 1964).

(C) PERIODICALS AND OTHER WORKS

AE   *L'Année épigraphique.*
AFA   *Acta Fratrum Arvalium* (all relevant texts in EJ,
                    Sm. 1 and 2, and MW—see below).
Ant. Journ.   *Antiquaries Journal.*
AJP   *American Journal of Philology.*
Barbagallo   C. Barbagallo, 'Il Governo di Galba', *Atti di
                    Accademia archeologica di lettere e belle arti di
                    Napoli*, 1915, 1 ff.
Boissier   G. Boissier, *Tacite* (Paris, 1903).
Braithwaite   A. W. Braithwaite, ed. to Suetonius' *Divus
                    Vespasianus* (Oxford, 1927).
Briessmann   A. Briessmann, 'Tacitus und das flavische
                    Geschichtsbild', *Hermes,* Einzelschr. 10
                    (1955).
Bull. arch. com.   *Bullettino della commissione archeologica comunale di
                    Roma.*
Bursian   *Bursians Jahresberichte.*
CAH   *Cambridge Ancient History* (vol. x, 1934, xi, 1936).
CGL   *Corpus Glossariorum Latinorum.*
CIL   *Corpus Inscriptionum Latinarum.*
Cisalpine Gaul   G. E. F. Chilver, *Cisalpine Gaul* (Oxford, 1941).
Courbaud   E. Courbaud, *Les Procédés d'art de Tacite dans les
                    Histoires* (Paris, 1918).
CP   *Classical Philology.*
CQ   *Classical Quarterly.*
CR   *Classical Review.*
CRAI   *Comptes rendus de l'Académie des Inscriptions.*
Degrassi   A. Degrassi, *I fasti consolari dell'impero romano*
                    (Rome, 1952).
Dom.-Dob.   A. von Domaszewski, *Die Rangornung des röm-
                    ischen Heeres,* edited by B. Dobson (Cologne
                    and Graz, 1967).

Domaszewski, *Fahnen* A. von Domaszewski, *Die Fahnen in römischen Heere* (Vienna, 1885).

Drexler H. Drexler, 'Zum Geschichte Kaiser Othos bei Tacitus und Plutarch', *Klio*, 1959, 153 ff.

Durry M. Durry, *Les cohortes prétoriennes* (Paris, 1938).

EJ V. Ehrenberg and A. H. M. Jones, *Documents illustrating the reigns of Augustus and Tiberius*[2] (Cambridge, 1955).

ESAR *An Economic Survey of the Roman Empire*, ed. T. Frank (Baltimore, 1932–40).

Fabia Ph. Fabia, *Les Sources de Tacite* (Paris, 1893).

Forni G. Forni, *Il reclutamento delle legioni da Augusto a Diocleziano* (Milan and Rome, 1953).

Fuhrmann M. Fuhrmann, 'Das Vierkaiserjahr bei Tacitus', *Philologus*, 1960, 250 ff.

GG A. Gerber, A. Greef, C. John, *Lexicon Taciteum* (Berlin, 1903).

Gerstenecker J. Gerstenecker, *Der Krieg des Otho und Vitellius in Italien im Jahre 69* (Munich, 1882).

Groag E. Groag, 'Zur Kritik von Tacitus' Quellen in den Historien', *Jahrb. class. phil.*, Supp. Band xxiii (1897), 761 ff.

Hammond, *AM* M. Hammond, *The Antonine Monarchy* (Rome, 1959).

Hanslik R. Hanslik, 'Die Auseinandersetzung zwischen Otho und Vitellius bis zur Schlacht von Bedriacum nach Tacitus', *Wiener Stud.* 1961, 113 ff.

Hardy E. G. Hardy, 'Tacitus as a military historian in the Histories', *Journ. Phil.* 1910, 123 ff.

Henderson B. W. Henderson, *Civil War and Rebellion in the Roman Empire* (London, 1908).

HRR H. Peter, *Historicorum Romanorum reliquiae.*

IG *Inscriptiones Graecae.*

IGRR *Inscriptiones Graecae ad res Romanas pertinentes* (Paris, 1914–27).

IRT J. M. Reynolds and J. B. Ward-Perkins, *Inscriptions of Roman Tripolitania* (Rome, 1952).

ILS H. Dessau, *Inscriptiones Latinae Selectae* (Berlin, 1882–1916).

Klingner	F. Klingner, 'Die Geschichte Kaiser Othos bei Tacitus', *Sächsische Sitzungsberichte, phil. hist. klass.* 1940, Heft I.
Kraft	K. Kraft, *Zu Rekrutierung der Alen und Kohorten an Rhein und Donau* (Bern, 1951).
K.–St.	R. Kühner and C. Stegmann, *Ausführliche Grammatik der lateinischen Sprache*[2] (Hanover, 1966).
LS	C. T. Lewis and C. Short, *A Latin Dictionary*, revised edn. (Oxford, 1922).
MAAR	*Memoirs of the American Academy in Rome.*
Miller, *It. Rom.*	K. Miller, *Itineraria Romana* (Stuttgart, 1916).
Momigliano	A. Momigliano, 'Vitellio', *Studi italiani di filologia classica*, 1931–2, 117 ff.
MW	M. McCrum and A. G. Woodhead, *Documents of the Flavian Emperors* (C.U.P., 1961).
Mus. Helv.	*Museum Helveticum.*
Nissen	H. Nissen, 'Die Historien des Plinius', *Rheinisches Museum*, 1871, 497 ff.
NS	*Notizie degli scavi.*
Num. Chron.	*Numismatic Chronicle.*
Paratore	E. Paratore, *Tacito*[2] (Rome, 1962).
Passerini	A. Passerini, 'Le due battaglie presso Bedriacum', *Studi di antichità classica offerti . . . a Emanuele Ciaceri* (Genoa, Rome, and Naples, 1940), 178 ff.
Passerini, *coorti*	A. Passerini, *Le coorti pretorie* (Rome, 1939).
Pflaum	H. G. Pflaum, *Les Procurateurs équestres sous le haut-empire romain* (Paris, 1950).
PIR	*Prosopographia Imperii Romani*: 1st edn. by E. Klebs and H. Dessau (Berlin, 1897–8); 2nd edn. by E. Groag and A. Stein (Berlin, 1933–), now continued to letter L by L. Petersen (1970).
Platner–Ashby	S. B. Platner and T. Ashby, *A Topographical Dictionary of Ancient Rome* (Oxford, 1929).
RE	Pauly–Wissowa–Kroll, *Realencyclopaedie des klassischen Altertumswissenschaft.*
RÉA	*Revue des études anciennes.*
RÉL	*Revue des études latines.*

Rev. phil.	*Revue de philologie.*
RhM	*Rheinisches Museum.*
RIC	H. Mattingly and E. Sydenham, *The Roman Imperial Coinage*, vol. i (London, 1923), vol. ii (1926).
Riv. class. e med.	*Riviste di cultura classica e medioevale.*
Riv. fil.	*Rivista di filologia.*
Rostovtzeff, *SEHR*	M. Rostovtzeff, *Social and Economic History of the Roman Empire* (Oxford, 1st edn. 1926, 2nd edn. revised by P. M. Fraser, 1957).
Sm. 1	E. M. Smallwood, *Documents Illustrating the Principates of Gaius, Claudius, and Nero* (Cambridge, 1967).
Sm. 2	E. M. Smallwood, *Documents Illustrating the Principates of Nerva, Trajan, and Hadrian* (C.U.P., 1966).
Starr	C. G. Starr, *The Roman Imperial Navy, 31 B.C.– A.D. 324²* (Cambridge, 1960).
S.-W.	A. N. Sherwin-White, *The Letters of Pliny* (Oxford, 1966).
Syme	R. Syme, *Tacitus* (Oxford, 1958).
Syme, *RR*	R. Syme, *The Roman Revolution* (Oxford, 1939).
Walser	G. Walser, *Rom, das Reich und die fremden Völker in der Geschichtsschreibung der frühen Kaiserzeit* (Basel, 1951).
Weber	W. Weber, *Josephus und Vespasian* (Stuttgart, 1921).
Wellesley, *RhM*	K. Wellesley, 'Suggestio falsi in Tacitus', *RhM* 1960, 286 ff.
——, Tr.	K. Wellesley, *Tacitus, the Histories* (Penguin Classics, 1964).
——, *JRS*	K. Wellesley, 'A major crux in Tacitus', *JRS* 1971, 28 ff.
——, ed. to III	K. Wellesley, *Cornelius Tacitus, The Histories Book III* (Sydney University Press, 1972).
Woch. f. kl. phil.	*Wochenschrift für klassische Philologie.*

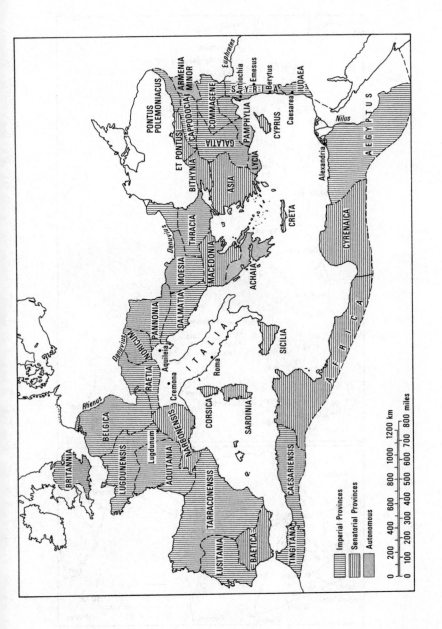

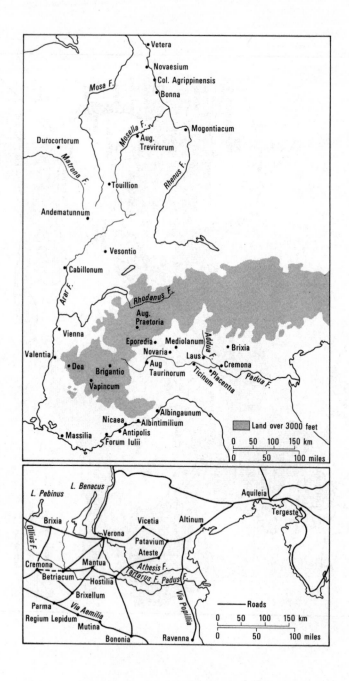

Top map labels:

Vetera
Novaesium
Col. Agrippinensis
Bonna
Mogontiacum
Mosa F.
Mosella F.
Durocortorum
Aug. Trevirorum
Matrona F.
Rhenus F.
Touillion
Andematunnum
Vesontio
Cabillonum
Rhodanus F.
Arar F.
Aug. Praetoria
Vienna
Eporedia
Mediolanum
Addua F.
Brixia
Novaria
Laus
Cremona
Valentia
Dea
Aug Taurinorum
Ticinum
Placentia
Padua F.
Brigantio
Vapincum
Albingaunum
Nicaea
Albintimilium
Massilia
Antipolis
Forum Iulii

Land over 3000 feet

0   50   100   150 km
0   50   100 miles

Bottom map labels:

L. Benacus
L. Pebinus
Aquileia
Tergeste
Brixia
Vicetia
Altinum
Ollius F.
Verona
Patavium
Ateste
Cremona
Mantua
Athesis F.
Betriacum
Tartarus F. Padus F.
Hostilia
Via Popilia
Brixellum
Parma
Via Aemilia
Regium Lepidum
Mutina
Bononia
Ravenna

Roads

0   50   100   150 km
0   50   100 miles

INTRODUCTION

I POLITICAL AND MILITARY PRELIMINARIES TO A.D. 69

I. THE FALL OF NERO

TACITUS devotes more consecutive space to the 'Pisonian' conspiracy of A.D. 65 than to any other item in the *Annals* (XV. 48–74). He was confident that he was drawing on reliable sources, above all the returned exiles, XV. 73, and we can reasonably take his account to be based on what has been called 'factual' material.[1] The affair was certainly considerable, and probably (though our evidence about earlier 'conspiracies' is inadequate) the most serious challenge the Julio-Claudian house had yet encountered. Powerful backing was provided by one of the praetorian prefects, *summum robur in Faenio Rufo, A.* XV. 50. But there was much more. The conspirators carried with them parts of a group which has been known as the philosophic opposition, and one of their prominent military members hoped that Seneca, rather than the futile Piso, would eventually emerge as *princeps*;[2] so it was on apparently unassociated members of the 'Stoic' sect among the aristocracy that Nero made assaults in the months that followed (see *A.* XVI*). The essential complaint of all the conspirators was that Nero was unserious as a *princeps*: his *scelera* were blatant, and were quickly included in the invectives used by his opponents; but what mattered above all was that he was diverting his attention away from his duties of governing an empire.[3] This at a time of severe financial crisis, which was already inciting the government to measures of taxation and confiscation of a kind bound to provoke dangerous discontent in Rome and abroad, *A.* XV. 45.

But the unrest was, so far, limited to the capital, and also tied to a tradition which affects much that happened in the ensuing years. The candidate selected to replace Nero, despite misgivings among some of the conspirators, was C. Piso. His character is described in a passage of Tacitean brilliance, *A.* XV. 48: his main recommendations were his lineage, his liberality, and his aristocratic affability. His collaterals within the *gens* Calpurnia are uncertain; but his son was son-in-law,

---

[1] B. Walker, *The Annals of Tacitus* (1952), cap. IV.
[2] *A.* XV. 65. Against the view that Seneca was actually implicated in the plot, Syme, 407, 575; on the other side B. W. Henderson, *The Life and Principate of the Emperor Nero* (1903), 279 ff., is still surprisingly useful.
[3] *finem adesse imperio deligendumque qui fessis rebus succurreret, A.* XV. 50. Yet some of the conspirators had more purely personal motives.

3

and previously related, to L. Piso (*cos.* 57), IV. 11, 49, and he had relations among many noble families. This social standard for a potential *princeps* was to show itself firmly again in 68.

The structure of Roman society, with its households of slaves and freedmen, made any conspiracy vulnerable inside the capital, and the conspirators themselves delayed too long: surely enough the efficient police service of the praetorian prefect Tigellinus not only brought the affair of 65 to nothing but launched a campaign of suspicion and bloodletting in the following months. On 25 September 66 (date from *AFA*) Nero felt able to leave for Greece, at the same time preparing an expedition to the Caucasus (I. 6. 12 n.) which he probably announced that he would lead in person (it was about this time that he assumed the *praenomen Imperator*). But shortly before he left (*AFA* after 19 June) a further conspiracy was discovered at Beneventum, Suet. *Nero* 36.1, the alleged leader being Annius Vinicianus, a young man sent to Rome as hostage for the good behaviour of his father-in-law Corbulo, who at that time held *maius imperium* over all the provinces on the Eastern frontier—for Vinicianus' arrival see Dio (= Xiph.) 62. 23. 6. Vinicianus, the son of one of the conspirators against Claudius in 42, was executed. His father-in-law was summoned to talk with Nero at Corinth, and despite his eminence and the effect his ruin might have on other army commanders, he was forced to suicide, see esp. Dio (= Xiph.) 62. 17. 6.

If Corbulo's elimination was the consequence of his son-in-law's conspiracy, then Nero's summons to him must have followed quickly and there is little doubt that it did. In the late months of 66 occurred a dangerous rebellion in Judaea; in September the Syrian governor, Cestius Gallus, took a legion and other troops south to attempt to quell it; on 25 November Gallus was defeated before Jerusalem; and Nero appointed Vespasian to conduct the difficult reprisals which ensued. The dates are given by Josephus, *BI* II. 499, 566, etc. But at no point does that author mention Corbulo, who had been appointed supreme commander in the East in 63. Corbulo was surely no longer Gallus' superior in November 66: he was already dead.

The Jewish War, which in many modern histories has been treated in isolation from other events in the empire, continued as a major military commitment during the year 67. Any plans made by Nero for a Caucasian expedition were postponed, and none of the three legions which had earlier been moved eastward to support his government's activities against Parthia was able to return to Europe. Meanwhile Nero continued in Greece, singing, playing, and competing in the games. But in the course of 67 he summoned the two brothers Sulpicius Scribonius Rufus and Sulpicius Scribonius Proculus (Dio = Xiph. 62. 17. 3), who for several years had been commanding the armies of

Upper and Lower Germany; and he forced them too to suicide. These men may have been sons of the Scribonius Proculus who was executed under Gaius, Dio. 59. 26. And it is with the great *gens* Scribonia, descendants of Pompey the Great through the marriage of his son Sextus, that they were evidently connected (their other *nomen*, Sulpicius, belonging to a *propinquus* of the Scribonii, namely the Augustan consular P. Sulpicius Quirinius, *A*. II. 30). Therefore two more significant links with persons who gave trouble to the Julio-Claudian house. First Furius (or Lucius) Arruntius Camillus Scribonianus (great-great-grandson of Pompey), who rebelled in Claudius' first year, with the father of the conspirator of 66, L. Annius Vinicianus, as his close ally. Secondly, the sons of Scribonia, wife of M. Crassus Frugi, *cos*. A.D. 27, see I. 14. 11 n.: of these the second, M. Crassus, *cos*. 64, a magnate with great estates in Histria, II. 72, was executed in this same year. His wife, it appears, was named Sulpicia Praetextata, IV. 42; and about the same time one Sulpicius Camerinus, a man of ancient lineage (but from Dio = Xiph. 63. 19. 2 we know no more) was put to death in Rome, together with his son.

Nero's victims in his last years were numerous and varied. Some of the best known were members of the 'Stoic' group. But the class which above all suffered was that of the older nobility,[4] the class which alone was thought to be capable of providing an alternative *princeps*—until the changes in social standards brought about by the 'long' year 69. Descendants of Augustus or his sister had been suspect from earlier years in the reign;[5] other families ennobled in Republican times were now involved as well.[6] And the suspicion now had also involved the commanders of major armies, causing insecurity all round: of this the government was probably conscious. The appointments in Nero's last years were mostly of men who looked safe. The successor to Scribonius Proculus in Lower Germany was Fonteius Capito, *cos. ord.* 67 (this gives a *terminus post quem* for the execution of the brothers), a man whose honesty and moral character were dubious, but who seems to have remained loyal to Nero, 7. 6 n.: to Upper Germany went L. Verginius Rufus, *cos. ord.* 63, whose origins, 52.1, were humble enough not only to make his candidature for the principate inconceivable, but to guarantee him immunity even if his troops tried, unsuccessfully, to proclaim him. Similar safeguards could have seemed to exist against any of the army commanders in 68.[7] One of them, the governor of Nearer Spain,

---

[4] Suet. *Nero* 36.1, *nobilissimo cuique exitium destinavit.* See M. Gelzer, *The Roman Nobility* (tr. R. Seager, 1969), 155.

[5] Syme, 555, 565 ff.

[6] For Corbulo too as *capax imperii* see II. 76. 20 f., but he was after all the half-brother of Caesonia, wife to Gaius Caligula.

[7] Against Nero, Mucianus admits that neither he nor Vespasian could have been
continued

certainly had ancient lineage, but he was thought to be a mild man (πρᾴῳ, and of *medium ingenium*, 49. 10 n.), and at the age of sixty-nine it was thought that he would attempt nothing rash, Plut. *G.* 3. 3.[8]

In the early days of 68 the freedman Helius, who had been left in charge of Rome and had repeatedly tried to persuade Nero to return, crossed to Greece and convinced the Emperor that a great conspiracy was about to break out in the capital, Dio (=Xiph.) 63. 19. 1. No such outbreak occurred, and we cannot tell the substance, much less the details, of Helius' fears. But Nero did go back, entering the city with great pomp as Olympian and Pythian victor, even perhaps as both Apollo and Hercules, Dio, cit., Suet. *Nero* 25. He started dispatching troops to the East, either reviving his plans for a Caucasian expedition or (conceivably) reinforcing Vespasian in Judaea (see note at end of this section).

But in the days of the *Quinquatrua*, in the third week of March, Suet. *Nero* 40 (cf. *A.* XIV. 12), it was announced that C. Iulius Vindex, son of an Aquitanian-born senator and himself the governor of Lugdunensis, had thrown off his allegiance. This was soon followed by news that Vindex had sought support from all other governors, and that Galba, governor of Tarraconensis, had, on or about 2 April (Dio=Xiph. 64. 6. 5) told an assembly at New Carthage that he would head Vindex' movement: he disclaimed the names of Caesar or 'emperor', but he would be the general of the SPQR. On all this the accounts of Plut. *G.* 4–5, Suet. *G.* 9–10, Dio 63. 23, are approximately in agreement.[9]

The aims of this rebellion caused prolonged disputes among writers of two generations ago.[10] Was Vindex a 'Gallic nationalist', or was he (as Dio's epitomators clearly represent him) a rebel against the tyranny of Nero? The argument, given the conditions of Roman provincial society and government in 68, was unreal. In the first place, everything in the history of that year, and of the two years that follow, shows that there was no effective unity among the Gallic tribes. Secondly, the

---

serious competitors, II. 76. In Britain Trebellius Maximus (*cos.* 56), even if T.'s *segnior* is unfair, given the condition of the province at the time (*Agr.* 16.3), was no danger. In Illyricum the governors in 69 were *divites senes*, without initiative, and Aponius Saturninus in Moesia was not a serious contender; even if they were Galbian, not Neronian, appointees, their predecessors have made no mark. Fonteius Capito, it is true, was probably son of a consular, but no distinction is known in his previous career, *PIR*[2].

[8] But he too claimed that Nero wanted to murder him, Suet. *G.* 9. 2.

[9] In *JRS* 1957, 32 I suggested that Galba, rather than Vindex, was the author of the whole movement. I no longer believe this: as P. A. Brunt, *Latomus*, 1959, 536, pointed out, it was a guess contradicted by every ancient source. I still think, however, that Vindex had prior assurance of support from Spain, and that Galba's party was built up early and with empire-wide links.

[10] Among many recent treatments of the affair in English, the article by D. C. A. Shotter, *CQ* 1967, 370 seems to me most valuable. See also J. B. Hainsworth, *Historia*, 1962, 89 ff., B. H. Warmington. *Nero: Reality and Legend* (1969), 135 ff, and Shotter's note on the chronology (though I have misgivings about this), *Historia*, 1975, 59 ff.

coinage of the period of the revolt, in Spain as well as Gaul, combined with Galba's coinage once he had become *princeps*, shows that he was prepared to support the slogans of Vindex and to continue them without shame after Nero's death.[11] But thirdly, on the other side, it is unlikely that a large army of Gauls, raised from among their clients by the governor and the landowners in an 'unarmed' province, were principally interested in Nero's tyranny and in atrocities at Rome. They had been the victims, as had been the Spanish provincials too (see above, and cf. Rostovtzeff, *SEHR.* 510 n. 6), of the exactions of Nero's last years. Their leaders, it may well be, had in some cases had to sell or mortgage their estates, and in their distress could call on their tenants or labourers to help them. These leaders have been described as 'local magnates';[12] they were the chief men of certain tribes in central Gaul, together with those of the Allobroges of Narbonensis with their wealthy city of Vienna.[13] These were not men seeking independence from Rome, indeed many of them must have shared the ideals of the average Roman senator: Galba was able, without loss of his patriotic face, to reward them with remission of taxation and with grants of land alienated from Lugdunum and from some of their other neighbours. Nothing in this seemed incompatible with his professed aim of achieving 'liberty' from a tyrant, and a later generation could remember his war as one fought *pro re publica*.[14]

Against the rising of an 'unarmed province' supported by a consular general with but one legion[15] the riposte of Nero was much more vigorous than might have been expected. The normal answer to Gallic rebellion[16] was intervention by the Upper German army, but this was not thought to be enough. Nero hurried on the conscription of a legion from the marines, and began to raise troops, including slaves, from within Rome.[17] More important, the detachments proceeding eastwards, some of which had already reached Alexandria, were recalled.[18] The legion XIV, which had been summoned from Britain as a crack regiment,[19] but seems not to have gone far to the East[20] was brought back to North Italy with its turbulent Batavian auxiliaries, and probably with other vexillations from the Illyrican armies. A consular

---

[11] C. M. Kraay, *Num. Chron.* 1949, 129 ff.
[12] Jos. *BI* IV. 440.
[13] Probably also the Vocontii, and possibly the Helvetii, I. 67. 3 n.
[14] *IRT* 537 = MW 31.
[15] Galba quickly raised another, the VII Galbiana with which he later marched to Rome.
[16] *A.* III. 42 ff., on the affair of A.D. 21.
[17] Suet. *Nero* 44, and on the marines I. 6 n. below.
[18] See additional note below, p. 9.
[19] *ut potissimos*, II. 11. 7.
[20] Where this legion was at this critical moment, and where it found a camp in Illyricum later (App. to Book II), is a major obscurity in the movements of these years.

command over these various units was established in the Po valley, under P. Petronius Turpilianus (*cos. ord.* 61).[21]

But those forces never had to take the field against Vindex or Galba. For in the later days of May[22] Verginius Rufus laid siege to Vesontio (Besançon), and Vindex' army tried to relieve it. The Rhineland troops fell on the Gallic 'rebels', destroying 20,000 of them, and Vindex committed suicide. We are told that Verginius mourned his death, and he was later able to plead that the battle had been fought against his will, for he had been conferring with Vindex when the troops took the initiative.[23] About that the truth cannot be known: the story of the parley was one which suited both Verginius and Galba when the new emperor had to decide what to do about the general whose force had eliminated his ally.

From all our sources it is clear that it was before Nero's death that the Rhine army offered the empire to Verginius: *tarde a Nerone desciverant*, I. 8. 11, i.e. they *did* desert, while Nero was still the emperor. Moreover one source indicates that the offer was made before the Vesontio battle,[24] and that the troops later threatened to return to Nero unless the offer was accepted. But Verginius steadfastly refused, not in terms of loyalty to Nero, nor indeed to Galba:[25] He declared, as Galba had done earlier,[26] that the decision to create a *princeps* must be taken by the Senate and People of Rome. It was this adherence to 'constitutional' principles which was recorded in the couplet inscribed on his tombstone; and it was of this that he boasted when Cluvius Rufus asked whether anything in his Histories had caused Verginius offence, replying that he had done what he did in order that historians should be free to write what they wished.[27]

On the news of Vesontio Galba retired to Clunia in some despair, for whatever was to be the future it did not seem to lie with him.[28] But the news of the Rhine armies' defection[29] was quickly reported to Rome and Italy; and it will obviously have had its effect on the behaviour of

[21] Dio 63. 27.

[22] *IRS* 1957, 32 n. 40, Brunt, cit., 541. D. C. A. Shotter, *Historia*, 1975, 59 ff., would put Vesontio a month earlier.

[23] Dio (= Jos. *Ant.*) 63. 25, Plut. *G.* 6. 3.

[24] Plut. *G.* 6. 1. Someone near Mediolanum, Verginus' birthplace, set up an offering for his *Salus* and *Victoria*, terms befitting an emperor, *ILS* 982 = MW 23.

[25] *nec statim pro Galba Verginius*, I. 8. 11.

[26] Plut. *G.* 5. 2.

[27] Brunt, cit., 539, may be right in suggesting that Cluvius' possible offence was frankness about the indiscipline of Verginius' army. Shotter, *CQ* 1967, 373, argues that Cluvius accused Verginius of incompetence and indecisiveness once the battle had happened. Perhaps no answer is possible, since we are dealing with a conversation between two evasive speakers, reported by a source who would have found it hard to understand them (Plin; *Epp.* IX. lg. 5.

[28] Plut. *G.* 6. 4.

[29] Troops from both German armies were concerned, I. 51. 11. with n.

the troops in the Po valley. Our evidence about this force is scanty and confusing,[30] but we are told that Nero learned of the defection to Galba of its commander, Petronius Turpilianus.[31] Petronius returned to Rome as a *privatus*, 'deserted and without an army',[32] and was later executed on Galba's orders, for what had happened had surely been the defection not of the commander but of his troops. And the news of this move completed for Nero and the praetorian guard the story that all the armies had deserted,[33] and the prefect Nymphidius Sabinus, colleague to Tigellinus (whose activities in this period are not recorded), promised the guard an enormous donative[34] if they would abandon Nero.

On 9 June Nero committed suicide. The Senate immediately offered the principate to Galba; his freedman Icelus brought him the news within a week,[35] and he now accepted his position as constitutionally valid.

ADDITIONAL NOTES

(a) *The eastward movement of troops in* A.D. *66–68*

In three passages of Book I (chapters 6, 31, and 70) Tacitus speaks of units which had been *praemissi* to the East, but were recalled to help in suppressing Vindex. When were they sent out, and why?

According to Dio (= Xiph.) 63. 8. 1, it was before Nero's departure to Greece that he was planning expeditions to 'the Caspian Gates' (I. 6. 12 n.) and to Ethiopia (cf. Plin. *NH* VI. 181). These projects were contemplated, but were not actually carried out: recognizing that they would take time and trouble, he sent scouting parties to make a report, hoping that the countries in question would capitulate of their own accord. Xiphilinus often lists items which illustrate a theme without regard for chronological sequence,[36] but here the context is clearly that in which Nero is planning, but has not yet embarked upon, his ἐκστρατεία. Moreover that chronology is confirmed by the imperfect *parabat* at Suet. *Nero* 19. 2: the 'Caspian' affair (Suetonius says nothing about Ethiopia) was being prepared when the emperor crossed to Achaia, i.e. in September 66.

This conclusion is the more probable when we consider the evidence about the units involved:

(i) The legion I Italica was certainly raised for the 'Caspian'

---

[30] See additional note (b) to this section, pp. 11–12.
[31] Dio (= Zonaras) 63. 27.
[32] Plut. *G.* 15. 2.   [33] Suet. *G.* 47. 1.   [34] Plut. *G.* 2.   [35] *Ibid.* 7. 1.
[36] See the long list of Nero's victims in 63. 17–18, which after dealing with the executions of the period of the Greek tour ends with the banishment of Caecina Tuscus, prefect of Egypt. Yet Tuscus' successor, Tiberius Alexander, was certainly prefect by the summer of 66, Jos. *BI* II. 492 ff., cf. Pflaum, 18 bis. Xiphilinus also misdates the deaths of Thrasea Paetus and Barea Soranus to the year 65.

expedition, Suet., cit., and there are strong grounds for thinking that it took service in 66, see I. 20. 14 n. The alternative birthday, 20 September 67, would seem a very perverse moment, given the history of the Jewish War.

(ii) At some point XIV Gemina was withdrawn from Britain. It had won a great reputation during the revolt of Boudicca, and Nero selected its men *ut potissimos*, II. 11. 7. In Nero's last days it was in North Italy, II.27.9 ff.; and in early 69 it was at an unknown camp in Pannonia or Dalmatia. But when did it leave Britain? Early editors of the *Histories* (Sp., V., and others) wondered whether the enemy against which it was summoned was not the 'Albani' but Vindex. Yet this is not really conceivable. The legion could not have received its orders, removed itself from the English Midlands to North Italy, and then engaged in operations, in the interval between the third week of March and Nero's death; and if a legion was urgently needed in the Po valley, the natural source would have been Illyricum. Furthermore, if XIV Gemina did move south in late 66, and was then stopped from a further movement eastwards, it had an obvious resting-place in Illyricum, where Pannonia was short of a legion since the departure in 63 of XV Apollinaris, which had been detained in Alexandria on its way back (see below). Late 66, then, seems the more probable date; but it must be admitted that the evidence still allows for a summons to XIV Gemina in the winter of 67–8, when the 'Caspian' project may have been revived.[37] For here again we must remember the Roman success in the Jewish War, which by that time may have made some such project seem conceivable.

(iii) There remain the various units which were actually dispatched eastward. Tacitus expressly states in I. 6 (see n. ad loc.) the destination of the *numeri* from Germany, Britain, and Illyricum to have been 'the Caspian Gates'; and in I. 31 we learn that the German *vexilla*, surely part of the same force, had proceeded to Alexandria, a reasonable assembly-point for a north-eastern campaign, cf. *CAH* X. 779.[38] Similarly the *ala* Siliana, I. 70, had Egypt as its immediate destination. All of these were *praemissi* sent ahead of the main army, which Neronian propaganda suggested the *princeps* himself would lead. But when did the first of such contingents set out?

(iv) The answer may be provided by a passage in Josephus, *BI* II. 494. In the late summer of 66 the prefect of Egypt was enabled to suppress a potential Jewish rising in Alexandria with the help of 2,000 (some manuscripts say 5,000) troops which happened to have arrived

---

[37] H. M. D. Parker, *The Roman Legions* (1928), 139, 'XIV Gem., which had probably reached Dalmatia on its way from Britain'. But for Parker this 'way' was prolonged, for two pages earlier he puts the departure of the legion in 66.
[38] Or more obviously one for a campaign in Ethiopia, if one was really envisaged.

from Africa. Josephus says they came εἰς τὸν Ἰουδαίων ὄλεθρον, but means not that they had been sent from Africa to deal with Jewish trouble, but that it was unlucky for the Jews that they arrived at that moment. This was two months and more before the Roman government knew that it was faced with a major Jewish rebellion, and about the time of Nero's departure for Greece. It could well have been the beginning of his movement of specially selected troops eastwards for his Caucasus campaign.

But that campaign never happened. When Nero heard of Cestius Gallus' defeat in November he gave Vespasian command of two legions which were then at Antioch, V Macedonica and X Fretensis, and also of XV Apollinaris, which had reached Alexandria on its way back to its old quarters in Pannonia, Jos. *BI* III. 8. The carefully constructed force, including legions I Italica and XIV Gemina, never left Italy, and XIV went to Illyricum. Vespasian broke the rebellion in Galilee and parts of Peraea in 67, and in 68 was prepared to besiege Jerusalem. So in that winter it was possible once more to contemplate a Caucasian expedition, and troops began to move (see ¶iii above). But not the legions; for in March 68 the revolt of Vindex was known in Rome, and units which had reached Alexandria or were on their way there were recalled.

(b) *The 'War of Nero' in North Italy*

The purpose of the force mobilized in the Po valley, and what it actually did, are obscure beyond most of the obscurities of Nero's last days. Was it intended to move into Gaul as reinforcement for the Rhineland armies? Or, as I would think, to be a second line of defence, one perhaps especially needed against the threat of advance from Spain through southern Gaul.[39] Some modern writers[40] have said that it actually crossed into Gaul before Nero's death, to which Syme[41] replied that there was no evidence whatsoever of such a movement in the ancient sources. He was undoubtedly right, if denying any actual text about troops crossing the Alps, but it is puzzling that the next evidence about legion I Italica finds it at Lugdunum. Conceivably it was Galba who sent it there,[42] but when and why did he choose that place, of all places, for stationing a legion which had been raised by Nero and which had no reason for loyalty to himself?

If, however, we return to North Italy, we have clear evidence that XIV Gemina, and the other troops from Illyricum, remained in the Po valley. There the legion had a fracas[43] with its Batavian auxiliaries, who later claimed that they had wrested 'Italy' from Nero, and who

---

[39] So also Shotter, *CQ* 1967, 373.   [40] e.g. Momigliano, *CAH* x. 740.
[41] *AJP* 1937, 12.   [42] Also maintained by Syme, cit.   [43] II. 27.

then proceeded to the territory of the Lingones where they were found by Valens on his southward march.[44] But the Illyrican troops, *dum in Italia cunctantur*, offered the empire to Verginius Rufus, I. 9. 11. What is implied by saying that they 'delayed'? That they had been intended (but were prevented by their trouble with the *auxilia*, or for other reasons) to cross into Gaul, or that they stayed on in Italy after the purpose for which they had been summoned became abortive (i.e. after Vesontio—or after Nero's death)? For the latter view see I. 70. 6 of another unit, *ob bellum Vindicis revocati ac tum in Italia manentes*: indeed it is almost certain, II. 17 with nn., that some units which operated in the Po valley were still there in early 69. The full legion XIV had gone back to Illyricum, but about other detachments it seems that Galba never took decisions—and he never took a final one about I Italica.

The evidence about all this is inadequate. If one must hazard a view, it could be that (i) I Italica pressed on to Gaul as a possible reinforcement before the news of Vesontio was known, (ii) that the other Neronian elements remained in North Italy while awaiting orders to depart, and (iii) that the Batavian cohorts proceeded into Gaul, and were felt by Galba's government to be a welcome counteraction to the anti-Vindician forces. And that the approach by the Illyrican troops to Verginius, *cunctantur*, was after Nero's death, when they had rid themselves of the Batavians but when it was not yet certain that Galba was going to be accepted by the Senate.

2. THE PRINCIPATE OF GALBA

Almost nothing in our sources[45] reveals what military or political plans Galba had evolved when he accepted leadership against Nero in the first days of April. Apparently he had staked all on the revolt in Gaul, which he may have hoped Verginius would join: the slaughter at Vesontio therefore reduced him to despair. Yet when Nero committed suicide, following his desertion by the guard, Galba had acquired allies in distant parts of the empire. The prefect of Egypt issued an edict in his favour less than a month after Nero's death; and it could even be that Nymphidius Sabinus' bribe to the praetorians, though later disavowed by the new emperor, had been concerted with him.[46] In Lower Germany the legionary legate Fabius Valens gave important support, but received no reward.[47]

The description of Galba's character in I. 49, a piece of superb Latin,

44 I. 64.
45 *IRT* 537 (= MW 31) appears to tell us (though not all its reading is certain) of naval operations by a *praefectus orae maritimae* during the war which Galba waged *pro re publica*.
46 For Galba's party cf. *JRS* 1957, 32.
47 I. 52. 14. Valens was perhaps felt to have been too precipitate in killing Fonteius Capito, I. 7. 5.

is probably derived in its essential judgements from the 'common source', though Plut. *G.* 29, has not made full use of it (below, p. 28). It makes excellent sense of a noble of Galba's lineage, his career, and his time. His military reputation was impeccable, his consular ancestry went far back into Republican days, and his wealth made him incorruptible in personal matters. Like many Roman nobles—and other nobles too—he assumed without serious question that his subordinates would be his faithful servants; and he therefore paid little attention to the possibility that they might be dishonest or disloyal. Yet of the two *amici* who were dominant from the start, I. 6. 1, T. Vinius for all his energy and intelligence was so widely unpopular that his reputation for corruption can hardly be groundless; for Laco see below. As ruler of the empire in 68 Galba was outdated, I. 18. 15 ff., for times had changed beyond his understanding.

The keynote of his propaganda was defence of the 'constitution'. When he accepted Vindex' offer he would not be Caesar or emperor, but 'general on behalf of the Senate and People'. That attitude was part of a theme which found currency in other events of the next year, cf. I. 55 13, 57. 7 nn., and it would be wrong to ignore the respect which was accorded to the Senate in this period of potential anarchy, cf. I. 74. 9, 76. 11, and Otho's speech in I. 83–4. Galba above all his contemporaries is likely to have seen the political scene in those terms, one familiar to the theorists of the late Republic, and welcomed by the propaganda of Augustus' days. In keeping with this attitude was his initial reluctance to use the furniture and other accompaniments of a *princeps* which Nymphidius had sent him from Rome—though about this Vinius persuaded him that he had to maintain the imperial dignity, Plut. *G.* 11. 1.

It was also in keeping with his character that he should demonstrate reaction against the more notorious features of Nero's regime and show sympathy to the people who had been objects of persecution in Nero's last years. He recalled exiles, among them Helvidius Priscus who immediately launched an attack on Eprius Marcellus as the prosecutor of his father-in-law, IV. 6; and the Senate passed a general decree *ut accusatorum causae noscerentur*, II. 10, with consequences Tacitus states were felt over a long period. Some of these measures may have been passed after Galba entered Rome, but it was certainly much earlier that he appointed Cornelius Laco to be his praetorian prefect, a man who had connections with the 'philosophic' opposition, and who next year promoted Piso Licinianus as Galba's successor, cf. I. 6. 1 n.

Laco's appointment, eventually ruinous to Galba, was immediately ruinous to Nymphidius, whose *coup*, in the Thermidorean situation of mid-68, was a fiasco: details of the way he was *in ipso conatu oppressus* (I. 5. 8) are given in Plut. *G.* 13–14.

Galba moved slowly towards Rome, by land, and met the Senate's envoys at Narbo. It was probably there that he interviewed Verginius (Dio = *Exc. Val.* 259 states that the two men met in person). The colloquy evolved the story which dominates our sources, namely that Verginius tried for an understanding with Vindex but that the troops got out of hand. So Galba was able to resist Vinius, who wanted Verginius' execution; but he felt bound to appoint a new commander to Upper Germany, and he chose the elderly and gouty Hordeonius Flaccus. Verginius seems to have accepted the decision without protest.

But various executions did take place. Cingonius Varro, whom Nero had designated as one of the suffect consuls for the following year, had drafted Nymphidius' speech of proclamation. P. Petronius Turpilianus had been Nero's general in North Italy. Fonteius Capito in Lower Germany had been slow to support Galba and was now put to death by Fabius Valens and another legionary legate, probably before Galba had been given an opportunity to pronounce on the case. And Clodius Macer in Africa, the legionary legate who had tried to advance his own position through his control of Rome's corn supply, was eliminated by a procurator on Galba's order. On all this see I. 6–7 nn. Galba incurred severe criticism over the first two of these cases, 6.6, for given that neither man was actually in arms, it would have been reasonable to hold a formal trial (the case of Turpilianus, Plut. *G.* 15. 2, was considered especially harsh). So when the emperor ordered the slaughter of a number of marines before his entry to Rome, 6.7 n., his reputation for *saevitia* had gained alarming ground among certain sections of society, probably most of all among the officers of the city garrison, 7. 13 n.

Yet if subsequent events had gone otherwise, these executions would probably have been forgotten, or looked on as the inevitable accompaniments of a revolution. What in the end brought Galba down was that he was confronted simultaneously by three quite formidable problems, and was unable to find a satisfactory solution to any one of them.

(a) The Rhine army claimed to have won a great victory and to deserve reward. No such thing was forthcoming, and its Rhineland allies, the Treveri and Lingones, had actually been punished by loss of territory, to the tribes which had supported Vindex, I. 51 ff. The recall of Verginius had been an insult to the Upper army, and a replacement for Capito in the Lower province was delayed for some weeks, I. 9.5 n. In late November A. Vitellius, whose appointment was recommended to Galba by Vinius, Suet. *Vit.* 7.1, took over the latter command. As the son of the greatest *privatus* since Augustus' day, cf. I. 9.6 n., he was an obvious challenger to any government if he was prepared to take up his army's grievances.

(b) The praetorians had been promised an exorbitant donative by Nymphidius Sabinus, I. 5.3 n. For Galba to pay it, even if ready cash had been available, would have been to sacrifice the stand he had taken in favour of discipline, and would almost certainly have been unfair to other elements of society. But his rigidity in this matter was extreme: some small sum on account (I. 18. 15, and 82. 15 on Otho's concession) might have conciliated the guard for the moment. Galba was racked between Vinius and Otho on the one side, the 'realists' among his advisers, and on the other side Laco and his friends. He remained *minantibus intrepidus, adversus blandientis incorruptus*, I. 35. 13. Yet his earlier ruthlessness was still in the minds of his officers, as also the belief that his incorruptibility was not transmitted to his advisers, *nec enim ad hanc formam cetera erant*, I. 5. 16.

(c) The adoption question, for a septuagenarian *princeps*, could not be long delayed, and became inescapable when the Rhine legions threw off their allegiance in the New Year. But once again Vinius and Laco disagreed; and Vinius, who was supporting Otho, was at a discount, for he had advocated the appointment of Vitellius, the new pretender. But Galba's dilemma would in any case have been painful, for he could not forget his *curam rei publicae, frustra a Nerone translatae si apud Othonem relinqueretur*, I. 13. 11. It had to be, Laco and Icelus argued, anyone rather than Otho. So he chose Piso Licinianus, whom Laco had known within Rubellius Plautus' 'philosophic' circle, and whose *nobilitas* could commend itself to the *princeps* more than that of any possible competitor.

One might speculate whether any man who became the first *princeps* to succeed the Julio-Claudian house, given the other difficulties in Rome and the provinces in the year 68, could have avoided disaster. Could he have compromised on part of the problems, and have then surmounted the rest? For example, by adopting Otho, giving the guard a small instalment, and taking the field quickly and resolutely against the Rhine army, with support from the many elements in the rest of the army which had brought him to power? Or by an immediate negotiation with Vitellius (to become the Trajan to his Nerva),[48] by moderate concessions to the Rhineland tribes, and then by a threat to the guard that legionaries might take their coveted places if they insisted on more than the minimum? Whatever the answer to such questions, it is clear that Galba was incapable of any of these solutions; and Tacitus gives him such credit as he deserved by reminding us that he belonged to an age *cui pares non sumus*, I. 18. 17.

[48] For T.'s complete acceptance of a hostile tradition about Vitellius see nn. to II. 57 ff. Against his account we must remember the obstinate loyalty of Vitellius' troops, both those who marched to Italy and those who were left in the Rhineland. They had their selfish motives, but their commander's understanding of his men, I. 52, was probably an important factor. See also P. A. L. Greenhalgh, *The Year of the Four Emperors* (1975), 105 ff.

Even in the military sphere, where his earlier achievements had made him seem *capax imperii*, his dispositions were curiously inept. It is not only that he took no effective measures when the news of the Rhineland rebellion arrived. When he had reached Rome in October, he had his new legion VII, I. 6. 9 n., and a number of marines whose comrades he had slaughtered but whom he made into the legion I Adiutrix. It was VII that he sent off to Pannonia, doubtless because he was advised that Otho had corrupted it:[49] but it was he himself who had raised it, and it might still have been loyal to him. But the Adiutrix legion he retained in Rome, and it of course deserted him when Otho rebelled. In addition Nero's I Italica, after its activities in North Italy, was either sent by him to Lugdunum, or at least allowed by him to remain there:[50] there could hardly be a less suitable place for an important unit owing no loyalty to the new Roman government. Such measures seem peculiar, but Galba's choice of a praetorian prefect who was *ignarus militarium animorum* may have been their cause.[51]

3. THE ROMAN ARMY OF A.D. 68–69

1. *The troops in Rome*

It is generally agreed that by A.D. 68 there were twelve praetorian cohorts and four urbans.[52] How large was each?

Dio 55. 24. 6 said that the praetorian cohorts of Augustus were 1,000 strong, i.e. *milliariae*, and that the urbans numbered 6,000, i.e. that each cohort had 1,500 men. In 1938 Durry[53] launched a strong attack on Dio's evidence, mainly on two grounds: that the *laterculi* which record dismissals from the guard in the mid-second century A.D. appear on the average to show that the strength of a cohort was 500 or less; and secondly that at II. 93. 11 Tacitus, by using the subjunctive *inessent*, implied that Vitellius altered the cohort strength. He claimed that both praetorians and urbans had hitherto been *quingenariae*, and that Dio's figures were anachronistically drawn from the situation of his own time, after Septimius Severus' reforms.

But the arguments developed by Passerini in the following year[54] make it likely that Durry was wrong. The *laterculi* are too few and incomplete to prove the case either way: similar *laterculi* from the third century suggest a strength of 1,000. But, more important, Dio had lived through the army reforms of Severus and was extremely critical of them:[55] had he known that Severus was the first to make a praetorian cohort 1,000 strong, he would surely have said so. And it should here be

---

[49] See Appendix, p. 272.   [50] Above, p. 11.
[51] I. 26. 13, and for Laco's origins, I. 6. 1 n.   [52] Durry, 12 ff., Passerini, *coorti* 53.
[53] cit, 84 ff.   [54] cit., 58–67.   [55] 74. 2. 5–6.

added that with a praetorian guard of only 6,000 men (paper strength) it is almost impossible to make sense of the operations in the Otho–Vitellius war.

I assume, therefore, that on 1 January 69 the twelve praetorian cohorts were *milliariae*, with a total effective strength of about 10,000.[56] What of the urbans? It is true that a cohort of 1,500 is otherwise unknown under the early Empire, and also that 6,000 urbans in the days before Nero, when there were only nine praetorian cohorts (*A. IV. 5*), is a surprisingly large figure. But if Dio was right about the praetorians, it is reasonable to trust him about the urbans too, especially because with them there is no occasion when the cohort strength is likely to have been raised.[57] In 69 Vitellius could have temporarily reduced it: there had been losses in the Ligurian expedition, and he himself would not have been anxious to restore the size of a force commanded by the city prefect, Vespasian's brother.[58] So at II. 93. 9 the *confusus ordo militiae* implies that the praetorian cohorts were increased in number from twelve to sixteen but were *milliariae* as hitherto; and that the paper strength of an urban cohort was reduced from 1,500 to 1,000, with the number of cohorts remaining unchanged. The extent to which the existing soldiers in the urbans were discharged and replaced raises another problem, see II. 93. 9 n.

Also quartered in the city were the seven cohorts of *vigiles*, again stated by Dio to have been *milliariae*. They had played a significant role when Tiberius decided to execute his praetorian prefect,[59] and were thought to be capable of doing the same again in the last weeks of Vitellius' life.[60] But they were freedmen; and they had their fire-fighting duties; and they were untrained for ordinary battle. It was probably for all three reasons that they saw no fighting outside Rome in 69.

But at 1 January 69, and still more a few weeks earlier, there was an abnormal addition to the troops in Rome.[61] Galba had brought in his new legion VII, and then sent it to Pannonia.[62] He had regularized Nero's recruitment of another new legion, subsequently called I Adiutrix, out of the clamant body of marines.[63] And there were units from Germany, Britain, and Illyricum, which had been destined for Nero's Caspian expedition but were then recalled. These last were still

---

[56] I see no way of deciding how far the effective strength normally fell below the paper strength of 12,000.

[57] From the praetorians Severus was excluding Italians: there is no evidence that he tampered with the urbans.

[58] III. 64. 3.   [59] Dio 63. 9.

[60] III. 64. 4, 69. 5.   [61] I. 6.

[62] I. 23 n., and Appendix, p. 272.

[63] This would have been a legion at full strength, for many applicants were disappointed, I. 6. 7 n.

in Rome, and were thought to be of consequence at the time of Otho's rising; it is strange that we never hear of them again.

Altogether we can assume at 1 January:

Praetorians	10,000
Urbans	6,000
Vigiles	7,000
I Adiutrix	5,500
Other units ('Numeri')	2,500 (at least)
Total	31,000

This was an *exercitus insolitus* (I.6.10), a force which added greatly to an emperor's powers of resistance were he to be challenged by a provincial commander.[64]

ii. *The legions*

Including I Adiutrix in Rome, there were now thirty legions, distributed as follows (I give the probable camps of the Rhine and Illyricum legions, with which in these Books we are chiefly concerned):

	Legion	*Station at 1 January 69*
I	(Germanica)	Lower Germany (Bonna)
I	Italica	Lugdunum[65]
I	Adiutrix	Rome
II	Augusta	Britain
III	Augusta	Africa
III	Gallica	Moesia[66]
III	Cyrenaica	Egypt
IV	Macedonica	Upper Germany (Mogontiacum)
IV	Scythica	Syria
V	Alaudae	Lower Germany (Vetera)
V	Macedonica	Judaea
VI	Ferrata	Syria
VI	Victrix	Spain
VII	Claudia	Moesia
VII	Galbiana (later Gemina)	Pannonia (Carnuntum?)[67]
VIII	Augusta	Moesia

---

[64] Then was also the possibility of employing large, additional numbers of marines, I. 6, cit.

[65] See above, p. 14.

[66] Sent there from Syria just before Nero's death, I. 10. 1 n.

[67] See p. 17 n. 62 above.

	Legion	Station at 1 January 69
IX	Hispana	Britain
X	Fretensis	Judaea
X	Gemina	Spain[68]
XI	Claudia	Dalmatia (Burnum)
XII	Fulminata	Syria
XIII	Gemina	Pannonia (Poetovio)
XIV	Gemina Martia Victrix	Pannonia?[69]
XV	Apollinaris	Judaea
XV	Primigenia	Lower Germany (Vetera)
XVI		Lower Germany (Novaesium)
XX	Valeria	Britain
XXI	Rapax	Upper Germany (Vindonissa)
XXII	Deiotariana	Egypt
XXII	Primigenia	Upper Germany (Mogontiacum)

iii. *Auxilia*

At *A*. IV. 5. 6 Tacitus estimates the number of auxiliary troops in A.D. 23 as being roughly equal to that of the remainder of the army, and there is no compelling reason for doubting that much the same was true of the situation in 69. But in emergencies, as Tacitus himself says, it was easy to raise additional auxiliaries and to dismiss them when no longer needed: so by Vitellius, I. 61, II. 57, and by the Flavians, II. 82, 84.

Yet the number of auxiliaries attached to individual legions[70] must have varied considerably, in accordance with the needs of the area in which the legion was quartered. To take an example from a later period, after Trajan divided Pannonia his Lower province with only one legion seems to have had a distinctly higher complement of *auxilia* than the Upper province where the number of legions was three; and in the same period there was a very heavy concentration of *auxilia* near the northern frontier of Britain and in Wales. It is therefore impossible to make close estimates of battle forces in 69, but it is probably not far wrong to calculate that groups of legionary troops were accompanied, or preceded, by auxiliaries in numbers not much lower than those of their own effectives.[71]

---

[68] This had been temporarily in Pannonia, but was returned to its former province by Galba.

[69] See above, pp. 7, 12.

[70] For the 'attachment' of *auxilia* to legions see I. 59. 4 n.

[71] I Adiutrix had presumably not yet acquired *auxilia*. It may also be doubted whether XIV Gemina had anything like a full complement after the Batavian cohorts had been detached from it.

iv. *The recruitment areas*

(a) Tacitus says that in Tiberius' time praetorians and urbans were recruited from Etruria, Umbria, and central Italy.[72] There is no strong reason for supposing that this system had been greatly modified by A.D. 68. By then there had been a significant number of praetorians drawn from the Po valley,[73] but recruitment outside Italy was still rare.[74] At I. 84. 17, II. 12. 8, T. implies that all these troops were Italians, and the epigraphical evidence abundantly confirms him.[75]

(b) In the earliest days of the Principate legionaries, who had to be Roman citizens, were normally Italians, but as Roman citizenship was spread to the provinces so also was provincial recruitment made easier. Under Claudius and Nero at least half of the men for the Rhine and Danube legions were being drawn from the provinces of the West.[76] But they had municipal origins, and some of them may have belonged to Italian emigrant families; those who did not may none the less have felt themselves to be as highly Romanized as their contemporaries from North Italy, who by now composed the vast majority among such legionaries as were Italian. Even between these elements and the praetorians and urbans there can have been no obvious difference in manners and outlook: Tacitus' picture of the *Germanicus exercitus* descending into Italy is too often overdrawn, so far as the legionary element is concerned.

The legions stationed east of the Aegean have left fewer epigraphic records. Some of them had garrisoned Syria from the earliest days of the Principate, and may have found it hard to maintain their Roman citizenship composition without recruiting Greeks and Orientals and giving them citizenship at enlistment (this certainly must have happened for the Egyptian legions very early, *ILS* 2483 = EJ 261). In Nero's reign new men needed for the Syrian legions were raised in Galatia and Cappadocia,[77] and in 69 the Eastern legionaries were closely attached, by family and other ties, to the provinces in which they were serving:[78] the men of III Gallica, whatever may have been their origin, had adopted a custom which was wholly eastern.[79] Moreover it is noticeable that Vespasian, though he moved the Western and Danubian legions fairly freely from one province to another, still stationed in Syria and the adjacent provinces all the legions which had been there in Julio-Claudian days.[80]

---

[72] *A.* IV. 5. 5. [73] *Cisalpine Gaul*, 125 f.
[74] Durry, 240, exaggerates from a small number of examples.
[75] Passerini, 148 f.
[76] Forni, *Reclutamento*, App. B. II. On the Danubian legions *A.* XVI. 13. 3 is an important text: they were being replenished from Asia, Africa, and Narbonese Gaul.
[77] *A.* XIII. 35. 4. [78] II. 80. 20. [79] III. 24. 15.
[80] For Vespasian's arrangements see Braithwaite, ed. to Suet. *Vesp.*, 8.4.

(c) A first principle in evaluating evidence about recruitment to the *auxilia* is that the 'ethnic' title of an auxiliary regiment is, from quite early days of the Principate, no guide to the origins of the men who composed it. The Roman government had two difficulties, which pulled it in opposite directions. In A.D. 6 it had seen the rising of Pannonians and Dalmatians, under chiefs leading their own peoples, who had been partially trained in Roman techniques. So the locally recruited men must be sent abroad, but in A.D. 26 it was precisely that policy which caused the Thracian rebellion.[81] So what did an army commander do if he wanted troops thereafter? It seems clear that normally, i.e. when the central government was not giving him close instructions on the matter, he reverted to local recruitment, for this was less cumbrous and less costly. So a *cohors Pannoniorum*, previously transferred to the Rhine, could soon be replenished by Gauls and Rhinelanders. Yet later it might be moved again, for some other province might need reinforcements. So we get the situation, amply documented for the first two centuries A.D., in which auxiliaries were serving neither in a regiment bearing an 'ethnic' title related to their origin nor in the province in which they were born. *Diplomata*, our main evidence, provide many examples, e.g. *ILS* 1998 (= MW 403), a Thracian in an Aquitanian cohort stationed in Upper Germany, *ILS* 2001 (= Sm. 2, 353), a Spaniard in a Pannonian *ala* stationed in Britain.

The process was studied closely by K. Kraft, *Zur Rekrutierung der Alen und Kohorten am Rhein und Donau* (1951), a work which has not been seriously superseded.[82] His analysis of individual soldiers led to the conclusion that by the mid-first century A.D. recruitment to all auxiliary regiments came from areas adjacent to those in which the regiment was serving—the word 'adjacent' being interpreted very broadly, e.g. the Rhine units could draw not only on the Rhineland but on the whole of Gaul. But regiments might then be moved away, either to meet emergencies elsewhere (Pannonian regiments composed largely of Pannonians were soon serving on the Rhine), or for political or disciplinary reasons (such as those which made Vitellius attempt to get the Batavian cohorts back to Britain, II. 59. 5). And there were other exceptions: specialist troops, such as Thracian archers, Cretan slingers, or Gallic cavalry,[83] might be needed anywhere; and sometimes (still more in the second century) the policy of sending new recruits far away from their homes was, at least temporarily, revived.

Exceptions such as these have made a decided mark on the surviving gravestones of first-century Rhineland auxiliaries. Yet Tacitus

---

[81] *A.* IV. 46.
[82] See H. T. Rowell's review, *JRS* 1953, 175, and my own in *CR* 1955, 189.
[83] Rowell, cit., was sceptical here, but seems to dismiss too easily the evidence for the large number of Gauls in the *alae*, as distinct from the *cohortes*.

persistently depicts the Rhineland cohorts and *alae* as almost wholly German or Gallic. This could be a picture as misleading as that which he draws of the legionaries.[84] But Kraft was surely right to emphasize that even by this period the 'auxiliaries' used by Rome, in the Rhineland above all, were not confined to those enrolled in units with permanent titles, and with regular conditions of service. For not only were there local forces defending their own homelands, a prime example being the Helvetian garrison of I. 67. 6. But it is also clear[85] that very substantial bodies of Gallic and German troops could be raised quickly to meet emergencies, and could then be returned to their homes long before they had served the official period of auxiliary service. If this be right, the auxiliary component of the Vitellian armies was something like the *Germanicus exercitus* which Tacitus depicts.[86]

The evidence about *auxilia* in the armies of Syria and Judaea is much less adequate. It is reasonable to guess that they, even more than the *auxilia* of the West and the Balkans, were recruited locally. But the force which Mucianus was leading to Italy[87] is never described in any detail, and it presumably went back before it crossed the Italian Alps.

II. THE COMPOSITION OF THE HISTORIES

Our first knowledge of Tacitus' operations on this work comes from A.D. 106, when Pliny, *Epp.* VI. 16, replied with style and readiness to Tacitus' inquiry about the eruption of Vesuvius in 79. He followed that with a further letter on the same subject (VI. 20), and later sent another offering (VII. 33) about an event in 93, a year when Tacitus was probably away from Rome (*Agr.* 45. 4). Probably this was Pliny's first acquaintance, and that of Roman society generally, with the fact that Tacitus was composing a historical work which concerned Domitian's reign. For at V. 8. 12, replying to Titinius Capito about historiography, Pliny refers to the treatment of *intacta et nova* as a subject open to generalization, not as something on which his friend had already embarked.[88]

(It should be said in passing that, if the above view be right, it renders something impossible which was already highly improbable, namely that Pliny drew on the *Histories* when he wrote up his *Panegyric*,

---

[84] Above, p. 20.   [85] Above, p. 21.

[86] Even so, the *Germanorum Gallorumque . . . corpora* of II. 93. 7 must be mainly 'regular' soldiers, for the emergency Gallic *auxilia* have already been sent home. The majority, however, are legionaries, see the preponderance of legionaries in the force with which Vitellius entered Rome, II. 89. 5.

[87] II. 83. 5.

[88] S.-W., 335. *Contra*, Syme, 117.

not later than 103. On the relation between the two works see the note which introduces I. 15–16.)

Nearly nine years, then, had elapsed since Tacitus had announced, with some pleasure (*Agr.* 3. 3), that he was contemplating a substantial work which concerned Domitian's principate, and to which his *Agricola* would be a book for publication meanwhile. How far had he changed his mind, either about the plan of this work, or about the thinking behind it? On both points some scholars seem to have exaggerated the change.

As to planning, Tacitus had promised *memoriam prioris servitutis, testimonium praesentium bonorum.* An account of Domitian's reign, therefore, all fifteen years of it, *grande mortalis aevi spatium.* But can he ever have thought of 81 as a suitable starting-point? Domitian's accession had to be tied to his membership of a dynasty, which had been *varia sorte laetum rei publicae aut atrox,* II. 1. 1. So back through the two previous Flavians, back to Vespasian's rising, and into the *longum et unum annum* (*Dial.* 41). At that point he may have pondered, but he eventually took his critical decision, and followed Sallust in starting at the beginning of a year, I. 1. 1 n.

But it is not about his beginning but about his ending that modern writers have often suggested that he changed his plan. *Testimonium praesentium bonorum*: what would that imply? When he wrote the *Histories* he forecast that he might write later about the reigns of Nerva and Trajan; but he did not do so (for possible reasons see I. 1. 17 n.). Had he promised that already in 98? He could not confidently have done so, when Trajan had become *princeps* only a few months earlier. Yet, though less extreme than many scholars, R. H. Martin writes[89] 'in the upshot the plan of the work was altered; the happy epilogue was omitted'. But was it? We do not know how Tacitus closed either of his two major works (or 'would have closed' perhaps we should say of the *Annals*), but two or three chapters of epilogue would have been enough to illumine the admirable features of Trajan's government (*A.* IV. 5–6 show what could be done, when Tacitus was in the mood). Or again, the books devoted to *memoria prioris servitutis* could, by themselves, by contrast, have been the *testimonium praesentium bonorum.*

For political thinking, we begin with Tacitus' claim (*Agr.* 3.1) that Nerva has been able to reconcile *principatus* and *libertas.* The words are striking, and there is no adequate ground for regarding them as just a perfunctory obeisance to a new regime: he wrote them after his consulship in 97, in which year he saw Trajan's adoption and may even have participated in the ceremony which consummated it.[90] In contrast,

---

[89] In an essay which is otherwise most shrewd and convincing, *Tacitus* (ed. T. A. Dorey, 1969), 126.

[90] The consulate, Plin. *Epp.* II. 1. 6; the ceremony, Syme, 129.

Galba's adoption of Piso seemed to him vicious—the wrong man was chosen and the procedure was autocratic;[91] but even in the speech he puts into Galba's mouth the promise of *libertas* is a forecast of what might emerge from the end of a bad emperor. So too in Book IV of the *Histories* (42) Curtius Montanus, in unusual language, describes the bright possibilities the future might bring, if only the Senate will show courage.[92] But Nero's death, and the coming of the Flavian house, turned out to be a false dawn, and in the *Histories* Tacitus was able to satisfy his own genius by concentrating on the horrors of the period he had chosen. Yet there is nothing in his actual writings[93] to suggest that in *c.* 106 the present seemed less bright to him than it had been in 98, and *rara temporum felicitate*, I. 1. 19, is surely a deliberate echo of *Agr.* 3.

Moreover it is now generally agreed that Tacitus wrote the *Dialogus* in the early years of the principate of Trajan.[94] At the end of that work the chairman Maternus accepts in the interests of peace a state governed by *sapientissimus et unus*. This too may reflect the thinking to which Tacitus had been driven—perhaps with reluctance—by the early days of the second century A.D. But in the *Dialogus* what stands out even more clearly is the comfortable affability and absence of acrimony which surrounds the closely textured argument, even though it becomes an argument about politics as well as about oratory.

(Syme, 219 f., uses the same passages in Tacitus to argue against Klingner, 26, and other scholars who have seen a change between the *Agricola* and the *Histories*. Yet for Syme, if I have understood him rightly, the main unchanging feature of Tacitus' thought was his scepticism, as fierce in 98 as in 106. That for Tacitus scepticism was inescapable is not to be doubted, but to me it seems to have been still moderated, in 106 no less than in 98, by a keen sense of relief.)

In 98 Tacitus had also published the *Germania*.[95] This was a piece of research, after the model of Posidonius and other Greeks, about the nature of 'barbarian' civilization and its contrast with Roman *mores*. That Tacitus felt the theme to have a bearing on Roman policy is certain: the famous ending to Chap. 33 is echoed in his later work, see (e.g.) I. 3. 9 n. But it is not a book which in any obvious way dealt with a contemporary situation, e.g. Trajan's tarrying on the Rhine during the first eighteen months of his principate. There is nothing to suggest a contribution to Trajan's foreign policy; moreover the research behind

---

[91] I. 14 nn.

[92] R. H. Martin, *JRS* 1967, 109 ff.

[93] Even though other evidence, especially the coinage, may suggest that Trajan abandoned much of the propaganda current in Nerva's reign.

[94] Syme, App. 28. Against the view that it was the book submitted to Pliny in 107, *Epp.* VII. 20, S.-W, 427, argues cogently. The most likely date seems 102, when Fubius Iustus, to whom it is dedicated, was consul.

[95] *Germ.* 37.

the *Germania* must have begun some time earlier, when the frontier situation, and the *princeps*, were entirely different. It has been argued, however, that the *Germania* was an offshoot from the work Tacitus was doing when preparing his *Histories*, analogous to the research he must have done before his description of the war in Judaea, but leading to material which he thought too ample for insertion in the *Histories* as ultimately compiled.[96] In reply one can say, first that neither in its scope nor in its emphases does the *Germania* read like an introduction to the events of 69–70 or to those of the Flavian period (even 29.4 reads like a clumsy afterthought); and secondly that the areas most affected by Roman activities in those years (the Rhineland and Holland) are singularly little described. But there is more. In 97, even if for only two months, Tacitus was consul, and both then and in the earlier months as consul designate, would have had special duties in the Senate. He began to compose the *Agricola*; can we suppose that the full planning and execution of the *Germania* were also accomplished in that year? It is surely more likely that his researches on Germany had been an occupation of the years when he had decided not to attempt publication, i.e. the last years of Domitian. And if this be right, there is no reason to suppose that in 98 he had progressed any distance with his planning of the *Histories*, to the point at which he was thinking about geographical offshoots. If he had got that far, his description of his literary biography at *Agr.* 3 would become at least as disingenuous as even his most hostile critics have made it.

All in all, it seems probable that Tacitus, born about 57,[97] was a man in his late forties when he began the composition of the *Histories*. There were men near his own age to whom he could turn for advice about events in the middle and later years of his chosen period—though few, one would think, who could, like Pliny, have had both the fortune to be present at a great event and the capacity to describe it with elegance. But for the period covered by the extant Books what participants were still alive? Tacitus must have talked with Verginius Rufus before his death in 97, even though he was not enthusiastic about Verginius' virtues, II. 51. 4 n.; Spurinna survived, and was used, we may be sure, about a limited piece of military history, II. 11. 14 n.; some source, possibly an oral one, seems to have described the bitter vicissitudes in the career of Marius Celsus, I. 14. 5 n.; Antonius Primus at Tolosa, II. 86. 3 n., was perhaps too difficult to reach, though others, perhaps including the young tribune of legion VII Claudia, Vipstanus Messalla, may have given evidence in his favour. But even Messalla, described as the one man who brought *bonas artes* to the wars of 69, III. 9. 14, had probably no career after the tribute Tacitus paid him as a participant in the *Dialogus*.[98]

---

[96] Paratore, 287 ff.   [97] Praetor in 88, *A.* XI. 11.   [98] Syme, 108.

So what were Tacitus' sources for 69? The question has been exhaustively discussed, and the following summary is intended to do no more than indicate the line taken in the notes:

(1) At II. 37. 1 Tacitus starts a discussion with *invenio apud quosdam auctores*, and at III. 51. 1 he has *celeberrimos auctores habeo*. Those who think he in fact followed, at least in the main, one source only, may claim that his plurals relate only to the various authors cited by that main source. But if they claim that, the burden of proof is on them, and in relation to the latter part of Book II and the whole of Book III they have never successfully borne it. On Book III see also 22.6 (*alii tradiderint*), 29.10 (*omnes auctores*), 54.23 (*quidam . . . tradidere*), 59.14 (*multi tradidere*). See also Wellesley, ed., 7.

(2) At the end of Book II (101.1) Tacitus cites *scriptores temporum qui potiente rerum Flavia domo monimenta belli huiusce composuerunt*, and implies that, in addition to these writers (more than one), he has a source which told him something different. Complicated problems arise (n. ad loc.), but the passage is almost unintelligible if Tacitus was using one written source only.

(3) Yet there is an extremely strong case for claiming that in Book I, and in Chapters 11–51 of Book II, Tacitus was *mainly* following a source which was common to himself and to Plutarch and Suetonius. Suetonius certainly used other material as well, and Tacitus surely did so too, e.g. at points like I. 79. Yet in this part of the work expressions like *varie prodidere*, I. 46. 8 (with subsequent expressions of doubt between differing versions), may do no more than repeat the doubts expressed by the author T. was following. Anyway there is adequate ground for speaking of a 'common source', used heavily by all three writers, and this expression has been freely used in my notes.[99]

(4) In Book III Tacitus cites and compares two authorities, Pliny (the Elder) and Vipstanus Messalla. The latter was a young man who played a part in the campaigns recounted in that Book, but is unlikely to have had anything to contribute on earlier events.

(5) For that and other reasons Fabia believed that it was Pliny who was the 'common source'. The case for that view is still strong, but for other candidates see Syme, App. 29. About possible contributions from Cluvius Rufus (though he cannot, for many reasons, have been a main source for 68–9) see G. Townend, *AJP* 1964, 337 ff.

(6) Comparison between Plutarch, Suetonius, and various points in I. 4–11 shows that the 'common source' covered also the later months of A.D. 68 (see nn.). But on Plutarch see Additional note.

Tacitus is said by Jerome, *Comm. ad Zachariam* III. 14, to have written

---

[99] Fabia's analysis provides overwhelming proof: particular points e.g. I. 12. 14, I. 80. 1 ff., II. 37, II. 65, are discussed in the notes.

thirty Books of history; and the Medicean manuscript labels the extant Books of the *Histories* with numbers from XVII to XXI. So, a well-known puzzle. One thing no solution must ever allow is that the *Annals* could have been completed to Nero's death in the rest of Book XVI of what we know of that work, which breaks off before the tour to Greece, before the deaths of Corbulo and many other prominent Romans, and before the catastrophes in Gaul and Spain. Therefore, if he survived, Tacitus would have written probably eighteen books of the *Annals*; and if Jerome had them, then there were only twelve Books of the *Histories*. But supposing Tacitus did not complete the *Annals* before his death, what then did Jerome know? The possibilities are analysed by Syme, App. 35.

If the *Histories* did contain only twelve Books, then the distribution favoured by Syme is surely right: Vespasian's death at the end of VI, one Book for Titus, and five for Domitian. But if Jerome's total of thirty was based on only sixteen for the *Annals*, a work which he did not realize was not completed, then fourteen Books for the *Histories* may still be allowed, and a more comfortable solution, assigning more space for the Domitianic Books (*prioris servitutis*), be tolerated.

What was Tacitus' degree of authority, in *c.* 106, as a contemporary historian? He was writing as a consular of ten years' standing, a man whose life had coincided with vital moments of the period he was recounting, and with at least one vital moment of the period which followed it. He had relatively close knowledge of the Senate of Rome and of its relations with the *princeps*, and does not seem to have made enemies in high circles at any time. But there is little evidence that he knew the Roman provinces at all well. Even if he had been a governor in the Greek-speaking world, his attitude to the Greeks, and of course also to the Jews, was contemptuous.[1]

Yet, so far as the Western provinces are concerned, his birth and social circle were considerable compensation for a man writing about the events of 68–9. 'Italicusne es an provincialis?', someone said to him at the circus;[2] and the incident, as recounted by Pliny, is reasonably regarded as enough to prove that he was born either in Narbonese Gaul (like his father-in-law) or in North Italy. Whichever view be right,[3] it is clear that he had an understanding of the 'new men' from both those regions. A familiar type of Roman vituperation was that directed at a man's birth-place. Tacitus forgoes this, and even omits altogether to tell us the birth-places of men he might have wished to wound.[4] He was well equipped to write of a period in which *novi homines e municipiis et*

---

[1] Syme, 504 ff.   [2] Plin. *Epp.* IX. 23. 2.
[3] E. Köstermann, 'Tacitus und die Transpadana', *Athenaeum*, 1965, 167 ff.
[4] In the *Histories* the best example is Antonius Primus.

coloniis atque etiam provinciis, A. III. 55, were setting the tone of society, and so also of the years when the storm centre of civil war lay in the border-lands between Italy and Gaul.

So Tacitus came to his *Histories* through biography, ethnography,[5] and a study of the place of oratory in politics. To compare his biography of a single man, and that his father-in-law, with the many character studies in his later works would be unhelpful; but it happens that two biographers, Plutarch and Suetonius, are our other surviving contributors to the history of Rome in A.D. 69.[6] At once be it said that Tacitus, no more than they, overcame the vice of ancient biography, that of assuming that a man's character remained unchanged throughout his life.[7] But in these two Books Tacitus is necessarily concerned only with brief moments in his subjects' careers, and not to any significant extent with the possibility that external forces might have altered the impact of their personalities.[8] Even his obituaries concentrate on the picture the subject would have presented to contemporaries at the time of his death.

His outstanding subjects are rulers and potential rulers, of whom Galba is the first and by far the most interesting. Tacitus' account of him appears at first reading to be inconsistent: between the man of *antiquus rigor, cui pares non sumus,* and the man who shows *mobilitas ingenii*; between the emperor's *facilitas* and his fierce maintenance of military discipline.[9] But a clear portrait gradually emerges, and it is then firmly drawn in the famous obituary at I. 49. Among the judgements in that chapter Plutarch gives enough to show that the two writers were using a common source. But to have neglected the elements used by Tacitus in the sentence beginning *famae nec incuriosus* . . . betrays Plutarch's lack of understanding of the Roman aristocrat (indeed of the aristocrats of other ages), a man who took his reputation for granted, once he had attained it, and who assumed his servants were loyal until it was proved otherwise.[10]

When we come to Otho, there is a looseness and thinness about Plutarch's account, as compared with Tacitus'.[11] What Tacitus brings out at every moment after Otho's elevation is the emperor's dependence

---

[5] Further developed in Books IV and V.

[6] Dio's epitomators contribute something, but we possess no analysis by Dio himself.

[7] See (e.g.) Syme, 421 ff.

[8] Otho's suicide surprised everyone, but simply because they had not appreciated the whole of his character, II. 31. 1 ff., 46 ff.

[9] I. 18. 17, as against 7. 10; 12. 14 as against 35 ff. See E. Köestermann, *Navicula Chilionensis* (1956), 191 ff.

[10] Yet D. M. Jones, *Plutarch and Rome* (1972), 77, can believe that the correspondences between the two writers derive from a reading of Plutarch by T.

[11] And topographical carelessness, though the author claimed autopsy, Plut. *O.* 7 (cf. 14).

on the soldiers who brought him to power and his unavailing attempts to free himself from their wishes.[12] With Vitellius Tacitus is not so happy. He makes a determined, and on the whole successful, attempt to discard Flavian propaganda (II. 1–7 nn.), but about the behaviour of Vitellius himself he is at the mercy of a senatorial tradition which saw wrong in every movement and which makes no effort to analyse the emperor's policies. On Vespasian and Titus, and on Mucianus, Tacitus has given us just enough to make it tantalizing that we have to miss his fuller account of Flavian rule.[13] He has also begun, with Vinius, his great series of obituaries (followed in Book III with those of Valens and Flavius Sabinus), which make one regret the loss of his words when he reported the deaths of Helvidius Priscus, or Eprius Marcellus, or Caecina.

As to oratory, whether or not his work on the *Dialogus* contributed to the change, it is obvious that in the *Histories* he progressed far beyond the artificial speeches which the *Agricola* reports before the battle of Mons Graupius.[14] In our two Books there are six speeches in oratio recta, Galba's speech on the adoption, Piso's address to the cohort on guard, three by Otho (his proclamation claim, the address to the mutineers, and his valedictory), and Mucianus' encouragement to Vespasian.[15] At first reading, one could readily believe, both that on each occasion such a speech was delivered, and also that Tacitus' rendering of it, though largely in his own style, reports faithfully the arguments each speaker used. It is only after more detailed study that one has to conclude that neither proposition is necessarily true. The first three of the six appear to relate to occasions when very few words were used.[16] The speech to the mutineers, unless Plut. *O.* 3. 7 has been even more than usually careless about interesting matter in the 'common source', seems to be Tacitus' own invention. And Mucianus' speech, though more carefully constructed than any, can be shown to contain material which has been introduced from other occasions, or which must have been conceived *post eventum*.[17] Yet one is left with a conviction that Tacitus' composition in all these speeches derives from careful thought, not only about the arguments which were apposite to each occasion, but also about the character of each speaker.[18]

For all these occasions for speeches are examples of the quality any reader of the *Histories* must most admire, namely Tacitus' descriptive

---

[12] Klingner, *passim*.

[13] K. H. Waters, *JRS* 1972, 226, claims that for T. Titus can 'do no wrong'. How does he know?

[14] Ogilvie–Richmond, *Tacitus, Agricola* (1967), 253, 265.

[15] I. 15–16, 29–30, 37–8, 83–4, II. 47, 76–7.

[16] Syme, 191–2.

[17] II. 76–7 nn. I do believe that Mucianus made a public speech, even though he could have been convicted of *maiestas* for going to Judaea to make it.

[18] See on Galba, I. 16. 1. n.

power. Perhaps no example can match parts of Book III—its ending, or the account of Cremona's fall. But there is much in these two Books which comes near to Tacitus' best—Galba's hesitations and bravery, with the scene in the Forum (esp. I. 40); the praetorian mutiny (I. 80); and the gradual approach to the determined suicide of Otho (II. 46–9).

COMMENTARY

BOOK I

1–11. *Introduction*

THIS introduction comprises a Preface (cap. 1), a Summary of Contents (2–3), and a Survey of Rome and the Empire (4–11). Of the many discussions which the whole, and each part separately, have provoked, bibliography is provided in three articles of relatively recent date: E. Koestermann, *Historia*, 1956, 213 ff., M. Fuhrmann, *Philologus*, 1960, 250 ff., and Heubner's edition; see also Bursian, 1943, 78 ff. (Koestermann). The following notes attempt to pose the main problems, but not in every case to analyse the views of earlier writers.

1.1. initium mihi operis. T. follows Sallust, and doubtless other predecessors, in starting annalistically at the beginning of a year (Sall. *Hist.* fr. 1, *res populi Romani M. Lepido Q. Catulo consulibus ac deinde militiae et domi gestas composui*); like Sallust, too, he proceeds straight to a comparison between himself and earlier historians (Sall. fr. 4), and then to an assertion of his own impartiality (ibid. 6, *neque me diversa pars in civilibus armis movit a vero*).

He has been criticized both for the substance of his decision to start at 1 Jan. 69 and for the way he has defended it. If he could have freed himself from anti-imperial bias (and so from reluctance to begin from the end of a dynasty), it has been felt, he would have started either at Nero's death in June 68 or at the proclamation of Vespasian on 1 July 69, i.e. at the end or at the beginning of a reign (yet the *Histories* did at least end at an emperor's death). For a summary of critics see Syme, 145, and add J. B. Hainsworth. *Greece & Rome*, 1962, 128. But the later of the two other possible dates, cutting in half *illum . . . longum et unum annum* (*Dial.* 17. 14), would have produced a monstrosity, and T. would have found it intolerable to introduce the Flavians in that context—his views on the planning of their rising emerge fairly clearly from the opening chapters of Book II. Yet for June 68 there was much to be said, since given that his main source for Galba's principate seems to have covered the whole of the year 68 (see Introd., and nn. below), T. was faced with difficult problems of adjustment when he selected a starting-point only a fortnight before Galba's death. True, had he begun with the death of Nero he would have had to bring in much that preceded that event, 'Vindex, Verginius, and the proclamation of Galba, with a vast military and political imbroglio' (Syme, cit.). But no writer of narrative history can escape the task of summarizing the forces which

33

led to his opening act, and it is not obvious that T.'s choice of 1 Jan. 69 made his own performance of that task any easier, especially as Vindex, Verginius, etc., had still to come in. What 1 Jan. did was to complicate for him certain connections within Galba's reign, notably the reasons for Otho's rising, on which his apparent divergence from our other sources may be due less to his deliberate judgement than to his self-imposed compression (see Fuhrmann, 258, and nn. to I. 23 below). We of course regret his decision all the more because of something he could not help, namely that we happen to possess no really adequate account of the events of 68; but this is not the only reason for dissatisfaction. The decision T. took was surely influenced by his determination to open his work on the lines laid down by his main model; but for that he paid a penalty, though he tried magnificently (not only in I. 4–11, but throughout the surviving Books) to render the penalty small.

Yet although T.'s decision may be questioned, one must sympathize with Syme's impatience at some of the strictures on the way our present chapter defended it. 'Si cette préface est brillament écrite, elle est faiblement pensée', wrote Fabia in a characteristic attempt to divorce thought from style (*RÉA* 3, 1901, 76)—for similar quotations from the same article see Syme, 146, and for criticisms by other scholars see Heubner, 9. What has caused trouble is the series of loose conjunctions, *nam, simul, sed* (line 16), *quod si*, which confuse efforts at schematic analysis. Yet they leave a piece of prose about the essential meaning of which there is no serious doubt: it would indeed have been difficult to achieve more in the course of twenty lines.

2. nam. This word is the main difficulty in the chapter. If T. meant what follows to give a logical explanation of his precise starting-point, then not only are his reasons inadequate but they are hardly even reasons, see Fabia, cit., 51. For he at once goes on to depreciate historians of the Principate before 69; so why not start earlier? And if the answer be offered that for the Julio-Claudians there were at least several historians, however biased, then not only is that not a good answer in this context, but one could also adduce the same argument against writing about Vespasian's reign, which T. expressly tells us had received treatment from more than one writer, II. 101. O. Seeck, *RhM* 1901, 227, put the point very pungently, but it is hard to accept his suggestion that the preface was recast when T. came to write the *Annals* and realized the deficiencies of the Julio-Claudian writers. How would he have been able to do this when his earlier text was known to his world? and was there ever a moment when he saw himself as the author of a single history (A.D. 14–96)—of the thirty Books known to Jerome and to the Medicean manuscript (see Introd., p. 27)?

So the explanation given by *nam* cannot precisely, or at any rate exclusively, apply to what immediately follows. What matters is the thinking of the whole chapter. T. is concerned above all to make two points, (i) that he is eminently qualified to write the history of 69–96 (13, *mihi Galba*. . . .), (ii) that this is now an age of free speech, as he prophesied when he wrote *Agr.* 2. 3, 3. The first point led him to his chosen period; the second, once he had made it, made him go back to reflect on the lack of *libertas*, enforced or self-imposed, shown by the people who wrote about the Julio-Claudians. There is no good reason to think that he saw their defects for the first time when he composed the *Annals*; indeed the point made at *A.* I. 1. 10 ff. is almost identical.

One omission from the chapter is remarkable. T. was writing contemporary history, but never tells us (did Sallust either?) how far he was an eye-witness. From *Agr.* 42 we know that the end of Domitian's reign embarrassed him, but what about the events of the surviving Books?

3. res populi Romani, 'the history of the Republic'; *A.* I. 1. 4, *veteris p.R. prospera vel adversa*, IV. 32. 1, *veteres p.R.res*; Livy 2. 1. 1, *liberi . . . p.R.res*.

4. pari eloquentia ac libertate. Earlier editors held that *eloquentia* was balanced by *magna illa ingenia cessere*, *libertate* by *veritas . . . infracta.* Heubner ad loc., following Klingner, 198, shows convincingly that this schematism is wrong, since the traditional components of a writer's *ingenium* were *libertas* as well as *eloquentia;* see Seneca, *ad Marciam*, 1. 3, on Cremutius Cordus, and *A.* I. 1. 2 on the *decora ingenia* broken by the growth of *adulatio* in Augustus' time.

Heubner, 11, goes on to ask whether T. claimed to have recovered the *eloquentia* and *libertas* which had disappeared after Actium. T. gives no explicit answer, but he surely leaves no doubt on either issue. Anyway, 'free speech' is the chief thing in his mind.

5. postquam. Heubner, 10, claims that the conjunction is purely temporal. But that T. intended no causal connection between writing and politics seems foreign to his whole method in this chapter.

6. pacis interfuit, cf. *A.* I. 9. 5, *non aliud discordantis patriae remedium fuisse quam ut ab uno regeretur* (spoken by Augustus' friends). But though this particular defence for the Principate is largely missing from T.'s more bitter analysis in *A.* I. 1 and 2, there is no need to suppose with Klingner that he had given the matter further reflection in the interval. *Potentia* here is not a friendly word, and *cum domino pax ista venit* had been said long ago (Lucan I. 670).

6. magna illa ingenia cessere. Here the antithesis takes T. to great extremes. Already *pari eloquentia ac libertate* may have been more than he really wanted to concede to Republican writers, but he now forgets his own praise of Livy (*Agr.* 10), Fabius Rusticus (ibid.), and Cluvius Rufus (I. 8. 3); and in the *Annals* (XIV. 19) he was to be even more laudatory of Servilius Nonianus (see also the arguments of Aper in *Dial.* 23, and on early Augustan writers *A.* I. 1). Sallust (*Hist.* I. 3 and 4) had been respectful of his predecessors; so was Servilius (Quintilian X. 1. 102).

7. simul... infracta. See again Seneca, *ad Marc.* I. 4. The Elder Seneca, according to his son (*HRR* II. 98), thought the process started as early as the beginning of the civil wars, the point at which he began his history. T. would perhaps not have wished to press Actium as a turning-point, but his two stages (*primum... mox*) are percipient and (as far as we know) his own.

inscitia... alienae. Dio too, 53. 19, in a passage which it was daring of an historian of his generation to write, finds this to be a problem from the first moment of the Principate; cf. Fergus Millar, *A Study of Cassius Dio* (1964), 37 f.

8. odio adversus dominantis. Heubner, 12, argues that at this point (as with *libidine adsentandi*) T. is talking only about the general tendencies of historians, and that *beneficium* and *iniuria* (lines 13–14) introduce for the first time the idea of prejudice for or against particular rulers, as distinct from antipathy to *dominatio* in principle. I find it hard to think that the sentence beginning *mihi* (13, without a conjunction) introduces an entirely new point. T. was surely concerned both with animosity towards absolutism and also with the consequence that the reputation of an emperor suffered after his death—*postquam occiderant*, *A.* I. 1. 10.

10. obnoxios. Cf. Livy 23.12.9, *aut superbus aut obnoxius... quorum alterum est hominis alienae libertatis obliti, alterum suae.* In T. generally with dative of the person to whom subjected, but used absolutely here and at II. 56. 8 (see also *A.* XV. 38). Wellesley's 'deeply committed' brings out the constraint imposed on these people by the regime they served, but perhaps not adequately T.'s contempt for them: 'servile', or at least 'submissive', seems needed.

sed ambitionem... inest. The judgement is shrewd, but it is astonishing that T. felt himself to be the man to make it. In what follows he disdains to give any reasoned defence for himself against any charge of prejudice in either direction. And when he does come to 'declare his interest' (14, *dignitatem nostram...*), he seems to fear that he might be accused not of *malignitas* but of *adulatio*. Did he really think that his contemporaries could have seen his work that way?

14. dignitatem... non abnuerim. There can be no certainty about the dates in T.'s early career, except that he was praetor in 88 and already then *XVvir* (*A.* XI. 11). Fabia consistently (see esp. *Journ. Sav.* 1926, 189 ff.) maintained that he received the *latus clavus* from Vespasian, the quaestorship from Titus, and the tribunate (or aedileship) from Domitian. This forced him to suppose a gap longer than the minimum between quaestorship and praetorship, and he supposed a setback caused by the 'disgrace' of his father-in-law Agricola in 83 (or 84). But it is almost impossible to connect with any 'disgrace' a *novus homo* who was granted a major priesthood by the time of his praetorship. More probably, T. was quaestor in 83. His *latus clavus* having been granted by Vespasian, he became military tribune and held office in the vigintivirate: at least one of those posts was owed to Titus. See Syme, 59 f.

17. quod si vita suppeditet. For *quod si* see GG, 1307; the nearest parallels are III. 9. 5, 66. 1, *A.* II. 73. 10, *Agr.* 16. 6 (*quod nisi*), in none of which is there an adversative sense. 'Indeed' is possible, if any word be needed.

T.'s failure to redeem the promise of this sentence has been used to argue that in Trajan's reign he suffered disappointment, and turned to write the *Annals*, which is held to be a work of greater bitterness than the *Histories* and one directed against the Principate as an institution: see, e.g., H. Bardon, *Les Empereurs et les lettres latines* (1940), 378 ff. Certainly the *Annals*, if our sentence be sincere, seem to derive from a change of plan. But there may have been other reasons for this, not least the growing interest in the Caesars which came to T. when he was reading his sources for the *Histories*. That the *Annals* contain some sinister allusions to contemporary events is probable (though they seem to point at Hadrian rather than at Trajan, cf. Syme, 481 ff.); but it is perhaps too often assumed that T.'s beliefs and activities were constantly modified by close attention to the world of politics (including his ambitions about his own career) rather than by the progress of his own study of history.

Even more commentators (see Fabia, *RÉA* 1901, 73, Courbaud, 18, Paratore, 345 ff., Klingner, *Mus. Helv.* 1958, 205 f., Heubner, 14) have held that this postponement of a work about Nerva and Trajan contradicts the promise made in *Agr.* 3. 3 that his next work would include a *testimonium praesentium bonorum*. Fabia even claimed that the present sentence could not have been sincere, since *uberior materia* was obviously unsuitable for a work of old age—a curious view of old age. But is the supposed promise in the *Agricola* a real one? T. had no *uberior materia* when he wrote those words in 98. His *testimonium* was going to emerge by contrast, when his readers compared their present happiness with his account of the servitude they had endured.

As to the promise here, we do not of course know whether T. ever deliberately abandoned it before his death. But it would not be surprising if he came to feel that Trajan's reign, and Nerva's too, did not provide material suited to his genius. *Uberior materia* certainly, and he would probably have relished Roman victories; but was he the man to write about an emperor whom he ostensibly, and perhaps actually, admired?

18. principatum divi Nervae et imperium Traiani. At *Agr.* 3. 1 Trajan was simply *Nerva Traianus*, at 44.5 *princeps Traianus*; at *Germ.* 37. 2 he is almost gratuitously called *imperator*. How much point has the variation here? It would be right to remind the world, as Pliny does often in the *Panegyric*, that the adoption of a military man had solidified the government; and by the time T. was writing Trajan had won some at least of his Dacian victories. But any suggestion that Trajan's rule was a 'persönliches Regiment' (E. Kornemann, *Tacitus*[2] (1947), 26) might have been dangerously offensive. For the view that Trajan's adoption was widely regarded as a military coup, and that his policies were little different from those of Domitian, see D. Kienast, *Historia*, 1968, 56 ff., K. H. Waters, *AJP* 1969, 385 ff., but I do not think either writer would claim this passage as significant support for their views.

19. rara . . . licet. Yet it was still apparently not wholly *securum* to write about the Flavian period; cf. Plin. *Epp.* V. 18. 12, *intacta et nova? graves offensae, levis gratia.* See Syme, 229. Heubner may well be right in seeing the sentence as a tactful exhortation to Trajan (he cites Cicero's *pro Marcello* as a parallel) on the principle enunciated by Pliny, *qui est acerrimus stimulus monendi, laudibus incitavi, Epp.* V. 17. 4.

I. 2. The two superb chapters which follow are well discussed by Heubner, and require no general discussion here. The *casus* (see 3.4) are 'events', not 'disasters', but except for *prosperae in Oriente . . . res* they included nothing which T. found agreeable.

1. opus adgredior †opimum casibus. The first adjective can never be confidently recovered. *Opimum* is read also by L., and is therefore adopted without obelus by K. (1961), the theory being that M. corrupted it by assimilation to *casibus*. But Madvig had objected (*Adversaria critica* (1878), ii. 559) (i) that the word is never used simply to denote abundance (i.e. without special reference to richness of soil or monetary possessions), (ii) that an adjective is needed to stand in direct relationship to *casibus*, as does *atrox* to *proeliis* and *discors* to *seditionibus*, rather than one which governs all the following substantives indiscriminately. On (ii) one may wonder: the adjectives get progressively less appropriate to *opus* and more to the contents of the *opus* (cf. the ambiguity of *res* in Livy, praef. 4); perhaps then the first one did look closely to the word *opus* (as would be true of *plenum*, suggested by a later hand in M.). But on the Latinity of *opimum*, never used elsewhere in T., and never (remarkably) in Lucan, Madvig's contention has never been successfully challenged. *Opibus* doubtless arose from *opus* as well as from *casibus*; and though *rapidum* (supposed haplography of r) is conceivable, the word written by T. may have had no resemblance to the letters found in M.

2. ipsa etiam pace saevum. It is hard to decide whether this is just a 'modal' ablative like the others. With a temporal ablative the word *ipsa* is slightly easier to construe; and there are many parallels for a temporal ablative without *in* (unwarrantably here inserted by Ritter), e.g. *proconsulatu* I. 48. 17, *motu Vindicis* I. 89. 4, *pace pessimus* II. 86. 11, *bello Sabino* III. 72. 10. But T. would surely have not been sorry to introduce a causal sense; cf. *recentia saevae pacis exempla* I. 50. 8, *pacem sine dubio post haec, verum cruentam A.* I. 10. 3, and the consequences of *immota pax* depicted in *A.* IV. 32–3.

   quattuor principes. Proof, if one were needed, that the work covered Domitian's murder: was Nerva's accession also described?

3. plerumque permixta. *Plerumque*, as normally in T., 'in a number of cases', cf. I. 87. 8 n. *Permixta* is surely more than 'the two types simultaneously', e.g. the invasion of the Rhoxolani (I. 79) or the Jewish War (so Sp., V., etc.). T. means civil wars which were inextricably connected with foreign, such as the Batavian rising prompted by Antonius Primus (*interno simul externoque bello*, II. 69. 6), the aid given by the Chatti to Antonius Saturninus (the third civil war was mentioned above, cf. Suet. *Dom.* 6. 2), and possibly domestic troubles in Illyricum (see n. to line 5).

4. prosperae in Oriente, adversae in Occidente res. Heubner follows Paratore, 541 ff., in referring this to the triumph over Judaea, in contrast with the disasters incurred during the revolt of Civilis. But surely T. is thinking at least as much of the Danubian catastrophes he recorded in the Domitianic books and of the quiet which ruled on the Eastern frontier throughout the Flavian period.

5. turbatum Illyricum. *Illyricum* may include Moesia, as in I. 9. 11, 76. 1, II. 85. 1, but even so this remains one of the few phrases in the Summary which we cannot illustrate from our other evidence for the period. It should, like *Galliae nutantes*, refer to internal trouble, not to invasions such as that recorded in I. 79; nor should it involve duplication of *coortae in nos Sarmatarum as Sueborum gentes.* It may be that the invading tribes in A.D. 88 and 92 were linked with discontented communities in Pannonia, and that in 70 too there was more happening in all the Danubian provinces than has appeared in our sources—see the rumour recorded in IV. 54. 6.

Galliae nutantes. Here clearly the reference is to the consequences of the Batavian rising. For the plural Galliae see I. 8.3 n.

perdomita Britannia et statim omissa. Against numerous cases (see GG for a complete list, but note esp. II. 65. 2, IV. 37. 4, 86. 9, *Agr.* 36. 5) in which *omittere* is used by T. to mean 'give up', 'leave to itself', 'lose interest in', there is no instance of the simple verb *mittere*, which is read by L. as well as by M. But the onus of proof is on those who wish to alter *missa.* It is now kept by G. and K., and was defended, with cogent arguments based on the rhythm of this very careful chapter, by E. Norden, *Altgermanien* (1934), 25; see also E. Löfstedt, *Spätlateinische Studien* (1908), 126. The meaning remains the same.

All commentators on this controversial phrase (still relevant is the prolonged discussion between G. Macdonald, *JRS* 1935, 187, 1937, 93, 1939, 5, and T. Davies Pryce and E. Birley, *JRS* 1935, 59, 1938, 141) agree in principle that two periods must be distinguished in Britain of the generation following Agricola: (i) the removal of troops, and especially of the legion II Adiutrix, with consequent failure to consolidate Rome's hold on the Scottish Highlands, (ii) the withdrawal of the 'frontier' to the Tyne–Solway line, and the building of the Stanegate, the precursor of Hadrian's fortifications. In period (i) Agricola's 'complete conquest' of the island (*Agr.* 10. 1, *tum primum perdomita est*) was not sustained, but forts beyond the Forth–Clyde line in Strathearn were still held (Ogilvie–Richmond, cit., 76); and the defence of Lowland Scotland was vigorously reorganized, with massive rebuilding at Newstead (near Melrose), see Richmond, *Roman Britain* (1955), 45. In period (ii) there was actual abandonment of extensive territory. But it was not 'Britannia' as such which was abandoned, nor is 'abandoned' the right translation of *missa.* Moreover the archaeologists cannot, at the earliest, allow period (ii) to begin before *c.* 94, and Macdonald was surely right to argue that this is too late for *statim.*

T.'s reference then is to period (i). II Adiutrix (brought to Moesia from Chester, and replaced there by XX Valeria from Inchtuthil in Perthshire), is securely attested on the Danube by 92, *ILS* 2719; moreover it took part in a Dacian war which was probably Domitian's (*ILS* 9193 = MW 371), and may have been the fifth legion of Moesia which occasioned the division of that province *c.* 87 (for the various possibilities see Syme, *JRS* 1955, 123). The legionary camp at Inchtuthil was abandoned before its finest buildings were complete, and 'its demolition-layers are associated with fresh bronze coins of A.D. 86 or 87' (Ogilvie–Richmond, cit., 71). Withdrawal of the legion frustrated all plans Agricola had formed for controlling the Highlands after his victory at Mons Graupius in 84. This is enough to explain T.'s words here, since anything other than full subjugation of the island was to him inconsistent with *virtus exercituum et Romani nominis gloria* (*Agr.* 23. 1).

There remains the question whether our passage can be used in any way to date period (ii). Macdonald maintained that T. could not have written it had the withdrawal to the Stanegate line already taken place and had Trajan shown himself contented with it. The earliest date for that frontier could then be *c.* 106 (or the date at which Book I of the *Histories* was published). But can we be sure that T. had access to detailed knowledge of what was happening on the British frontier under Nerva and Trajan? Moreover, though to leave Agricola's *novas gentes* (*Agr.* 22. 1) outside the frontier might have shocked him, we must beware of thinking that all the technical military arrangements of which we learn from archaeology would have been of serious interest to him. The decisive step had been taken by Domitian within the period on which he was researching, when his father-in-law's work seemed to have been wasted. The chronology of period (ii) must be settled (if it can be) on archaeological evidence without help from this passage, 2. 5. (S. S. Frere, *Britannia* (1967), 116 f., argues with ingenuity (not to me convincingly) that the real reason for abandoning the Highlands was a shortage of auxiliary regiments—'the withdrawal of Legio II Adiutrix will be seen as the result rather than as the cause of the loss of Scotland.' The argument of the above note would not be affected were this view to be right.)

6. coortae in nos Sarmatarum ac Sueborum gentes. The Sarmatae Rhoxolani invaded lower Moesia in early 69 (as they had done a year earlier), I. 79; and in 70 Sarmatians defeated and killed the Moesian governor, Jos. *BI* VII. 89. But the concerted attacks referred to here are those made on the Pannonian front by the Sarmatae Iazyges (west of Dacia) in alliance with the Marcomanni and Quadi: these began in 88–9 and were renewed in 92. For details see Syme in *CAH* XI (1936), 175 ff., C. Patsch, *Der Kampf um den Donauraum unter Domitian und Trajan* (1937), 32 ff.; and for the description of the two German tribes as Suebi cf. *Germ.* 41–2. The cause of the trouble is obscure. The Iazyges were immigrants to the area between Danube and Tisza (Plin. *NH* IV. 80–1), but their arrival took place before A.D. 50 (*A.* XII. 29), and all three tribes were loyal clients of Rome in 69 (III. 5, cf. *Germ.* 42). T.'s *coortae in nos* does not suggest the wanton Roman aggression implied by Dio (= Xiph.) 67. 7. 1, but a reasonable guess is that Roman levies both sides of the Danube during Domitian's Dacian wars had been provocative (see n. on *turbatum Illyricum* above).

7. nobilitatus cladibus mutuis Dacus. The Dacians invaded, *gens numquam fida*, when the frontier seemed weak in the autumn of 69; but they were beaten back by Mucianus, who happened to be passing through Moesia at that moment, III. 46. In 85, under their new king Decebalus, they came again, and this time defeated and killed the Moesian governor, Oppius Sabinus, Suet. *Dom.* 6. Domitian himself went to the front, but his prefect of the guard, Cornelius Fuscus (II. 86. 16 n.) was killed at the head of his troops with heavy losses. In 88 the tide turned when Tettius Iulianus won a victory at Tapae near the Iron Gate pass; and Domitian was able to make a compromise peace with Dacia, despite troubles which by then had broken out with the German and Sarmatian tribes on the Pannonian frontier. For details, and for the consequent movement of troops to the Danube provinces (and for the division of Moesia) see *CAH* XI. 168 ff.

T. at least admits Domitian's victories as well as his defeats. It would be interesting to know whether *nobilitatus* was written after Trajan's extermination of the Dacians in 106.

8. falsi Neronis ludibrio. The pseudo-Nero of A.D. 69 (II. 8–9) did not enlist Parthia and is not in point here. Dio 66. 19 (=Zonar. XI. 18; cf. Jos. *Ant.* fr. 106 M) tells of one Terentius Maximus who posed as Nero with Parthian support in Titus' reign; and Suet., *Nero* 57.2, remembered another impostor when he was a young man about 88. The latter was *vehementer adiutus et vix redditus* by the Parthians, and the former may have occasioned the *Parthica laurus* of Trajan's father (Plin. *Pan.* 14. 1; cf. *ILS* 8970 = MW 263); but as Syme, *CAH* XI. 243, points out, the word *prope* shows that there was no actual war with Parthia during the Flavian period.

The circumstances of Nero's death gave impostors a good chance. Only Alexandria, Acte, and Claudia Ecloge knew about his burial; Icelus had perhaps seen his corpse, perhaps not (Suet. *Nero* 50, Plut., *G.* 7. 2). Even in Trajan's time Dio Chrysostom could write XXI. 10, Νέρωνά γε καὶ νῦν ἔτι πάντες ἐπιθυμοῦσι ζῆν, οἱ δὲ πλεῖστοι καὶ οἴονται. On Nero's posthumous activities see also Syme, *CAH* XI. 144.

9. post longam...repetitis. Perhaps previous burnings of the Capitol, the last of which was in 83 B.C. (III. 72), perhaps also eruptions of Vesuvius, of which there had been a *longa series*, the last occasion being the disaster to Pompeii in A.D. 63 (*A.* XV. 22, recounted without any hint that far worse was to come).

10. haustae...ora. For *haustae* of places destroyed by earthquakes (not tidal waves, for in Campania in 79 the sea receded, Plin. *Epp.* VI. 20. 9) cf. Sen. *Ben.* VII. 31. 5, *Epp.* 91. 9. The deletion of *urbes*, proposed by Wölfflin (*Philologus*, 27. 21) because of the awkwardness with *urbs* in the next line, is unnecessary; cf. *A.* XVI. 13. 4, *ut amissa urbi* [sc. *Lugduno*] *reponerent; quam pecuniam Lugdunenses ante obtulerant urbis* [sc. *Romae*] *casibus.* Fisher is probably right in placing a semicolon after *ora* and taking the word as a nominative: the whole stretch of coast was overwhelmed by the lava.

11. consumptis antiquissimis delubris. For a list of the shrines destroyed in the terrible fire at Rome in A.D. 80 see Dio 66. 24, cf. Suet. *Tit.* 8.3.

12. civium manibus. See III. 72 for T.'s passionate development of this theme.

    pollutae caerimoniae. In 83 three Vestals were found guilty of adultery and were allowed to choose the manner of their deaths, their lovers being relegated; in 90 the Chief Vestal, for the same reason, was buried alive, her lovers being beaten to death. See Suet. *Dom.* 8, Dio (=Xiph.) 67. 3. 3, Plin. *Epp.* IV. 11. 6.

13. magna adulteria, 'in high places', especially Domitian and his niece Julia, Suet. *Dom.* 22, etc. That T. joins this item with the previous one probably reflects the same picture so pungently drawn by Juvenal, II. 29 ff., *qualis erat nuper tragico pollutus adulter concubitu*, etc.

14. plenum . . . scopuli. Stock phrases, for which it is most unlikely that T. was copying Plin. *Pan.* 35. Cf. also Juv. XIII. 246.

15. omissi . . . pro crimine. Herennius Senecio's offence, Dio (=Xiph.) 67. 13. 2 alleges, was in part that he failed to stand for office after the quaestorship. Flavius Sabinus (*cos.* 82), Domitian's cousin, was executed for arrogating too much to himself when Domitian's colleague in the consulship (if this be the meaning of the story in Suet. *Dom.* 10. 4 but see *PIR*[2] F 355); and M'. Acilius Glabrio (*cos.* 91) was exiled in or soon after his consulship and later put to death, Dio (=Xiph.) 67. 14. 3, though the story that his offence was a successful battle against wild beasts must conceal something else (it is not clear, despite *CAH* XI. 32 and other writers, that Dio means involvement in the charge of impiety).

16. praemia delatorum. The regular reward under the *Lex Iulia de Maiestate* was one quarter of the condemned man's property, *A.* IV. 20. 3; but for far greater monetary rewards see IV. 42. 20 (Regulus), *A.* XI. 4, XVI. 33, in all of which cases steps in the senatorial *cursus* were also bestowed. Regulus was alleged to have received *consularia spolia* and a priesthood, but no other case of that kind is known from the Flavian period. The general taunt goes back to Sallust, *BI* 84. 1, *sese consulatum et victis illis spolia cepisse*.

18. interiorem potentiam, 'power behind the scenes', of which *procurationes* are a possible example, though the phrase is not quite a hendiadys.

20. per amicos oppressi. Once again the most famous case is Neronian rather than Flavian, namely Celer's accusation of Barea Soranus, IV. 10 below. See however also Plancius Varus' evidence against Dolabella, II. 63.

3. 3. secutae ... coniuges. See Plin. *Epp.* VII. 19. 4 of Fannia, wife of the elder Helvidius, *bis maritum secuta in exsilium est* [i.e. under Nero and under Domitian], *tertio ipsa propter maritum relegata.*

4. constantes generi. No example known except Helvidius' loyalty to Thrasea (see IV. 5–6), which is again an example from Nero's reign.

servorum fides, e.g. L. Piso's slave, IV. 50. 8.

5. supremae ... toleratae. See Fisher's app. crit. Madvig's conjecture must surely be discarded: it hopelessly weakens the force of any *exemplum.* Those who, like K., retain *ipsa necessitas* (usually with the simple change of *tolerata* to *toleratae*) suppose that *necessitates* in the plural are the preliminaries and preparations for death as distinct from death itself: so Heubner (following Andresen, *Woch. f. kl. Phil.* 1914, 1025), who contrasts *A.* XI. 37. 4 and Sen. *Epp.* 17. 9 with 72. 3 below and *A.* XV. 61. 7. But it would be extraordinary of T. to expect this distinction to be understood from the conjunction of *necessitates* and *necessitas* in the same sentence, when he could (see H.'s emendation) have written *ipsae neces.* A different distinction is drawn by Meiser's emendation, that between death (*necessitates*) and the 'necessity' (the evils of the time) which made men die. It is not perhaps surprising that Fisher felt happier with the conjecture of the *deteriores.*

7. caelo ... praesagia. When such claims are made in practice, T.'s scepticism, and even contempt, are apparent: above all at II. 50. 5 (though he feels bound to recount the instance which follows as at least a curious coincidence). See also I. 10. 15, II. 78. 5, with nn., and Syme, 521 ff. In suggesting that these things were an especial feature of his period T. was probably influenced by the many portents which found their way into Flavian propaganda, see Suet. *Vesp.* 5.

9. nec enim ... esse ultionem. To believe, with Heubner, that for this magnificent ending T. should have needed any help from a passage of Pliny on the treatment of informers (*Pan.* 35. 4, *divus Titus securitati nostrae ultionique prospexerat ideoque numinibus aequatus est*) is distasteful and surely unnecessary. The converse view (K. Büchner, *Hermes*, 1955, 308) that Pliny drew on T. is perhaps not ruled out by any ineptitude it ascribes to the borrower, but use of the *Histories* for the *Panegyric* is almost certainly impossible on chronological grounds, see Introd., pp. 22–3.

Yet (*pace* Syme, 143, who supposes community of theme rather than an actual debt) it is hard to think that T. was not conscious of Lucan IV. 808, *felix Roma quidem civesque habitura beatos, si libertatis superis tam cura placeret quam vindicta placet*, perhaps also of VII. 454, *mortalia nulli sunt curata deo, cladis tamen huius habemus vindictam.* For the influence of Lucan see Paratore, 358 ff., and for comparison of the thought of the two authors on this particular topic P. Zancan, *La crisi del principato nell'anno 69 D.C.* (1939), 59. But (as Zancan emphasizes) T. is not concerned here with the possibility that the gods are uninterested in human affairs (something he discusses, without hinting at his conclusion, at *A.* VI. 22, cf. XVI. 33), nor indeed with their attitude towards *libertas.* Moreover, although in the generation he is describing their sole concern seemed to be to punish, they still had power, or even desire, to bestow blessings, *propitiis, si per mores nostros liceret, deis*, III. 72. 3. Yet he has departed a long way from the traditional view (e.g. Cicero, *Har. Resp.* 19) that Rome was protected by the gods.

How strong was T.'s conviction, when he wrote the *Histories*, that the failure of Roman *mores* was irretrievable? His *deum ira* in II. 38. 14 has perhaps not yet acquired the generalized force which gives such pessimism to *A.* IV. 1. 3 and XVI. 16. 3. The question cannot be divorced from that of the interpretation of *urgentibus imperii fatis, Germ.* 33. 2. That passage must inevitably mean that T. saw pressing dangers, already in 98; for a relatively mild version of his fears see R. Heinze, *Vom Geist des Römertums* (1938), 255 ff., "da das Reich, durch Schicksalsfügung, in schwerer Bedrängnis ist', and see also J. G. C. Anderson ad loc., and Syme, 46. But the passage normally adduced for comparison, Livy V. 6. 3, must (if it be relevant) show that at the outset of Trajan's reign T. was not without hope of a successful future; and J. M. C. Toynbee, *CR* 1944, 40, made a good case for thinking that he was then still making a claim for lasting world dominion.

An excellent bibliography on the *Germania* passage is given by H. W. Benario in *Historia*, 1968, 37 ff. His ensuing discussion is surely right in attempting to interpret T. there in the light of his other writing of the year 97–8 (and esp. of the optimism of the *Agricola*), rather than in submerging it in a general pool of Tacitean pessimism. See also K. Kraft, *Hermes*, 1968, 591 ff.

4. 1. ceterum antequam destinata componam ... Though once again we start with a reminiscence of Sallust (*BI* 5. 3), the survey which follows, first of Rome (4–7) and then of the armies and provinces (8–11), has no known precedent in ancient historiography (Syme, 147), and must have been enough to announce T. to his contemporaries as an historian of individual genius; for an appreciation which is still of great value see Boissier, 182. Although Fabia, 89 ff., has established with some certainty that T. had one main source for the events of A.D. 68 and that this was also the source of Plutarch, yet T.'s selection of the vital material is almost as telling as his style, if anyone were inclined to doubt whether a 'one-source' historian could be original.

T.'s selection is addressed to the *ratio causaeque*, and can discard anything which he considered irrelevant (although we may not always agree with him) to the character and strength of the forces which burst into action from 1 Jan. 69. Among the names which find no place in this survey the most striking is that of Otho (first introduced at I. 13. 6 as M. Otho). For what mattered to T. in his general analysis of the situation on 1 Jan. was not the personality or behaviour of that individual but the temper of the praetorian guard: they were ready for trouble whether it was Otho or another who presented himself to take the lead (I. 5. 1 ff.). In contrast the Eastern commanders must be named, and one of them given a fairly full description; for there personalities mattered, both that of the carefully chosen general who had been given a special command in Judaea, but even more that of his colleague in Syria who had ambitions as a king-maker but not as a king. Similarly, both Spain and Upper Germany might have played a different role had not Cluvius Rufus and Hordeonius Flaccus been the men they were. But for the names of the proconsul of Africa, or of the legates of Britain and of the Danubian provinces, we must wait until appropriate parts of the narrative are reached (indeed the legates of Pannonia and Dalmatia are not named before the victory of Vitellius, II. 86).

On all this the analysis by Fuhrmann (254; cf. Heubner, 26 ff. and his n. on I. 4. 4) is admirable, but the extent to which T.'s survey looks constantly to the future must not be overdrawn. For instance, is it really true (see Fuhrmann, 263) that particular attention is paid to the three 'crisis points' (the Guard, the Rhine armies, and the armies of the East) only because each of these in turn produced an emperor in 69? Like any historian T. is of course conscious of what came later, and openly so (*per omnis civilium belli motus*, I. 9. 8; *Oriens adhuc immotus*, I. 10. 1; *in pretium belli cessura*, I. 11. 12). But it is only fair to him to ask whether an intelligent observer, writing in the later months of 68, would have given different weight to the various areas, or said about them things which were substantially different from what T. reported. The Guard, the vast concentration of strength on the Rhine, and the great but less easily calculable resources of the East—these were clearly the centres of power which no one in that generation would ignore. Writing with knowledge of the actual campaigns of 69 T. might have felt temptation to give more prominence to the Danube armies, but he resists it: instead he confines himself to important points entirely appropriate to an assessment of the situation at the beginning of the year. In addition it was natural to ask how heavily preoccupied were the forces in Britain; to cast a glance at Spain and Africa; and to emphasize the vital importance of Egypt. Nor could a contemporary observer have been unmindful of the two features in the military situation which in early 69 were abnormal: the Jewish War, and the exceptional concentration of troops in Rome.

Yet although he may have exaggerated the extent to which T. was influenced by hindsight about these military matters, Fuhrmann was surely right to emphasize the predominance of *mens exercituum* over the other elements in the Survey. In the chapters on the provinces this is obvious. On only one area is there any report about provincial feelings, and that one was inescapable, namely the Gauls, I. 8. 3 ff. Nothing about Spain, though there the *habitus provinciarum* might have been interesting; and nothing (except *apud subiectos . . . potens* of Mucianus, I. 10. 9) about the Syrian provincials and their relations with the armies, contrast II. 4 ff. and II. 80. 17. In Africa it is at least in part the attitude of the legionaries rather than the provincials which is described, see I. 11. 6 n.

When one comes to look carefully, it seems that *mens exercituum* is also the main feature in the analysis of *status urbis*. In cap. 5 we pass quickly to the concerns of the troops; in 6 too the criticisms of Galba derive from military circles; and when in 7 we are told that the emperor was already unpopular, we must wonder how he could have incurred unpopularity among upper-class groups, in contrast to what has been said in 4. 10 f. Was it really the Senate, rather than certain army elements, who were outraged by the executions of Macer and Capito (see 7. 12 n.)? In any case chapters 5–7 have constructed a dark and hostile picture of Galba's reign, which has been brilliantly studied by Köstermann (see also his article in *Navicula Chiloniensis* (1956), 191); for it was his relations not with the Senate but with the soldiers which destroyed Galba. It is only in parts of the narrative chapters that we get the indulgent view of the emperor which prevailed among the upper classes of T.'s own generation (cf. IV. 40. 5, Juv. VI. 559, *IRT* 537 = MW 31). Had that view been more prominent, the almost insuperable financial difficulties of the new regime might have found a place in these introductory chapters (cf. Boissier, 149); and we might (with whatever consequences for Galba's reputation) have been given a clearer picture of the way the adoption problem developed.

In the chapters on Rome, as Heubner rightly observes, there are distinct marks of the passage of time. First the death of Nero (4. 6), with Galba still away from Rome (4. 11), a situation which persists throughout 5 (though the *sermones* of 5. 10 are those current in the city). Then the journey (6. 3), and the entry to the city (6. 7); and finally the *nova aula* (7. 15). But one may doubt whether T. here was showing conscious artistry ('den kunstvollen Aufbau', Heubner, 26). All he has done, for the most part, is to turn over the pages of his source and record items which seemed to him significant, as he came to them; and in doing so he has produced anachronisms in relation to 1 Jan. 69 (*inducta legione Hispana*, 6. 10, but the legion had now departed; and *Africa ac legiones in ea*, 11. 6 n.). So much does he regard the last months of 68 as (in a sense) timeless that he can shift two items from the contexts in which they appear in Plutarch (and therefore surely in their common source, for Plut. had no ground for moving them) and use them to illustrate certain general points he was making (the remark reported at 5. 15 n. and the judgement about the *invisus princeps* at 7. 12; see Heubner, 26 f.). Yet the time-sequence can still be seen, and Heubner's recognition of it helps, at one point at least (the deaths of Macer and Capito, see 7. 1 n.), to establish a chronology.

4. non modo casus ... noscantur. Despite the subtle distinctions drawn by Heubner ad loc., there can be little doubt about the sense: the difficulty is to find a satisfying translation. *Rerum* (cf. 1. 3 n. above) are surely 'history'. Perhaps 'the actual events of history and their consequences ... the logic and reasons which lie behind them'.

8. urbanum militem, here the whole garrison of Rome, cf. I. 5. 1, II. 94. 3. Only if the context explains it, e.g. I. 89. 12, does it mean the urban cohorts only.

9. posse principem ... fieri. The arbitrament of the army (see already Livy 26. 2. 2, though there of course *mali exempli*) was hardly by now an *imperii arcanum* in the sense in which T. elsewhere uses the phrase (*A.* II. 36. 2, 59. 4). But though thoughtful men of the preceding century must have regarded the happenings of A.D. 68 as a theoretical possibility, no one had actually witnessed a process such as led from Galba's acclamation by VI Victrix to his formal adoption, in absence, as *princeps*; and the effect on all classes in the empire was probably as sharp as T. makes it. Note however that the kindred phrase from Mucianus' speech, *posse ab exercitu principem fieri* (II. 73. 23), refers to Vitellius, whose acclamation was not quickly followed by senatorial recognition, rather than to Galba.

10. libertate, principally freedom of speech. See nn. to cap. 1 above.

11. primores equitum. It is reasonably certain that there was a class of *equites inlustres*, perhaps those who possessed the senatorial census of 1 m. HS, cf. A. Stein, *Der römische Ritterstand* (1927), 100 ff. The class was definite enough to be the subject of administrative regulation (e.g. *A.* II. 59. 4), but whether T. intends it here is uncertain.

12. pars populi integra ... D. van Berchem, *Les Distributions de blé ... sous l'empire* (1939), 74 ff. identified this group with the *plebs* *frumentaria*, who on his view were Roman citizens officially domiciled in Rome, as distinct from non-citizens and immigrants. He assumed that the suspension of the *frumentationes* after the fire of 64 (Dio 62. 18. 5) had continued until Nero's death, and that Nero was meanwhile favouring the other group, the *plebs sordida*, by making corn available to them at low prices; this would be why the (rest of the) *plebs* put on caps of liberty after Nero's suicide (Suet. *Nero* 57), and why a Galbian denarius (*RIC* I. 200) shows Libertas flanked by two ears of corn.

On the qualifications for receiving free corn van Berchem was probably right, but such qualifications would obviously have included people whom T. would have labelled *plebs sordida*; for the phrase see III. 74. 11, and the careful analysis by Z. Yavetz, *Athenaeum*, 1965, 295 ff.* Moreover Nero's posthumous popularity is almost inexplicable if he deprived 200,000 people of free corn over a period of four years; and the Galbian coin was more probably an answer to the activities of Macer and Calvia Crispinilla in Africa, I. 73. 5.

The *plebs integra* was a more select body, Suet. *Nero* 12. 1, *quosdam fortunae atque existimationis integrae*. As clients of noble houses they were a recognized group in Roman society, A. von Premerstein, *Vom Werden und Wesen des Prinzipats* (1937), 115 f., but not one defined by Roman statute or ordinance.

5.1. longo Caesarum sacramento, an oath which had been actually embarrassing to Nero, when the praetorians showed obstinate devotion to his mother and his wife, *A*. XIV. 7. 5. For its derivation from the oaths taken to late Republican generals see P. Herrmann, *Der römische Kaisereid* (*Hypomnemata*, Heft 20, 1968), 90 ff., 116 ff., against the contention of Premerstein, cit., that it derived from the relationship of *cliens* to *patronus*. The city troops had of course no tradition before Augustus created them.

2. arte magis et impulsu. The important story how the praetorians were induced by Nymphidius to abandon Nero is told inadequately by Plut. (*G*. 2. 1, implying that he had dealt with it more fully in his *Nero*), and never by T. Nor does T. explain the timing and causes of Nymphidius' rising against Galba, which Plut., *G*. 8–9, 13–14, shows to have been a more complex and prolonged affair than might be supposed from *in ipso conatu oppressus* (line 8), cf. Köstermann, *Navicula Chiloniensis*, 220 ff. When he came to write *A*. XV. 72 T. had evidently decided to fill the gap, at least of the events before Nero's death. In the *Histories* his only interest in the man is that his rising foreshadowed, and even (*conscientia*) made more likely, another revolt by the praetorians.

C. Nymphidius Sabinus was born to a freedwoman who was daughter

---

* This seems to me a clearer presentation than in his *Plebs and Princeps* (1969), 143 ff.

to Callistus, the powerful freedom of the emperor Gaius (and subsequently of Claudius). He claimed that Gaius was his father, and T. (*A.* XV. 72) thought this not impossible, given the emperor's tastes for promiscuous girls, but Plut. *G.* 9. 2 is confident that the father was a gladiator called Martianus. In 65 he was made praetorian prefect in succession to Faenius Rufus, and was also given *ornamenta consularia* for his part in suppressing the conspiracy in which his predecessor had been involved. The Pannonian inscription *ILS* 1322 (=Sm. 1, 269) is generally thought to record an earlier military post held by him, but it is not impossible that he visited the province during his command of the Guard.

3. donativum. Claudius and Nero had each given 15,000 HS to each praetorian at their accession, Suet. *Cl.* 10, Dio 61. 3. 1. Plut. *G.* 2. 2, says Nymphidius promised 7,500 drachmae i.e. denarii, for troops in the city and 1,250 for men serving outside Rome. On a rough computation, and leaving *auxilia* out of account, this might mean

$$16,000 \times 30,000 \text{ HS} = 480 \text{ m. HS}$$
for praetorians and urbans
$$160,000 \times 5,000 \text{ HS} = 800 \text{ m. HS}$$
for legionaries

or a total of 1,280 m. HS, on which Plutarch comments mildly 'a sum which it was impossible to raise without inflicting on the world ten thousand times more evils than those inflicted by Nero'. The figures have been challenged on the ground that a donative of this size was unparalleled for years to come; but Nymphidius was unparalleled too.

6. legionibus. In fact there was only one legion (VI Victrix) in Spain when Galba was first proclaimed; the second (VII Galbiana) was raised afterwards. For the difficulties of such plurals see I. 11. 6, 70. 22, nn.

10. nec deerant . . . It is almost certainly wrong not to make a heavy break before these words. Long ago W. Nesbitt, *Hermathena*, 3. (1879), 402 saw this part of the Survey as a prime example of the way the traditional division of T.'s work into chapters can mislead. In reality chapters 4–6 have three themes, which do not correspond with the three chapters: (a) 4 and 5 to the present point (ending in *conscientia*), the effect of the change of regime on the various elements in Rome, (b) the remainder of 5, and the first sentence of 6, Galba's growing unpopularity and its causes, (c) the rest of 6, Galba's journey, and his entry to Rome. Wellesley's translation illustrates these divisions with clarity.

12. celebrata severitas. The reputation was gained during his governorship of Upper Germany in A.D. 40, Suet. *G.* 6.

15. vox ... honesta, ipsi anceps. The other sources, Plut. *G.* 18. 2, Suet. *G.* 16. 1, Dio 64. 3. 3, all record the remark in a context after, perhaps well after, Galba entered Rome. See above, 4.1. n.

ipsi anceps is a comment made by T. alone, and is taken by K., cit. 220, to mean that one must hesitate before giving Galba credit for what looks like a patriotic utterance, because it really sprang from the meanness which was so grave a defect in the emperor's character. But surely most editors have been right in thinking of the two-edged consequences for Galba, for his reputation in patriotic circles, and for his personal safety: Heubner cites Velleius II. 125. 4, where despite the difficulties of the text it is clear that *ancipitia* means 'hazardous'. *Pro re publica honesta* (Plut. has ἡγεμόνι μεγάλῳ πρέπουσαν) is therefore unqualified praise of Galba, the only instance in the Introduction.

6.1 Titus Vinius et Cornelius Laco. For Vinius' career (he had lately been proconsul of Narbonensis and had considerable influence on Galba's policies on Gaul and on the Upper German command, as also on other matters, Plut. *G.* 10. 4, 18. 1, etc.) see I. 48.5 ff. with nn. For Laco's earlier career all we have is Suetonius' statement (*G.* 14) that he was promoted to command the Guard from being an *assessor* (legal assistant, cf. *ILS.* 1404, presumably serving Galba in Spain), and the interesting detail given by T., I. 14. 9, that he had been a friend of Piso Licinianus in the home of Rubellius Plautus, see Introd., p. 15. Given what we know of Plautus (*A.* XIV. 57), and of Piso (I. 14. 12 ff.), we can guess what inspired the words *adrogantia socordiaque intolerabilis* (Suet., cit.) and the devastating judgement at the end of 26 below.

Again it is important to recognize that all this sentence links with the latter part of cap. 5 (see 5.10 n.) and has no special relationship with the story of Galba's march to Rome.

2. deterrimus ... inertiae. The two men are entirely different characters; *deterrimus* is picked up by *odio flagitiorum*, *ignavissimus* by *contemptu inertiae*, though each in his way was gradually ruinous to Galba. The construction (described by K. O. Brink, *CR* 1944, 43, as a double zeugma or double syllepsis) is discussed by V. in *Riv. fil.* 1908, 374, though he does not make clear whether he had repented of his deletion of *oneratum* (surely unnecessarily) from his earlier text. R. M. Rattenbury, *CR* 1943, 67, shows that I. 62.10, 79.13–15 are parallels; and Brink, cit., adds several other examples, among which see II. 92. 10 n.

3. tardum Galbae iter. The chronology cannot be confidently constructed, but Fluss, *RE* IV A, 783 ff., gave good ground for thinking that Galba left Spain in July and did not reach Rome before the beginning of October. He spent some time at Narbo on the way, Plut. *G.* 11.

4. Cingonio Varrone. The period for which he had been designated consul was probably the latter half of 69, cf. I. 77. 10 n. All that is known about his earlier career is his authorship of a severe proposal about the slaves of a murdered master, *A.* XIV. 45.

5. Petronio Turpiliano, *cos.* 61 and then governor of Britain, *A.* XIV. 39. Dio 63. 1 (= Zon. XI. 13) described his command of an advanced guard against Vindex: this assembled in North Italy, Introd., p. 8. Zonaras says he eventually deserted to Galba, but surely what in fact happened was that his army deserted: otherwise Galba's action is quite inexplicable. Petronius returned to Rome, and Plut. *G.* 15. 2. emphasizes the bitterness generally felt at the execution of a man who was isolated, and had no arms at his command.

6. tamquam innocentes. *ut . . . ut* simply record the charges: on the question of either man's guilt (about Varro Plut. has no doubt) T. expresses no opinion. Cf. Plin. *Epp.* IV. 11. 8, on the Vestal under Domitian, *nescio an innocens, certe tamquam innocens.*

7. trucidatis tot milibus. This reference to the slaughter of marines at the Milvian bridge presents the first of many obscurities connected with the use of marines in 68–70 and with their formation into legionary units.

T. writes as if there were no connection between slaughtered men and the legion *quam e classe Nero conscripserat,* which he mentions in his very next sentence. Some editors, e.g. Heraeus, have taken him at his word and supposed that the men who met Galba at the bridge were marines who had *not* secured admission to Nero's legion (see V's Excursus). Heubner, too, thinks that *diffidebatur* in I. 31. 8 would be quite inappropriate had Galba massacred men from the actual legion: in that case he could never have entertained hope of aid from them. It is maintained, therefore, that the survivors of the massacre (*reliquos caesorum,* I. 87. 4) were given no kind of favourable treatment, but were kept in prison until Otho released them and promised them legionary service. The legion, already designated by Nero, was a different matter: it still had to be made *iusta* by Galba, but this was a proceeding accomplished without bloodshed.

Much though that view saves the credit of T. in this chapter, it is difficult to reconcile with *commilitonum* in I. 31. 8, and impossible to reconcile with the evidence of Suet. and Plut. Suet. *G.* 12. 2 has *cum classiarios, quos Nero ex remigibus iustos milites fecerat, redire ad pristinum statum cogeret, recusantis atque aquilam et signa pertinacius flagitantis, non modo inmisso equite disiecit, sed decimavit etiam.* This is surely T.'s legion, *quam e classe Nero conscripserat,* awaiting its formal insignia; and Plut. *G.* 15. 3 speaks explicitly of the incident being caused by men οὓς εἰς ἓν τάγμα ὁ Νέρων συλλοχίσας ἀπέφηνε στρατιώτας.

Galba, then, was met by a very large body of troops. Some of them were massacred on the spot, but Dio's figure of 7,000 (64. 3. 2) and T.'s *tot milibus* are probably gross exaggerations (*inermibus* too seems to challenge Plut.'s story that the cavalry charged men who had already drawn their swords—but perhaps *inermibus* means 'without defensive armour', cf. I. 79. 20). From the survivors Galba made some into a *iusta legio* a few weeks later (see below), perhaps diluting them with other men (from Britain, Germany, or Pannonia) who wanted legionary service. The remainder, still a substantial number (II. 11. 20) were kept in captivity until Otho's Narbonese expedition.

Whether or no this view be right (and Heubner strongly contests it), we clearly have impressive testimony to the size of the Misenum fleet. Starr, 17, concludes that it was 10,000 strong, and even that may be an underestimate. No doubt new recruits could quickly be provided to make the fleet still *valida* in March for the Narbonese campaign (see similar measures taken about the Ravenna fleet later, III. 50), but there is no actual record of new recruitment by Otho in I. 87. Yet from the fleet as it had been in Nero's time there had been drawn off (a) the majority of the men required for the new legion (I Adiutrix), (b) men put *in numeros legionis* by Otho (87. 6), who were equivalent to *classicorum ingens numerus* (II. 11. 20), and (c) the men who perished at the bridge. And Vitellius formed a new *e classicis legio* late in 69, III. 55. 4.

As to the origin of I Adiutrix, it seems clear that Dio 55. 24. 2 was right in calling Galba the official founder. The words *Nero conscripserat* (repeated by Suet.) mean that it was Nero who had brigaded the men as legionaries: this is action similar to that taken by Otho over the remaining survivors, *in numeros legionis composuerat,* and probably also by Vitellius when he too formed a legion, cf. Ritterling, *RE* XII. 1267, 1382. What Galba did was to make the legion *iusta* by giving it an eagle, and it is almost certain that he took that step on 22 Dec. 68, the day on which time-expired men from the legion I Adiutrix, i.e. men who on becoming legionaries were at once entitled to discharge, having had twenty years of military service, were given citizenship and *conubium.* So H. Nesselhauf on *CIL* III. 2014, who agrees with Ritterling, cit., and with Mommsen, *CIL* III. 2014, that the birthday of the legion cannot have been significantly earlier, because non-citizens would not have been retained as such in a *iusta legio.* Against this it was argued by Parker, *Roman Legions,* 101 ff., that *ILS* 9059 (= *CIL* XVI, App.

12 = MW 404) showed that some soldiers of X Fretensis recruited in 68–9 received citizenship only on their discharge twenty-five years later. But though that inscription presents notorious difficulties, it is not (as *CIL* XVI. 7–9 are) a *diploma* in regular form: it evidently deals with men recruited in a hurry for the Jewish War, and it probably constitutes a certificate for citizenship deemed to have been granted from the moment of recruitment (for which there would otherwise have been no documentary evidence, since legionaries *instrumentum accipere non solent*, *CIL* XVI, App. 13). Parker's view that the marines of Nero's 'legion' got their citizenship gradually as each became time-expired is hard to accept against the fact that we possess three *diplomata* from the single day 22 Dec. and none from later days. It is true, as he said, that the *diplomata* say nothing of a grant of citizenship to men who continued to serve. But that was not their function: the evidence of the way in which such a grant was made has not survived.

T. continues to call the legion *classica* or *classicorum* until he reaches the first battle of Bedriacum, when it receives its name Adiutrix to distinguish it from I Italica, which was fighting on the other side, cf. II. 43. 4.

9. inducta legione Hispana. i.e. VII Galbiana. But this legion was in Illyricum in March 69 (II. 11. 4), and had evidently left Rome before 15 Jan., since it is not mentioned in the story of Galba's downfall. Had it still been there its behaviour might have been interesting; for it owed its origin and name to Galba, but had been corrupted by Otho on the march from Spain, I. 23. 3 n. and Appendix, pp. 272. In the present passage T. does no more than record its entry to Rome in October, but the Survey as a whole (*hic fuit rerum Romanarum status*, I. 11. 13) purports to be a description of the situation on 1 Jan.; and since, given the news from Germany and the silence of T. in his narrative chapters, it is hardly conceivable that its departure took place as late as the new year, T. has here been seriously misleading.

Heubner insists that to T. the point was unimportant. To him the fall of Galba was caused by his character and by the state of Rome and the empire (and especially of the whole army) at this time. The whereabouts of particular legions were irrelevant, and if anyone had questioned him he might have doubted whether VII Galbiana would have been loyal when it came to the point. All that may be so, but the evidence for such judgements by T. is scanty. He liked accuracy about troop movements, and it is probably wiser to admit that he has here made an oversight.

10. exercitu insolito. The normal complement of troops in Rome was rather over 16,000 (see Introd., p. 16ff). In October, with the two extra legions, and with say 6,000 for the *numeri*, this figure may have been doubled.

11. numeri. For the movement of these and other troops see Introd., p. 10ff. The word *numeri* is used at *Agr.* 18. 3, Suet. *Vesp.* 6. 3, and on several inscriptions (e.g. *ILS* 2660, 2713, *AE* 1933, 107), of any detachments or groups of soldiers for which there was no obvious alternative description. It need not follow that the members of such groups were not enrolled in legions or regular auxiliary regiments. Indeed *in numeros referre* became (though it is doubtful when) the technical term for enrolment on Roman army lists, see Plin. *Epp.* III. 8. 4, X. 19. 2, and J. F. Gilliam, *Eos*, 1956, 207 ff. It is so used by T. of the *classici* put into legionary service, I. 87. 6, II. 69. 10 (though the latter passage is more ambiguous, see n. ad loc.)

12. ad claustra Caspiarum ... parabat. See Introd., p. 4, 9ff. Nero described his new legion, I Italica, as *phalanx Alexandri Magni*, Suet. *Nero* 19. 2, and one can well understand why the Caspian Gates, famous in the story of Alexander, were named as his objective. But Alexander's Gates were at the southern edge of Mt. Elburz, the road from Media over to Parthyaea; and though one cannot confidently ascribe ordinary prudence to Nero in 66, one would expect that Parthia would have reacted had he planned an expedition through Media. Anyway how would the Albani have been involved (they lived north of Media Atropatene, on the western shore of the Caspian)? That T.'s words are at least misleading, and probably mistaken, appears from Plin. *NH* VI. 40, where it is asserted that the 'Iberian gates', properly called 'Caucasian' (as Pliny had explained in § 30), were wrongly labelled 'Caspian' by Corbulo's men, and that this error appeared on a plan sent to Rome; moreover *Neronis principis comminatio ad Caspias portas tendere dicebatur, cum peteret illas quae per Hiberiam in Sarmatas tendunt.* By 'Iberian' Pliny must mean the Darial pass, which runs through the central Caucasus north from Tbilisi: in defiance of his censure later writers continued to call this the 'Caspian Gates' (Suet., cit., Jos. *Ant.* XVIII. 97), and T. himself again uses the phrase *Caspia via* when he describes the Sarmatian irruption into Armenia in A.D. 35 (*A.* VI. 33. 4). That pass then was Nero's objective, and it also almost certainly follows that his main enemies would have been not the Albani but the Alani. It was in his reign that this Sarmatian tribe (see Pliny, above) was first known to Roman writers (Lucan VIII. 223, Seneca, *Thyestes* 630); its branch, the Rhoxolani, were encountered by his legate Plautius Silvanus (*ILS* 986), apparently moving south-west under pressure from a more northerly Sarmatian migration (see also I. 79. 2 n.); they invaded Media in 72 (Jos. *BI* VII. 244 ff.); and Vespasian was (unsuccessfully) invited by the Parthians to conduct a joint expedition against them in 75 (Suet. *Dom.* 2. 2, Dio 65. 15. 3). For fuller discussion of the facts see J. G. C. Anderson, *CAH* X (1934), 776 ff.; and against the view that *claustra Caspiarum* meant the Derbend pass, in the south-east corner of the Caucasus leading over to the Caspian Sea, ibid. 883 f.

The mistake is puzzling. MS. corruption of the tribe's name (the explanation given by Mommsen, *Provinces of the Roman Empire* (1909), II. 62 n., E. Taübler, *Klio*, 1909, 14) is unlikely: *Alanos*, one of the most notorious barbarian invaders of the later empire, would have been infinitely *facilior lectio* to a scribe. But in any case how did T. come to write *claustra Caspiarum* if Pliny was his source? Fabia never discusses the problem. Pliny may have done his research on the point after he had finished the *a fine Aufidi Bassi*; or he may have written something like *ad claustra Caspiarum, quas recte Caucasias portas accepimus vocari*, and had his parenthesis disregarded by T. Neither explanation leaves one happy, and we would still have to account for *Albanos*. It is just possible that that tribe did figure in Nero's plans. In T. they are commonly associated with the Iberi (*A.* IV. 5. 4, VI. 33. 3), and through Iberian territory an expedition to the *Caucasiae portae* would certainly have had to have passed. Perhaps the Iberi were resistant to the building of forts in their country (for Vespasian's later fort at Tbilisi see *ILS* 8794 = MW 237), and relied on their old allies the Albani to support them.

13. opprimendis . . . coeptis. For the chronology of these movements see Introd., pp. 7–9, 11f.

7. 1. forte congruerat. With one another, or with the entry to Rome? The sequence of thought, running on from the previous chapter, certainly favours the latter view; and even though we may doubt whether T. himself thought the matter out with precision, he presumably found the item at this point in his source.

Heubner takes this argument to imply that the news arrived, not just about the time when Galba arrived, but actually after his entry. So, following A. Alföldi, *Insignien und Tracht der römischen Kaiser* (1935), 49 n. 1, he believes that Galba retained his uniform inside the city; for Suet. *G.* 11 records that he refused to resume the toga until he had overcome all his enemies, including Capito and Macer. But for Galba to do such a thing would have been an enormity (see II. 89. 1 on Vitellius); the numismatic evidence cited by Alföldi proves nothing about time or place; and Suetonius' *iterque ingressus est paludatus* is very mild if the dress was still worn in Rome. If *forte congruerat* implies the timing suggested above, surely the answer is that Galba did not enter Rome until he had learned that the executions had been carried out; he then took off the *paludamentum*, pressed on from the Milvian bridge to the *pomerium*, and in his toga made public announcement of his successes, perhaps in the senate the next day.

But there is still room for doubt about the timing. Galba arrived in

early October; Lower Germany was *diutius sine consulari* (I. 9. 5);
Vitellius arrived there before the end of November (I. 52. 1). Does
diutius mean a period of only six to seven weeks? About the date of the
executions Suet. *G.* 11 gives no help, but Plut. *G.* 15. 2, connects them
with the deaths of Nymphidius and Turpilianus, presumably during
Galba's march. Maybe T.'s source was not paying strict attention to
timing, but dealing with the topic of *saevitia*, and going on to *avaritia* in
line 13 (for Galba's two vices see Suet. 12. 1).

Clodi Macri. See Introd., p. 14. He was undoubtedly legate of III
Augusta, not proconsul of Africa, see IV. 49. 28, Suet. *G.* 11.

Fontei Capitonis, *cos. ord.* 67 (the name is obliterated by the Antiate
Fasti, but see *PIR*² F 467). As governor of Lower Germany he had
popularity with the legionaries (I. 8. 13, 58. 9, Dio 64. 2), whereas some
of the native officers of his auxiliary regiments favoured Galba (I. 58.
6 f., IV. 13).

3. procurator iussu Galbae. With Trebonius, it seems (IV. 49. 27),
was Papirius, the centurion executed by the proconsul Piso a year later.
A procurator, Baebius Massa, played a decisive part in the execution of
Piso; cf. also the use of *rei familiari impositi* to execute Iunius Silanus in
Asia in 54 (*A.* XIII. 1), and Nero's unsuccessful attempt to use his
procurators to check Galba (Suet. *G.* 9. 2). Contrast Tiberius' attitude
to a procurator's use of military force, *A.* IV. 15.

5. antequam iuberentur. Plut. *G.* 15. 2 makes Galba wholly
responsible. G. Townend, *AJP* 1964, 353, thinks Cluvius may be behind
T.'s account, and certainly it seems to be one which was unknown to
Plut. or Suet. (*G.* 11). Conceivably T. derived the story from an oral
source: it was one easily believed when Valens, allegedly because Galba
was ungrateful for the watch he had kept on Capito and Verginius
(52.15), promoted Vitellius' rising. T.'s doubts about Capito reappear
at III. 62. 11.

10. mobilitate ingenii, not a quality attributed to Galba elsewhere—
unless it be identical with *segnitia.* But T. does not necessarily support
it here. See Introd., pp. 12ff.

12. inviso . . . adferebant. Similar words are used by Plut. *G.* 18. 1
(cf. also Suet. *G.* 14. 1), and Bezzenberger's conjecture (see app. crit.)
can be regarded as reasonably certain; but Plut. makes the point in a
different context, namely that when Galba had spared Tigellinus even
his sensible measures in Gaul were censured. One may doubt whether
the rewards given to the Gallic states could have found general favour
in Rome, whatever the 'common source' may have said. But the
remarkable thing about T.'s account is the way in which, starting from

the extreme pleasure of the upper classes with the new regime, he has now convinced us that Galba was *invisus* everywhere (see above, p. 14). Yet if that was what he meant to imply, he has given evidence to the contrary later, IV. 40. 5 ff. on the Senate's restoration of Galba's *honores* in early 70.

13. venalia cuncta. Suet. *G.* 15 is a bit more specific, asserting the sale, or free gift, of *vectigalia*, *immunitates*, convictions of the innocent, and acquittals of the guilty. But apart from the matter of Vinius' intervention for Tigellinus (details in Plut. *G.* 16–17), and a bribe administered to Otho (Suet. *O.* 5), no source brings concrete instances to support the charge; and in taxation matters free gifts were not necessarily corrupt.

14. servorum ... avidae. *manus* could mean 'crowds' (see Heubner's note for parallels), but surely their 'grasping hands' were what T. had in mind. For the temporal ablative *subitis* see above, 2. 2 n. (a dative with *avidus* would be without parallel) and cf. *A.* I. 69.

18. forma ... corporis. As usual, Suet., *G.* 21, is ready with physical details which T. prefers to avoid.

8.1. tamquam ... multitudine. In a different context, the waves of opinion which beset Galba in the Forum (see I. 40), Plut. *G.* 26. 3, has οἷα δὲ ἐν πλήθει τοσούτῳ, which undoubtedly means 'as was natural in so great a crowd'. It is possible that T. was borrowing such a phrase from the 'common source', and in any case probable that he means that so large a population would produce the variety of opinions he has just analysed. The alternative (accepted by Irvine from many previous editors) is 'in so far as one can judge from so large a population', i.e. T. is entering a reservation to his own account. No parallel for the former view is quite decisive: e.g. Hor. *Sat.* I. 6. 79, *in magno ut populo* (cited by H.) seems to be equally ambiguous; and both I. 75. 5, *per tantam hominum multitudinem*, and Plin. *NH* IX. 157, *non omnibus id contingit ovis in tanta multitudine* (cited by Heubner), fail to throw light on the main issue, which is the meaning of *tamquam*. Yet there is really no parallel at all for the alternative translation; and it is in any case conceivable that the thought goes back ultimately to Thuc. II. 65. 11 ὡς ἐν μεγάλῃ πόλει καὶ ἀρχὴν ἐχούσῃ. See also I. 55. 16.

2. Hispaniae. Galba and Otho had been legates of Tarraconensis and Lusitania respectively, and the proconsul of Baetica had probably come to grief after Galba's rising (I. 37. 14 n.). Cluvius was probably, at this moment, in charge of all three Spanish provinces, appointed by Galba: at any rate T. tells us of no other Spanish governor, and in II. 58. 9 Cluvius is operating near the Straits of Gibraltar.

3. Cluvius ... inexpertus. To take *pacis artibus* as an ablative of quality, 'a man of the arts of peace', is surely intolerable: V. lists several passages which have been suggested as parallels, but is rightly dissatisfied with them. If M.'s reading be kept, *expertus* must be supplied from *inexpertus*, as *quibat* from *nequibat* at *A.* XII. 64. 3, *quae filio dare imperium, tolerare imperitantem nequibat*; cf. *A.* XIII. 56. 1, *deesse nobis terra in vitam, in qua moriamur non potest.* For defence of this view see P. Persson, *Eranos*, 1914, 113. K. (1961) reads *artibus clarus* from L.: of other suggestions perhaps the best is *artibus aptus*, E. von Leutsch, *Philologus*, 1882, 139.

Cluvius is often assumed to have been an old man by this time, since Jos. *Ant.* XIX. 91–2, appears to speak of him as consular in A.D. 41. But both Groag, *PIR*² C 1202 and 1206, and Syme, 294, have reservations about that evidence; moreover for what it is worth, Suetonius Paulinus (still praetorian in 42) is called *vetustissimus consularium* in II. 37. 7, and since there were not many consulars actually in Otho's camp T. may mean that he was the most senior consular alive. Cluvius was certainly consular by 65, when he accompanied Nero to Greece (Suet. *Nero* 21. 3, Dio 63. 14. 3). On his career and works see L. H. Feldman, *Latomus*, 1962, 248 ff., and above all G. B. Townend, *Hermes*, 1964, 237 ff., who gives a very low estimate of him. See also Introd., p. 26.

4. Galliae. Syme, 456 n. 3, claims that in T. and other authors the plural 'normally and firmly excludes Narbonensis'. To press the point too far could create difficulties over one or two *Histories* passages (e.g. I. 61. 3, III. 2. 10, 13. 5), but it does much to explain certain usages in Book IV; and see esp. III. 41–2, IV. 49, where the Narbonese province seems almost directly contrasted with the warlike *Galliae* (perhaps also I. 87. 2, see n. ad loc.). In the present passage too T. clearly means that part of Gaul which had taken part in an armed rising, i.e. he includes Vienna and the Vocontii, but not the greater part of Narbonensis. It follows that Narbonensis, despite its wealth and importance, and despite T.'s own connections with the area (on Syme's view he was born there) is nowhere mentioned in the Introduction, except in the general reference to *inermes provinciae* (11. 11). This is a striking commentary on the military content of T.'s conception of *habitus provinciarum*, see above, p. 47.

dono Romanae civitatis. Plut. *G.* 18. 1 also speaks of this (saying it was bought from Vinius), but equally gives no details. See further I. 78. 3 n., and cf. I. 58. 22.

5. tributi levamento, remission of a quarter, I. 51. 21. What T. fails to mention, in either passage, is Galba's complete remission of the XL Galliarum, the customs duty levied at the Gallic frontiers with Spain and Italy. The numismatic evidence for this considerable concession is conveniently set out by S. J. de Laet, *Portorium* (1949), 122, 170 ff. The tax was soon restored, evidently by Vespasian, Suet. *Vesp.* 16. 1.

proximae ... civitates, developed in I. 53.

10. alias partis. This implies no more than what is said in the next sentence. Note that the Lower German *vexilla* (see I. 53. 10 n.) passed to Galba, because of Valens' activities, more quickly than did Verginius' troops. As well as arguing (not necessarily rightly) that T.'s judgement here is derived from Cluvius Rufus (cf. Plin. *Epp.* IX. 19. 5), K. criticizes T. for not analysing Verginius' attitude more thoroughly and especially for not explaining what he thought of the programme put forward by 'the majority of the Senate' (i.e. various brands of *Libertas*). But even if there was such a programme, T. was perhaps entitled to regard it as of little relevance to the situation of 1 Jan. 69.

13. conveniebat. This is the point which matters most for T.'s theme, for it explains the fear, as well as the indignation, which the Rhine legions were feeling. Plut. too, *G.* 6. 1–2, has no doubt that Verginius received several offers, and that one of them preceded the battle of Vesontio. See Introd., p. 8.

14. qui queri non poterant, 'were in no position to complain' (rather than 'could not get their complaints heard'): see parallels cited by Heubner, and esp. Plin. *Epp.* X. 17a. 2. In other words, though possibly guiltless of intrigues against Galba, Capito was *foedus ac maculosus*, I. 7.7.

dux, a deliberate double entendre. Galba had withdrawn their commander, *dux exercitus*; whom could they back as *dux partium*?

15. per simulationem amicitiae. After surrendering his command without protest, Verginius joined Galba's company on the march to Rome, and was treated by him without clear sign either of anger or of regard, Plut. *G.* 10. 3. Galba had compromised. Vinius would have liked Verginius to be not only recalled but punished; but the soldiers were certainly wrong in thinking that he was ever put on trial.

9.1. superior exercitus. It is curious that T. in these chapters never makes clear that this was Verginius' army, and that Capito had been in Lower Germany.

senecta. T.'s standards vary. At III. 66. 7 Vitellius is addressed as a *senex* at the age of fifty-four; and we are uncertain whether the *divites senes* of II. 86. 15 were all that old (one of them, agreed, had been consul in 45)? Plut. too, *G.* 15. 2, calls Petronius Turpilianus 'an old man', only seven years after his consulate.

2. debilitate pedum, characteristic Tacitean evasion of the technical word *podagra*, cf. Plut. *G.* 18. 4.

3. adeo. Cf. III. 39. 10, *nullius repentini honoris, adeo non principatus adpetens,* III. 64. 9, *Vitellium ne prosperis quidem parem, adeo ruentibus debilitatum,* IV. 39. 16, *ne paratis quidem corrumpi facilis, adeo metuens incerta.* Though in appearance the meaning is 'Y is so emphatically the case that we can also assert X', yet Y (the clause introduced by *adeo* = *a fortiori*) is the one which matters in the context. So too IV. 80. 4, *aequalium quoque, adeo superiorum intolerantis,* which might be ambiguous if it stood alone. See *TLL* I. 607. 56 ff.

5. diutius sine consulari. 7. 1 n. above.

6. censoris . . . filius. For the career of the father, whose eminence was unparalleled for a *privatus* of the Julio-Claudian period, I. 52. 23 n. But A. Vitellius was chosen for qualities other than military experience, *nullis stipendiis, nulla militari fama,* II. 76. 24. One should remember that it was Galba, on Vinius' advice (Introd., p. 15), who initially chose him, and it may be that he seemed a promising statesman, despite his eventual collapse.

7. id satis videbatur. That the words are heavily ironical is clear, but editors have disputed whether the judgement is one ascribed to the soldiers (so Goelzer following Lipsius) or represents Galba's hopes when he appointed Vitellius. But is not the ambiguity both deliberate and deadly? Those who thought Vitellius' parentage qualified him for leadership of a disaffected army were Galba and his advisers (especially Vinius, Suet. *G.* 7. 1); but the troops too found these qualifications highly satisfactory (*velut dono deum oblatum,* Suet. *G.* 7. 3), not because Galba had appeased them but because they now had a commander whose birth and standing made him *capax imperii.*

8. non sane . . . innocentius egerunt. For some exceptions see I. 60, II. 65.

11. dum in Italia cunctantur. Classen's *cunctatur* (with Nero as the subject), adopted by V. 1 and H., involved a strange judgement on Nero's 'war'; for though one might criticize him for dallying near Rome, to move out of Italy altogether would have been pointless until it had been seen whether the Rhine legions would suppress Vindex. The emenders claimed that there was no evidence of Illyrican troops entering Italy; but II. 27. 9, *ablatam Neroni Italiam* (the Batavian cohorts speaking of their operations against XIV Gemina) is clear enough. Probably XIV was the only whole legion which left Illyricum cf. *eligendo ut potissimos,* II. 11. 9); for the plural *legiones* = *legionarii* see I. 11. 6 n. For other Illyrican units see II. 11. 7, and on Nero's mobilization Introd., pp. 9ff.

12. Verginium legationibus adissent. For this there is no other evidence, and it is not certain whether the embassy was sent before or after Nero's death; but *cunctantur* suggests to me the latter. See Introd., p. 12.

longis ... exercitus. Apart from that of XIII Gemina (Poetovio, III. 1. 2), the camps of the Pannonian and Dalmatian legions at this time are not known with complete certainty. But it is unlikely that any of the four were in two-legion camps; and in any case T. probably includes here the legions in Moesia, which were even more spread apart from one another, and distant from those of Illyricum proper.

10. 1. Syriam et quattuor. But III Gallica had departed for Moesia before Nero's death, Suet. *Vesp.* 6. 3, leaving only three legions in Syria. T. forgets this at II. 4. 16, 6. 15 (he is aware of it at II. 74. 6), and it is surprising that he was not reminded of the movement when he came to describe the legion's victory over the Sarmatians in I. 79.

2. Licinius Mucianus. Of the portrait which follows (supplemented at II. 80. 14, *omniumque quae diceret atque ageret arte quadam ostentator*), there is an excellent appreciation by Courbaud, 173. See also Syme, 195 f., who points out that for a character-sketch of Vespasian we have to wait until II. 10: it could be that T. regarded Mucianus, for the moment at least, as the stronger candidate for the empire.

Mucianus eventually, though he remained a *privatus*, won an exceptional position. He held three consulships (all suffect, the first in the mid-sixties, the others in 70 and 72); he directed affairs in Rome before Vespasian's return in October 70, and was called 'brother' by the emperor he had made (Dio 66. 2, though for Vespasian's more characteristic reactions to his *nimiae voluptates* see Suet. *Vesp.* 13). He was also responsible, presumably in agreement with Vespasian, for much of the money-raising in Italy which earned the emperor his reputation for *avaritia* (Dio 66. 2. 5; see below, II. 5. 4 with nn.), and he took a prominent part in the hostility shown to the 'philosophers'. Yet his earlier career, and the explanation of the sentences which follow (in particular the reasons for his fear of Claudius), remain obscure, except that he was at some time governor of Lycia–Pamphylia, and that as consular legate of Syria, appointed presumably in 67, he was until Nero's death on bad terms with Vespasian. For the sources see *PIR*[1] L 147, and for speculation about his birthplace (possibly Spain) Syme, App. 85. He was a prolific writer, *Dial.* 37, and his works on geography are frequently cited in Pliny's *Nat. Hist.* He died before Pliny's work was published in 77, *NH* 32. 72.

3. famosus. Most commentators have translated 'notable': Paratore, 58 (following Wolff) stands out for 'infamous'. *TLL* gives ample support for both meanings, and both are current in T. (see GG).

Paratore argues that when T. gives a preliminary sketch rather than an obituary he is always hostile; but of preliminary sketches he cites but seven examples of which two do not support his thesis; and anyway T. here explicitly ascribes *virtutes* as well as *vitia*.

5. in secretum ... sepositus, 'removed into private life in Asia; cf. II. 100. 13 n. but without further evidence we cannot tell whether *sepositus* (surely the right reading) implies an actual order by Claudius, nor what the trouble was.

8. quotiens expedierat. In the very next chapter (line 3) *expedire* means 'to be expedient', but here it surely bears the sense it has in I. 88. 6, II. 99. 2, 'to be on campaign', as contrasted with *vacaret*. Madvig insisted on *expediri* in both the parallel passages, and therefore inserted *se* here: see however Valmaggi in *Boll. fil. class.* 1924, 173.

palam. Generally agreed by editors to equal *palam facta*, though no absolutely convincing parallel has been found.

10. et cui expeditius. Madvig's *set* was regrettable.

11. bellum Iudaicum ... administrabat. Probably Vespasian's official title was *legatus* in charge of this war: up to this time there had been no senatorial governor of Judaea.

13. tribus legionibus, V Macedonica, X Fretensis, and XV Apollinaris, the last commanded by Vespasian's son Titus, Jos. *BI* III. 65. See Introd., pp. 18–19.

14. votum aut animus. For *votum*, 'hope for Galba's welfare', see GG b)a). *Adversus* in itself is neutral, 'in relation to' (see Heubner's n.).

venerationem cultumque. The words are surprising, because either, or both (*A.* IV. 37. 3), can be used of the imperial cult, and it was clearly not divine honours which Titus was going to pay to Galba. But see Cic. *de Inv.* II. 161, *observantia, per quam homines aliqua dignitate antecedentes cultu quodam et honore dignantur*; and for the two words together Sen. *Dial.* XII. 5. 2, *praestitit venerationem tamquam parenti, cultum tamquam superiori.* Heubner also cites *A.* IV. 52. 2, where T. speaks of *cultus* paid by Claudia Pulchra to the elder Agrippina.

15. miserat. But Titus heard of Galba's death when he had only reached Achaia, II. 1. 13. See introd. to that chapter for the reasons why T. considered it the appropriate point at which to tell the story further.

occulta fati ... The whole sentence surely implies that T. did not take such manifestations with seriousness, see 3. 7. n. above; contrast Zancan, *La crisi del principato nell'anno 69 D.C.*, 73. *Fortunam* (line 17) means no miraculous fortune of Vespasian, but simply his 'rise to the principate'; cf. I. 15. 27 (Piso), 62. 6, 77. 2, II. 59. 18 (Vitellius), II. 80. 6, 81. 15, III. 43. 2 (Vespasian).

11.1 Aegyptum. T.'s other summary of Roman rule in Egypt, *A.* II. 59. 4, deals with the prohibition on entry imposed on senators and *equites inlustres*. *Domi retinere* (the emendation *domui* is wanton) implies that the *domus Caesarum* controlled it beyond the normal usages of the *res publica* (cf. *A.* XIII. 3. 2), but does not mean that Augustus regarded Egypt as his private property: at *RG* 28. 1 he expressly says he added it to the *imperium* of the Roman people. But the elaborate nature of its administration sharply distinguishes it from any other province, see Brunt's first n. to his survey of its government in *JRS* 1975, 124. Its *praefecti* were viceroys for an emperor who had succeeded to the Ptolemies (*loco regum*, line 2), cf. Strabo XVII p. 797, ὁ μὲν οὖν πεμφθεὶς τὴν τοῦ βασιλέως ἔχει τάξιν. They received the marks of divinity which had been given to previous rulers, and like the kings these *praefecti* were 'forbidden' to sail on the Nile when it was in flood, Plin. *NH* V. 57. For judicious discussion see H. I. Bell, *CAH* X (1934), 284.

5. ignaram magistratuum, for they had been governed by a *regnum*, which implied absence of laws and magistrates as Rome would understand such things. And so their new *praefecti*, technically speaking, were not magistrates either, for they were not senators. But one of the early measures of the Principate was to let them give decisions *ac si magistratus Romani constituissent, A.* XII. 60. 3, and in that passage T. gives Egypt as the first example of the new policy.

6. Tiberius Alexander. Tib. Iulius Alexander was born a Jew, nephew to Philo, and son to Alexander the alabarch of Alexandria (his brother was the first husband of queen Berenice, II. 2. 2 n.). He abandoned the Jewish way of life, and was thought by Claudius' government to be an appropriate procurator of Judaea in 46: he had been a friend of Herod Agrippa I. In 63 he held an important post under Corbulo in Armenia, *A.* XV. 28. 4, and by the middle of 66 had become prefect of Egypt, *PIR*² i. 139, where he played a significant part in connection with Galba's rising (see Introd.) and next year was the first commander to proclaim Vespasian, II. 79 with nn. In 70 he was chief of staff to Titus in Judaea, Jos. *BI.* VI. 4. 3, and it has been commonly assumed that this was the position described in Pap. Hibeh 215 (=MW. 329 (b)) as τοῦ ἡγεμο[νεύσαντ]ος γενομένου καὶ ἐπάρχου πραι[τωρίου . . .]. But E. G. Turner, *JRS* 1954, 61 ff., argued ingeniously that these words referred to an actual prefecture of the guard at Rome, as colleague of Titus after his return in 71. I am not wholly convinced, since I doubt whether Titus would, without protest, have accepted an older colleague in the prefecture at this stage in his own advancement. But perhaps we know too little about this period of Vespasian's principate to feel confidence about any judgement.

Africa ac legiones in ea. Normally III Augusta was the only legion in Africa, but see II. 97. 9 for *legio cohortesque delectae a Clodio Macro.* Mommsen, *CIL* VIII. p. xx, who objected to the reading here on grounds of Latinity, maintained that all Macer did was to put fresh drafts into III Augusta and to rename it I Macriana. But Macer's coinage (*RIC* I. 193–4, R. Cagnat, *L'Armée romaine d'Afrique* (1892), 144 ff.) refutes this view: the word LIBERATRIX is applied on some coins to a legion named III Augusta, on others to one named I Macriana, and the emblems of the two legions are different from one another. Moreover, since Galba cashiered Macer's legion, Africa would on Mommsen's view have been left without a legionary garrison until Vitellius revived it. There were therefore clearly two legions in Africa during Macer's rising.

Yet Macer's units were *mox a Galba dimissae*, II. 97. 9, so it is unlikely that there was more than one legion in the province on 1 Jan. 69. If then the MS. reading produces historical inaccuracy, is it reasonable to tolerate (a) the 'hanging' prepositional phrase *in ea*, and (b) the singular *contenta* following the plural *legiones*? Ritter regarded *legiones in ea* as a gloss, but the author of such a gloss would have been surprisingly learned if he knew of Macer's legion, and surprisingly lucky if he did not. V. 1 and H., and also Mommsen, followed Lipsius in emending to *legio*, though V. later observed that *contentae* would be an equally easy way of overcoming objection (b). Equally easy, and equally arbitrary; and anyway that objection is less formidable if one realizes that T.'s thought is concentrated on the first subject *Africa* and that his mention of troops in the province is parenthetic.

Objection (a) is of a different order, for the phrase is a curiously inept one, quite apart from the fact that no Tacitean parallel seems to exist for a prepositional phrase wholly dependent on a noun. Yet in earlier prose writers this usage, though exceptional, is not entirely unknown. K.–St. II. 1. 216, cite Cic. *de Orat.* II. 352, *quum cenaret Crannone in Thessalia Simonides apud Scopam*, and Caes. *BC* III. 22. 2, *Cosam in agro Thurino oppugnare coepit*; and though in both these it could be argued that the prepositional phrase is related to the action in the verb, there are more convincing instances where the preposition is *cum*, in Cic. *Dom.* 23, *bellum cum pacatissimis gentibus . . . dedit*, and Livy 26. 28. 3, *ut . . . Italia bellumque cum Hannibale provincia esset*. On the whole it would seem that we ought to explain the present passage without emending, and K. in his last two editions does not even question the MS. reading.

Why then did T. write *legiones* if there was only one? V.2, now reconciled to the MS. but still worried by the singular *contenta*, pointed out (*Riv. fil.* 1908, 374) that *legiones* in T. (and in Suetonius) often means just *legionarii*; cf. (besides I. 5. 6, a doubtful case), I. 22. 1 (only one legion then in Rome), 70. 22. 2 (see n. below), II. 22. 2, 25. 5 (three passages about Caecina's army, in which only one legion was present entire), and probably also IV. 25. 18. About these other passages he was surely right, but (apart from the fact that he did not by these means solve his own difficulty about *contenta*) he makes T. introduce an irritating ambiguity if he (T.) was fully conscious that the garrison had been two legions but was now reduced to one. A much more likely explanation lies in a feature of T.'s Survey which has been emphasized above (see n. on I. 6. 9, *inducta legione Hispana*, and introd. to cap. 4), namely that he tends to treat the last months of 68 as if they were a single moment and takes from his source items which were no longer operative on 1 Jan. 69. Our present passage could be based on a source which surveyed the provinces as they were when Galba entered Rome in October. Macer (see I. 7. 1 and n.) had been executed while Galba was on his way, but soon after his arrival measures would have been taken to deal with the African troops and reduce their numbers to normal.

(For further discussion see V.'s note; Cagnat, cit.; P. Romanelli, *Storia delle province romane dell'Africa* (1959), 279 ff. I am also most grateful for valuable advice from the late Mr. T. F. Higham and from Mr. J. D. P. Bolton on the questions of Latinity, though they must not necessarily be taken to have agreed that the passage is tolerable as it stands in the MS.).

8. domini minoris, not even a consular, *PIR*² C 1170. On his character and aims we have only the hostile sentences of Plut. G. 6. 2.

9. quae aliae . . . For the momentary troubles in the two Mauretanias, at this time controlled by a single procurator, see II. 58–9. Raetia and Noricum, *ut cuique exercitui vicinae*, followed the one the German army (I. 58. 12, III. 5. 11), the other that of Illyricum (I. 70. 16, III. 5. 13). For Corsica/Sardinia see II. 16, and for the Alpes Maritimae II. 12. 14, III. 42–3. Thrace and the minor provinces of the East gave Vespasian such support as he needed (III. 81. 8 ff.), but saw no fighting.

15. rei publicae prope supremum. So we return to his opening words. When one reads the Younger Pliny, and feels the complacency current among upper-class circles in Trajan's early and middle years, one can wonder both whether T. really looked back to 69 as a year of so extreme crisis (but cf. Suet. *Vesp.* 1. 1, *incertum diu et quasi vagum imperium*), and also whether he was right to do so. But in the light of all the evidence, especially that provided by T., we must surely believe that, had Vespasian's victory been less decisive and quick, the disruptive forces, both from beyond the frontiers but still more from inside the various provinces, might have created a very different world from that in which T. was writing. And if that judgement be right, it is surely unfair to suggest that T. did not make it sincerely.

12–49. *The Fall of Galba*

12. 1. paucis ... diebus. This gives us very precise information about the speed with which important dispatches could travel. Like Vitellius at Colonia Agrippinensis (I. 56. 10), the procurator, who at Augusta Trevirorum was slightly closer to Mogontiacum (141 km), could have got the news in the late afternoon of 1 Jan. If his message reached Rome, 1,692 km away, before the 10th (I. 18. 1), the post must have travelled rather over 200 km a day. This was not of course the normal speed of the *cursus publicus*, but for urgent messages, which despite the revised arrangements of Augustus (Suet. *Aug.* 49) may have been carried by relay riders, there are near parallels, see Köster, 12 f. A. M. Ramsay, *JRS*, 1925, 60 ff., probably exaggerates the exceptional nature of this incident, and adds a bit to the distance by supposing (wrongly) that the procurator was at Durocortorum = Reims, rather than at Trier (see following n.).

Pompei ... Belgica. This man, about whom nothing else is known, was executed before his dispatch reached Rome, I. 58. 5. The headquarters of the procurator of Belgica were at Augusta Trevirorum (O. Hirschfeld, *Der kaiserlichen Verwaltungsbeamten*[2] (1905), 379—in Strabo's day, IV. 194, the legate of Belgica had been at Durocortorum), and he was responsible for matters affecting the Rhineland as a whole, an arrangement continued even after Domitian created a province of Germania Superior.

2. superioris Germaniae legiones. Strictly speaking, as Fabia, *Klio*, 1904, 42 ff., pointed out, only two of the three Upper German legions had refused allegiance, I. 55. 10 ff.; and the dispatch must have made this clear, *duae legiones* 16. 17, *quartam et duetvicensimam* I. 18. 9. In Rome the intentions of legion XXI Rapax, which at Vindonissa was considerably further from Mogontiacum than either Vitellius or the procurator, may not have been known. But it is surely likely that Vitellius' agents had concerted action with this legion, as also with commanders in Britain, I. 59. 13, see ad loc.

3. rupta ... acciperetur. The constitutional formality with which the revolt of the Upper German army began was modelled on the actions of Galba and Verginius Rufus in the previous year. The implications, which were probably left in no doubt in the procurator's dispatch, are made fairly explicit in I. 55.

8. licentia ac libidine, not a tautology. Freedom of discussion generated the taste for it.

10. rei publicae amor. The number of instances where this phrase means 'public spirit' is so great that it is astonishing how often historians have asserted that Plautius Lateranus, *A.* XV. 49., was a 'republican'.

12. in Titi Vinii odium, 'to gratify their dislike of Vinius'. V.'s parallels for *in* with accusative after *corruptus* are hardly adequate, but *A.* XV. 44, *tamquam . . . in saevitiam absumerentur* is what we need—see Furneaux's n. ad loc.

15. infirmum et credulum, an important contribution to T.'s complex sketch of Galba; obstinate on principles he remembered from the past, I. 18, fin. (where Syme, 204, dismisses him as an 'anachronism', but perhaps ignores the wistfulness of T.'s words), yet unable to make up his mind on unfamiliar issues. Such a man would easily trust his subordinates once he had chosen them, see I. 49. 13 and the various references to Vinius and Laco, without reflecting that the advice they gave him might be less frank (as well as concerned with newer sorts of problem) than that which Tiberius (say) had received from his *amici.*

13. 3. Icelo, who had travelled to Spain with the news of Galba's adoption by the senate, Plut. *G.* 7, Suet. *G.* 14 and 22.

anulis donatum, cf. Suet. *G.* 14. 2, *paulo ante anulis aureis et Marciani cognomine ornatus ac iam summae equestris gradus candidatus,* Plut. *G.* 7, δακτυλίους τε χρυσοῦς ἔδωκε καὶ Μαρκιανὸς ὁ "Ικελος ἤδη καλούμενος. The same privilege was granted to Vitellius' freedman Asiaticus, II. 57. 9, Suet. *Vit.* 12, and to the slave who betrayed Tarracina, IV. 3. 10. Suet.'s words about Asiaticus, namely that earlier Vitellius *detestatus esset severissime talem equestris ordinis maculam,* suggest that he (and Vitellius) thought that the consequence of the grant would be membership of the equestrian order; similarly Hormus, Vespasian's freedman, is regarded as having been given *dignitas equestris,* IV. 39. 5, and this may have meant a grant of *anuli aurei.* From a full review of the evidence A. Stein, *Der römische Ritterstand* (1927), 30 ff., concluded, following Mommsen, that in our period (i.e. before Hadrian, *Dig.* XL. 10. 6) the grant meant the conferment of equestrian status.

This conclusion was challenged by A. M. Duff, *Freedmen in the early Roman Empire* (1928), 214 ff., who maintained that from the time of Augustus the technical effect of the grant was only to confer on freedmen a fictitious *ingenuitas*: to give the recipients equestrian rank was a further step, and Dio 48. 45. 9, when he calls such recipients τοῖς ἱππεύειν δυναμένοις strictly meant that they might become *equites* but were not necessarily so. This view is hard to reconcile with the

Suetonius text about Asiaticus, and still more with the well-known
passage of Pliny about the *equites* (*NH* 33. 32–3, though it must be
admitted that this contains some inescapable confusions). It is dangerous
to attribute to Augustus, simply because he 'founded the Principate',
social reforms with which no known text connects him, and it also
seems that Duff's argument rested on a misunderstanding. He asked
why, if the grant of *anuli* conferred equestrian rank, it was not made to
ingenui as well as to freedmen. Surely the passages about the army,
which he cites on p. 219, show that it was so made, as it had been made
in Caesar's time and just after, Suet., *Iul.* 39, Cic. *Fam.* XIII. 32. 2: there
was until Septimius Severus' reform (Herodian III. 8) a distinction
between on the one hand centurions and private soldiers, who could
not wear the gold ring, and on the other hand senior officers, who
could. Now the equestrian public service of the first century A.D. was
recruited almost wholly (a) from the army, (b) from freedmen who had
been given the ring. There was small reason for wishing to promote to
the equestrian order any number of civilian *ingenui*, unless they were
already qualified by the requisite property census. Under Hadrian
there came a change, presumably because it was thought necessary to
limit the accretions to the equestrian order. So the gold ring, from then
on, was regarded as simply conferring the fiction of *ingenuitas*; and
when under Severus larger numbers of soldiers were stationed in Italy,
the emperor felt bound to treat them no worse than the favoured
freedmen. But T. (and Suet.) were writing before Hadrian's reform.

The plural *anuli(s)* is constantly used in passages about the grant (see
also Martial XI. 59. 2, Juvenal I. 26). Most editors have agreed with
Mommsen that this was a 'technical' plural, but H. C. Nutting, *CQ*
1928, 172, gave strong ground for thinking that these people were
given several rings.

7. non tam unum aliquem. Yet surely Plut. *G.* 23, is right in
recording that Cn. Cornelius Dolabella was among those mentioned.
This man was a relative of Galba (probably a great-nephew, *PIR*²
C 1347), though the emperor (or perhaps Vinius?) suspected that he
had gained too much favour from the German 'corporis custodes'
because his gardens were near their camp, Suet. *G.* 12. 2. T. knew about
the relationship and about Dolabella's subsequent fate, I. 88. 3 (see n.),
II. 63–4, and it is curious that he fails to mention him in the present
context.

10. vidua filia, Crispina, I. 47. 11 n. *vidua* (see passages cited by
Heubner) probably means simply 'unmarried', Plut.'s χήρα (*G.* 17. 5)
being a mistranslation of his Latin source.

gener ac socer. T. gives this project only as a rumour; Plut. *G.* 21. 1
as a fact.

11. frustra ... translatae. T. from the start (see also last words of the chapter) introduces Otho as the 'Nero-type' candidate, and prepares the way for the high moral tone he allows Galba in the speech adopting Piso. See Klingner, 11 ff.

13. aemulatione luxus. He taught Nero to put ointment on the soles of his feet, Plin. *NH* 13. 22, and replied to Nero's sprinkling him with a particularly expensive oil by having the same one gushing from gold and silver pipes in his house next day, Plut. *G.* 19. 3.

14. eoque Poppaeam Sabinam ... This affair has been taken by all sides as critical in the consideration of T.'s sources. Fabia, 13, made it a key point for his view that T., Plut., and Suet. were using a common source for this period; his critics, for various reasons, have thought it to be a prime reason for refuting him; and other scholars have made it their base for different theories. The acute discussion by G. Townend, *Hermes*, 1961, 242–8, showed that the problem was even more complex than many writers had allowed; above all in his use of Dio 61. 11, and in showing that Suet.'s evidence must not be limited to the passage in *O.* 3.

The main discrepancies in our extant sources can be identified as follows:

(a) At *A.* XIII. 45–6 T. makes Poppaea the wife of Otho before Nero fell in love with her. This is inescapably divergent from any other account, and Townend claims that T. produced it 'for his own purposes, and almost certainly out of his own head'. He could be right, but his case is not really proven, nor does he provide a parallel for this sort of inventiveness by T.

(b) Was this affair, as T. would have it in the *Annals*, an important part of the politics of A.D. 58–9, leading to the murder of Agrippina? Townend shows that Dio, though his epitomators quickly fade out on this aspect, introduced Otho as a prime factor in those matters; but that Plut., who seems in *G.* 19 to be mentioning 'Marcus Otho' for the first time, had probably ignored him (in contrast to Poppaea) in his life of Nero. Suet. gives us nothing before *O.* 3, despite all that his *Nero* has on the events of 59: T. in our present passage does not contribute to the question. On this issue, which affects the sources of the *Annals* rather than of the *Histories*, Townend's analysis seems essentially sound.

(c) Was Poppaea the mistress of Nero before she was mistress (or wife) of Otho? Taken literally, T.'s *principale scortum* and Suet.'s *tunc adhuc amicam* imply that she was; Plut., though clear that Nero was already interested, gives Otho priority with προμοιχεύσας; Dio leaves the question open, αὐτῇ ἀμφότεροι ἅμα ἐχρῶντο. It is doubtful whether any of them gave the matter much thought, and certain that no source could have supplied compelling evidence either way.

(d) Did Otho actually marry Poppaea? Townend, 246 n. 2, says that T. in the *Annals* provides the only 'straightforward' evidence that he did; but there is at least corroboration in Suet. *O.* 3. 2, *diducto matrimonio* and in Plut. *G.* 19. 2, τὸν Ποππαίας γάμον. Indeed the whole story in Suet., ending in the two lines of verse, is not unreasonable, given what all our sources tell us about Nero's court. But it is curious that in listing Nero's wives at *Nero* 35. 2 Suet. should describe Poppaea as *equiti R. antea nuptam* (i.e. Crispinus) and no more.

(e) How greatly was Otho endangered? Plut. says he was saved by the intervention of Seneca, Suet. that Nero could not afford to make the ridiculous affair public, T. in the *Annals* that he had to get his obvious rival out of the way. Moreover Plut. *G.* 23. 4 says the soothsayer Ptolemaeus predicted (but when?) that Nero would not kill Otho, whereas T. (in a different context, I. 22. 12) speaks only of a prediction that Otho would survive Nero. One can only comment that Nero left Otho in safety in Lusitania for nearly ten years.

(f) What of Suet.'s story that Otho gave a banquet for Agrippina and Nero on the evening Nero had chosen for his mother's murder? According to the *Annals* Otho was by then in Lusitania, and there is nothing about him in Dio's story of the murder.

There must remain uncertainties about all these things, though perhaps they are uncertainties more about the transmission of the stories rather than about what actually happened. Yet despite the divergences noted above, especially at (c) and (e), the similarity between the *Histories* and the accounts of Plut. and Suet. is surely more fundamental—the 'pawning' (*deposuerat*) of Poppaea to Otho, and Nero's fear that the pledge would not be honoured. A common source seems almost certain, and it could be that the divergences are due only to the different temperaments and varying degrees of attention paid by the three authors using it. But the existence of a common source does not preclude the possibility that each one of these authors from time to time made use of other material, especially oral evidence.

For the *Annals* T. may still have had that 'common source' before him; if the source was Pliny, he certainly did (*A.* XIII. 20, XV. 53). But by then he was making extensive use of other authors as well; and in one of them, perhaps Cluvius Rufus, he found the variant about Poppaea which he (probably rightly) preferred. Remarkably, but perhaps characteristically, he says nothing in the *Annals* about the matter being controversial, and that he had earlier given a different account, see Syme, 290.

17. specie legationis, 'ostensibly as a legate'. Yet he was not only ostensibly but actually a legate, though only of quaestorian standing, Suet. *O.* 3. 2. For the usage see I. 74. 9 n.

18. comiter ... provinciae. On this point T.'s view in the *Annals* is unchanged, *non ex priore infamia, sed integre sancteque egit*, XIII. 46. Suet., cit., and Plut. *G.* 20. 1, agree.

primus transgressus, with lavish gifts of gold and silver plate and of slaves, Plut. *G.* 20. 6.

19. praesentis, 'his staff': cf. Sall. *BI* 93. 7.

22. aula Neronis, above all the procurators and freedmen, Suet. *O.* 7. 1. For further light on Otho's revival of Nero see I. 78.

14. 2. quamquam nihil ... certum, i.e. Galba as yet had only the procurator's dispatch about the refusal of the legions at Mogontiacum to take the oath on 1 Jan. Plut. *G.* 23. 1, who describes Vitellius' proclamation and then says Galba has learned of τὸν ἐκεῖ νεωτερισμόν appears to be in conflict with T., but as Townend, *AJP* 1964, 355, points out, his phrase need only mean 'the disturbances in the Rhineland'.

4. comitia imperii transigit. After this piece of irony ('the deadly constitutional thrust', M. I. Henderson, *JRS* 1954, 125), however much one may analyse the origin and meaning of Galba's ensuing discourse on the Succession problem, one must surely have little confidence in the strength of T.'s own convictions on the subject.

adhibitis ... praefecto urbis. The holding of any council is implicitly denied both by Plut. *G.* 23. 1, who says Galba made his choice μηδὲν προειπών, and by Suet. *G.* 17, who depicts Galba as suddenly picking out Piso from among the crowd at his morning reception. Yet T.'s circumstantial account, with the names of the four colleagues, can hardly be his invention; and Townend, cit., 354, plausibly derives the story from a source (probably Cluvius Rufus) familiar with 'inner history'—adding that such a story would have been of keen interest to T. had he attended a similar council in 97 (see Syme, 129).

5. Mario Celso. The sympathy with which Celsus is treated, e.g. I. 45. 6, 71. 4 ff., and the attention given to his views by Plutarch as well as by T. during Otho's war, have made many scholars wonder whether he was not available as a source, directly or at second hand. Legate of XV Apollinaris under Corbulo in 63, *A.* XV. 25, he is probably the writer on tactics cited by Lydus, *de Mag.* III. 33, and may have written other works besides, Syme, App. 32. Moreover T. must have known Ti. Iulius Candidus Marius Celsus (*cos.* 86, *cos.* II 105), who may have preserved memoirs of our Celsus given him orally or in writing.

After being spared and then used as a general by Otho, Celsus survived to hold under Vitellius the consulate to which Otho had designated him, II. 60. 13. Yet the words *fataliter* and *infelix* in I. 71. 12 suggest that ill fortune (worse than the defeat at Bedriacum) overtook him before the faction fights were over. A P. Marius Celsus was governing Syria in 73, *ILS* 8903 = MW. 93, but may, as Dessau suggests, be the consul of 62.

6. Ducenio Gemino. Already consular by 62, when he was appointed to a special treasury commission, *A.* XV. 18, Ducenius was presumably made city prefect by Galba, who dismissed Flavius Sabinus as one of Nero's appointees, Plut. *O.* 5. 2. For possible conjectures about the order, though not the precise timing, of his earlier career see Groag, *PIR*[2] D. 201, who assigns to him *ILS* 963. His subsequent fate is unknown.

7. Pisonem Licinianum. See stemma, p. 71.

8. seu propria ... instante. There is here a remarkable discrepancy among the sources in that Suet. *G.* 17, says that Piso had for long been a favourite of Galba and had been made heir to both name and property in the emperor's will. Plut. shows no knowledge of this; and if T. had heard the story he has firmly suppressed it in *seu propria electione.* Townend, *AJP* 1964, 354, claims both that the story is 'manifestly improbable' and that Suet.'s source for it was the Elder Pliny. But (a) to ourselves the story may seem improbable, or at least surprising, but only because T. and Plut. ignore it; (b) is not this the sort of thing Suet. might have discovered (or thought he had discovered) from his own researches? In any case, whether or not Suet. be right, and whether or not Laco had heard about the will, his behaviour as recorded by T. remains credible. All he had to say to Galba was 'this young man, although I don't know him personally, seems from your account of him to be an admirable candidate, and certainly preferable to Otho', *callide ut ignotum fovebat.*

9. Rubellium Plautum, son of C. Rubellius Blandus and of Julia, granddaughter of Tiberius, executed in 62 *adsumpta Stoicorum adrogantia, A.* XIV. 57.

11. Piso ... nobilis utrimque. His father, *cos. ord.* A.D. 27, was, if Syme's conclusions (see stemma, p. 74) be right, son to a Piso Frugi (*cos.* 14 B.C.) who had been adopted by a Crassus (the consul of 30 B.C., grandson of the 'triumvir'). His mother was the great-granddaughter of Scribonia, wife to Sex. Pompeius the younger son of Pompey the Great. Note also that our Piso's sister (*PIR*[1] L 185) had married L. Piso (*cos.* 57, the ill-fated proconsul of Africa, IV. 39 ff.), who was son to

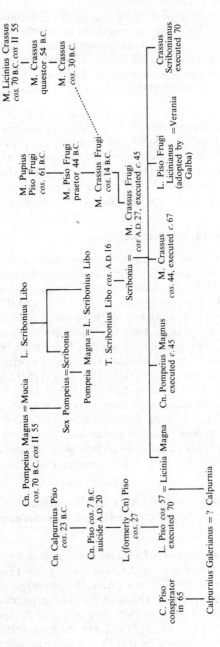

THE PISONES AND THEIR COLLATERALS

For the stemmata of both the Pisones and the Libones see Syme, *RR*, Table V, following Groag, *PIR*² C, facing p. 54. But Syme made an important correction, and added other probable conjectures, in *JRS* 1960, 13–20. M. Crassus, *cos.* 14 B.C., was shown to have been a Frugi, i.e. he was not the adopter of a Piso, but a Piso adopted by a Crassus (see dotted line above) was almost certainly the consul of 30 B.C., the grandson of the 'triumvir'. Syme's case for supposing that the Pisonian father of the consul of 14 B.C. was the grandson of M. Pupius Piso (*cos.* 61 B.C.) is also most attractive. Particularly significant are the two consular colleagues of A.D. 27.

74

their father's consular colleague and grandson of Cn. Piso (*cos.* 7. B.C.) the enemy of Germanicus.

So if M. Gelzer, *The Roman Nobility* (tr. R. Seager, 1969, 141 ff.), was right in interpreting *nobilitas* under the Principate as limited to descendants of 'Republican' consuls (but see I. 30. 1 n.), then clearly Piso Licinianus had the appropriate ancestry on both sides. For a claim based on maternal descent, which Gelzer believed to be also a new usage under the Principate, see *A.* XIV. 22, of Rubellius Plautus, *cui nobilitas per matrem ex Iulia familia*, and also Gelzer's comments (ibid. 147) on the Volusii. Yet I wonder whether this usage was not a Tacitean fancy.

13. tristior, a stock charge against Stoics, *A.* XVI. 22. 3. Piso's lack of emotion after the ceremony was probably seen as typical, I. 17. 1 ff. See Introd., p. 15.

15–16. *Galba's speech*

One thing is inescapable, namely that both T. and his audience would have had vividly in their minds the adoption of Trajan by Nerva in October 97, together with the events which preceded and followed that act. Galba's act was different from Nerva's in its outward form, and is criticized as such by Pliny (see 15. 2 n.), but T. makes no explicit allusion to the differences. H. Nesselhauf, *Hermes*, 1955, 495, is surely right in emphasizing that for T. the less said about 97 the better, whatever he might imply. For the many other modern treatments of the affair see Heubner's n.

As to the treatment of *adoptio** as the ideal means of imperial inheritance, many scholars have asked whether either T. or Pliny drew on the other. There is no adequate means for determining this. It is not a question of verbal correspondences, but simply of community of theme; and the theme would, in the first decade of the second century, have been in every senator's mind. Probably the two friends discussed the subject, possibly they showed one another their drafts, but how can we say more? See M. Durry, *Panégyrique* (1938), 60 ff. and his nn. to *Pan.* 7 ff., and Syme's review of that edition in *JRS* 1938, 219.

What respect, then, did T. have for the carefully modelled arguments he ascribes to Galba? About the actual affair of 69 he has already indicated contempt, see 14. 4 n. above, and particular sentences in the speech are clearly a travesty of the realities, as T. has described them, of Galba's regime, see nn. below. But could the speech, none the less, be offering a considered defence of *adoptio*, provided it was carried out in

---

* Here, and in what follows, I use *adoptio* to mean an emperor's choice of someone *in re publica*, 15. 13, as against retention of a dynasty *in domo*.

different circumstances and with more proper procedures? In other words, has *loco libertatis quod eligi coepimus* a serious place in T.'s political thinking? Heubner rejects this on the ground that T. would never have chosen as his mouthpiece a man who was *capax imperii nisi imperasset*; but this is not a convincing ground, since T., in the tradition of Thucydides, often introduced arguments he believed to be plausible, or even important, into speeches delivered by characters of whom he disapproved. But a fairly decisive reason for rejection is that T. allows a contrary view about imperial succession to be developed, with almost equal force, by Mucianus in II. 76–7. The whole question was beyond doubt being widely discussed in T.'s day, but it would have been uncharacteristic of him to have seen the principle of adoption as a permanent contribution to *libertas*. For an historian writing in Trajan's early years it was a reasonable solution to let the theme be developed, in opposing directions, by speakers of whom he indicates neither whole-hearted approval nor wholehearted condemnation.

2. lege curiata . . . *Adrogatio*, the adoption of a man *sui iuris* as Piso was, involved an investigation by the *pontifices* followed by the formality of a *Lex curiata*: so *comitia pontificibus arbitris*, Gellius V. 19. 6, cf. W. Buckland, *A Textbook of Roman Law*² (1932), 124. By these traditional means Augustus had adopted Tiberius, Suet. *Aug.* 65; and it was probably a *Lex curiata*, rather than some special law, which Claudius had used in adopting Nero, *A.* XII. 26. Galba, and all subsequent *principes* who used adoption, proceeded by simple *nuncupatio*, which they may have claimed was permitted to the *pontifex maximus*. In 69, on T.'s showing, the formal *nuncupatio* was deemed to have taken place in the camp, I. 17. 6, but the decision that mattered had been made in Galba's small *consilium*. It was that which enabled Pliny to claim that the procedure in 69 was disreputable in comparison with that of 97, *nec modo iudicium hominum, sed deorum etiam consilium assumpsit* etc., *Pan.* 8. 1; for Nerva had organized a ceremony on the Capitol, cf. Dio (= Xiph.) 68. 3. 4. See Hammond, *AM* 1.

3. Cn. Pompei et M. Crassi. T. would be right in thinking that an emperor who thought the *respublica* had ended with Caesar (16. 2) would have selected these two among Piso's ancestors.

5. Lutatiae. For Galba's ancestry see the careful researches of Suet., *G.* 2–3. His mother Mummia Achaiica was granddaughter of Q. Catulus, *cos.* 78 B.C., and great-granddaughter of the destroyer of Corinth. For the omission of *gentis* (supplied unnecessarily by some editors) Heubner compares *SHA M. Ant. Phil.* 5. 5, *pro Annio Aurelius coepit vocari, quod in Aureliam . . . transisset.*

6. deorum hominumque consensu, but also on his own admission *bello . . . adsciti*, 16. 15. The language is that used by loyal supporters of the Principate, Val. Max. 1, *praef.*, or Plin. *Pan.* 10. 2. See Hammond, *AM* 10, 23.

8. maiores nostri. If Galba was thinking of himself and Piso alone, the reference could be to Ser. Galba the conspirator, unsuccessful candidate for the consulate of 49 B.C., and to Cn. Piso, *cos.* 23 B.C., *qui civili bello resurgentes in Africa partes . . . adversus Caesarem iuvit, A.* II. 43— but also, of course, to Pompey the Great.

9. Marcellum . . . privignum. None of this should be enlisted to help over problems about the way in which Augustus actually handled the succession question. But it is interesting that Augustus is taken as the antithesis of the ideal envisaged by Galba (or by T.?), in that he adopted *malgré lui.* Yet so did the emperors beginning with Nerva: if Trajan could have a son of his body, Pliny is satisfied that that son should be his successor, *Pan.* 94. 5. But if one had no son, then one elevated adoption into a virtue, and it was of course a virtue dear to many theorists of the Flavio-Antonine period, cf. J. Béranger, *RÉL* 1939, 179. See again 16. 9. n.

13. propinquos . . . socios, clearly Dolabella and Otho, though T. has failed to mention the former, 13. 7 n. above. Nerva too was praised for passing over his relations, Dio (=Xiph.) 68. 4. 1.

16. frater . . . natu maior, Crassus Scribonianus, see stemma, p. 74.

19. fortunam . . . adversam, in exile for a long time under Nero, I. 48. 3, but we are not told on what charge.

24. blanditiae et . . . The parallel to which Fisher refers in his app. crit. is Plin. *Pan.* 85. 1, *adsentationes, blanditiae et peior odio amoris simulatio*; see his note in *CR* 1909, 223, and also Cic. *Lael.* 91 (cited by Heubner, which must have been in the mind of Pliny, and (if Fisher be right) of T. too. It so happens that L. reads *blanditiae et . . .*

16. 1. si immensum . . . posset, echoing the sentiment of an historian (probably the elder Seneca) who compared the story of Rome with the ages of man, and ended, after the civil wars, with the monarchy as the age of second childhood, *tamquam sustentare se ipsa non valeret, nisi adminiculo regentium niteretur* (Lactantius 7. 15. 14=*HRR* II. 91). The idea became a commonplace on monarchy, cf. Sen. *de Clementia* I. 4.

2. res publica. The meaning is unmistakable, 'Republic' (more normally in T. *libera*, or *vetus*, *respublica*) as opposed to monarchy, i.e. *imperium sine rectore.* But this usage by T. is relatively rare. In the *Histories* the only certain parallel is I. 50. 15 (see n.); in the *Annals* we have I. 3, *quotus quisque reliquus qui rem publicam vidisset* (of A.D. 14), IV. 9, Tiberius meditating *de reddenda re publica*, and IV. 19, T.'s sarcasm over Tiberius' use of a consul to initiate a prosecution, *quasi aut legibus cum Silio agemretur aut Varro consul aut illud res publica esset.*

Yet at the beginning of that book of the *Annals* (IV. 1) T. has described the early part of Tiberius' reign as a period of *compositae rei publicae*, and many passages throughout his works show that his normal meaning for the word is 'commonwealth' (or the 'institutions of the Roman State', Syme, 130). To it responsible men were prepared to devote themselves, and are then said to possess *amor* (or *cura*) *rei publicae*, 12. 10 n. above. With that meaning T. is quite clear that the *res publica* survived even into evil days of the Principate, in that *principes mortales, rem publicam aeternam esse, A.* III. 6. Indeed those who gain the supreme power are said *suscipere* (or *capessere*) *rem publicam*, II. 1. 20 etc.; and even the last days of Domitian were *rei publicae tempora, Agr.* 41.

Is it possible that T. thought the rarer sense of the words to be *ben trovato* in a speech by Galba—a man who desired to be οὔτε Καῖσαρ οὔτ' αὐτοκράτωρ, Plut. *G.* 5. 2, but who eventually found that a *res publica* in the only sense he could recognize it was now an impossibility? Or even (cf. above, 14. 4 n.) that he had learned something, at second or third hand, about 'the general sense' of what Galba actually said?

6. Tiberio . . . Claudio, but not Nero, because he had no potential Julio-Claudian heir.

7. loco . . . coepimus. Here again the thought may be Galba's own, for *libertas* clearly means 'Republic', an institution opposed to *principatus*, and not reconcilable with it as at *Agr.* 3. 1 or *Hist.* IV. 8. 21.

9. nam generari . . . fortuitum . . . Plin. *Pan.* 7. 7. has the same doctrine in delightfully naïve terms. It became the subject for many essays, until *SHA Sev.* 21 can issue congratulations to a series of great men for being so clever as not to have sons. *Adoptandi. . . monstratur* is also echoed by Pliny, *Pan.* 10. 2, *non unius Nervae iudicium illud, illa electio fuit*; but though this may have been true, for harsh reasons, in 97, it was not the case, if T. be right, in 69.

13. una legione. Not surely his newly raised VII Galbiana (so Irvine), but VI Victrix, the legion which initially proclaimed him.

14. neque adhuc . . . exemplum. Claudius had rescinded the acts of Gaius, but vetoed his *damnatio memoriae*, Dio 60. 21, Suet. *Cl.* 11. But Nero was declared a *hostis* by the Senate, Suet. *Nero* 49.

15. ab aestimantibus adsciti. Galba, though he won his place through war, 15. 8, was chosen *deorum hominumque consensu*; Piso's advocates are made no clearer by this speech.

17. duae legiones, above, 12. 2 n.

26. imperaturus . . . libertatem, here we come closer to *Agr.* 3. 1, and also to *Dial.* 13. 15 (of Crispus and Marcellus), *nec imperantibus umquam satis servi videntur nec nobis satis liberi.*

29. tamquam principem faceret, 'speaking as a man would who was creating a *princeps*'; but could he in that gathering adopt a son, and then assume that that son would succeed him? On the purely legal point regarding adoption T. never expresses doubts, even on the question whether adoption made Piso a Caesar, see I. 30. 12. For the irony on the question of succession, see 14. 4 n. above.

17. 1. Intuentibus, a dative, rather than an ablative in agreement with the words that follow, see Heubner's n. But Plut. *G.* 23. 3, puts this description of Piso's lack of emotion into the scene in the camp, and this is doubtless where the 'common source' put it. It is doubtful, therefore, whether (as Heubner thinks) T. deliberately distinguished the *intuentes* from the *omnes*, and meant by the former the small company assembled at the *consilium*—an affair which he is alone in mentioning.

6. in castris. A site well known, partly because Aurelian used part of its walls to build his own wall of the city. It lay outside the Servian *agger*, on the north-east of Rome, south of the Via Nomentana.

9. Palatium. Most topographical discussion of the Roman chapters of the *Histories* is bedevilled by the ambiguity of this word. *Capitolium* can mean the hill or the temple upon it; but the context normally leaves the reader in no doubt. The means of distinguishing between the Palatine hill and the palace buildings which by Galba's, and still more by T.'s, day occupied most of the summit are much less easy to determine.

Until Augustus' time *Palatium* was the regular Latin (and, transliterated, the Greek) for the hill; see Platner–Ashby, 374 f., and the careful examination of texts by K. Ziegler, *RE* XVII. 3, coll. 6 ff. The adjective *Palatinus* of course existed (indeed the Palatina was one of the city tribes), but it is only applied to *mons* in some such context as Livy I. 12. 5 (*inter Capitolinum Palatinumque colles*, another hill being mentioned). These usages persist into imperial times, especially in the Elder Pliny, who frequently uses *Palatium* of the hill rather than of a building. But already Ovid, *Met.* I. 175, has *Palatium* of the residence of Augustus, and this meaning is regular in the Flavian poets (who incidentally lengthened the first syllable for the singular, though keeping the short 'a' which dactylic poets had often found useful for the plural). Ziegler, col. 11, claims that T. too invariably used the word of the palace and not the hill, the latter being *mons Palatinus*, as in *A.* XII. 24, cf. XV. 38.

Unfortunately the problem is not so simple. We could, if necessary, be persuaded that a cohort bivouacked in the palace, I. 29. 2, or that the common people were allowed to surge about the building, I. 32. 1, 72. 17. But III. 70. 9, *Vitellium in Palatium, in ipsam imperii arcem*, is another story. Ziegler, who boldly cites that passage as characteristic, presumably thought that T. believed the imperial residence to be the *ipsa imperii arx*; or that he depicted Vespasian's brother Flavius Sabinus as so believing, even when the *princeps* was Vitellius. But at this moment Vitellius was not in the imperial house, for we are told three lines earlier that he had gone to his brother's house, *imminentem foro*. So *Palatium* there means the hill, and T.'s usage must be allowed to be variable. In passages like I. 35. 3, 82. 1, *A*. XII. 69 (where doors are mentioned), and in that before us now, he means the palace; in those cited earlier in this note, and in III. 67. 8, 84. 17, *A*. II. 40, he means the hill; in others, most of all *A*. XV. 39, we are left to guess.

The difficulties do not end there. Augustus' official palace (which developed from the house that had once belonged to Hortensius, Suet. *Aug.* 72) adjoined the temple of Apollo, Ziegler, cit., col. 52. The controversy surrounding the site of that is outlined on I. 27. 1 below; but did the emperors of our period still use the Augustan *Palatium*? Vitellius sometimes resided, or dined, in the *domus Tiberiana*, Suet. *Vit.* 15; but it was probably always designated as such (as at 27. 11) and cannot be intended here. There is however great probability that what had been built of Nero's Golden House continued to be occupied, and it may be this which the crowd now surrounded. It is surprising that T. should have left his readers to guess; for they were familiar with a different building again, Domitian's *Palatium*, and might have needed reminding what preceded it.

18. 1. quartum Idus. The date (10 Jan.) is confirmed by the *AFA* (MW 2, line 25), *adoptio facta L. Li(ciniani)*. It is surprising (for the restoration must be right) to find Piso's other names suppressed.

3. observatum id antiquitus, cf. Livy, 40. 59. 5, *comitia tempestas diremit*, Cic. *Phil.* V. 7, *Iove enim tonante cum populo agi non esse fas quis ignorat?*, Vatin. 20, *Iove fulgente cum populo agi nefas esse*.

5. seu ... vitantur, an odd concession for T. to make, cf. 3. 7 n. Moreover *seu* does not introduce a genuine alternative, for a believer in the inevitability of fate could maintain his position whether or not Galba was *contemptor talium*; and a *contemptor* like Galba, when he decided on his next move, would have had no interest in the weather.

8. vir virum legeret, i.e. the man first summoned chose a comrade, who chose another, and so on, until the required number was reached; according to Livy (e.g. 9. 39. 5, 10. 38. 12) the practice was governed by a Lex Sacrata, and was followed by Etruscans, Volscians, and Ligurians as well as by Romans. Augustus apparently made deliberate use of it in filling the Senate, Suet., *Aug.* 35, 54.

9. quartam ... legiones, I. 12. 2 n.

16. quantulacumque ... Plut. *G.* 18. 2, says they would have been satisfied with what Nero had given them, i.e. 15,000 HS or half the sum promised by Nymphidius, cf. 5. 3 n. above.

19. 3. patrum favor aderat, but the judgement is immediately qualified. As Köstermann, *Historia*, 1956, 217, points out, T. never makes clear whether the Senate's initial sympathy with Galba (I. 4. 10) was sustained.

4. medii, "neutral": cf. IV. 8. 23, *etiam mediis patrum adnitentibus retinere morem,* a use known in Livy 2. 27. 3, 40. 2. 4.

5. quadriduo. i.e. in the four days intervening between 10 and 15 Jan., cf. I. 48. 3, Plut. *G.* 24. 1. The more usual expression employs an ordinal; so *sextus dies,* I. 29. 10.

7. crebrioribus ... nuntiis. So far T. (12. 1, 14. 2) has been precise about the news from Germany: the procurator's dispatch had reported the mutiny at Mogontiacum, but not the acclamation of Vitellius; and at I. 50. 3 he states that a message reporting the latter event was concealed until Galba's death. Yet miscellaneous messages, semi-official or private, were naturally reaching Rome about the behaviour of both German armies; so we need not believe with Courbaud, 145, that T. has improved on the story of his source in order to enhance the air of mystery at the time of Otho's rising. It is true that the time-table is tight, see Fabia, *Rev. Phil.* 1913, 52. The embassy actually set out before Galba's death; and since there was jockeying, and consequent delay, about its composition, the decree which promoted it can hardly be dated later than 12 Jan. Yet on 10 Jan. the only official news was Pompeius Propinquus' dispatch, so *crebrioribus in dies* seems a bit exaggerated. The difficulty disappears, however, if we allow for unofficial news. (To avoid making the decree a consequence of fresh messages, Fabia punctuated with a comma at *factumve* and a full stop after *tristia sunt,* but this makes obscure the logic of the sentence about Piso's silence during the *quadriduum.*)

9. censuerant. i.e. before the private debate about Piso's participation, not necessarily before the adoption.

Germanicum exercitum, presumably to both armies, and possibly also (cf. *rursum,* I. 74. 7) to the troops at Lugdunum. See Fabia, cit.

11. praetextu. Cf. I. 76. 12, *praetexto senatus*, but whichever declension is used, the meaning is the same, "pretence" and so a facade. So Sen. *Epp.* 71. 9, *illud pulcherrimum rei publicae praetextum, optimates.*

12. Caesaris. For Piso's assumption of the name see also I. 29. 12, 30. 12, 48. 3, Plut. *G.* 23. 2. It appears to be confirmed by the official record in *AFA,CIL* VI. 2051. 1.28 = MW. 2. But after Galba's death his acts were cancelled, and Piso's gravestone (*ILS* 240) treats him as if the adoption had not occurred, cf. E. Nesselhauf, *Hermes* 1955, 489 n. 1.

It was clear to Galba that even after the extinction of the Julio-Claudians a properly constituted *princeps* must be "Caesar": this is as much implied by his initial refusal of the name (οὔτε Καῖσαρ οὔτε αὐτοκράτωρ, Plut. *G.* 5. 2) as by his taking it immediately he heard of the senate's action in his favour, Suet. *G.* 11. The decision is understandable, but it is remarkable that it passes without comment from any of our sources. Henceforth only Vitellius, II. 62. 10, hesitated: all others used the name both for the reigning *princeps* and for his recognized heir or heirs.

20. 1. proxima. Even if this means not 'next in time' but 'next in importance' (i.e. to the questions of the adoption and of the German mutiny), T. has given the impression that the appointment of this commission occurred between 10 and 15 Jan. This cannot be right: both Plut. *G.* 16. 2, and Suet. *G.* 15. 1, put its appointment well before the adoption, and Dio (= Xiph.) 62. 14 says that its effects were felt in Greece. It probably began soon after Galba reached Rome in October 68.

Imprecision about time-sequences in the opening Survey (see introd. to cap. 4 above) was understandable: elsewhere in his main narrative (*per illos mensis*, I. 12. 8; *iam pridem*, I. 23. 2) T. does at least hint when he is referring to events before 1 January. His reason for introducing finance at this point is presumably to provide an additional reason for Galba's unpopularity, but it is difficult to acquit him of carelessness. (I cannot follow Heubner's view ad loc., that *proxima* takes us back to *iam pridem* in I. 12. 6 and consequently to a date in the previous year. It certainly does not do so clearly, nor does a comparison with *proximus* in II. 67. 1 seem to help.)

2. ubi inopiae causa erat. What Plut. and Suet. make clear, but T. does not, is that Galba sought recovery even from men who had bought property from the first recipients of Nero's largesse.

3. appellari, 'to be sued for payment'.

7. faenus, 'interest-bearing capital': cf. *A.* VI. 17, *duas quisque faenoris partes in agris per Italiam conlocarent.*

8. instrumenta vitiorum, furniture, slaves, jewellery, clothes, etc.

9. ambitu ac numero onerosum. The points at issue are (a) was the commission burdensome to its members or to the city at large? (b) are the burdensome numbers those of the commission or of the persons with whom they had to deal? (c) what sort of *ambitus* and exercised by whom? Plut. *G.* 16. 3 answered (b) in terms of those affected, πόρρω νεμομένου καὶ προϊόντος ἐπὶ πολλούς, and many editors, including Heubner, have assumed that T. too intended this. But his words are almost intolerably obscure if the *numerus* was other than the numbers included in the *novum officii genus*; and a commission of thirty (Suet. says fifty) was certainly large by Roman standards. So T. seems to mean 'burdensome to the citizens from the large numbers of the commission' (so approximately Ritter), 'who tried to outdo one another by their officious zeal' (for this I am indebted to Mr. J. D. P. Bolton). But if this view be right, then either T. or Plut. misunderstood the 'common source'; or else (Townend, *AJP* 1964, 350) T. has 'deliberately applied the wording of the common source to make a different point'. No doubt the *facts* of what was happening in Rome would have supported every interpretation which has been given to the words.

13. per eos dies. Here we are back at the early days of 69. The officers dismissed, to judge from their subsequent careers, were all friends of Otho.

14. Antonius Naso. His career, known from the Baalbek inscription *ILS* 9199 = MW 355, followed a pattern which is familiar from Flavian times onward. After a primipilate he was tribune in a legion, then held four tribunates in the various regiments in Rome, received a second primipilate (see Pflaum, 36, following Ritterling in *RE* XII, col. 1408), and after other military posts held the important procuratorship of Bithynia/Pontus (for his road-building there in 77/8 see *ILS* 253 = MW 421).

The legion in which he was tribune was I Italica. This was raised by Nero for his abortive 'Caspian' expedition, 6. 12 n. above, its birthday being 20 Sept. Naso's career (*pace* Ritterling, cit.) is strong ground for thinking that the year of its birth was 66 rather than 67 (anyway even Nero would hardly have planned his expedition while the Jewish War was on), for surely Naso cannot have held five different posts in fourteen months.

During his tribunate of a praetorian cohort Naso was decorated, presumably by Nero. His next post was temporary charge of legion XIV Gemina: if Dessau was right in thinking Otho was the emperor who gave him that post (but Vespasian is a possibility), then he may have been sent to bring the legion from Illyricum to the Po valley, II. 11.

Aemilius Pacensis, restored by Otho and made one of the commanders of the Narbonese expedition, I. 87. 12, II. 12. 5. He was killed in the defence of the Capitol in December, III. 73. 12.

15. Iulius Fronto, tribune in Otho's army and brother of Caecina's *praefectus castrorum* Iulius Gratus, II. 26. 8.

21. 3. inopia. Plut. *G.* 21. 2, gives the amount of his debts as 50 m.— presumably drachmae, i.e. 200 m. HS.

4. fingebat. Is this what Otho said to his friends (so H.), or a guess at his private thoughts (Heubner)? The question is perhaps unreal: the chapter describes his psychological condition, which may have been modified, or intensified, by talking to others. See V.

10. occidi Othonem posse. Emendation here (see app. crit.) is unnecessary. Otho uses the third person, with his name, to describe himself in II. 47. 9, 48. 18; so does Mucianus in II. 77. 2.

14. oblivione . . . distingui, 'but some men's deaths are remembered with honour, the rest forgotten'. So, for the first time, T. looks forward to Otho's suicide.

22. 3. matrimonia. Cf. Suet. Cal. 25. 1, *matrimonia contraxerit turpius an dimiserit an tenuerit, non facile est discernere.*

5. ut aliena. Was Otho really led to believe that Piso would enjoy these things?

6. mathematicis, the Chaldaei; cf. Gell. I. 9, *vulgus quos gentilicio vocabulo Chaldaeos dicere oportet, mathematicos dicit.* Believed to have predicted imperial power for Libo Drusus under Tiberius, and for Furius Scribonianus under Claudius, they were banished from Rome in A.D. 16 and 52, *A.* II. 31, XII. 52, and were again removed by Vitellius, II. 62. 11. Yet *principes* regularly consulted them, not least Vespasian, II. 78. 3, Dio, 66. 9.

10. principalis matrimonii instrumentum. Although there is no other evidence that Poppaea used astrologers to gain her position, the most likely meaning is 'the means by which marriage with a *princeps* was achieved'.

11. Ptolemaeus. Suet. *O.* 4 and 6, by confusion with Vespasian's astrologer, II. 78. 4, calls him Seleucus. Plut. *G.* 23. 4, introduces Ptolemaeus only at the moment of the conspiracy, but unlike T. allows

Otho little credit for being ready to act independently of Chaldaean promptings. Moreover Plut. appears to put the prophecy of Otho's rule before Nero's death, whereas T. and Suet. clearly mean it to be later. But I agree with Townend, *AJP* 1964, 352, that Plut.'s words are ambiguous, and that all three authors are making the same point, namely that the success of an earlier prophecy that Otho would survive Nero made Ptolemaeus, after Nero's death, insistent that Otho would go further. But Dio 61. 11. 2, who records some prophecy of Otho's principate as early as 58–9, must therefore have been using a different source, possibly Cluvius Rufus.

23. 3. in itinere . . . stationibus. Heubner is probably right in taking *in itinere* as a general phrase which is made more specific by the two which follow—'on the journey, both on the march and in camp'. Anyway for *in agmine atque itinere* see *A.* III. 9 (of Cn. Piso's return to Rome): there is no good ground for bracketing *in itinere*, which would have been quite superfluous as a gloss.

Without doubt (*iam pridem* with the pluperfect, cf. *sed tum*, 25. 1) T. is consciously taking us back to a time before 1 Jan. Like Plut. *G.* 20. 3, he thought, rightly or wrongly, that this march was the one from Spain (line 10, *Pyrenaeum et Alpes*). Plut. tells the story soon after his first mention of Otho, when Galba considered adoption as a means of facing the disaffection he encountered on his entry to Rome. This may, Fabia 14, have been the context indicated by the 'common source'; but T.'s introduction of the story here is simple and effective, for it develops the point Plut. *G.* 24. 1, himself made, that four days would not have been long enough to corrupt so large an army.

But the main question is whether any of the troops who brought Otho to power in Rome were identical with those who marched with him from Spain. Obviously not I Adiutrix, nor the *numeri* of I. 6. 11: T. means the praetorians, who alone had been of Nero's *comitatus* and had visited the lakes of Campania and the cities of Achaea. Editors have suggested (Alford, and now Heubner also) that some praetorians were sent by the Senate as escort for Galba, just as Nymphidius had sent him other types of imperial accoutrement, Plut. *G.* 11. 2. But for this there is no evidence, and there would have been little time for the escort to get to Spain, even if they went by sea; moreover we are told that Galba formed his own bodyguard, Plut. *G.* 10. 3. It is more likely that T., in expanding his source by the words at the end of the chapter, failed to realize that on the march a different body of troops was involved. Otho had first ingratiated himself with the legion VII Galbiana (with significant consequences later, see Appendix, pp. 272); then, when that legion was removed from Rome, he turned his attention to the praetorians. See *JRS* 1957, 33 for the consequences of this view.

It remains remarkable that T. failed to mention Otho's activities in the introductory Survey, see above, 4. 1 n.

4. memoria ... comitatus, yet since 58–9 Otho had been in Lusitania. The phrase is consistent with T.'s conviction that Otho represented a return to Nero's regime, I. 13. 11 n., 25. 11.

6. requirere, 'ask after'.

9. Campaniae lacus, for praetorians with Nero on his journeys see Dio 63. 8 ff.

24. 2. mobilissimum ... praecipitem. i.e., as Heubner shows, two types of man, the natural revolutionaries, and those who wanted money.

5. per speciem convivii. Nero had commuted the public banquets, hitherto given by the *princeps*, for a gift of money, Suet. *Nero* 16; and private individuals seem to have followed his lead, L. Friedländer *Roman Life and Manners* (E.T. 1908–13), I. 196.

The normal *sportula*, even in Domitian's time, was 25 *asses*, Martial I. 59 etc.; so 100 HS (= 400 *asses*) was an enormous bribe.

6. excubias agenti. The practice of having a cohort on guard during dinner was begun by Claudius, Suet. *Cl.* 35, Dio 60. 3. It was evidently there during Otho's famous banquet, I. 80 ff.

9. speculatori. By the end of the Republic *speculatores*, troops who were employed on special missions (see Caes. *BG* II. 11. 2, with Rice Holmes's n.) were acting as an élite corps, attached closely to the chief commanders, Durry, 108 ff. Under the Principate there were still *speculatores* in the provinces, apparently ten to each legion, *ILS* 2375, 2382, etc., but the most important unit was one used close to the *princeps* in Rome, Suet. *Cal.* 44, *Cl.* 35, *G.* 18. This unit was considered part of the praetorian guard, though distinguished from the ordinary *milites*, see the Vespasianic diploma *CIL* XVI. 21 = MW 400; and from I. 31. 1 it is clear that *speculatores* were adjoined in some sense to each cohort; but they do not specify their particular cohorts on inscriptions and were probably not regarded as fully members of any one, Passerini, *coorti* 71 ff. On occasions a substantial number of them was used as a single force, II. 11. 18, *speculatorum lecta corpora*, and individuals from them might be detached for a special mission, II. 73. 2. The title given to an officer of considerable seniority, *exercitator equitum speculatorum*, e.g. *ILS* 2648 = Sm. 1, 283, implies that some (but not all, Passerini, 72) of them were mounted.

Their numbers have caused controversy. Dom. Dob., 99, maintained that the high-ranking centurion called *trecenarius* was their commander, replacing the *centurio speculatorum* in Nero's reign; and that consequently they were 300 strong, twenty-four and an officer to each of twelve cohorts, i.e. the equivalent of twelve *turmae*. This estimate of strength is perhaps nearly right, I. 27. 11 n., but Passerini, 92 (accepted by Dobson), showed fairly effectively that *trecenarii* had no connection with any part of the guard. These men were the germ which produced the secret police of the middle and later Empire. In the first century they have been described as 'a special body of imperial guards who tend to appear in moments of military intrigue', A. N. Sherwin-White, *Roman Society and Roman Law in the New Testament* (1963), 109. This is true, but the evidence for their development in the Julio-Claudian period does not exist.

25. 2. tesserarium ... optionem. Plut. *G.* 24, who was puzzled by *speculatori* in the previous chapter, says that these were Latin names for διαγγέλων and διοπτήρων, whatever those may have been. Veget. II. 7, defines a *tesserarius* as one who passes on the watchword *per contubernia militum*; but his definition of *optiones* (*ab optando appellati*) is inadequate. Festus 184 M. has *optio in re militari appellatus is quem decurio aut centurio optat sibi rerum privatarum administrum, quo facilius obeat publica officia*, i.e. a non-commissioned man (*principalis*) chosen by his superior officer, not by his subordinates, Dom.–Dob. XIX. 1 ff., 10, Durry, 101 ff. From several inscriptions it can be shown that an *optio* was senior to a *tesserarius*, and that there was probably no other rank until the centurionate.

6. manipulares. Although T. in this splendid sentence was not unduly concerned with technical terms, it is likely that his word could properly include the *principales*, i.e. all men under the rank of centurions. See n. on *gregarii*, I. 36. 5. Suet. *O.* 5. 2 explains the enterprise more fully. It was entrusted to five *speculatores*, each of whom chose two more; and each of the fifteen received 10,000 HS with a promise of 50,000 HS on completion. Otho's financial resources had been more than exhausted by his earlier largesse; but he had, a few days earlier, obtained a stewardship for one of Galba's slaves, and had received 1 m. HS as his reward.

9. primores militum, again probably non-technical, in T.'s manner. But the connection with Nymphidius' *beneficia* suggests that his source referred to the class of *beneficiarii*, see IV. 48. 8.

12. mutandae militiae. The threat is not otherwise attested, but could be connected with Galba's economy campaign.

26. 1. legionum, but only one legion, cf. above, 11. 6 n.

4. postero Iduum die. G. Andresen, *In Taciti Historias Stud. crit.* (1899), I. 11, refuted any palaeographical excuse for emending the text. On its meaning Mommsen, *Hermes,* I. 433, argued for *postero die qui fuit Id. Ian.* (i.e. 13 Jan.), and cited Cic. *Sull.* 52, *nocte ea quae consecuta est posterum diem Nonarum Novembrium.* But that passage is no less ambiguous than ours, so far as the Latin goes, and it is certain from the fact that T. has not mentioned 12 Jan. in any context that the day he means is that following the Ides, i.e. 14 Jan. The enterprise here is different from the abortive plan for a *coup* on the day of the adoption reported by Suet. *O.* 6.

5. rapturi fuerint. *Rapi* becomes almost a technical term for being acclaimed emperor, I. 27. 14, 29. 2.

6. tota urbe, illustrated in the accounts of various units in I. 31.

12. praefectus Laco. Nothing of this stage of the plot is in Plut., who as usual seems ignorant of things affecting Laco. Townend, cit. 356, suggests that the story came from Cluvius, who got interested in Laco in Spain. No single word will satisfactorily translate *elusit*, but it clearly implies that Laco avoided any action or discussion on the reports. Sp.'s 'parried' has merit.

27. 1. pro aede Apollinis. The position of this temple must still be regarded as a vexed question, and on it hangs the interpretation of Otho's activities as described in this chapter. He went from the temple through the House of Tiberius into the Velabrum, and thence to the Golden Milestone. The Velabrum is the low ground to the west of the Palatine, and between the Palatine's north-west spur (the Germalus) and the Capitoline; from it the vicus Tuscus led past the Capitoline's south-eastern slopes to the Forum, where the Golden Milestone stood before the temple of Saturn. The Domus Tiberiana, from which the top of the Capitol could be seen (Suet. *Vit.* 15), was close to the northern end of the Palatine (the area near the present-day Farnese Gardens), from which Otho *could*, had he wished, have gone down to the Forum at a point not far from his destination. Suet. *O.* 6. 2, confirms that the Milestone was where the conspirators were awaiting him; and Plut. *G.* 24. 4, confirms that he went through Tiberius' palace. On the topography so far Platner–Ashby, supported by G. Lugli's *Roma Antica* (1946), supply references the bearing of which is not seriously controversial.

The one thing certain about the temple of Apollo is that it adjoined Augustus' house, Ov. *Trist.* III. 1. 33 ff. Both Platner–Ashby and Lugli accept the identification of that house with the ruins known as the 'House of Livia', and so put the temple between those ruins and the

Flavian Palatium, on the south-south-west side of the Palatine. On that
view Otho had a long way to go, and it is not surprising that he
descended into the Velabrum; but his route through the Domus
Tiberiana was curious, since he had an easy descent immediately down
the 'scalae Caci'. With that difficulty in mind, but basing his case more
on evidence from the Augustan poets, J. H. Bishop, *CQ* 1956, 187 ff.,
revived the view that Apollo's temple (and Augustus' house with it)
was at the north-east corner of the Palatine, in which case a journey to
the Velabrum would take Otho 'through but not into' (Bishop, 190)
Tiberius' palace. But then why did Otho, if (as Bishop insists) he was in
a hurry, go to the Velabrum at all? He could have directly descended
into the upper part of the Forum, and have proceeded down the Sacra
Via to the Milestone.

Yet on either view any difficulties presented by this passage could be
answered by supposing that for security reasons Otho was concerned to
avoid the most direct route. And in his answer, *CQ* 1961, 128, to an
impressive rejoinder by O. Richmond (*CQ* 1958, 180), Bishop admits
that T.'s words can be used to support either conclusion.

2. Umbricius, a seer accounted the most learned of his day, Plin. *NH*
X. 19.

4. ut laetum . . . But Plut. *G.* 24. 3 has it that he was in confusion and
changed colour. Fabia, 25, thought the 'common source' reported Otho
as affected by both kinds of emotion, and this (*pace* Townend, *AJP*
1964, 357) is not unreasonable. For Otho was certainly believed to be
superstitious, I. 22. 6 ff.; and if so, he would have been elated by omens
hostile to Galba, but frightened that his plot had been disclosed before
he had an excuse for joining his conspirators. Moreover even if he was
a sceptic, he might have believed that Umbricius and, through him, the
rest of the audience, had acquired knowledge of what was going on.

10. innixus liberto. Here T. is probably drawing on the alternative
version of the excuse Otho gave, namely that he had a fever, Suet.
O. 6. 2.

11. miliarium aureum, set up by Augustus in 20 B.C., Dio 54. 8. 4,
to be the meeting place of all roads of the empire. Lugli claims to have
found traces of it near Saturn's temple, by which it certainly stood,
Suet. *O.* 6. 2.

12. tres et viginti, used by Dom. Dob. to confirm the view that
twenty-four *speculatores* formed a unit and were attached to a single
cohort, cf. above, 24. 9 n.: they belonged to the cohort at the palace,
I. 29. 7; and the 24th, Iulius Atticus, was still there, I. 35. 9. Passerini,
70 n. 6, objects that Otho ought then to have known the precise situation

and not to have been alarmed *paucitate salutantium*. But perhaps he expected more than one *turma*; perhaps he had no time to count; or he could not quickly recognize that those awaiting him were members of a single unit rather than a few casual soldiers.

28. 1. Iulius Martialis. Plut. *G.* 25. 3, claimed authority for saying that he was not an accomplice but was overcome by the sudden irruption. The man was unfortunate enough to be on duty again at Otho's dinner-party next month, I. 82. 3.

2. magnitudine … sceleris, described by Heubner as a causal ablative. But the alternatives given by T. are not really alternative reasons for suspecting Martialis' loyalty, but reasons why he might have been afraid; so (see V.'s note) some such word as *territus* should be supplied with *magnitudine*.

6. habitus animorum, an acute appreciation of riot psychology, to which T. returns over Vitellius' proclamation, at I. 55–6.

29. 7. cohortis, that from which the *speculatores* had already slipped away to acclaim Otho, I. 31. 1. For the Palatine cohort, *quae more militiae excubiis adest*, cf. *A.* XII. 69, Suet. *O.* 6.

9. pro gradibus, 'from the steps', a common usage, cf. Caes. *BG* VI. 3. 5, *hac re pro suggestu pronuntiata*, Sall, *BI* 67. 1, *pro tectis aedificiorum … saxa … mittere*, *A.* II. 81, *Agr.* 35. The same position was taken by Vitellius, III. 74. 13.

10. Piso's speech, though dignified, and also prophetic about future disasters, is quite unrealistic about Galba's rise, about the adoption, and about the severity of Otho's threat.

commilitones, a usage abandoned by Augustus after the civil wars, *ambitiosius id existimans quam aut ratio militaris aut temporum quies aut sua domusque maiestas postularet*, Suet. *Aug.* 25. 1. But even Galba, I. 35. 11, realized that *temporum quies* was gone; and for Otho see I. 37. 1, 84. 7.

18. incruentam urbem. The slaughter of the *classici*, I. 6. 7, had been outside the city, but T. was perhaps deliberately evoking it.

30. 1. nobilitatis, too commonly taken by earlier editors as 'nobility of mind'. (Not so by Heubner, though I cannot follow his objection that Piso in T.'s portrait of him could not lay claim to that quality, for see I. 14. 11 ff., 17. 1 ff., or that reference to it would have been pointless in an address to the soldiers.) But against abundant instances (see GG) where T. by *nobilitas* means 'noble birth' (or 'the nobility'), only one can conceivably be adduced with the sense 'nobility of mind' (*A.* I. 29, *nobilitate ingenita* of Drusus' speech in Pannonia, but even there the meaning is doubtful). That Piso's noble birth was one of his greatest assets we have been told already, e.g. I. 15. 5; and no doubt he, if not T. also, would have assumed that *virtutes* were the natural accompaniment of high lineage. So of Galba, I. 49. 9, *vetus in familia nobilitas . . . ipsi* (i.e. despite what his ancestry should have conferred on him) *medium ingenium*, etc.

A famous article by M. Gelzer in *Hermes*, 1915, 395 ff. (tr. by Seager as pp. 141–61 of *The Roman Nobility*) argued for a precise meaning of *nobilitas* under the Principate: previously accorded to descendants of consuls in the male line, it was henceforth confined to men and women of whom an ancestor (possibly now in the female line, see above, 14. 11 n.) had held the consulate under 'the Republic'—so *posteros libertatis*, Plin. *Pan.* 69. 4. Two years later E. Stein, accepting the view that there was a change in meaning, argued that the last consuls to confer nobility of their descendants were not those of (say) 42 B.C. but those of A.D. 14, after which the elections were transferred from the People to the Senate (*Hermes*, 1917, 564 ff., cf. Syme, 654).

Yet even in this modified form Gelzer's doctrine is not easy to sustain. For a summary of the passages in T. and other writers which appear to contradict it see H. Hill, *Historia*, 1969, 230 ff. (with bibliography of earlier discussion): Barnes, *Phoenix*, 1974, 444, gives especial emphasis to *A*. XI. 28. 1 where C. Silius, son of the first consul in his family, is called *iuvenis nobilis*. But the most serious difficulty is one not developed by Hill, namely that the situation in which such a change in usage came about is almost unimaginable. Gelzer, it is true, insisted (Seager's tr., 151) that he was not supposing an amendment to 'constitutional law'; but to deprive an increasingly large group of consulars and their progeny of their social status must have required either an obvious change in the nature of society or a decision by some recognized body. For instance T. himself, and Pliny, would have had somehow to be convinced that they themselves were (as ex-consuls) not the potential of *nobilitas*. Could this really be achieved by reminding them that they were chosen not by the People but by their colleagues in the Senate?

I share, therefore, the view of those who think Piso is simply claiming that any *nobilitas* Otho possessed (see I. 78. 12) was much less than his own, i.e. that one *nobilis* could be inferior to another. The generation of T. and Pliny valued, and carefully assessed, *nobilitas*, because it was a concept dominant in the days of *libertas*, and emperors such as Trajan (see *Pan.* 69–70) had no need to challenge their values. In the century that followed, as Gelzer admits (Seager, 157), the word denotes social distinction, without any kind of precision.

9. penes, 'belongs to'. For a full analysis of T.'s use of the word in the *Histories* see Heubner's n. to II. 6. 13.

16. et Nero quoque ... The same argument is put by Plut. *G.* 2. 3, into the mouth of Nymphidius, and this may be where the 'common source' recorded it, cf. Townend, cit., 349. The alternative version used by the praetorians was that Nymphidius had deceived them, see I. 5. 3, Plut. *G.* 14. 2.

17. minus triginta. Piso can see that the *speculatores* attached to the cohort he is addressing have left the palace, and it suits him to assume that few, if any, praetorians have yet joined them.

20. transcendet ... in provincias. It is ironical that a Galbian should make this prophecy, for Galba was the first *princeps* to be acclaimed outside Italy.

23. quam ab aliis ... A curious omission from our sources is any record of the way Otho satisfied the obvious expectations of the troops, see I. 82. 15 n.

31. 3. rapit signa *quam*. For M.'s *par signas* Madvig's *pars magna* is inadequate: a main verb is needed, for *non aspernata* is not all that T. thought the cohort did. K.(1961) takes *parat signa* from L., 'prepared for action' (so Wellesley), but *rapit* is perhaps more appropriate to *ut turbidis rebus evenit.*

The cohort's action is not mentioned by other writers, and it may be that T.'s view about its motives is his own.

4. electos Illyrici exercitus. Celsus may have been regarded as a suitable emissary because he had been legate of XV Apollinaris, a Pannonian legion transferred to the East, 14. 5 n. above.

5. Vipsania in porticu. This was some way to the north, on the east side of the Via Lata (in modern terms the Corso just south of the Via del Tritone), forming part of the Campus Agrippae. For its construction, completed after Agrippa's death, see Dio 55. 8. 3; and on the topography Platner–Ashby, 90, 430, and Lugli's map. These colonnades in the Campus Martius (a term extended to include land east of the Via Lata, I. 86. 17) often opened on to large gardens, where at this time it was found convenient to bivouac troops.

6. primipilaribus. Men who had served as *primipili* but were retained in service without being (as yet) assigned to specific duties were an important element in the army, especially in Rome itself. Both there, cf. I. 87. 10, III. 70. 2, and in provincial armies (*A.* II. 11, see also XIII. 36) they seem to be part of a *numerus*, which (given the relatively small number of ex-*primipili* likely to have been available) was probably a single unit for the whole empire. See Dom. Dob. XXX. 116, Passerini, *Diz. Epig.* iv. 600 f., also Durry, 21, 142–3, though the evidence about their numbers and functions is still disappointingly thin.

7. Libertatis atrio, built to house the censors' archives, Livy XXV. 7. 12, and restored by Pollio, Suet. *Aug.* 29. It was near Caesar's forum, Lugli, 111. G. Bartoli, *Bull. Arch. Com.* 1949–50, 77 ff., attempts to place it more precisely, but his evidence from the fifth century A.D. proves no more than that it was near the Curia. It is clear from the story (true or false) of the German troops losing their way, Suet. *G.* 20, that it did not actually adjoin the Forum Romanum.

legioni classicae. 6. 7 n. above.

8. diffidebatur. This correction of M.'s *diffidebat* is generally accepted, though K.[1] tried *diffidebant.*

10. Cetrius Severus. The early part of the career of a man of this name is given on *ILS* 2073 (Pisaurum): first *speculator,* then (A.D. 48–51) *beneficiarius* of the praetorian prefect, then *a commentariis custodiarum.*

Subrius Dexter, subsequently *procurator et praefectus* of Sardinia, *CIL* X. 8023–4 = MW 337. Perhaps brother to Subrius Flavus, conspirator in 65.

11. Pompeius Longinus. A man of this name governed Judaea in 86 and was consul in 90, *PIR*[1] s.v. Conceivably an oral source for these events, Syme, 176 n.

si ... flecteretur. For *si* (with subjunctive) as εἴ πως, expressing hope or effort, cf. III. 30. 8, 52. 2, K–St., II. 2, § 219. 3 (p. 425).

14. non ordine ... amicis. To balance an ablative of cause with a prepositional phrase dependent on an understood participle is remarkable, but Nipperdey's insertion of *provectus* after *militiae* was not only gratuitous but unhelpful. Both elements depend on *fidus,* and the *et* before *desciscentibus* is 'consecutive' (see V.'s n.). GG, followed by Heubner, seem to have mistaken the sense of *ordine militiae,* which refers not to Longinus' rank but to his duty as a soldier: the phrase should have fallen within their classification I.A. (b), where the meaning is 'military propriety' or 'discipline', cf. II. 38. 14, 93. 9, and *ordinem disciplinae* I. 60. 5. Longinus was suspect because his loyalty derived not from his position as a member of the army of his emperor, but from his friendship with Galba.

17. Germanica vexilla, in I. 6. 11 called *numeri*: it is impossible to tell from either word whether legionaries or auxiliaries are intended. See II. 83. 5, where the interpretation matters more. There were auxiliaries from Britain in Rome, I. 43. 10, but also legionaries from the Rhine, I. 41. 14.

diu nutavere. Suet. *G.* 20, says they rushed to Galba's aid but lost their way. Fabia, *Rev. Phil.* 1912, 95, could not believe that no one was available to direct them. This objection, given the confusion, is not decisive; but we do know that the soldier of legion XV, I. 41. 14, joined Otho, and T.'s view that the 'Germans' were at best hesitant is plausible.

18. invalidis. E. Hohl, *Klio*, 1939, 323 n. 1, suggests that the trouble was at least more serious than the effects of sea-sickness—probably scurvy.

19. Alexandriam praemissos, see Introd., p. 9ff.

32. 1. Palatium, 'the Palatine', above, 17. 8 n.

8. duae sententiae. T. gives much more prominence to this debate than does any other writer, but never makes clear on which side he would have been, see I. 34. 1 n.

13. regressum. V. 2, G., K. (1961), and Heubner are all content with M.'s *regressus*, a genitive after *facultatem*, though *facultatem . . . in aliena potestate* is then tautologous.

33. 6. Capitolium adeat, to sacrifice on becoming *princeps*, cf. I. 47. 8.

8. et praeclarum . . . The unlaboured sarcasm is splendid, but the rest of the sentence robs Laco and Icelus of any great credit for their argument; for the real artistry lies in the way T. reminds us of the vast, but obviously ineffective, mob which was clamouring outside the doors. To place reliance on that sort of support destroyed much of their case.

13. Icelo. Plut. *G.* 26, makes Celsus an ally of Laco.

34. 1. nec diutius . . . accessit. Clearly the *speciosiora* are the aggressive-looking plans of Laco and Icelus, and it is remarkable that at the end of the previous chapter T. should have suggested that their advice was given *in publicum exitium.* Even if he thought some of Laco's arguments futile, did he really believe that Vinius' advice was sounder? Probably Galba was by now lost whatever he did, but the one hope for an emperor with military renown was surely to put himself at the head of such troops as he could trust and show himself in public forthwith. So one may well wonder whether Vinius' advice was not that of a traitor, but on that point T. (like Plut. *G.* 27. 4) says nothing until the moment of Vinius' death, I. 42. 3 ff.

There is also some conflict among the ancient authorities about the decision now taken. T. means that Laco's view prevailed, but that it was agreed to send out Piso first. But Suet. *G.* 19. 1, says that, despite pressure on him to go out at once, Galba decided to remain on the defensive with the aid of legionaries, *nihil amplius quam continere se statuit et legionariorum firmare praesidiis*; he was then lured into changing his mind by the false report of Otho's death. Plut., *G.* 26. 1, though saying that Galba wanted to go out, also implies that the issue was unsettled until the false report came in. Moreover neither Suet. nor Plut. mentions Piso's mission (Townend, cit., 357, suggests that T.'s account of it may be a doublet of Piso's address to the palace cohort).

Throughout the chapter what T. wants above all to convey is that no one was giving Galba sound, disinterested, advice, and that his decision was therefore taken on irrational grounds.

3. infensus Tito Vinio. In T.'s view the general dislike of Vinius, I. 12. 14, had spread to the praetorians. So he makes Otho attack Vinius in his speech, I. 37. 25, though Vinius had been his supporter; and Laco, I. 39. 8, suggests killing Vinius to satisfy the soldiers.

4. et facilius . . . creditur, 'one finds it easier to believe in a quarrel': i.e. Laco and Vinius found it so: T. is not committing his own judgement.

7. fama, personified—there is no parallel for Sp.'s suggestion that *credula* has a passive sense.

8. arbitrabantur. The imperfect, parallel to *adnotabant* in III. 37. 13, A. XIII. 3, means simply that T.'s source reported that this view used to have currency—Heubner seems too precise in referring it to the period directly after Galba's death. Suet. *G.* 19. 2 has no doubt that the rumour was a ruse; Plut. makes no comment.

35. 3. intus, for *intro*, a usage regarded by Quintilian, I. 5. 50, as a solecism.

9. resistens. K.[2] reads insistens, from L., which Heubner (rightly, I think) dismisses as 'einer unnötigen (wohl durch *ann*, XV. 57. 2 hervorgerufenen) Humanistenkonjektur'. The *Annals* passage is that in which Epicharis cannot, after torture, stand on her feet (*membris*); what would such a dative here imply for Galba?

But Heubner supports K.'s earlier view (1957) in keeping M.'s *sistens*, and this is very difficult too. It involves an extreme use of the dative if *turbae* is taken directly with *levaretur*, and anyway Galba's litter was surely carried by his own bearers, not by the crowd. Moreover it is unlikely that anyone would want to explain an emperor's use of a litter by saying that he was unable to stand up.

Galba was certainly both old and infirm; for detail see Suet. *G.* 21, Dio 64. 3. 2. But the point here is surely not that his infirmities made it impossible for him to stand up, but that he could not stand fast against the surging crowd; and that given all the other factors (*inopia veri et consensu errantium*) he decided to move at once. Plut. *G.* 26. 2 takes the litter as quite normal: on his version Galba was going to the Capitol to offer sacrifice for his deliverance.

Iulius Atticus, in Domaszewski's view the twenty-fourth member of the *speculatores* attached to the palace cohort, I. 24. 9, 27. 1 nn.

11. 'commilito ... quis iussit'. Plut., cit., gives Atticus' reply, τὴν πίστιν ... καὶ τὸν ὅρκον ὃν ὤμοσε. He was interested in the discipline of the soldiers: T.'s preoccupation here is with the character of Galba. Suet. and Dio omit the reply.

36. 2. non contenti ... circumdarent. The point is not that they surrounded him with flags, but that, having carried him on their shoulders (*succollatus*, Suet. *O.* 6. 3), they set him among the standards, on the platform where Galba's statue had stood.

3. aurea Galbae statua. For the statue of the *princeps* among the *signa* (golden presumably only in Rome) cf. *A.* XV. 24, *iturum ad signa et effigies principis*; for its symbolism in the Rhine camps, I. 55–6, IV 37.

4. signa ... vexillis. *Signa* were in this period the regular standards of cohorts, in all branches of the army including the Guard. They were plated lances, highly ornamented with medallions and other decoration; see Domaszewski, *Fahnen*, 35 ff., 76 ff., Durry, 197 ff. with his Planche IV. A *vexillum* was a flag, probably vermilion, hanging from the crossbar to a staff. It was carried not only by the detachments known as *vexillationes* (themselves called *vexilla* by T.) but by special units which included the legionary and praetorian cavalry. See Domaszewski, cit., M. Rostovtzeff, *JRS* 1942, 92 ff.

5. gregarius miles. Despite I. 57. 13, *manipulus quoque et gregarius miles*, it is unlikely that T. made, or that usage of his time required him to make, a distinction between soldiers below the rank of centurion, cf. above, 25. 6 n.

9. complecti armis. All commentators (rightly) cite Verg. *Aen.* XII. 433, *Ascanium fusis circum complectitur armis*, yet there too it is not undisputed whether *armi* or *arma* are intended. Most of the soldiers in our passage were not yet armed, 38. 12, but some doubtless were; yet an embrace is surely T.'s meaning, if not Virgil's too.

12. adorare. This act was not performed to Roman individual mortals (other than the Emperor Gaius, Suet. *Vit.* 2.5). When given to the gods, the salaam involved bringing the fingers to the lips, Plin. *NH* XXVIII. 25, *in adorando dextram ad osculum referimus*, Apul. *Apol.* 56, *si fanum aliquod praetereat, nefas habet adorandi gratia manum labris adorare*. But all we have here is a crowd throwing kisses to their favourite, cf. Juv. IV. 117 f. and

A. XVI. 4 (Nero posing as *citharoedus*). Otho was abasing himself before the mob, but not doing anything to shock religious feeling.

37. Otho's speech. There *was* a speech, in which Otho's main promise was that he would have no more than what the soldiers left for him to have, Suet. *O*. 6. 3. But what T. gives us is his own, and Courbaud, 225, thought he was too much carried away by the servility to remember (*pro dominatione*, I. 36. 13) that Otho wanted power. Yet all the arguments are carefully directed to what the army would enjoy: the key is given by *princeps a vobis nominatus*, line 2, which in T. governs Otho's story for the future, cf. Paratore, 478 ff.

It is a hymn of hate, Klingner, 12, but T. works in points which seem closer to the facts than those he had put into Piso's mouth, e.g. the slaughter of the marines, contrasted with *incruentam urbem*, I. 29. 18. So he contributes here to the blacker side of his portrait of Galba, Heubner, 85.

8. cuius . . . Galba, "G.'s clemency being what it is": cf. Cic. *Sull*. 18, *qua mollitia sum animi ac lenitate*. The object of *promisit* is *poenam meam et supplicium vestrum*.

12. deprecantis in fidem. Confirmed neither by Suet. nor by Plut., though both are anti-Galbian over this incident.

14. Obultronii . . . Gallia. The first three names are obscure. H. Mattingly suggested, *BMC*, I. p. ccix, that Obultronius and Marcellus were to be seen on Galba's QUADRAGESIMA REMISSA coins, being procurators in Spain who objected to his leniency (cf. Plut. *G*. 4). The suggestion was applauded by Rostovtzeff, *SEHR*. 510, but is impossible as it stands: Obultronius Sabinus certainly (*A*. XIII. 28, a quaestor in A.D. 56), and Cornelius Marcellus probably (if the identification be right he was praetor-designate in 65, *A*. XVI. 8; cf. *ILS* 6767), were senators. Syme, *AJP* 1937, 9, following a conjecture by Groag, claimed that these two were the proconsul of Baetica and his legate, and it is hard to improve on this view. Betuus Cilo or Chilo (for Betuus as *gentilicium* see *ILS* 6615 from Perugia) could on Syme's thesis be a Gallic governor, perhaps the legate of Aquitania (succeeded by Iulius Cordus, I. 76. 5): any of them, if they did not support Galba, must have been in danger from him.

20. falsis nominibus. For the theme in earlier Latin authors, surely all conscious of Thuc. III. 82. 4, see Heubner's n.

23. Polycliti . . . Aegiali. Polyclitus (cf. *A.* XIV.39, Dio, 63. 12. 3) was executed by Galba, Plut. *G.* 7, and so doubtless were the other two. Vatinius is the cobbler from Beneventum, Mart. XIV. 96. 1, Juv. V. 46, cf. *A.* XV. 34, *Dial.* 11; of Aegialus (Lipsius read Helim) nothing is known. For the plurals, still characteristic in modern Italian, cf. II. 95, 16.

24. perdiderunt. Madvig, *Adversaria critica* ii. 561, made an attractive case for *quam ⟨ob⟩ quod perierunt,* but the plurals would be less appropriate if Otho had meant to recall the deaths of particular freedmen than if he was speaking of the rapacity of Neronian freedmen generally.

25. T. Vinius. Heubner maintains that Otho, though Vinius had been his friend, now wanted to be rid of him as a possible future rival. But there is no hint of this in any source: Otho felt guilt at Vinius' death, I. 44. 4, and it is fair to assume that he would have saved him had he dared. In T's view Vinius was detested by everyone, including the soldiers, see above, 34. 3 n.

26. una illa domus. For Vinius' great property see I. 48, 21. (Wolff ingeniously, but surely wrongly, took these words to refer to the fact that all three of Galba's favourites lived with him in the Palace, Suet. *G.* 14).

38. 2. ab exilio, I. 48. 2 n.

8. cohors togata, so Martial, VI. 76. 1, calls the praetorian prefect Fuscus *ille sacer lateris custos Martisque togatae.* The cohort on guard wore not the *sagum* but the toga, and under it concealed their swords, *A.* XVI 27. They appear to have had no defensive armour, Durry, 207.

11. quis . . . imputet, "who will put most against my account?" For the metaphor from book-keeping, which sometimes leaves doubt whether a credit or debit is intended, e.g. 55. 18, see GG s.v. *imputo* (α) (β).

12. aperire. K. reads *aperiri,* but for *iubeo* with active infinitive without accusative cf. I. 40. 6.

13. armamentarium. The only known arsenal, and arms factory, in Italy was in the praetorian camp.

14. ordine . . . distingueretur. For *ordo militiae* cf. 31. 14 n. above, but what *insignia* would have distinguished praetorian from legionary arms is not clear, cf. Durry, 195. That there were legionaries actually present in the praetorian camp is probable from I. 41. 14, though the main units were elsewhere in Rome, I. 31. 5 ff.

39.1. Piso ... adsecutus erat. T. finds no need to say that Piso turned back before reaching the camp, nor what he said to Galba on his return. For an excellent appreciation of the drama evoked by this and the two following chapters see Courbaud, 161 f.

4. Palatium, hill or palace (above 17. 8 n.)—it does not matter.

5. rostra. The Rostra Iulia were near the temple of Saturn. During the riots preceding the recall of Cicero they were considered a vantage point, Cic. *Sest.* 35, but it is unlikely that advice to occupy them now made much sense., see Heubner's n.

8. occidendo. above, 34. 3 n.

12. turbavere consilium ... The confusion of counsel here and earlier in the chapter is attributed by T., not as Plut. *G.* 26. 3 to the crowd, but to Galba's entourage.

40. 1. agebatur. The metaphor of the storm derives from T.'s source, cf. Plut. *G.* 26. 3, τοῦ φορείου, καθάπερ ἐν κλύδωνι δεῦρο κἀκεῖ διαφερομένου. But his artistry diverts the word *fluctuantis* on to the crowd which drove Galba's litter to and fro; and in the rest of the chapter, though sacrificing some details (e.g. the Basilica Aemilia), he easily outdoes Plut. in rhetorical effect. See Fabia, 29 f.

4. non tumultus... Orelli reported a surprising origin, in Xenophon, *Ages.* 2. 12, κραυγὴ μὲν οὐδεμία παρῆν, οὐ μὴν οὐδὲ σιγή, φωνὴ δέ τις ἦν οἵαν ὀργή τε καὶ μάχη παράσχοιτ' ἄν; and early editors (e.g. Sp.) took the *quale* clause to be illustrative of all the previous words, i.e. that the absence of riot or silence was typical of a situation in which the people were deeply afraid and deeply angry. But angry at what? At Galba's misgovernment, or at Otho's coup? Despite Otho's fears (next sentence), the *plebs* seem from T. and the other sources to have shown neither emotion: they were indifferent, as later over the fate of Vitellius III. 83. It seems more likely, then, that the *quale* clause defines *non silentium* only, "there was no silence of the kind associated with fear or deep anger", and that the sentence is reminiscent of Livy 1. 29. 2, *non quidem fuit tumultus ille nec pavor, qualis captarum esse urbium solet ... sed silentium triste ac tacita maestitia ... defixit omnium oculos* (whether or not Livy was conscious of Xenophon). See R. W. Husband, *CP* 1915, 321.

7. quasi Vologaesum, a comparison not found in the other accounts, but both Plut. and Dio express themselves in terms which suggest that the "common source" was greatly moved.

10. proculcato senatu. This prepares the way for *per stragem iacentium,*

I, 47. 8. Yet the only senators T. reports as killed are Galba, Piso, and Vinius, and on such a point he is unlikely to have withheld evidence.

rapidi equis. Suet. *G.* 19. 2 says it was the cavalry who had been given definite instructions to kill Galba. But Groag's contention, 766, that there is discrepancy among the sources (Plut. and Dio vs. T. and Suet.) about the use of infantry in the Othonian attack is fruitless: T. showed that all types of soldiers were mixed up, I. 38. 13, and it was probably an infantryman who killed Galba, I. 41. 13.

12. priores et futuri principes . . . The point is made more explicit in I. 44. 14. Here T. may be actually invoking the sight his readers could see—the statues (including those of later emperors) which were on the Capitol.

13. cuius . . . successit, "the kind of crime which any successor must punish".

41. 1. vexillarius, here, unusually, the carrier of a flag, i.e. a *signifer*, Domaszewski, *Fahnen*, 24. T. is not concerned to be technical.

3. imaginem, from the *signum*.

5. Curtii lacum. Near where the column of Phocas now stands, i.e. in front of the Basilica Aemilia and east of the Rostra, this pool was surrounded by a balustrade containing an altar, Ov. *Fast.* VI. 401 ff., Lugli, cit., 157 f.

extremam eius vocem. Dio 64. 6. 3, gives only the first version, Plut. *G.* 27 only the second, δρᾶτε, εἰ τοῦτο τῷ δήμῳ Ῥωμαίων ἄμεινόν ἐστι. Suet. *G.* 20, has as his first alternative *Quid agitis, commilitones? ego vester sum et vos mei,* and as his second *ut hoc agerent ac ferirent, quando ita videretur.* Whether the vital words *e re publica* were added by T. or omitted by Suet. cannot be decided, but the latter seems more probable.

12. de percussore . . . constat. The same three names, without any description of Terentius, are in Plut. *G.* 27. 2, and Plut. adds a fourth, Fabius Fabullus, who cut off the head and carried it on a spear to Otho. But Suet. *G.* 20. 2 says the body was left lying by the lake until a soldier came and cut off the head; no doubt this soldier was Fabius Fabullus, and Plut. has been careless in thinking he may have been the killer, cf. Groag, *RE* vi, col. 1769. As to the other three names, it is likely that the "common source" recorded them all, and Plutarch's ὡς οἱ πλεῖστοι λέγουσιν is identical with T.'s *crebrior fama traditit,* i.e. "as most people say" rather than "as the majority of my written sources state", cf. Townend, *AJP* 1964, 357.

The enormity of Fabius Fabullus' prance through Rome, like a

Bacchanal with the head on a lance, was to Plut. the most horrifying incident in the whole story, and the echo of some of his words in Dio 64. 7. 3 shows that the horror was already expressed in his source. It is certainly very striking ("enorme stranezza", Momigliano, 117) that T. says nothing of the man either here or in 44 or 49; and Köstermann, *Hermes*, 1965, 184, tries to show that Fabullus and T. were both Transpadanes, and that T. therefore suppressed his compatriot's part in such an outrage. But Townend, cit., n. 48, is surely right (see also Syme, 189) in arguing that the differences among the sources here "simply illustrate the sort of details which interested each writer". What T. has established is that the common soldiers have been given unbridled licence; and if one of them now behaves in a way he would have thought characteristic of a common soldier, the details would not attract him, especially if they included physical features like Galba's baldness, see Suet., cit., and Syme's n. 6.

14. quintae decimae legionis, from Vetera in Lower Germany, cf. 31.17 n. above.

42. 1. ambigitur. Plut., *G.* 27. 4 has no doubt.

6. cuius causa erat. But how, unless he was *conscius*? After all, he had supported Otho and was emphatically no friend of Piso. But T. (or his source) was convinced that Vinius was hated by all, including the soldiers, and that he was the main reason for Galba's unpopularity, cf. 34. 3 n. above.

  aedem divi Iuli, close to the Lacus Curtius, but further up the Ima Sacra Via.

43.1. Sempronium Densum. This is the most puzzling of the discrepancies among the sources. T., with circumstantial detail (*a Galba custodiae Pisonis additus*, and that Densus' action gave Piso temporary *effugium*) makes this centurion the defender of Piso; Plut. *G.* 26. 4 and also Dio 64. 7. 5 say he defended Galba; and Suet. *G.* 20. 1 says Galba was defended by no one. Furthermore T.'s sentence *insignem ... vidit* must surely echo the same source as Plut.'s ὃν μόνον ἥλιος ἐπεῖδεν. There is no satisfactory solution. Plut. could, as Fabia, 146, thought, have been excited by the story of Densus' bravery, and then told it without remembering who was being defended. But then did Dio copy Plut.? or was he, by strange coincidence, guilty of the same piece of carelessness? Townend, cit., 358–9, must be right in thinking that different sources lie behind our writers, but it is hard to accept his suggestion that T. "has admired Pliny's story of Densus sufficiently to incorporate it in an entirely different setting", i.e. that Plut. and T. used Pliny and that T., believing from the story followed by Suet. that Galba was not defended, proceeded to an invention of his own. There must, as Townend suggests earlier, have been two versions available to T.: one (probably also used by Suet.) described the defence of Piso, the other provided the basis for the first words of our chapter. But who gave T. these versions we cannot tell. Nor can we be sure that the version accepted by T. is right, though the probability is that it is.

3. stricto . . . armatis. He belonged to the *cohors togata,* and so had no defensive armour, above, 38. 8 n.

6. aedem Vestae, the round temple (just south of the temple of Divus Iulius), of which a partial reconstruction, with slender Corinthian columns, stands in the Forum today.

7. contubernio, as at III. 74, the dwelling-place of the *aedituus* of a temple, who was a public slave.

    non . . . caerimoniis. *caerimoniae* at *A.* III. 60 indicate a formal right of asylum. There is no clear evidence that the temple of Vesta provided an absolute sanctuary, but the Vestals claimed to offer a strong protection, cf. Plut., *Numa* 10, Cic. *Cael.* 34, *Fam.* XIV. 2.2 (Terentia takes refuge with them after Cicero's exile).

10. nuper . . . donatus, presumably given him as an individual rather than in a general grant to time-expired men in his regiment, although Galba *civitates R. raro dedit,* Suet, *G.* 14. 3.

11. Statius. The editors of *PIR*¹ suggest that the name was Staius, derived from Staius Murcus, the legate of Caesar the dictator.

44. 4. maiestatis. Not simply an abbreviation for *maiestatis laesae,* i.e. his treason; but his memory (as of Vinius his friend) of a man who had been an emperor. After all Otho had made him so, and had profited thereby. Cf. *A.* I. 42 (of Tiberius by Germanicus), *illum quidem sua maiestas* [sc. *defendet*].

8. aquilam legionis, presumably I Adiutrix.

11. libellos, "petitions". Here at least the same precise number is reported by Plut. *G.* 27.5.

14. tradito principibus more. The accusatives which follow in apposition to the sentence are clear in their meaning: potential murderers of a *princeps* will be deterred, or, if not that, at least the *princeps* can expect to be revenged. The classic case was Claudius' execution of Gaius' murderer Cassius Chaerea, ἐπ᾽ ἀποτροπῇ τοῦ μέλλοντος χρόνου, Jos. *Ant.* 19.265: he disapproved (ἐδυσχέραινεν) of anyone killing an emperor, says Dio 60. 3. 4, πόρρωθεν τό καθ᾽ ἑαυτὸν ἐς ἀσφαλείαν προορώμενος. But what other instance contributed to a *mos* by T.'s day?. Vitellius' effort was not significant: was Vespasian's any more? The murder of Domitian must have been in T.'s mind, though Nerva took his time before pressure made him follow this "tradition".

45. 1. alium ... populum. The parallel passage in Plut. *G.* 28. 1 relates to the meeting of the Senate, which T. does not reach till I. 47. 2.

6. Marium Celsum, above 14. 5 n.

12. vinciri iussum. H. maintained that this was part of what Otho asserted, but this cannot be: the soldiers would have wanted to see the arrest made before they were satisfied, and anyway Otho cannot have said *simulatione irae.* For the construction, in which *et ... adfirmans* has been inserted as an additional point between *vinciri iussum ... subtraxit* see Heubner's n.

13. maiores poenas. Plut.'s version is that Otho said he must first subject Celsus to cross-examination. Fabia, 33, objected to T.'s account on the ground that no punishment could be worse than death. But death is worse than arrest, and anyway there is more than one way of dying.

T. now leaves Celsus until after the digression on the German rising, but it is clear from Plut. *O.* 1. 1 that the reconciliation with Otho took place next day.

46. 2. Plotium Firmum. Nothing is known of this man outside the *Histories*, but he may have been father of C. Tullius Capito Pomponianus Plotius Firmus, *cos.* A.D. 84; conceivably also related to Plotius Grypus, III. 52. 11 etc., whom Vespasian made a senator. Ascent from the ranks of the praetorians to the prefecture is most remarkable (even the successful ranker Vettius Valens, *ILS* 2648 = Sm. 1,283, did not reach the highest posts), but the spectacular steps in his promotion had been due to Otho's predecessors. The appointment of the *praefectus vigilum* to command the guard had recent precedent with Tigellinus; earlier *praefecti praetorio*, including Burrus, had been holding inferior posts at the time of their elevation; Vitellius appointed a *praefectus cohortis* and a centurion, II. 92. 1, at the same time disappointing a *praefectus alae*, II. 100. 15; and Arrius Varus thought he ought to have received the post from a primipilate, IV. 2. 3. T. is silent about the previous career, as distinct from the politics, of Licinius Proculus, but it may be that there was nothing very revolutionary about any of the appointments now made.

5. Flavium Sabinum. For the career of Vespasian's elder brother see III. 75. 1, with Wellesley's n.; also Braithwaite's n. to Suet. *Vesp.* 1. 3, and *PIR*² F 352. Plut. *O.* 5. 2 places this appointment in March, just before Otho's departure for the front, and says it was made by Otho himself. About the timing he is probably wrong: it was then that Otho left Rome in charge of his brother Titianus, I. 90. 19, and Plut. may have found a mention of Sabinus in a source recording that his regular duties were being overshadowed. But equally suspect is T.'s attribution of the appointment to the troops (anyway it would presumably be the urban cohorts, not the praetorians, who would be interested in appointing a *praefectus urbi*, see E. Hohl, *Klio*, 1939, 321 n. 6): Otho himself had good grounds for choosing Sabinus, whose character as described in III. 75 is not that of a common soldier's idol. The two grounds mentioned by T. are also in Plut. and go back to the "common source". There can be little doubt that *plerique* were right: a gesture to the greatest political *dux* of the time was an obvious one for Otho to make. But *iudicium Neronis secuti* reopens the theme, which interested T., of Otho's revival of the Neronian regime (see I. 14. 21); for a useful discussion of that see Paratore, 482, though he greatly underrates the importance of Vespasian, whether the appointment was made in January or in March.

8. vacationes, exemptions from military *munera*. These abuses by centurions were of long standing, cf. *A.* I. 17, 35, and the problem was evidently regarded as pressing in 69, for Vitellius was taking a similar measure to Otho's, almost simultaneously, I. 58. 3. Despite T.'s vivid description, one thing that remains unclear is whether the men were claiming, and whether they obtained, an entitlement to specified periods of leave each year. If not, what prevented the centurions from continuing chicanery about the issue of grants from the sum made available from the *fiscus*? Much later, a *princeps* is accused of selling exemptions himself, *SHA, Pertinax* 9.

14. tum, "moreover", GG. 1681 (b).

20. ad extremum .. An echo of Sall. *Hist.* I. 12, *seditiones et ad postremum bella civilia orta sunt.* In 69 the soldiers were as ready for civil war after the reform as before.

    vulgi largitione, a rare objective genitive, for which H. cites as parallel *Bell. Hisp.* 1. 4, *ut . . . ex ea pecunia latronum largitio fieret.*

21. fiscum suum. To add here to the vast literature on the origins of the imperial *fiscus*, and on its resources and legal status, would be pointless. In English see Fergus Millar, *JRS* 1963, 29 ff. (with whom I agree that Sen. *Ben.* VIII. 6. 3 remains a fundamental text), and the reply by P. A. Brunt, *JRS* 1966, 75 ff. The places where the word is used in the *Histories* throw no light on the real problems. We simply know that both Otho and Vitellius, immediately on their elevation, laid their hands on funds which T. was prepared to call a *fiscus*, cf. I. 65. 5, 90. 2.

24. tamquam . . . seponeretur. T. omits the antecedent, i.e. that he was removed from Rome; Otho sent an executioner after him.

25. Marcianum . . . libertum, with easy sarcasm, cf. I. 13. 3. In *palam* the contrast may in part be with the concealed death of Laco, but the manner of Icelus' death was *servile supplicium* (i.e. crucifixion), as with Asiaticus, IV. 14. 20.

47. 1. exacto . . . die. So also *vergente iam die*, Suet. *O.* 7. 1 and Plut's εὐθύς, is not in disagreement. The thing that both Plut. and T. emphasize is that the corpses were still lying in the Forum.

2. praetor urbanus, this being the *mos maiorum* when both consuls were dead, Cic. *Fam.* X. 12. 3. Similarly, the consuls being away, Frontinus summoned the senate at the beginning of 70, IV. 39. 1.

3. decernitur . . . honores. Plut. cit., says the *honores* included the names of Caesar and Augustus (see above, 19. 12, n.), and the oath of loyalty was taken to Otho, the one "he had sworn to Galba but not kept". Otho also, Suet., cit., made a speech explaining how he had been "compelled" to take the principate.

The senate decreed similarly for Vitellius, *cuncta longis aliorum principatibus composita*, II. 55. 8; and for Vespasian, *cuncta principibus solita*, IV. 3. 11. But we know from *AFA* (*ILS* 241 = MW 2) that the decrees for Otho and Vitellius were later ratified by the Comitia, and in Otho's case after an interval which suggests a surprising respect for formal procedures. His *comitia trib. pot.* were on 28 Feb, with *comitia sacerdotiorum* on 5 March and *comitia pont. max,* on 9 Mar.; yet from the first mention of him as ruler (probably 16 Jan.) he is called Imp. M. Otho (the *praenomen Imperator* had been revived by Nero in 66, but not assumed by Galba), though there is no mention of *comitia imperii.* Vitellius' *comitia trib. pot.,* on 30 Apr., followed the Senate's action more quickly (he presumably claimed that a free Senate would have acted earlier); and the following day, 1 May, is described as his *dies imperii,* possibly because *comitia imperii* were then held. When and how Vespasian obtained formal ratification of his powers is not known, for the *Acta* are missing; the *Lex de Imperio* (*ILS* 244 = MW 1) implies that the *comitia* purported to have done something, but that in this case little trouble was taken over protocol.

These procedures are part of an artificial world, one which it is odd to find surviving into 69. Vespasian exploded most of it when he took 1 July, the day the troops acclaimed him, as his *primus principatus dies* (II.

79. 3, with n., Suet., *Vesp.* 6. 3) and also as that on which his *trib. pot.* began. For further discussion see M. Hammond, *MAAR* 1938, 26 ff., P. A. Brunt, *JRS* 1977, 106, and II. 79 n.

8. cruento adhuc foro. Both Plut. and Suet. place the sacrifice on the following morning, the normal time for sacrifice, but the accession of a new *princeps* was not normal (cf. I. 33. 6) and T. could be right. See Townend, *AJP* 1964, 361.

10. Verania (Gemina), daughter of Q. Veranius, *cos.* 49, who died as governor of Britain; her last illness is recorded by Pliny, *Epp.* II. 20. The funeral urn which she shared with her husband (on whose name his unhappy adoption is not recorded, *ILS* 240 = MW 76) was found in the Villa Buonaparte near the Via Salaria, with that of Piso's father and eldest brother (*ILS* 955–6, see I. 48. 2).

11. Crispina, presumably the daughter whom Tigellinus saved from Nero, 72. 11, and who was believed to be a possible wife for Otho, I. 13. 10. Plut. *G.* 28. 2 says she paid 10,000 HS for the head.

48. 1. Piso. Even now we have only a few lines on him and his family, which had been prominent in the politics of the Julio-Claudian age, and we are still not told how he came to be exiled. T. gives four times the space to Vinius, whom he saw as a much more important character in the history of Galba's fall, see Köstermann, *Navicula Chiloniensis*, 193.

explebat, presumably not yet thirty-one, cf. III. 86. 2.

2. fratres eius. See stemma, p.74. Pompeius Magnus, the eldest brother, was made Claudius' son-in-law, resuming the *cognomen* Magnus of which Gaius had deprived him, Dio 60. 5; but about A.D. 45 he was executed, and (almost certainly at the same time) his father Crassus and his mother Scribonia suffered death, Dio 61. 29, Sen. *Apocol.* 11. M. Licinius Crassus, the second brother, husband of Sulpicia Praetextata (IV. 42. 6), was consul in 64, but perished on the accusation of Regulus in Nero's last years, see also Plin. *Epp.* I. 5. 3; it may have been at the same time that Piso Licinianus was exiled, though *diu* is odd. The death of the third brother, Crassus Scribonianus, presumably under Vespasian, is not recorded in the extant Books; he was alleged to have been urged by Antonius Primus to seek supreme power, but declined, IV. 39. 13.

5. Titus Vinius quinquaginta septem ... The figure is probably wrong. It would be possible for a man, after a discreditable early career, to come back to the proconsulate of Narbonensis and a consulate at this kind of age, but the tenure of a military tribunate at age twenty-eight is unlikely, especially as his father was of praetorian rank.

7. maternus avus. Dio 47. 7. 4 records the proscription of a T. Vinius, saved by his wife, so perhaps our Vinius took the name of his mother's family.

8. Calvisium Sabinum, *cos.* 26, legate of Pannonia under Gaius, Dio 59. I. 18. 4; *numquam vidi hominem beatum indecentius,* Sen. *Epp.* 27. 5. Both he and his wife Cornelia committed suicide in 39, the charge against Cornelia being that she had visited the sentries and looked at the exercises of the troops. The incident, especially the connection of Vinius with it, is mysterious, but Calvisius had already been involved in a *maiestas* charge in 32, *A.* VI.9; and since he had been the consular colleague of Gaetulicus, whose execution during his command in Upper Germany was a major event in Gaius' reign, it is likely that Gaius suspected that something serious was afoot, see J. P. V. D. Balsdon, *The Emperor Gaius* (1934), 71. Perhaps the charge of *stuprum* against Cornelia was concocted after the event, to avoid dwelling on the graver suspicions of her husband's activities.

9. situm, "the lay-out". In whatever way the offence was later represented, it looks as if Cornelia was accused of something more dangerous than *lascivia.*

10. temptasset, for M.'s *temperasset,* cf. the corruption in *A.* XV. 42. Yet *temerasset* (V.) seems a more likely reading. For *temerare* implying a camp's disgrace see IV. 58. 35 and *A.* I. 30; and for the strong feeling against women in camps *A.* I. 69. II. 55.

13. mutatione temporum, released on Gaius' death, Plut. *G.* 12. 2, so kept in prison for about fifteen months.

cursu honorum inoffenso. Yet despite the ensuing story of the cup there is something odd about it. When was he praetor, and when did the cup incident take place? But more, did he hold any post after his blameless governorship of Narbonensis? It is only Suet. *G.* 14. 2 who says he was a legate of Galba in Spain. It seems likely that it was as proconsul of Narbonensis that he was *Galbae amicitia . . . tractus,* and that as such his consulate came naturally to him as a man in his forties, though with a dubious past. See Domaszewski, *RhM* 1890, 7.

21. eadem vi, to be taken with all the preceding adjectives, from *audax* onwards. Wellesley's tr., "with equal effectiveness", is hard to better. The chapter's ending is almost as brilliant as that of the much more famous one that follows. (It needs more than a tentative suggestion (see G. B. A. Fletcher, *CR* 1940, 186) to convince most readers that *Vinius . . . vi* was intended as a pun).

21. magnitudine opum. Otho had said, I. 37. 25, that Vinius' fortune was by itself enough to pay the guard their donative. It could be that this confiscation of his property enabled him to pay both for the *vacationes* and for the advance of 5,000 HS given after the riot, I. 82. 15 (see n.). See E. Hohl, *Klio*, 1939, 322, though his figures need correction.

49. 1. Galbae corpus. T. avoids the details, especially about the head, which are given by Plut. *G.* 27 and Suet. *G.* 20. 2. He also omits the story, found in Plut., that Helvidius Priscus was allowed by Otho to take the body. That story, given Helvidius' friendship with Galba, is not unlikely (see Groag, 746), but T. may not have wished to record devotion, by one of his heroes, to an emperor he had come to despise.

3. privatis eius hortis, on the Via Aurelia, Suet. *G.* 20. 2.

4. lixas calonesque, a group which in T.'s view was capable of any ruffianly action: cf. III. 33. 1. But this one was not part of a general riot by the lower orders or by Neronians. A freedman of Patrobius bought the body for as much as 10,000 HS, and cast it on the ground where his patron had been executed, Suet. *G.* 20. 2.

7. hunc exitum... The great obituary which follows, when compared with the parallel at the end of Plut.'s *Life*, gives a fine test for assessing T.'s power and his originality. See Fabia, 35 f., Syme, 182.

Servius Galba. The *praenomen* Servius, which betrayed T. into a surprising blunder, II. 48. 16, was not used by Galba during most of his life. He was adopted by his stepmother Livia Ocellina, and called himself L. Livius Ocella (or Ocellaris ?) Sulpicius Galba, Suet *G.* 4. 1. In the edict of Tib. Alexander (*SEG* XV. 873 = MW 328) he is called L. Livius Augustus Sulpicius Galba, but he ultimately decided for the title *Ser. Galba imperator*.

tribus et septuaginta. Galba was born on 24 Dec., Suet. *G.* 4. 1, Dio (= Xiph.) 64. 6. 5, but the sources differ about the year. Suet. gives it as 3 B.C., which would make him only seventy when he died, and this is supported by Dio's statement, 56. 29. 5, that he assumed the *toga virilis* in A.D. 14. But with T.'s seventy-three years Plut. *G.* 8 is in agreement; and that fits with Suet.'s story, *Nero* 40. 3, that Delphi told Nero to fear the seventy-third year. Yet a third version comes from Xiph., cit., namely that Galba lived seventy-two years and twenty-three days, i.e. born in 5 B.C. and only seventy-one when he rebelled, and Suet. too, *G.* 23, says he died in his seventy-third year. In all this the date for the assumption of the *toga virilis* is perhaps the least likely to be wrong. The number seventy-three could have been introduced to echo the oracle, though what Delphi was really thinking about when Nero went there is quite obscure.

9. vetus ... nobilitas, details provided, with considerable learning, by Suet. *G.* 2–3. See also 15. 3 n. above.

10. magnae opes. Plut. *G.* 3. 1 says he was the wealthiest *privatus* who attained the principate. His fortune was greatly increased by his stepmother, Livia Ocellina, who adopted him.

medium ingenium. For the rarity of the phrase see *TLL* VIII. 590. 10 ff. T. must have been remembering Livy 1. 32. 44, *medium erat in Anco ingenium, et Romuli et Numae memor.* But the addition of *magis ... virtutibus* is (as Ed. Fraenkel once said to me by letter) a "truly Tacitean variation": Livy was concerned with Ancus' foreign policy, and found a compromise between Romulus' aggressiveness and Numa's pacific temperament to have been admirably suited to the problems of the time. T. is assessing Galba's character, and in particular his capacity as a ruler, and his findings are very different. For the shortcomings which T. had most in mind (in the main, I would think, contained in the rest of this chapter), see Introd., pp. 12. ff.

11. venditator, "nor did he show it off"; the noun is found elsewhere only in two passages of Gellius, Syme, 721 n. 3.

alienae ... parcus, recalling, but reversing, Sallust on Catiline, *BC* 5. 4, *alieni appetens, sui profusus.* That passage again attracted T. when he wrote II. 86. 9 f.

16. quod segnitia ... Cf. *Agr.* 6. 3, *gnarus sub Nerone temporum, quibus inertia pro sapientia fuit.* Galba's *segnitia* was first noticed, precisely because of *metus temporum*, during the later years of his governorship of Spain, Suet. *G.* 9.

17. Germanias ... Africam. Consul in 33, he governed Upper Germany after the execution of Gaetulicus in 39, and received triumphal ornaments for a victory over the Chatti in 41, Suet. *G.* 6–7, Dio 60. 8. His African proconsulate was held for two years, probably from 45, and he was then given the ornaments again, a rare honour after Gaius had put the only legion under a legate of the emperor.

18. iam senior, from 60 or 61, Suet. *G.* 9. 1. Nero kept him there for an exceptionally long time, having appointed him because he thought he would "be careful", Plut. *G.* 3. 3. Had Delphi's intelligence service reason for believing Nero wrong (see n. to line 7 above)?

19. maior ... privatus fuit. Any possible misunderstanding of the famous epigram that follows (there ought to have been none) is removed by these words. It is not just that Galba, had he died a *privatus*, would have been acclaimed *capax imperii* by posterity, but that in his days as a *privatus* he was in fact so regarded. See *A.* VI. 20. 3 with Furneaux's n., and Suet. *G.* 14. 1, *maiore adeo et favore et auctoritate adeptus est quam gessit imperium.*

omnium ... imperasset. And even the epigram (but I have not been able to see the article by F. Hampl criticized in Heubner's n.) seems in relatively recent times to have been labelled as a piece of rhetoric designed to justify T.'s condemnation of Galba. If one calls a brilliant use of language "rhetoric", and then regards the word "rhetoric" as pejorative, one's interest in T. will soon flag. For more restrained, but well chosen, words see Heubner's n.

I. 50 *Transition*

For similar pauses between different themes cf. II. 8 ff., III. 36 ff, etc. This chapter contains verbal echoes of I. 2, and like it has unmistakable reminiscences of Lucan, esp. *Phars.* II. 60 ff. In lines 18–19 T. probably also remembered Sen. *Epp.* 14. 13, *potest melior vincere, non potest non peior esse que vicerit.*

It is a curious chapter. Nothing in it diverges from what T. and other sources tell us about the actual events of 69: yet the political analysis contains striking contrasts with the immediately preceding chapters. *Veteres Othonis mores paventem* perhaps; but against I. 45 and 47 (Plut. is even more fulsome about the early days of Otho's rule) the *palam* of line 8 is hard to credit; and though Rome, *tamquam in tanta multitudine* (I. 8. 1), doubtless embraced a diversity of sympathies and forebodings, it would be surprising if the *vulgus* was unanimously depressed at this moment. In the future it was only "gradually", I. 89. 1, that they became concerned at the economic consequences of the coming civil war. Similarly one can wonder whether T.'s summary here entirely conforms with his account of Otho's regime in 71–90.

3. novus ... nuntius. On the events this completes a reasonable story. The official dispatch about the Mogontiacum legions arrived on 9 Jan.; followed by unofficial news circulating before Galba's death; followed by a further official *nuntius* just before the 15th. This last was now revealed. Cf. above, 19. 7 n.

9. saevae pacis exempla. Cf. 2. 2 n. above.

11. Pharsaliam ... Mutinam. Editors have tried in various ways to explain the order of the four names (geography, euphony, etc.), even to the absurd extent of suggesting emendation because they are not arranged chronologically.

The asyndeton, followed by variation of conjunctions, has its closest parallel in *A.* XIII. 64. 1, *quaestore aedili tribuno ac praetore et consuli,* where the point, presumably, is to pile heavily on the list of sudden deaths. Perhaps the best-known parallel for variation, but without asyndeton, is in *A.* I. 1, *Tiberii Gaiique et Claudii ac Neronis,* possibly (see Furneaux's n.) designed to distinguish two Julian *principes* from two Claudians; see also *H.* II. 76. 14, *contra Gai quidem aut Claudii vel Neronis fundatam longo imperio domum,* where Heubner is probably right in suggesting some such translation as "the long-established house of Gaius or Claudius, or even that of Nero" (the last without progeny, and with crumbling support). Yet even in these instances it could be that T. indulges in variation for its own sake.

In the present passage it is possible that T. thought first of the two most decisive, and bloody, battles of the civil wars, and then added the other two, mainly perhaps because they had been fought on Italian soil.

14. bonos, a striking contrast with T.'s comments on Republican *principes* in II. 38.

15. mansuram ... rem publicam. If Pompey or Brutus had won, not only would Rome and her empire have survived, but there would still have been a *res publica. Rem publicam* here must mean 'free state'. Cf. above, 16. 2 n.

19. erant ... augurarentur. T. is alone among our sources in mentioning Vespasian at this stage, and it would be interesting to know what evidence he had for saying that men in Rome already thought of him as a possible contender. So far as our own evidence goes, (a) Vespasian was the only commander who had won significant military successes in the later part of Nero's reign, (b) on Nero's death he had composed his differences with Mucianus, and had also, ostensibly awaiting fresh orders, stopped fighting in Judaea. Was the significance of this latter activity, or inactivity, appreciated in Rome; and, if so, was it a "Flavian" writer who recorded it for T., or did he put his own interpretation on the story he received? The question is discussed more fully in nn. to the earliest chapters of Book II.

20. potior utroque Vespasianus. If *potior* means "more powerful" this is clearly true, provided he had Mucianus and Egypt with him. But, more probably, "preferable" to his rivals.

21. ambigua de Vespasiano fama ... Apart from his military distinction, nothing to Vespasian's credit is recorded (e.g. by Suet.) of his career under the Julio-Claudians; and his proconsulate of Africa, II. 97. 12, Suet. *Vesp.* 4. 3, was remembered to his discredit. But it is the judgement *solus ... in melius mutatus est* which is of vital importance to our understanding of T.'s political standpoint when he wrote the *Histories—contra* Paratore in many passages.

51–70. *Acclamation of Vitellius and advance of the Rhineland armies.*
51. 1. nunc ... expediam. Plut. describes the revolt in its chronological

setting, inside Galba's reign. He felt no reason for altering the order given by his source, whereas T. was determined not to break the story of the praetorian mutiny. See Fabia, 16.

2. caeso, not intended as a contradiction of his suicide, Plut. *G.* 6. 3, Dio 63. 24. 4.

3. ditissimi belli. For the reputed riches of Gaul cf. *A.* III. 46. 2 (the Aedui), XI. 18. 1 (the northern coast). And strong support of Vindex had come from Vienna, which was probably (cf. I. 66) richer still.

4. expeditionem... malebat. War was what they positively wanted, without any other considerations, I. 64. 3. For the Latin cf. 8. 3 n. above.

9. ad usum et ad decus. The contrast ("for use as well as for ostentation", immortalized by Gibbon, cap. vii on Gordian II) is made more pointed by the unusual repetition of the preposition, see Heubner's n.

10. finibus provinciarum. The boundary was approximately at Rheinbrohl, between Remagen and Andernach, cf. Mommsen, *Provinces of the Roman Empire,* I. 119 n. 2.

11. contractae legiones. This reinforcement to Verginius from Lower Germany is not mentioned in our main accounts of Vesontio, but see again I. 53. 11.

15. ac tum acerrima instigatrix. Many commentators take this to mean that earlier, during the Vindex war, the Treviri and Lingones had urged the legions to take the field, i.e. that *tum* relates to the past and *nec deerat . . .* records similar behaviour during Vitellius' rising. But a contrast between *tum* (i.e. the time of which T. is now speaking, cf. I. 89. 11) and the immediately preceding past participle *secuta* is surely more likely: they had supported the anti-Vindex party before, but *now* they had come to describe the pro-Vindex tribes as *Galbiani* and were actually eager for rebellion. Whatever view was taken of Vindex at the time—anti-Roman or anti-Neronian—it would hardly have needed pressure from the Rhineland tribes to persuade the armies to suppress him; if they wanted to desert Nero, they could do so on their own account, and they would of course have no hesitations against anything which could be labelled "Gallic rebellion". (But the "Gallic" view of Vindex, if expressed in any crude form, must fail before the next sentence, *hoc enim . . . indiderant,* for Galba's enemies could not have allowed the term Vindiciani to pass into oblivion if Galba had supported an enemy of Rome, see *JRS* 1957, 30, and Introd,. pp. 6 ff.).

17. Sequanis. Their capital was Vesontio (Besançon), which they held for Vindex. For their later activities see IV. 67.

ac deinde. H., followed by GG and Heubner, said that *deinde* was equivalent to *deinceps* (a rare word in T.), and saw a parallel in *Dial.* 26. 28; but there is no parallel there for using the word absolutely, i.e. without a noun or verb corresponding to what has gone before. If we take it to mean "the states further on", these might be the important ones in northern Narbonensis (esp. the Allobroges and Vocontii), or perhaps some in central Gaul, such as the Arverni, IV. 17. 15.

22. publice donatos, "that their communities had received rewards"—of land, (I. 8. 7., 53. 12), and by reduction in tribute and remission of customs duties (above 8. 5 n.): citizenship was now bestowed on individuals—I. 8. 4, but not (so far as our evidence goes) on whole communities. For *publice* cf. *publice . . . multati*, I. 66. 9. also IV. 55. 13, *A.* IV. 36. 5, 45. 3.

23. decimari . . . dimitti. The rumours were presumably based on what Otho had alleged in his speech, I. 37. 13, and on the events mentioned in I. 20. 12.

26. pertinaci pro Nerone fide. Nero had back paid 4m HS to Lugdunum after its fire in 65, *A.* XVI. 13. 3. The words are causal ablative with *facunda rumoribus*.

52. 1. sub ipsas . . . Decembris, "before that actual 1 December", i.e. in the last days of November 68. For the chronology see 7. 1 n. above.

3. cum cura adierat, "had made a careful visit of inspection". For *adire* of official visits by commanders cf. Livy 26. 21. 1. A more racy account of Vitellius' behaviour is given by Suet. *Vit.* 7. 3–8. 1.

redditi plerisque ordines . . . In cashiering or reinstating centurions probably neither Capito nor Vitellius was exceeding the functions normally permitted to a consular legate, though the known parallels (Cn. Piso in Syria in A.D. 18, *A.* II. 55, and Antonius Primus later in 69, III. 49. 8) could conceivably both have been actions *ultra vires.* See Th. Mommsen, *Römische Staatsrecht* ii 3 (1887), 265, 851.

5. sordis et avaritiam. For T.'s indecision about Capito, cf. I. 8. 14, 58. 9, and above all III. 62. 11. V. and others take the ablatives as instrumental with *mutaverat*; but by these means Vitellius was not altering Capito's regime, for Capito had done exactly the same. Surely they are ablatives "of circumstance", explaining *sordis et avaritiam.*

7. consularis legati mensura, ablative, and the meaning is not that a consular legate had no right to do these things (see n. to line 3), but that the cumulative effect of Vitellius' actions was measured by a more exalted standard than that normally applied to a legate.

8. humilis, "demeaning himself", see *TLL* s. v., II. B. 3.

10. imperitandi, Fisher' conjecture for M.'s *imperandi*, supported by G. and K.[1] But despite the parallel from IV. 25. 17, where the Gauls join Civilis *cupidine imperitandi*, the idea that Vitellius' soldiers wanted to "rule", i.e. that Vitellius was simply their puppet, is very sudden, and not really supported by anything said so far. For other suggestions see app. crit.: I take Wellesley's "eager enough for favours" to be a translation of *impetrandi*, though the absence of an object to this verb would surely be odd. Heubner suggests that *aviditatem imperandi* was a gloss on *vitia*: this is hazardous, but he is right (as were many previous editors) in feeling unhappy about the passage.

12. mali et strenui. The second adjective is unexpected and challenging—their very energy added to the evil. So Sall. *BC* 60. 4, *BI* 7. 1, and the epigram on Vinius, I. 48. 20, *pravus aut industrius eadem vi*.

13. Alienus Caecina. Born at Vicetia in the Transpadana, III. 8. 6, (but the *nomen* is Etruscan, and Cicero's client was born at Volaterrae) he was almost certainly legate of IV Macedonica, P. Fabia, *Studi romani* ii. 156, Ritterling, *RE* s.v. *Legio*, col. 1554.

Fabius Valens, without doubt the legate of legion I, I. 57. 1. His obituary is given at II. 62.

15. Verginii cunctationem, I. 8. 11. What exactly Valens alleged to Galba about Verginius is as uncertain as many other things about the events of 68.

20. panderet modo sinum. Almost certainly the metaphor is not from the sail, but from the toga spread to receive a gift: cf. Sen. *Epp.* 74. 6, *ad haec quae a Fortuna sparguntur sinum expandit*, Iuv. 14. 327, *si nondum implevi gremium, si panditur ultra*.

21. equestri familia, ignoto patre. For Verginius' family at Mediolanum see *Cisalpine Gaul*, 98 f. How much nobility was needed for a *princeps* is a more ample theme in Mucianus' speech, II. 76. 16 f.; and the position attributed to Verginius here, *tutum si recusasset*, is an interesting contrast with Mucianus' claims for Vespasian, a man no more nobly born.

23. consulatus, A.D. 34, 43, 47, the last two, as in the censorship of 48, as Claudius' colleague. L. Vitellius, son of a Roman knight in Augustus' service, entered the Augustan senate with his brothers, and made his reputation in the government of Syria in Tiberius' last years. His loyalty to Tiberius, and then also to Gaius and Claudius, secured him, after his death, a statue inscribed PIETATIS IMMOBILIS ERGA PRINCIPEM (Suet. *Vit.* 2–3), and he lived to see both his sons consuls in 48 (for Aulus' earlier career see above 9. 6 n.). He was the only man other than a *princeps* to hold a third consulate between Agrippa (*cos.* III 27 B.C.) and the accession of Vespasian.

All this is fine, but it is remarkable that at no point does Valens give Vitellius any actual argument for revolt against Galba, such as those given by Otho in I. 37–8, or by Mucianus in II. 76–7.

53. 4. legioni praeposuit, i.e. made him a legionary legate when he had held only the quaestorship. In the event, Caecina became consul without being tribune or praetor. But the story remains unclear. Was he posted forthwith from Baetica to Germany, and what happened about the charge Galba had against him?

6. flagitari, "put on trial" (= *postulari*), a Tacitean variant found only here.

9. universus adfuerat. This does not necessarily mean that legion XXI Rapax from Vindonissa had subscribed to the activities of the two legions at Mogontiacum—though that may well have occurred. The point is that the Mogontiacum force was at full strength, including *auxilia*, whereas Lower Germany was at that time represented only by *vexilla*. Yet it was the *vexilla*, and not Verginius' main force (above, 8. 11 and n.), which deserted Nero first. It was perhaps Valens who was in charge of the detachments sent to the Upper province, for we are told that he had been prominent in taking the oath to Galba, Plut. *G.* 10. 3.

11. Treviri ac Lingones. The attitude of the Rhineland Gallic tribes is shown from a different angle at IV. 56.

12. damno finium. I. 8. 7, 51, 22.

14. paganos. Originally the inhabitant of a *pagus* as distinct from an *urbs*, the word is used by T. and his contemporaries to mean "civilian", and this is later the normal usage of the jurists. There is no longer any implication about the birth-places of the people so described: see II. 14. 11 and 19 (Maritime Alps—but the chapter needs separate discussion), 88. 3 (near Rome), III. 24. 12 (Antonius to the cashiered praetorians now serving in his army—see Wellesley's n.), 43. 7, *ipsique pagani favore municipali et futurae potentiae spe* (Forum Iulii), 77. 10 (Campania), IV. 20. 8 (Rhineland); also Suet. *Aug.* 27. 1, *G.* 19. 2 (both on the Roman populace), Plin. *Epp.* X. 86 b., *et milites et pagani*. The change in meaning, though unmistakable, is not entirely easy to explain. It is assumed, e.g. by Kornemann, *RE* xviii. 2295 ff., to derive from a time when soldiers, or at least the legionaries and praetorians, came almost exclusively from cities: this, if right, provides important evidence about the principles of recruitment in earlier periods. It is unfortunate that the new usage was not noticed by Rostovtzeff, when in *SEHR* he argued that A.D. 69 saw a contest between legionaries and "city bourgeoisie". But although he was wrong (see index to his 2nd edn.) to overlook the new meaning of *paganus* in literary texts, it remains true that the word (and its cognates) still often carry the old meaning on inscriptions (see, e.g., n. 60 to his cap. VII).

54. 1. civitas Lingonum. In T. the phrase could mean either "the community" or "the tribal centre" (in this case Andematunnum = Langres). In most instances (but see I. 63. 7 n.) the context removes any ambiguity; and here the former meaning seems obvious.

2. dextras, hospitii insigne. Cf. II. 8. 12 (the Syrian army greeting the praetorians). The clasped hands were made of bronze, or sometimes of silver; and the custom was believed to originate from the Persian empire, Xen. *Anab.* II. 4. 1, Nepos, *Datames* 10. 1, *more Persarum*.

3. per principia, per contubernia, "through the headquarters block and the men's quarters".

6. pericula et contumelias, their suppression of Vindex, and Galba's subsequent treatment of Verginius and of themselves, I. 8. 8 ff.

13. tamquam ... pararetur, "the belief being that there was a plan to surround the legions with auxiliary regiments, and attack them". Hyginus, *de munit. castr.* 2, describes a camp in which several auxiliary regiments were enclosed by the barracks of legionary soldiers (who were *in vallo tendentes*), and some editors, followed by Heubner, suggest that the legionaries here suspected an attempt to reverse that arrangement. But was Hyginus' camp the normal *hiberna* of mid-first century troops on the frontiers, rather than one used by units on active service? It is more likely, though pre-69 evidence from the Rhineland is not decisive, that the majority of Upper German *auxilia* were quartered in forts away from the double legionary camp at Mogontiacum.

55. 1. sollemni ... sacramento. See 12. 3 n. above.

3. primorum ordinum. This, although a technical term for "chief centurions", here means the common soldiers in the front ranks, cf. I. 18. 13, *proximi militum*, the men who stood nearest to the tribunes and centurions.

6. primani ... sexta decima. These two groups each contains one of the legions (V and XV) brigaded together at Vetera.

7. imagines. For the emperor's statue on the platform see 36. 3 n. above.

10. isdem hibernis, at Mogontiacum (Mainz).

14. senatus ... nomina. See 12.4 n. above. The soldiers are not, even ostensibly, suggesting a return to the Republic: indeed in Republican days the military oath was taken to the commander, not to the SPQR. All they are doing, for the time being, is to proclaim the virtuous doctrine that the choice of a *princeps* is one for the senate and people. For *oblitterata*, "forgotten", cf. *Dial.* 8. 1, *A.* XI. 14.3, XIII. 23. 2; the army had not recently been accustomed to think about constitutional theory, and their *sacramentum* quickly seemed *inane* I. 56. 14.

16. ut in tumultu, "given the riot which was raging", cf. Livy XXX. 6. 4. They took the situation as an opportunity to behave (for they were in the plot) in a way senators would not normally behave.

17. non tamen ... locutus. Here Plut. *G.* 22 inserts a speech which clearly derives from the same source as that used by T. for Valens' speech in I. 52. Cf. Fabia, 17 f.

18. cui imputaretur, "with whom to establish a credit", cf. 38. 11 n. above. There was as yet no openly chosen candidate, though it is likely that Caecina and others knew they were acting for Vitellius.

56. 3. socordia innocens, "kept from guilt only by his indolence": cf. the *segnis innocentia* of Faenius Rufus, *A.* XIV. 51. 2.

4. quattuor centuriones. None of these men is elsewhere known, yet T. recites their names again in I. 59. 6. Were their descendants among his acquaintances?

8. propris sacramenti, the oath taken to Galba in the summer of 68; cf. I. 12. 3, 53. 10.

10. nocte ... secura est. The dates in the next chapter leave no doubt that T. meant this to be the night of 1–2 Jan., cf. Dessau, *Geschichte* (1926), II. 321. Mainz is about 112 miles from Cologne, but if the administration of the oath occurred at daybreak a fast rider could surely cover the ground in the day, Hölzapfel, *Klio*, 1913. 297.

15. legiones legatosque. i.e. those in the Lower German army. It is likely that Valens and others, if not Vitellius himself, were ready for the message from Upper Germany.

18. si concordia ... placeat, and so no war? The irony shows to perfection T.'s understanding of revolutionary slogans.

57. 1. proxima . . . hiberna, Bonna.

2. die postero. Suet. *Vit.* 8. 1 says the salutation, made by "the soldiers", was in the evening, *neque diei neque temporis ratione habita.* Hölzapfel, cit., suggests that it was the unlucky nature of all *dies postridiani,* here 2 Jan., which made the day unsuitable. This is probably right, but Suet., who has not said what day it was, may not have realized the point.

3. equitibus legionis, 120 men, Jos. *BI* III. 120.

6. speciosis . . . relictis, taken very closely from T.'s source, cf. Plut. *G.* 22, τοὺς καλοὺς ἐκείνους καὶ δημοκρατικοὺς εἰς σύγκλητον ὅρκους . . .

8. non penes . . . fuisse, "had not been on the side of the constitution". For *penes* see *A.* IV. 16, *plures . . . causas adferebat: potissimam penes incuriam virorum feminarumque;* for *rem publicam* see above, 55. 14 n. (and also 16. 1 n.); I cannot agree with Wellesley (tr.) that anyone had thought of "republican government".

10. corpore, opibus, ingenio, "in accordance with their various physical, material and moral resources" (Wellesley). *ingenio* would include any kind of support which could come from people's brains, whether their eloquence or their actual help in planning.

11. principes . . . castrorum, civil and military leaders, without any technical sense in either case. Even coloniae should not be taken too literally, though besides Colonia Agrippinensis there was certainly Augusta Trevirorum = Trier (probably a colony of Claudius, cf. Rau, *RE* vi *A* 2, col. 2321), and conceivably Andematunnum of the Lingones, *CIL* xiii. 2. 1, p. 85 (but see I. 78. 3 n.).

13. manipuli . . . miles, probably a tautology (except that *manipuli* should not include the cavalry), but "whole companies and the men in them" is a possible translation.
    viatica, "savings", *A.* I. 37, Suet. *Iul.* 68.
    balteos phalerasque. The *balteus,* from the left shoulder to the right hip, carried the sword, and could be decorated with gold or silver, Plin. *NH* 33. 152. *Phalerae,* part of the decorations given to soldiers for valour, were medallions worn on the chest. Lammert, *RE* xix. 2, col. 1659, describes finds of *phalerae,* including some of bronze from Vetera now in the British Museum (one bears the legend PLINIO PRAEFEC); see also J. Curle, *A Roman Frontier Post* (1911), 174.

15. instinctu et impetu, under the impulse of their own feelings, of the pressure put on them (by Valens, Caecina, and others), and on their greed. *Instinctus* and *impetus* are again joined by T. in a curiously different context, about Nero's poetry, *A.* XIV. 16; cf. also Plin. *Epp.* I. 22. 10.

58. 1. ministeria ... disponit. Some writers (e.g. A. M. Duff, *Freedmen in the Early Roman Empire* (1928), 179 f.) have perhaps exaggerated the significance of this. Vitellius is unlikely to have had freedmen of any consequence in Germany, and until he could acquire some (Blaesus, governor of Lugdunesis, helped him here, II. 59. 10), his obvious recourse was to use officers in his army. We cannot therefore tell what he intended as his permanent arrangements (though we know that his freedman Asiaticus later became notorious). Yet it is true that the employment of *equites* in important *ministeria* was a feature of Flavian government (Suet. *Dom.* 7. 2, *ILS* 1448 = MW 347); and Otho had an equestrian secretary (Secundus, Plut. *O.* 9).

One of Vitellius' appointments is seen on *ILS* 1447 = MW 338, a tribune of IV Macedonica who became the emperor's procurator *a patrimonio et hereditatibus et a libellis*, the pluralism reflecting the shortage of personnel.

3. vacationes ... ex fisco. 46. 21 n. above. It is obvious that Otho and Vitellius were acting independently, and that the grievance had been felt generally in the Roman army.

4. saepius ... raro. In what follows T. is hard put to it to justify these words. When he compares the two emperors, II. 31. 5, it is not to Vitellius but to Otho (despite his *clementiae titulus*, I. 71. 7) that he ascribes the vice of *saevitia*: for Vitellius the *primum specimen* was Dolabella's death, II. 64. 6. Suet., however, says Vitellius indulged in sadistic cruelty, as notorious as his *luxuria* (*Vit.* 13. 1. 14).

5. Pompeius Propinquus. I. 12. 1.

6. Iulium Burdonem. Later in the year important elements in the Lower Rhine fleet quickly joined the cause of Civilis, of whom Burdo may have been a friend. See IV. 16.

9. grata ... Capitonis. Cf. I. 8. 14. As Wolff pointed out (see also H.'s n.), the popularity is at first sight surprising, given that one of Capito's vices was *avaritia*, 7. 6, 52. 5: the former passage may record only the opinions of people in Rome, but in the latter he is remembered in the Rhineland on account of *sordis et avaritiam,* which is precisely what made Trebellius Maximus an object of hatred to the British army, I. 60. 1. But (see Heubner's n.) we need not suppose that the common soldiers suffered from Capito. He was probably accused of selling promotions to higher grades, and he also (IV. 13) had his enemies among the auxiliary officers.

12. stratis. See app. crit. Those (e.g. K.) who retain *statis* explain it as a past participle of *sistere*, but there appears to be no parallel. For *stratis* cf. Stat. *Silv.* II. 5. 1, *quid tibi constrata mansuescere profuit ira,* Verg. *Aen.* V. 763, *placidi straverunt aequora venti.* Not entirely convincing, perhaps; and Heubner argues that T. uses *stratus* to mean "removed" or the like only in contexts which imply the use of force, e.g. II. 43. 5, III. 25. 13, and that this is inappropriate here. But surely all T. means is that deliberate measures, not necessarily brutal ones, were taken to quell the men's passions.

59. 1. Iulius deinde Civilis. Why Civilis should have been sought as a victim by the Vitellians we are not told; perhaps he was considered to be a Galbian, just as later he posed as a supporter of Vespasian (see Book IV, *passim*). But there is nothing here to support Walser's doctrine that he was not, in his ultimate aims, a clear rebel from the Roman Empire. T. here, as in the later books, commits himself to the view that the Batavians, with their eight cohorts quartered in one place, were an uncertain quantity to any government. See Brunt, *Latomus*, 1960, 495 n.4.

4. quartae decima . . . auxilia. For the movements of XIV Gemina and these cohorts in 68 see Introd., p. 10 f.; for their subsequent relations II. 27 and 66. They were mounted men, *cohortes equitatae*, IV. 19. 5.

This passage, given that XIV Gemina was now in Illyricum and the cohorts in Gaul, has been used as important evidence that *auxilia* were always regarded as attached to a particular legion. On the other side it has been argued (e.g. Cheesman, *Auxilia* (1914), 49 ff.) that *auxilia* moved often from province to province, and that the auxiliary regiments of a single province, which might contain several legions, are treated as a single unit when the auxiliary troops are given discharge. But the latter argument can now be shown to be invalid, see *CIL* XVI. 175. The use, in epigraphy as well as literary texts, of phrases like *legio et auxilia eius* must imply some form of attachment, at the least that in normal times (of which this is not one) the *praefecti* of the auxiliary regiments were responsible to a legionary legate. But whether legio XIV had other auxilia assigned to it once the Batavians had departed, we are not told.

5. digressae. They were supposed to be going back to Britain, II. 27. 10. Vitellius again tried to send them there later in the year, II. 66. 7, but once more in vain. For their background, and their aims, see Brunt, cit., 501.

8. fidei crimine. See I. 71. 8.

9. Valerius Asiaticus. This man made his peace with the Flavians, to the extent of proposing honours for the victors while he was consul designate early in 70, IV. 4. 12. But he died soon afterwards (*CIL* VI. 1528 = MW 257), and for his widow, Vitellius' daughter (coins show but one), Vespasian arranged a distinguished marriage, Suet. *Vesp.* 14. 1. He was presumably (*PIR¹*) the son of the twice-consul from Vienna whom Messalina, with Vitellius' father's support, destroyed in A.D. 47. V. Scramuzza, *The Emperor Claudius* (1940), 87, uses his present connection with Vitellius to discredit T.'s story, *A*.XI. 1 ff., of L. Vitellius' part in the father's condemnation. That story does indeed present puzzles, but family feuds in Roman history seldom outweighed immediate problems of power. Asiaticus' position in Vienna, and his father's connection with the Rhine armies, made him a man worth conciliating by all contenders in 68–70; cf. Townend, *AJP* 1962, 127–12–9.

10. Iunius Blaesus, generally agreed to be the grandson of Q. Iunius Blaesus (*cos. suff.* A.D. 10), who was uncle to Seianus and the last non-member of the imperial house to be allowed the salutation *imperator*, *A.* III. 74. See *PIR²*, and Wellesley's n. to III. 38.

11. ala Tauriana, a name derived conceivably from Augustus' general (*cos.* II, 26 B.C.), more probably from a later member of his illustrious family. There are no other records of it at Lugdunum, but it may, in the Julio-Claudian period, have formed part of the 1200 men who were said to have been the garrison of Gaul, Jos. *BI* II. 373. Under Hadrian there was an ala Tauriana in Mauretania, *CIL* XIV. 73.

12. nec ... dubitatum. If assurances from Britain and Raetia had arrived before the Rhine armies moved, it seems almost certain, especially in view of the speed of Valens' march, I. 64. 1, that reliable contacts had been made with those two provinces (and also with Belgica and Lugdunensis) before the proclamation was made. This point has some bearing on subsequent chronology, but its main implication is to challenge any suggestion that the proclamation was spontaneous and unprepared.

60. 1. Trebellius Maximus, colleague of Seneca in a suffect consulate, almost certainly in 56, and governor of Britain from about 64, *Agr.* 16.

The account in the *Agricola* makes this chapter's elusive story even more difficult to interpret: it is unclear who was playing for what, and who was supporting Vitellius. In *Agr.* there is a quarrel between

Trebellius and his legates (ending with *pacta exercitus licentia, ducis salute*, though there is dispute about the exact reading), but nothing about the governor's flight. J. G. C. Anderson's edn. (1922) (cf. R. G. Collingwood, *Oxford History of England* ² (1937), 106) maintained that T. was there describing an earlier phase of the mutiny, perhaps not concerned with Vitellius: in the *Histories* Trebellius, an ardent Vitellian, who had to meet the charge *spoliatas et inopes legiones* because he was trying to send troops across the Channel. That the *Agricola* records an earlier "flight" by Trebellius is possible, see Ogilvie–Richmond, 203. But Anderson's interpretation of the *Histories* is unlikely (a) because the legate of legion XX who supported Vitellius later in the year, *Agr.* 7, was presumably the Roscius Coelius mentioned here, and (b) because it was after Trebellius' departure that troops were sent to Vitellius, and in substantial numbers, II. 57. 5. More probably, then, Trebellius, who was not well received by Vitellius, II. 65. 13, was advising caution against the Vitellian partisanship of the the legate; and *spoliatas ... legiones* could mean that bribes offered to the legionaries were withheld, i.e. that Trebellius was not one who *largiretur aliena*, I. 52. 10.

3. Coelius. Q. Roscius Coelius (the spelling used by the Arval Brothers) was suffect consul in 81: probably the man here, delayed in his career because of his Vitellian past; and probably also adoptive father to Pliny's polyonymous and important friend Pompeius Falco, *cos. suff.* 108, *ILS* 1035.

9. adgregantibus ... alisque. Whether these words are ablative absolute or governed by *desertus* (or even conceivably *proturbatus*) is unclear. The sense must be that Trebellius had tried to use the *auxilia* as a counterweight to the legions; but unlike the Flavian plotters in Germany later in the year, he had no success.

61. 1. adiuncto ... exercitu. For the forces sent a few weeks later to Vitellius see II. 57. 6. At this moment Britain had only three legions (Introd., p.18 f.), but it was probably already a province with an abnormally high complement of *auxilia*.

ingens viribus opibusque. With the British and German armies Vitellius had more than a third of the legions of the empire; and the reserve manpower of the Rhineland was believed to be vast, III. 15. 6, and King Agrippa's speech in Jos. *BI* II. 376. Agrippa also regards the Gauls as proverbial for wealth, ibid. 364, see I. 51. 3; and this fits with other evidence, cf. Rostovtzeff, *SEHR* ² 103 ff. Yet those resources had to be mobilized, *adlicere vel si abnuerent, vastare*: even after Galba's death many of the richer tribes were loyal to his memory.

2. duces ... destinavit. The numbers assigned to the two legates, 40,000 to Valens and 30,000 to Caecina, could be too large, the main argument being that too little is then left in the Rhineland to provide Vitellius with *tota moles belli* (line 10) and also to explain the operations described in Book IV. Anyway there is a distinction between what is said of legion V (Alaudae) and of XXI (Rapax). V took its eagle, and presumably went in greater strength than did the other legions of Lower Germany; but it left a recognizable force behind, IV. 35–6. XXI, without reservation, was the *robur* of Caecina's army, and in II.43. 2 it seems to be operating at full strength. So Caecina was probably allowed, after the Helvetian affair, I, 67 ff., to take it in its entirety, given that at this time a legion at Vindonissa was less vital for frontier defence than was the case further north.

For the eventual entry of their forces into Italy, supplemented for Valens' army by troops he picked up on the way, see Appendix.

4. Cottianis ... Poeninis, cf. IV. 68. 21. For the Cottian Alps, with a province embracing territory on both sides of the mountains, see *Cisalpine Gaul*, 26 f. The one pass through the Poeninae is the Great St. Bernard (8, 114 feet), which despite its name was certainly not crossed by the Carthaginians, and over which Caecina's crossing in later winter was a remarkable event.

9. addita ... auxilia. These were probably "Germani" from both sides of the Rhine, for II. 69. 7 speaks of *Gallorum auxilia, ingens numerus* who were recruited at the outset of the rebellion and after Vitellius' victory were sent back from Italy to their homes; they would naturally be from friendly tribes, including the Treveri and others which were often accounted as German. For Batavos Transrhenanosque See II. 17. 11.

63. 3. Hispaniae. I. 76. 3.

6. fortunam. 10. 15 n. above.

10. strenuis ... metumque. For the construction see 6.3 n. above.

11. nomen ... Caesarem. So also Plut G. 22. 7, Suet. *Vit.* 8. 2. All Vitellian coins and inscriptions show the title Germanicus: some eastern coins show the name Caesar, which for some reason he continued to resist, II. 62. 9, though at the last he took it, III. 58. 17.

14. ipso profectionis die. See Appendix. Köster (see I. 63. 1 n.) reckoned that Valens started directly the rebellion had received messages of support from Britain and Raetia; he took this to mean about 15 Jan. Almost incredibly early given his premises: but if British support had been assured *before* the proclamation (59. 12 n. above), this date is entirely possible. What matters most is the evidence about the news of Galba's death.

Suet. *Vit.* 9. 1, says the news reached Vitellius at Cologne before the armies moved, but he is highly inaccurate elsewhere about the Vitellian rising (cf. *O.* 8), and we should trust the precise statement of T., 64. 1, that Valens got the news at Toul, 340 km from Cologne (or on Köster's computation fourteen days' march). Now the news of the New Year rebellion at Mainz reached Rome in nine days, 12. 1 n. above, and we can reasonably expect that Vitellius' agents (for surely, whatever the extent of his detailed planning, a commander of his eminence would have his agents) would have alerted him with not much less speed: in addition, Otho's government, for their own reasons, would be sending quick messages to the armies. Possibly all these dispatches had to reach Cologne before they were passed to Valens, but some responsible agent at Mainz, or even Windisch, might well have communicated with Valens directly. Consequently, though for different reasons, Köster's 15 Jan. is probably not too early for the departure: it could be a few days too late. If this be right, it is clear proof that the rising had been carefully planned, especially as parts of Valens' army had to come south from Xanten and Neuss.

(The Helvetii, I. 67. 3, had not heard of Galba's death when the events described in that chapter began. But that passage helps little: the exact point in time is not defined, for the tenses imply that Caecina had not yet reached Vindonissa, see n. ad loc. and anyway the tribe would not get official news.)

63. 1. et Treviros . . . Divoduri. The march presumably started up the Rhine, where the detachment of Valens' legion I could join the column at Bonn. Then up the Mosel through Trier to Metz; across the Meuse near Toul, and up the Marne valley to Langres; over to the Saône valley and down it to Lyon. Then passing through Vienne and Valence they ascended the Drôme valley, through Luc and the col de Cabre to Gap; up the Durance to Briançon; and so over Mt. Genèvre to come down on Turin.

The itinerary and its timing was analysed in a careful dissertation by F. Köster (Münster, 1927), who offered a chronology taking account of distances and road difficulties, and also of the events which retarded the army on its way. The details are clearly vulnerable, expecially those which concern the end of the journey. But Köster's analysis has stood the test of time, and it is worth listing the dates at which he thought the army entered various centres, because they provide a fair guide to subsequent chronology.

Augusta Trevirorum (Trier)	21 January
Divodurum (Metz)	25 ,,
Toullium (Toul)	28 ,,
Andematunnum (Langres)	2 February
Cabillonum (Chalon-sur-Saône)	9 ,,
Lugdunum (Lyon)	15 ,,
Vienna (Vienne)	17 ,,
Lucus (Luc)	28 ,,
Vapincum (Gap)	2 March
Brigantio (Briançon)	20 ,,
Augusta Taurinorum (Turin)	30 ,,

7. excidio civitatis. See 54. 1 n. above. Does T. mean, here or in I. 69. 2, ruin of the urban centre, or extermination of the tribe? There can be no confident answer, but probably he would have thought that the first practically implied the second.

10. cum ... precibus, taken by H., and seemingly by *TLL*, as Hendiadys, "prayers offered by the magistrates". It is surely, since whole crowds came out in supplication, much more nearly a zeugma, "with their magistrates leading, and with entreaties".

64. 1. nuntium. 62. 14 n. above.

2. civitate Leucorum. of which Ptolemy calls the centre Τούλλιον or Τοῦλλον (Toul); the tribe lay between Mosel and Marne. Köster, 21, suggests that the army reprovisioned here, after its fourteen days' march.

4. cunctatio exempta est. This applies to Gallic tribes which the army had not yet reached: many of them had supported Vindex and been rewarded by Galba. The Treviri and Lingones, and possibly also the Mediomatrici and Leuci (cf. *alias civitates* I. 53. 12), had been ardent Vitellians from the start.

7. cohortium intemperie. M. Woodside, *TAPA* 1937, 281, suggests that the cohorts were expressing disapproval of Otho's grant of *civitat* to the Lingones. But even if there was such a grant, see I. 78. 3 n., news of it could hardly yet have arrived; and anyway it could not have been blamed on the Vitellians.

13. Aeduos. The army has now entered Lugdunensis, and the Saône valley. Cabillonum was an Aeduan town, Köster, 8.

14. pecuniam atque arma. At Vienna, I. 66. 9, arms were surrendered for security reasons, but here probably for use by Valens' army.

16. cohortem duodevicensimam. There was a cohort at Lugdunum at least from Tiberius' early days, *A.* III. 41, mainly to guard the mint. Despite doubts implied by Durry, 12 n. 6, it must have been an urban cohort: to make an auxiliary regiment the garrison of a Roman colony was no part of the policies of that period. But the number XVIII is not confirmed from epigraphy: there was a *cohors XIII urbana*, probably early, *ILS* 2124–6, and at uncertain date a *cohors XVII Lugduniensis a moneta*. The urban cohorts must often have moved about: Vespasian placed his *I Flavia urbana* at Lugdunum, *ILS* 2119, but it was soon moved to Carthage.

17. Manlius Valens. A man of this name was consul in 96 in his ninetieth year, Dio = Xiph. 67. 14, and *Fasti*, but if he was identical with any homonym it would be with the legionary legate in Britain in 50, *A.* XII. 40. The man here was surely younger than either.

18. bene ... meritus. Heubner suggests that his chief service had been to bring the well-born and wealthy Blaesus over to the Vitellian cause.

20. infamaverat ... laudatum. Köster, 59, argues that the praise must have been given at a council held by Vitellius before the army left Cologne; and that T.'s source (Pliny?) inferred "secret charges" from the fact that Fabius was given command over Manlius, though the two were hitherto of equal standing. In other words, the source, hostile to Fabius, inferred that he had been behaving in character, cf. *et fovit Verginium et infamavit*, III. 62. 11. All this could be: it is certainly probable that the praise was given at Cologne, for there would have been no point in sending it by dispatch from Lugdunum and accompanying it with *criminationes*.

65. 1. veterem ... discordiam. The foundation of Lugdunum in 43 B.C. followed the expulsion of some Italians by the Allobroges, Dio 46. 50. 4. Vienna, the centre of the Allobroges, was made a Latin colony by Augustus, or so it would seem, (evidence in F. Vittinghoff, *Römische Kolonisation und Bürgerrechtspolitik* (1952), 29. 3), and was then given full Roman citizenship by Claudius, or possibly Gaius, *ILS* 212, II. 15. No doubt it had lost territory to Lugdunum originally, and had been trying to use the success of the Galbian party to get it back.

2. multae ... clades. The disturbances in Gaul in late 68 were clearly more serious than anything described in detail by extant sources.

4. reditus ... in fiscum. For *fiscus* see above, 46. 21 n. Did T. here find the word in his source or convert into these terms some such word as *publicaverat*?

occasione irae, "making his resentment a pretext", as Nero had done after the revolt of Vindex, Suet. *Nero* 40. 4. There is no need, with H. and editors who followed him, to confine the diverted revenues to the grant made by Nero in 65 (51. 26 n. above): as well as owning land like other important towns, Lugdunum probably exacted tolls on the Rhône; and Galba was desperately short of funds.

6. uno amne discretis. Lugdunum was on the right bank of the Rhône just below the Saône confluence, Vienna on the left bank about 30 km lower down.

9. conscriptas . . . legiones. Though the plural need not mean more than *legionarii* (above, 11. 6 n.) and though the Lugdunenses are clearly exaggerating, this is a significant piece of evidence about the seriousness of Vindex' military preparations and about the status in society of his supporters; cf. Jos. *BI* IV. 440.

13. cuncta illic externa. The Vindex war could be seen as *velut externum* because it was fought *inter legiones Galliasque*, i.e. between the regular Roman army and Gallic levies led by the chief men in Romanized (often enfranchised) Gallic cities, see previous n. But the palpably tendentious plea here cannot be allowed to refute the view that it was essentially a *bellum civile*, see Introd., pp. 6 ff.

14. partem exercitus. Syme, *RR* 478, took this to refer to the military potential among Lugdunum's own citizens. This is attractive, but at this moment the Lugdunenses could point more convincingly to the presence in the city of I Italica and other forces. It is unfortunate that we do not know whether the legion was already there during the Vindex war, see Introd., p. 11.

66. 2. duces partium, a phrase used often from II. 87 onwards of the Flavian leadership, meaning sometimes the party headquarters, sometimes the council of war in the field. Here it is unlikely that there was consultation with Vitellius at Cologne: Valens and the other *legati* are likely to have taken some tribunes and senior centurions into their councils.

4. velamenta et infulas, as at Cremona, III. 31. 13, and see Heubner's n. for parallels in Livy. The *velamenta* were boughs of laurel or olive, bound with wool.

5. vestigia, "feet"; again see Heubner for parallels, this time from poetry.

6. trecenos . . . sestertios. 300 HS a man, if the *auxilia* were included (but perhaps they got less), required at least 12 m. HS. For the legionaries it would mean a third of their annual pay.

7. vetustas dignitasque coloniae. See 65. 1 n. above. The impertinence of Lugdunum's claim to be the unique *colonia* is now exposed.

9. publice ... militem, "the town as such was disarmed, and its inhabitants assisted the troops with all kinds of supplies". For *promisci* (or *promiscui*) in this sense see *GG* 1210 B. The commoner meaning, "ordinary", though accepted by H., makes little sense here; but an alternative possibility is "indiscriminately", cf. II. 69. 11, *promiscae missiones* (so Alford).

10. fama constans, still current when the army reached Ticinum, II. 29. 3 f. When the army there ransacked Valens' quarters and (presumably) found no gold, they forgave him, but T.'s source remained hostile: cf. Köster, 37.

14. lento deinde agmine ... The route to the Alps which starts by ascending the Drôme valley (63. 1 n. above) is described in the *Itin. Antoninianum* (ed. Cuntz, 357). There seems to have been no recognized road from Lugdunum or Vienna through Grenoble to the Mt. Cenis; but in any case Valens probably wanted, for money-raising purposes, to come south to the Vocontian country.

The Vocontii had two centres, Vasio (Vaison) far to the south, and Lucus, Plin. *NH*. III. 37: there was also the less Romanized town of Dea (Die) on the Drôme, for which see Vittinghoff, cit., 65 n. 1. T. tells us nothing of this, nor of the long march under winter conditions from Lucus to the pass, which on Köster's reckoning took three weeks of the journey. It is surely not about this part of Narbonensis that T. is "full and accurate" (Syme, 806), though it is a different matter about the region near his father-in-law's birthplace, II. 12 ff. The present context illustrates rather the more general judgement made by Syme, 170, about T.'s narrative of the march, that he is concerned not with times and stages, but with "the behaviour of men and armies when the restraints of peace are suddenly removed".

16. venditante. The *stativa*, with actual construction of camps as well as actual billeting, were what the landowners and magistrates chiefly wanted to avoid. But it was also worth paying for long detours being made when the army was near their estates or towns.

17. magistratus civitatum. These would be mainly *praefecti* of *pagi* (O. Hirschfeld, *Kleine Schriften* (1913), 75). But Brigantium in the Cottian province had *duoviri*, *CIL* xii. 95, and T. here calls Lucus a *municipium* (Vittinghoff, cit., 44 n. 2, argues that it was in fact a Latin colony).

20. sic ad Alpes perventum. In the last week of March (above 63. 1 n.), by which time the early operations in North Italy (II. 17 ff.) had taken place, and Otho himself had left Rome, I. 89. 18 n., and Appendix pp. 265 f.

67. The topography of the Helvetian affair has often been closely studied, e.g. by F. Stähelin, *Die Schweiz in römischer Zeit*[3] (1948), 187 ff., G. Walser, *Schweizerische Zeitschrift für Geschichte* (1954), 260 ff., A. Deman, *Collection Latomus* 23 (1956), 90 ff. But some of the identifications have been over-confident, largely because the following points have been misunderstood (on all of them I owe much to Heubner's n.).

(a) the initial events, i.e. the Helvetian refusal to accept Vitellius, the legion's appropriation of the pay for the fort, and the arrest of the Vitellian embassy to Pannonia, all occurred before Caecina reached Vindonissa. This is shown by the pluperfect *rapuerant* (line 5), and by the imperfect *retinebant* (line 10) which describes the situation when Caecina arrived. The legion had taken swift action (*festinatio*) directly they heard, by rapid messenger, of Vitellius' proclamation.

(b) There is nothing to indicate that it was the garrison of the fort which arrested the embassy.

(c) We have therefore no evidence about the route taken by the embassy. If (a) above be right, it started not from Caecina's army at Vindonissa, but from Vitellian headquarters at Cologne; and this is what one would expect, for it was a matter of urgency to make contact with Illyricum directly Vitellius had been proclaimed. For the embassy's intended destination see n. to line 8 below.

3. memoria clari nominis, for Caesar had praised their *virtus* over that of all other Gauls, *BG* I. 1. 4.

de caede . . . abnuentes. Although they are not recorded as having assisted Vindex, they evidently thought of themselves as Galbians. Whether the legion had yet heard of Galba's death we cannot tell.

5. unaetvicensimae . . . rapuerant, probably a deliberate play on the legion's name Rapax: cf. E. Norden, *Germ. Urgeschichte* (1923) 252 n. 1.

6. olim . . . tuebantur. *olim*, as often in T. (cf. I. 60. 3 and GG, but contrast line 2 above), means "for a long time past", and we need not assume that the arrangement was discontinued after 69. How far back it went is uncertain, but Caesar says, *BG* I. 28. 4, that he deliberately resettled the Helvetii to keep out invading Germans. For similar use of local units 70. 17, *concitis auxiliis*, II. 14. 9, *Ligurum cohors, vetus loci auxilium*.

8. epistulis. Heubner takes this to be a true plural, i.e. one dispatch for the legion at Carnuntum, a second for that at Poetovio. But there was only one centurion; the matter was urgent; and the plural is common enough in T. (V. cites several cases, and there are others in Pliny's *Letters*) to mean one letter, on analogy with *litterae*. If the destination was only one camp, Poetovio seems the more likely: it was important, if possible, to anticipate an approach from the government in Rome, and there is reason (see III. 1. 2) to think that at this time it was the headquarters camp of the Pannonian army. In that case, pace Stähelin, cit., the embassy probably planned to cross the Arlberg into Noricum, though there was no military road over that group of passes.

13. in modum municipii, "which had grown to the size of a town": cf. IV. 22. 4 (the settlement near the Vetera camp), *A.* 20. 4 (Nauportus). The place, frequented for its waters amid beautiful scenery, has always been identified as Baden on the Limmat (Aquae Helveticae), just east of Vindonissa.

14. Raetica auxilia, already in the Vitellian party, 59. 12. Early in the second century there were four *alae* and up to fourteen cohorts, of various origins, stationed in Raetia, cf. *CIL* XVI, App. V. Probably less in 69, if the *Raetorum iuventus* was then, but not later (I. 68. 6 n.), doing a significant part of the work.

68. 3. non arma noscere, non ordines sequi, a standard phrase for incompetence on active service, cf. II. 12. 17, *non castra non ducem noscitantibus,* 93. 2, *non principia noscere* (of the Vitellians in Rome), with also *A.* IV. 25, *non arma non ordo non consilium* and *Germ.* 30. 2, *nosse ordines.* Perhaps "showed no training in weapons or battle-order".

4. obsidio. The reference cannot be to the single *castellum* of I. 67. 6. There were several such forts in this region, normally of cohort size (for examples from an earlier period see C. M. Wells, *The German policy of Augustus* (1972), 35 ff.), and the Helvetii would not have contemplated crowding their army into one of them; moreover they were part of the active defence of the frontier, and their walls would not have been allowed to crumble. The walls are probably those of the capital, Aventicum, see line 13 below.

6. ipsorum Raetorum iuventus, cf. II. 12. 15 (Maritime Alps), 58. 6, *ingens Maurorum numerus,* III. 5. 13 (Noricum). Similar units do not figure in records of the next century of the Empire, and it may be that they were an untidy element in army organization eliminated by the Flavians (though if we relied on epigraphical evidence alone we should not know of their existence in the Julio-Claudian period either).

The contrast between the discipline of the Raeti and that of the Helvetii is marked. Although ethnic titles of regiments are not an entirely secure guide, it is noticeable that a dozen or more cohorts of Raeti are known from *diplomata* of the next century, only one of Helvetii.

9. Vocetium, probably the Bözberg, through which, east of Windisch, an important road-pass ran between Gaul and Raetia. See Stähelin, cit., 194, though he also suggests that the name *mons Vocetius* was applied to a larger group of Jura outcrops, both to north and to south.

10. cohorte Thraecum. If they were actual Thracians, specialized in archery, their employment here would have been clearly deadly.

13. Aventicum. Avenches lies about midway between Fribourg and the lake of Neuchâtel, on the ancient road from the neighbourhood of Vindonissa to the northern side of Lake Geneva. It became Colonia Pia Flavia Constans Emerita Helvetiorum, Stähelin, cit., 205, possibly as Vespasian's recognition of the tribe's opposition to Vitellius. For its earlier prosperity see Syne, cit., 136.

16. Vitellii. The affair had now raised important questions of politics and also strategy (communications with Illyricum). But I suspect that the ultimate fate of the tribe was something which would always have been referred to an emperor, especially if the man in the field had other cares.

69. 2. placabilem. Note that here to 75. 10 a page in M. is missing.

civitatis. See above. 54. 1, 63. 7 nn. Here the word immediately follows 68. 14, where the meaning "commune" is almost certain, and immediately precedes the last line of this chapter, where that meaning is hardly less probable. Yet Heubner subscribes to the view of V. and H. that what they wanted was the destruction of the town of Aventicum.

7. ut est mos ... See app. crit. But there is no compelling need for emendation, and for these three words see I. 80. 12, and parallels from other authors cited by Heubner. *Mox* at the beginning of the sentence would suggest an interval after *animum mitigavit*; but this is surely the description of a single scene at which Claudius Cossus showed his oratorical powers.

70. 1. sententiae. i.e. what he should do about the Helvetii, not whether he should press on into Italy, about which his earlier instructions must have been that he should do so at the earliest opportunity.

2. transitum parans. Yet we may still be in early February, see

Appendix pp. 264 ff. If I. 89. 17 can be taken at its face value, the actual crossing of Caecina's main army was reported to Rome before Otho left on 14 March. This was astonishingly early, but even so Caecina had time for elaborate preparations, and perhaps also for considering an invasion of Noricum (see 16 n. below).

3. alam Silianam. An *ala* of this name was in Lower Germany in 78, *CIL* xvi. 30 = *ILS* 9052. It may have owed its name to C. Silius, governor of Upper Germany under Tiberius, but we do not know how long it had been in Africa. For other units remaining in North Italy after the *bellum Neronis* see II. 17. 7, Syme, *AJP* 1937, 10 ff.

4. proconsule ... in Africa. II. 97.

6. exciti. See app. crit., and for the movement of troops in early 68 Introd., pp. 9 ff. Heubner accepts *acciti*, i.e. "summoned (to Italy)", but for the following reasons his grounds are not compelling.

We can agree that, if T. be right, (a) the *ala* was in Africa when it was needed for dispatch to the East, (b) either before or after it reached Alexandria (the German *vexilla* actually got there, I. 31. 19), it was summoned "back" to Italy and stayed there (*manentes*), (c) it was needed for the *bellum Vindicis*, and so wherever it may have landed it went to the Po valley, where we find it now.

Heubner claims further that (1) *revocati* implies that it came back to the place from which it had recently embarked, i.e. it had crossed from Utica (?) to Brundisium (?) before it started eastward, and that consequently (ii) it had been ordered in the first instance to Italy, making *acciti* the more appropriate participle.

But surely the point of *revocati* is that these and many other units were recalled from the operation for which they had set out because they were needed *opprimendis Vindicis coeptis*, I. 6. 13. There need be no thought, by T. or his source, about the port from which this *ala* had last embarked. And anyway why should it have gone from Africa to Brundisium? Would not these advance units have proceeded to Alexandria by the most direct route, rather than being brought first to a place "Woher die ganze Aktion ihren Ausgang nahm" (Heubner, 148 line 8)? They were not part of the main body, but *praemissi*.

7. decurionum, commanders of *turmae*, Dom. Dob., 53, XVI.

10. transpadanae regionis. In the Augustan division of Italy Regio XI in the extreme north-west, bounded by Alps, Po, and Adda, was called Transpadana, Plin. *NH* III. 123: it included all these four towns, and it can reasonably be described (line 13) as *latissima Italiae pars*. In II. 17. 5 T. loosely speaks of the *ala* as having won the whole area between Alps and Po, but he mentions no early Vitellian operations east of Cremona (which was on the western edge of the adjoining Regio X).

It is interesting to find no mention of the veteran colony Augusta Praetoria: presumably its military potential had disappeared, see *Cisalpine Gaul*, 25.

14. Gallorum ... cohortibus. Presumably T. refers to the ethnic titles of the regiments, though these can be no sure guide to the origins of the men who composed them: see (e.g.) Cheesman, cit., 73 ff.

15. Germanorum vexillis. These would be some of the German *auxilia* given to each commander at the outset, I. 59. 9. Whether they included cavalry is uncertain (the plural *alae* in line 19 is not decisive), but *vexilla* can undoubtedly mean detachments from any type of regiment: cf. I. 31. 17.

ala Petriana. The *ala Augusta Gallorum Petriana* (origin of *cognomen* unknown) was at Mogontiacum in 56, *ILS* 1491, and in Britain after 70: its *praefectus*, evidently an ardent Vitellian, crossed to Africa to encourage L. Piso early in 70, IV. 49. 10.

16. paulum cunctatus ... One can at once dismiss the theory of Henderson, 66 f., that Caecina's idea was not an attack on Noricum, but a descent into Italy down the Adige after a crossing of the Arlberg and Brenner. With no military road across the Arlberg or other *Raetica iuga*, cf. Stähelin, cit., 193, 367, such an operation would take time, even when the snow melted; and even if it could be effected, there could be few less healthy places for Caecina's relatively small army than Verona, where it might be caught by the Danubian troops advancing through Aquileia, and pinched between them and the Othonian army of Italy before Valens arrived.

The motives ascribed by T. himself to Caecina for pressing on to Italy are so compelling that it is difficult to believe that he even hesitated once the news from the ala Siliana reached him: quite apart from the prospects of *gloria* (a characteristically Tacitean addition to his source?), it was his clear duty to protect his advanced units and contain the Othonians in the Po valley until he was reinforced. Yet T.'s source may have recorded something genuine, namely the delay which at first seemed inevitable before the Great St. Bernard became passable. Caecina may at least have considered a preliminary diversion, with part of his forces, to deal with potential trouble from Noricum. That province did not have the strategic importance it possessed in the Flavio-Vitellian war (cf. III. 5; Hardy, 126, does not bring out the difference between the two situations); but strengthening of the Vitellian left flank against a possible westerly move of troops from the

Danube was a project which Caecina's council might have responsibly debated. But in the outcome it became clear that the Norican procurator was acting only defensively, *interruptis fluminum pontibus*, and Caecina decided on an early Alpine crossing against all obstacles.

On this passage see also Momigliano, 130, who emphasized the difficulties of a winter crossing, but thought that the story here was invented by an amateur who failed to understand the reasons for Caecina's halt.

17. Petronium Urbicum, mentioned on a Norican inscription, *CIL* iii. 11557.

18. fluminum pontibus, the Inn above all, III. 5. 14, but also possibly the Danube above Lorch.

22. subsignanum ... agmen, the legionaries and their baggage train, cf. II. 87. 4. This time (cf. 66. 14 n. above) T.'s failure to describe Caecina's military feat may be due to his (or his source's) prejudice against the commander rather than to unwillingness to follow those of his predecessors who liked the picturesque (Syme, 170). We cannot here be at a later date than early March: *hibernis adhuc Alpibus* is one of the greatest understatements in military history.

71–90 *Otho as Princeps in Rome*

71. 1. interim. We go back to the morrow of Galba's murder, on which day Plut. *O.* 1, puts the reconciliation with Celsus; see above, 47. 8 n., with the possibility that T. was right in placing the sacrifice on the evening of the same day.

Heubner and others imply that T.'s division of the story and also the way he recounts the Celsus affair play down, perhaps deliberately, the dramatic change in Otho's behaviour depicted in the early chapters of Plut. *O.* Yet in speaking of Otho's ἀναγκαῖα πολιτεύματα and of his need δημαγωγεῖν, Plut. *O.* 4 is surely emphasizing, no less than T., that Otho was the slave of the armies which elevated him: all his attempts at conciliation, even though many are directed at winning senatorial support, are conditioned by these beginnings, see Klingner, *passim*. So chapters 51–70 may have been inserted where they are because T. was increasingly feeling that he had neglected the formidable events in the Rhineland rather than because he wanted to present an idiosyncratic view of Otho. As to the latter, what does impress the reader is the emphasis on Otho's restless activity, something which Plut. ignores. Yet it remains true that *falsae virtutes et vitia reditura* are words more openly hostile than anything in Plut.

3. decorem imperii, "the behaviour expected of an emperor", but in T.'s view Otho soon fell from grace, I. 77. 4, 82. 8.

4. Marium Celsum. 14. 4 n. above.

8. ultro imputavit, "actually claimed credit for setting such an example", the same two words used of Paulinus and Proculus when they claimed not loyalty but treachery, II. 60. 7. For *imputare* see 38. 11 n. above.

10. deos testis . . . See app. crit. (note that M. is still missing). Nipperdey's emendation, accepted by K., is appropriate to a reconciliation which took place not in the palace but on the Capitol. Plut. says nothing of an oath here, but his sentence at least makes it unlikely that the word *hostis* was in his source. At the same time it is here peculiarly obvious that his source was not T., cf. Fabia, 37.

72. 2. Ofonius. The name is read here (Ophonius) and in *A.* XIV. 51 without any initial S, see *PIR*[1] s.v. He succeeded Burrus as praetorian prefect in 62: his prefecture of the *vigiles* is not elsewhere recorded.

3. impudicia, a misprint in the O.C.T.

7. postremo . . . proditor. Both Plut. *G.* 8. 2, 13. 2 and Jos. *BI* IV. 492 agree that Tigellinus betrayed Nero, but in no source is there any account of his part in the events of 68.

10. Titi Vinii . . . defensus. Suet. *G.* 15. 2 blames Galba; possibly from an anti-Galbian source (Cluvius?), cf. Paratore, 483. Plut. *G.* 17, though he develops the story of Vinius' alliance with Tigellinus, omits any reference to Vinius' daughter.

11. filiam, the Crispina of I. 47. 11. Her life would have been in danger from Nero once it was known that Vinius had promoted Galba. It is interesting that Tigellinus so quickly sought an *effugium* in Vinius, i.e. that he thought Galba had a good chance of defeating Nero.

17. Palatium, here fairly certainly the Palatine hill, see 17. 8 n. above.

19. donec. T.'s artistry conceals gaps in the narrative. Above all, in contrast to Plut., he has omitted Otho's own part in the condemnation.
    Sinuessanas aquas, *A.* XII. 66. The baths, near Mondragone, on the borders of Latium and Campania, are now known as the Terme di San Ricco.

73. 1. Calvia Crispinilla, a woman of high rank (ἐπιφανής, Dio 63. 12), who owned considerable property in Histria and Pannonia, to judge from *amphorae* and tiles stamped with her name. From one *amphora*, inscribed TRAUL ET CRISP, Dessau, *ILS* 8574, concluded that she married the Roman knight Sex. Traulus Montanus, condemned in 48, *A.* XII. 36. About her *consulare matrimonium* we have no clue. Plut. never mentions her, and it could be that T. derived the whole item from Cluvius, see Townend, *AJP* 1964, 353.

4. transgressa . . . molita. For Macer's part in this affair see Introd. p. 14 Crispinilla presumably crossed to Africa while Nero was mobilizing support against Vindex and Galba; but the arrest of the cornships surely happened after Nero's collapse, since the Neronian government would not have wanted to add to their difficulties by provoking famine in Rome. Already they had been blamed for high prices, Suet. *Nero* 45. 1.

T. tells us practically nothing about the timing or effects of the shortage, but Galba's CERES AUGUSTA coinage (*RIC* I, Galb. 52–3) was probably an attempt to allay fears about the coming winter. The legend is continued by Otho; and Vitellius put out ANNONA AUG S. C. and CERES AUG. See R. F. Newbold, *Historia*, 1972, 316. For the vital importance of Africa to Rome's supply see Jos. *BI* II. 383, 386 (allegedly eight months of the year, compared with Egypt's four).

74. 1. crebrae . . . epistulae. From this point until the end of the Book it becomes important to know whether the items are presented by T. in the order in which they actually occurred. The first, relatively minor, problem arises here. Plut. *O.* 4 recounts the exchange of letters only after the news arrived that the Danube armies had declared for Otho; (in T. *A.* 76); and both Fabia, 44 f., and Heubner argue that this was what the "common source" said. Yet there is room for thinking T. was right.

Certainly the recall of Galba's embassy, which in view of the chicanery recorded in I. 20. 13 ff. cannot have got far, must have happened directly after his murder; and the reconstitution of the delegation, with the addition of praetorians, should not have taken long. This new party doubtless carried the first of the *crebrae epistulae,* the one which led T. to make Otho alone the subject of the chapter's first sentence: the second sentence takes us to a period at which both contenders were writing. It is conceivable, though improbable, that the first message was not *delivered* before its carriers had heard about the Danubian support: we cannot tell how fast the embassy travelled (see n. to line 11 below). But other letters followed, one of which, stiffening Otho's terms, may have secured an entry in the "source" and led to Plut.'s dating.

2. offerebant. About the nature of Otho's offers Suet. *O.* ᴄ 1 is more precise: Otho was to marry Vitellius' daughter and give his father-in-law a share in the empire. On the latter point Dio 64. 10, agrees: Plut., like T., suggests a more limited offer.

3. e quietis locis, "one of the quiet spots", an awkward piece of Latin restored by Madvig to a passage on which M.'s copyists give little help; but the general sense is clear. The favourite spot was Campania, cf. III. 66. 10.

7. rursus, simply meaning that after the recall of the first embassy another was sent in the same direction: see Drexler, in Bursian 1929, 360. Fabia, *Rev. Phil.* 1913, 52 ff., criticized T. for forgetting that on the earlier occasion the forces at Lugdunum were not known to be among the defectors. But there was no need to spell this out here, and Fabia would not have known the facts but for T.'s own earlier narrative.

9. specie senatus, "ostensibly in the Senate's name", but not necessarily implying (as some translators and *GG* 1532 suggest) that the Senate's part was unreal: cf. I. 13. 17, *in Lusitaniam specie legationis seposuit* (Otho was a genuine *legatus*, but what mattered to Nero was that he should be *called* one, as an excuse for removing him from Rome). It would have been inconsistent with Otho's policy in the period covered by the next few chapters not to consult the Senate on such a matter. To T., who regarded the Senate as a pawn in the game, the question whether an actual s. *c.* had been passed was unimportant.

11. praetoriani ... remissi. Fabia, *Sources* 44 f., followed by Heubner, insisted that the praetorians could not have been allowed to proceed further than Lugdunum. If Fabius Valens had reached Lugdunum ahead of them (Köster's date for entry is 15 Feb.), that could have been so. But if he was still short of it, then Manlius Valens would surely have sent them on to someone authorized to listen to them, rather than keeping them in the town where they might start fraternizing with his troops. The speed of their march is impossible to determine confidently; but if we compare the embassy sent by Tiberius to the mutinous Danubian legions in A.D. 14, *A.* I. 16 ff., it seems that a similar party could reach Siscia (or Poetovio?) from Rome between 17 and 26 Sept., see R. Seager, *Tiberius* (1972), 60 f. For Lugdunum, the embassy would have left Rome by sea, and could well have reached the town by the earliest days of February.

The civilian members of the embassy went on past Valens to Vitellius. Since they were only too willing to be *retenti*, there was no reason to stop them.

per simulationem officii, "under pretence that they performed some duty", i. e. of acting as a bodyguard to the main delegation. Their real purpose was to watch the behaviour of the senators, but still more to make contact with the Vitellian legionaries.

12. epistulas ... Germanici exercitus. C. M. Kraay, *Num. Chron.*

1952, 78 ff., suggested that it was these dispatches which were accompanied by the issue of coins (discussed by him and H. Mattingly in the same number) to emphasize FIDES EXERCITUUM and attempt to seduce the praetorians.

13. tanto ante, thirteen days.

75. 1. promissis ... minis, followed by a paradigm chiasmus. But *bello impares* would have been a threat less convincing to the praetorians if the news of support from the Danube had by now reached them.

3. insidiatores ... in Germaniam. These may have included the Gallic *primores* who were sent by Otho to inflame anti-Vitellian feeling in Gaul, IV. 54. 13.

7. gnaris. As in II. 56. 6 L. reads *ignaris*, missing the antithesis, and suggesting something quite unreal about the German army.

Titianum. L. Salvius Otho Titianus, *cos. ord.* 52 and an Arval Brother by 58, had been proconsul of Asia, (*ad omnem aviditatem pronus*, *Agr.* 6), when Agricola was quaestor there, probably in 63–4. He became *cos.* II with his brother, I. 77. 5.

9. mater, Sextilia, II. 64. 8.
  liberi, a son and a daughter, II. 59.

76. 1. Illyrico. Not only does Illyricum report for Moesia, but the term itself may be meant to include all three military provinces of the Balkans, cf. I. 2. 5 n., II. 85. 1.
  nuntius. Here the chronological question (above 74. 1 n.) becomes more acute. The consular elections described in the next chapter took place on 26 Jan. (*AFA*): does T. imply that this first message (not of course those from the far-eastern provinces) reached Rome before that date? The question is ignored by, e.g., H. G. Pflaum, *Essai sur le cursus publicus* (19—) and A. M. Ramsay (12. 1 n. above), but it is at least worth considering.

  The elections were only eleven days after Galba's death. But (a) Galba's government may have sent an alert to Illyricum a few days earlier, and (b) the three Danubian commands may (cf. II. 5. 11 for Syria and Judaea) have already to act in concert, Pannonian headquarters being empowered to answer for all of them. If we take those headquarters to have been at Poetovio (cf. III. 1), then Otho's message to them had to cover about 726 km (= 586 m.p.); with speed equal to that of Pompeius Propinquus' dispatch from Trier to Rome (I. 12 n.), it could have arrived in four or five days. If a reply could be sent without consultation with the other two provinces, five more days should have been enough. Moreover, though the message from Rome had to go *in extenso* (saying that it was now Otho who required their support), all that was needed in reply was a simple "Yes". Could the latter not have been flashed by signal? About such devices the sources are silent, but it is surely not unlikely that the empire had by now organized signals to indicate whether there were disaffected provinces when oaths were taken each 1 Jan. and perhaps at other moments of expected crisis. Yet I suspect that on this occasion the necessary organization had been arranged by the officers of Legion VII Gemina and its commander Antonius Primus (see Appendix).

As between Rome and Pannonia there is comparable example in 193. Pertinax was murdered on 28 Mar.: Septimius was proclaimed at Carnuntum, 1078 km (= 735 m.p.) from Rome on 9 Apr. (date from *Feriale Duranum*; cf. C. W. J. Eliot, *Phoenix*, 1955, 76 ff.).

5. Aquitania ... Iulio Cordo. Curious that an unarmed province (not elsewhere mentioned in the Histories) should receive a notice. Maybe T. derived information from Agricola, governor there in 74–7. Cordus is otherwise unknown, except that a man of that name (conjectured in *PIR*[2] to be an elder brother) governed Cyprus about A.D. 50.

8. Narbonensem, more significant for its wealth but above all for the naval base at Forum Iulii.

11. grande ... senatus, a point later underlined by Otho, I. 84. 13 ff., and one too easily forgotten in the story of Otho's helplessness before the soldiers. Even as late as A.D. 238 the Senate was able to mobilize widespread support against Maximin.

12. praetexto. 19. 5 n. above.

16. Carthagine, the provincial capital, more famous in civil wars for its part in the rising of the Gordians in 238.

17. Vipstani Aproniani, *cos. ord.* 59, and an Arval from 57 to 86. His appointment must have been due to Nero and began on 1 July 68; his successor for 69–70 was L. Piso (IV. 38).

18. nam et hi ... cf. III. 12. 17 on Vespasian's freedman Hormus, and *Germ.* 25.

20. pleraque, not explained, but Heubner (who suggests replacement of Galba's statutes by Otho's and an address of loyalty to the new *princeps*) is surely right in thinking that it is not the actions which T. is

COMMENTARY

criticizing but the haste with which they were performed. But it is less certain that Heubner is justified in seeing here any real distinction between *populus* and *plebs* (as there was in I. 35. 1).

77. 2 fortunam. 10. 15 n. above.

3. quaedam ... properando. H. took both the neuter plurals with *obibat*; but surely both are governed by *properando*, the latter part of the sentence showing an antithesis between *ex dignitate r. p.* and *ex praesenti usu*. So also Heubner; but he is less convincing in seeing a zeugma when *properando* is taken with *quaedam*, which word he thinks required some such verb as *administrando*. Everything Otho did had to be done in a hurry, yet some things are admitted to have been *ex dignitate r. p.* : others (some described in the next chapter) were *ex praesenti usu* and *contra decus*. There was, for example, nothing *contra decus* in making rapid designations to consulates, given that both consuls were dead; but the choice of Verginius and Vopiscus was *ex praesenti usu* (Wellesley 'based on a policy of quick returns'), and the measures mentioned in the last sentences of this chapter were more clearly disreputable.

5. consul ... The arrangements now made by Otho, and the subsequent alterations by Vitellius (II. 71. 7 ff.) are discussed with great acuteness by G. Townend, *AJP* 1962 113 ff. His conclusions, with which in the present state of the evidence (see also Plut. *O.* 1 and *AFA, ILS* 241 = MW 2) I agree entirely, can be summarized as follows.

(a) Nero had designated two pairs, one for each half of 69, the two Sabini as *ordinarii*, and then Cingonius Varro (above 6. 4 n.) and Arrius Antoninus,

(b) Galba, with Vinius, took over the ordinary consulships—this being the first calendar year of his principate—and pushed the Sabini on to April (or possibly an earlier month). He substituted Marius Celsus for Varro (now dead), and put Valerius Marinus and Pedanius Costa (II. 71) into the last three months of the year: Celsus and Antoninus now had only the three months July to September,

(c) Otho and Titianus took over from their deceased predecessors, and gave Verginius and Vopiscus the month of March (that the Sabini were consuls on 30 Apr. and therefore presumably throughout that month, is attested by the *AFA*),

(d) when T. (line 9) says *ceteri consulatus ... mansere* he only means that no other person already designated lost his consulate *altogether* at this stage: he does not state (his source probably said nothing on the point) that no one had his consulate curtailed or rearranged. What Otho did do was to bring in Martius Macer and Quinctius Atticus for November and December, taking those months away from the three which Galba had given to Marinus and Costa. So

Otho and Titianus	to end February
Verginius and Vopiscus	March
Caelius and Flavius	1 April to end June
Celsus and Antoninus	1 July to end September
Marinus and Costa	October
Macer and Atticus	November and December

This construction entails two mis-statements by T. here: (i) the plural *mensis* is wrong for Verginius and Vopiscus: they had one month only (T.'s source here, cf. Plut., was probably vague), (ii) Celsus and Antoninus were still given three months, i.e. to 1 Oct. It was Vitellius who deprived them of September: if not, then of whom else were *consulatus coartati* (II. 71)?

in Kalendas Martias. Here and in line 11 *in* undoubtedly means 'up to', although *designatus in Kalendas* of consulates normally indicated the initial date, see Townend, *AJP* 1962, 122.

7. Pompeius Vopiscus. Nothing else is known of him. Vienna had already received a consulate from Galba—C. Bellicius Natalis in the last three months of 68, see Syme, 592.

10. Caelio ac Flavio Sabinis. Cn. Arulenus Caelius Sabinus was a distinguished lawyer, who reached the peak of his career under Vespasian, *PIR²* A. For Flavius Sabinus see Townend, *JRS* 1961, 54 ff. He held a second consulate, with Mucianus *cos.* III as his colleague, in 72, and was therefore beyond doubt a close connection of Vespasian: Townend argues convincingly that he was his nephew, i.e. the son of the urban prefect (above 46. 5 n.). For his part in Otho's war see II. 36. 7, 51. 8: if the above reconstruction of the consulates of 69 be right, T. was mistaken in calling him *consulem designatum* a few days before Bedriacum, for he will have entered office on 1 Apr.

It is interesting that a diploma of A.D. 94 (*ILS* 9059 = MW 404) cites this pair as the *consules ordinarii* of the year, as Nero had originally intended them to be. Not only Galba and Vinius, and Otho and Titianus, but even Verginius and Vopiscus, have been suppressed. Dessau (n. 29 to the inscr.) was surely right in suggesting that Flavius' connection with the imperial house was responsible for this way of dating.

11. Arrio Antonio. See several references in Pliny's *Letters*. He was maternal grandfather of Antoninus Pius, was proconsul of Asia, and then *cos.* II in 97. His wife was Boionia Procilla, and his daughter married the Narbonese T. Aurelius Fulvus (*cos. ord.* 89), son of the legionary legate of 79. 25 who later became city prefect. His Narbonese origin can hardly be doubted, and Syme (App. 87) argues that Marius Celsus was Narbonese too.

COMMENTARY

12. quorum ... intercessit, although Vitellius did take away from Celsus and Antoninus the month of September, see n. to line 5 above.

13. sed, 'But he did more ...'. I do not think T. implies any severer criticism of the measures recorded in this sentence than of the consular designations, though *honoratis iam senibus* is perhaps contemptuous (some people are never satisfied, cf. Sen. *de Ira* III. 31).

16. Cadio Rufo, Pedio Blaeso, condemned in 49 and 59, *A.* XII. 22, XIV. 18, the former a governor of Bithynia, the latter of Crete and Cyrene. If this is the Pedius of Pers. *Sat.* I. 85, his guilt was presumably notorious, but the identification is far from certain.

Saevino P ... Ritter reported M.'s reading as 'pqse', on the strength of which Hirschfeld, *Kl. Schr.* 853, suggested Scaevino Paquio, supposing a descendant of Paquius Scaeva, proconsul of Cyprus under Augustus, *ILS* 915. But Saevinius is a known name, and PIR[1] accepts it.

19. videri maiestatem. It must have been hard to persuade anyone that their offence had really been *maiestas*, since all they had suffered was *infamia* (together with simple restitution of the stolen property), whereas the penalty for *maiestas* at its lowest would have been exile. Presumably Otho declared a general amnesty for all who had been in the Senate.

78. 2. Hispalensibus ... adiectiones. Hispalis (Seville) was a *colonia Iulia,* founded almost certainly by Julius Caesar, see M. I. Henderson, *JRS* 1942, 13, Vittinghoff, cit., 74; an important trading station near the mouth of the Baetis (Guadalquivir), its share in the wine exports of this period is proved by many sherds from the Monte Testaccio in Rome, *ESAR* III. 184. Emerita (Merida), another Julian colony but founded by Augustus (Vittinghoff, 109), was the capital of Lusitania. There is no evidence that either town was suffering economic difficulties, but new settlers would be welcome, especially if land had been left unallocated in the original centuriation, cf. Kornemann, *RE* s. v. *Colonia,* col. 578. The settlers may have been legionary veterans, as in Italy under Nero, *A.* XIII. 31, XIV. 27.

Lingonibus. Lipsius has been followed by many commentators in objecting (a) that Otho could hardly have wasted largesse on a tribe so notoriously Vitellian (I. 53. 12 etc.), and (b) that a Gallic community fits badly between two references to Spain. He suggested *Lusonibus* or *Illurconibus,* the former accepted by C. H. V. Sutherland, *The Romans in Spain* (1939), 180. Against this Momigliano, 171 ff., argued that at this stage Otho was bound to go to desperate lengths to win support in all parts of Gaul. In itself a grant of citizenship to a whole community in

Gallia Comata is not in this period an absurdity, and Fisher was therefore reasonable in finding the case against M's reading non-proven (so too Heubner).

4. Maurorum ... dedit. Plin. *NH* V. 2 says that Iulia Constantia Zulil, a colony in Mauretania Tingitana, was included in a *conventus* of Baetica, presumably that of Gades. Here, however, Otho was dealing not with judicial arrangements, but with the assignment of *contributae civitates*, which would pay taxes to the Baetican cities: it may be that he was reviving Augustan arrangements which had been reversed by Claudius, Sutherland, cit., 176.

5. Cappadociae ... Africae. Of these *nova iura* no detail survives. Since *Lex Banasitana* (A. N. Sherwin-White, *JRS* 1975, 90) omits Otho and Vitellius from the catalogue of emperors who granted citizenship, T.'s *non mansura* is probably correct.

7. statuas Poppaeae, upset and restored in 62, during the events leading to Octavia's death, *A.* XIV. 61; upset again after Nero's death, despite Poppaea's deification.

9. per senatus consultum. At this moment Otho is careful with constitutional niceties; cf. 74. 9 n. above.

10. imagines Neronis. Cf. Suet. *Nero* 57.

78. 11. nobilitatem ... abstruerent. For the concept of *nobilitas* see above, 30. 1 n. Hill's criticism of Gelzer here (*Historia*, 1969, 234) misfires when he attempts to analyse T.'s use of *adstruere*. In some of his examples this verb is followed by a dative, and can of course involve an addition to something already there: with an accusative it could mean that Otho's *nobilitas* was previously non-existent. Yet I share Hill's doubts whether in fact it does.

12. Neroni Othoni. Important though this passage is for revealing Otho's political attitude, its chief interest has been in the light it might throw on T.'s sources. For Plut. *O.* 3 says that *diplomata* were sent out with the name Nero, τὸ τοῦ Νέρωνος θετὸν ὄνομα, in Otho's titulature; and he cites Cluvius Rufus as authority for his statement. But that Cluvius' writings were his immediate source is most unlikely; for he fails to mention the prima-facie ground for respecting evidence from Cluvius, namely that the man was a provincial governor. Contrast Suet. *O.* 7, who only cites *quidam*, but does speak of *diplomata* and *primae epistulae* to governors of provinces.

But if it was the 'common source' which provided Cluvius' name to Plut., why does T. neglect him? Momigliano, 185 f., suggested that it was because T. disapproved of him; but if he did, he has missed many chances of saying so, and he must have largely forgiven him by the time he wrote the *Annals*, e.g. XIII. 20, XIV. 2. Moreover the problem is not so much the failure to mention Cluvius as the failure to tell us that the name Nero was actually affixed to documents: *ipse in suspenso tenuit* is contradicted by Suet.'s testimony.

A solution was suggested by O. Seeck, *RhM* 1901, 230 (see also Syme, 675), namely that Cluvius, whose history may never have covered 69, dealt with the matter in connection with Nero's death. The 'common source' could then have used his evidence when speaking of June 68, and have been copied by Plut.; and T. did not draw heavily on that section of the source. On early 69 the source said little more than T. has transcribed.

79. 1. sine cura. These words are almost directly contradicted by this chapter's account of the efficient counter-measures. But T is thinking of the preoccupation of the central government with other things: the local commanders had to repel the invaders, and had they received earlier instructions to move their troops to Italy they could not have done so. He introduces a theme of great importance to him, namely the threat to Rome's frontiers created by the year of civil war; cf. III. 46, and the account of Civilis' rebellion in IV and V.

2. eo audentius. if the incursion was really stimulated by the internal condition of the empire (see previous n.), it must mean that the tribe had heard of the revolts against Nero. But in fact they were simply trying to repeat, with booty, their success of the previous winter.

Rhoxolani. The 'Red Alans' are first found pressing on the Danube in Nero's reign, at the same time as their kinsmen on the Caucasus (6. 13 n.). They were in negotiation with, and gave hostages to, M. Plautius Silvanus Aelianus during the expedition described on *ILS* 986 (for the date see *RE* xxi. 37 ff., where Hofmann favours 57 rather than *c.* 63). Their invasion here, repeating one in winter 67–8, was apparently followed by a third attack in the last months of 69, IV. 4. 9; and in January 70 they defeated and killed Fonteius Agrippa, the newly appointed governor of Moesia, Jos. *BI* VIII. 90. A reorganization of the Lower Danube frontier, which had been doubtfully adequate even in normal times, was then at last undertaken, cf. C. Patsch, *Der Kampf um den Donauraum* . . . (1937), 3 n. 3.

Adequate descriptions of these heavy cavalrymen, the *catafracti*, are not available before the Flavian age, but Syme, *CQ* 1929, 129 ff., gives an interesting comparison between T.'s account here and that in

Valerius Flaccus, *Arg.* VI. 162, 231 ff. For later evidence see R. M. Rattenbury, *CR* 1942, 113 ff., 1943, 67 f. The horseman was encased in mail from neck to knee, and wore a helmet covering his whole head. His horse, too, was mailed, and a loop from the horse's neck supported the long spear (*contus*) of which the butt end came up against the horse's thigh. The horseman had only to steady himself and direct his spear with his right hand, so that when a whole regiment charged *vix ulla acies obstiterit* (lines 11–12). A sword was carried as a secondary armament, mainly in case the rider had to dismount.

Plut. says nothing of this campaign, though his source must surely have recorded the victory and the resulting awards. For the description of armour and tactics T. surely relied on his knowledge of the fighting against the Sarmatae Iazyges in 89 and 92 (2. 6 n. above), but above all of the defeat, during Trajan's first Dacian war, of a Sarmatian invasion in the winter of 101–2. For illustration see still the two works of C. Cichorius, *Die römischen Denkmäler in der Dobrudscha* (1904), and *Die Reliefs der Traianssäule* (1896–1900); also L. Rossi, *Trajan's Column and the Dacian Wars* (1970), 125, (but his text can be misleading). The Column shows Sarmatians shooting bows, which must have been very difficult for men with the armament described above; but it is probable that their mounted men had two types of unit.

4. ex ferocia et successu. Cf. IV. 28. 12, *successu rerum ferocior*. But in our passage the two nouns are not causally connected: the Rhoxolani had natural *ferocia*, and they also relied on their victory in the previous winter.

6. tertia legio. III Gallica was transferred to Moesia from the East just before Nero's death, Suet. *Vesp.* 6 and above, 10. 1 n.

13. neque conti... pondere. See Rattenbury, *CR* 1943, 67. The *conti* were no good because the horses slipped; the *gladii* because the mail was too heavy when the riders dismounted. The construction (cf. above, 6. 2 n.) is one in which two words or phrases in the early part of a sentence are picked up by two elements later, each of the first pair being related only to one member of the later pair. The clearest example is at I. 62. 10: for others see C. O. Brink, *CR* 1944, 43.

14. catafractarum. *Alae* get the name *catafractatae* from at latest the time of Pius, see *CIL* xvi. 110. An *ala I Ulpia contariorum* appears in Pannonia in 133, ibid. 76.

19. lanceis. This is the only clear evidence for lances being used by legionaries before Hadrian's day, but II. 29. 6, III. 27. 13, could also refer to legions. See Parker, *Roman Legions*, 251.

24. M. Aponius, who reappears, without great consequence, in the Flavio-Vitellian war. The date of his consulate is unknown, but he was an Arval by 57, and was proconsul of Asia in some year after 73, *ILS* 8817.

25. Fulvus Aurelius, from Nemausus, paternal grandfather of Antoninus Pius: cf. above 77. 11 n. He was already legate of III Gallica in 64, *ILS* 232; but some time in 69 he had given place to Dillius Aponianus, III. 10. 2. Syme, 166, conjectures that he had gone to join Vespasian: certainly his career under the Flavians was distinguished—consul twice, and city prefect. His son, who predeceased him, was consul in 89.

25. Iulianus Tettius. II. 85, IV. 39–40. This man did flee to Vespasian in mid-69, because Aponius Saturninus was trying to murder him. He was legate of VII Claudia (Vipstanus Messalla took his place, III. 9. 11), but only of quaestorian status—he was praetor in 70. He was consul in 83, and in 87 or 88 was victorious in Domitian's last campaign against the Dacians.

Numisius Lupus, still legate of VIII Augusta in the Flavian invasion of Italy, III. 10. 2.

consularibus ornamentis, though these did not excuse Tettius from the need to hold the praetorship, IV. 39. The honour is a generous one for the two legates who took no part in the battle. Nor of course had Otho had any part in its planning, but in claiming credit he was being no more exorbitant than some of his predecessors in the principate.

80. 1. Parvo interim initio. But the origins of this riot, important for an understanding of the political and military situation, are hard to determine with any confidence. The two parallel accounts must be quoted in full:

Plut., *O.* 3.2–3:

οἱ μισθοφόροι χαλεποὺς παρεῖχον ἑαυτούς, ἀπιστεῖν παρακελευόμενοι καὶ φυλάττεσθαι καὶ κολούειν τοὺς ἀξιολόγους ... Κρισπῖνον δὲ πέμψαντος αὐτοῦ τὴν ἑπτακαιδεκάτην σπεῖραν Ὠστίας ἀπάξοντα, κἀκείνου νυκτὸς ἔτι συσκευαζομένου καὶ τὰ ὅπλα ταῖς ἁμάξαις ἐπιθέντος, οἱ θρασύτατοι πάντες ἐβόων οὐδὲν ὑγιὲς τὸν Κρισπῖνον ἥκειν διανοούμενον, ἀλλὰ τὴν σύγκλητον ἐπιχειρεῖν πράγμασι νεωτέροις, καὶ τὰ ὅπλα κατὰ Καίσαρος, οὐ Καίσαρι παρακομίζεσθαι.

Suet. *O.* 8. 2:

placuerat per classiarios arma transferri remittique navibus; ea cum in castris sub noctem promerentur, insidias quidam suspicati tumultum excitaverunt; ac repente omnes nullo certo duce in Palatium cucurrerunt caedem senatus flagitantes, repulsisque tribunorum qui inhibere temptabant, nonnullis et occisis, sic ut erant cruenti, ubinam imperator esset requirentes perruperunt in triclinium usque nec nisi viso destiterunt.

The divergent account in Suet., the obscurities in Plut., and T.'s failure to explain why a cohort was being summoned from Ostia to Rome, baffled most commentators until Hohl attempted a coherent account in *Klio*, 1939, 307 ff. After castigating T. for inadequacy, and Plut. for a version little short of fantastic (for it appeared to end with a midnight dash of the cohort on foot from Ostia to Rome, at the end of which they still found Otho's party in progress*), he claimed that only Suet. gave the essential clue to what was happening, i.e. that the naval expedition to Narbonensis (see I. 87) was in preparation. All the urban cohorts, and some of the praetorians, were to take part, and the 17th cohort was entrusted with the transport of all the necessary arms from Rome. *Classiarii* meant 'men detailed for naval service', for which Hohl found a parallel in *A.* XII. 56 (the miscellaneous criminals enlisted for Claudius' mock naval battle in A.D. 52—Suet. *Cl.* 21. 6 calls them *naumachiarii*). The affair was later than 1 Mar. could be seen, he claimed, from I. 81. 10; for the magistrates who discarded their *insignia* could not be Otho and his brother, but were Verginius and Vopiscus, who succeeded as consuls on that day.

This analysis was strongly contested by Heubner, *RhM* 1958. 339 ff. Plut., he argued, had been misunderstood. σνσκευαζομένου does not imply that the σκεύη of the cohort were being packed at Ostia, but is a general term introducing the tribune's action in loading the arms to go to Ostia from Rome; ἥκειν means that the tribune arrived, not at Ostia, but at the praetorian camp; and that it was a riot of the praetorians in that camp, not something which started at Ostia is clearly implied by Plut.'s opening words (οἱ μισθοφόροι). As to Suet., his account is brief and unsatisfying; it was he who had introduced fantasy with his *omnes . . . cucurrerunt*, for it was not every man of the twelve praetorian cohorts who invaded the palace, but just the cavalry; and *classiarii* cannot include an urban cohort. Moreover Hohl's *terminus post quem* at 1 Mar. cannot stand, for the *magistratus* need not be the consuls.

All this reasoning is cogent, and Heubner maintained his position in his Commentary (where he also criticizes the article by H. Drexler in *Klio*, 1959, 153 ff.). He concludes that the 'common source' of T. and Plut. (who in his next section includes a few more details) was essentially right. Urban cohort XVII was instructed to march to Rome under full armour, and a praetorian tribune was detailed to supervise

---

*An account accepted by P. R. L. Greenhalgh. *The year of the Four Emperors* (1975), 62, but surely incredible.

the dispatch of such arms as they did not have with them at Ostia, presumably in the main their defensive material. The riot, he agrees, began in Rome.

Yet there remain serious grounds for discomfort:

(a) Why was the cohort being moved—and moved to Rome? To be ready for an expedition northwards (see Wellesley's fn. to his tr.)? If so, the intention was never carried out, for no urbans are included in the list of forces sent to the Po valley, II. 11.

(b) How did Suet. come to include *classiarii* and *naves* in his story? Heubner replies that his account was based only on memory, not on direct consultation of a literary source; and that he assumed that to take arms to Ostia implied naval operations. Was Suet. really so careless, or so simple-minded?

(c) What of the chronology? Hohl's *terminus p. q.* at 1 Mar. is ill founded, but has Heubner (art. cit., 351–2) any better ground for claiming that the incident must belong to the first days of Otho's reign, when he was consolidating his power? T. only comes to it after recounting not only the consular elections (26 Jan.), but also the measures of I. 78 and the news from the Lower Danube (I. 79); and his next events are the series of prodigies which preceded Otho's departure from Rome, and then the Narbonese expedition (I. 86–7). When that expedition started is discussed in the Appendix, pp. 265 ff.: the date must be earlier than Hohl supposed, but can hardly be as early as the immediate aftermath of Otho's accession. For we have reached a point at which T. (I. 83. 17) can make Otho say *imus ad bellum* and emphasize the consequent need for extreme security. This was not the attitude T. ascribes to him in the days immediately after his elevation: it would have become explicit only after the failure of negotiations with Vitellius.

So the possibility of an alternative version still exists, as follows. In the third week of February a naval expedition was being mobilized at Ostia, and a praetorian tribune was instructed to send down the necessary arms. As he assembled them, some praetorians somehow identified the arms destined for the urban cohort stationed at Ostia, and assumed, wrongly, that it was being summoned to Rome. The 'common source' recorded, correctly, that this assumption was the cause of the riot, but did not bother to investigate whether the assumption had been right or wrong. So it could be that Hohl's analysis, when stripped of some unmistakable errors, comes near to the truth.

2. prope urbis excidio. T., who now devotes six chapters to the riot and its aftermath, almost certainly worked up the story to a pitch much higher than that attained by the 'common source'. In this part of the Histories, *militaris seditio* was one of his key themes; and that not necessarily (as suggested by Treu, 26 ff.) because he had the events of A.D. 97 in his mind.

septimam decimam cohortem. If its number be correctly reported, this must be an urban cohort, not one of the praetorians or *vigiles*, see Durry, 12 n. 6. It is generally assumed that this was the cohort which Claudius stationed at Ostia for fire-fighting purposes; Suet. *Cl.* 25. 2; in that capacity it would not have needed its defensive armour and could have left it in the armoury in Rome. There was still a cohort at Ostia (again not expressly designated as an urban) when Vitellius arrived in Rome, II. 63. 8; that it should have returned to its quarters is compatible with any hypothesis about the movement envisaged here. But it was probably replaced before long by the regular Ostian corps of *vigiles* (see R. Meiggs, *Roman Ostia* (1972), 75, for the construction of their regular barracks under Hadrian). There is no extant epigraphical record of an urban at Ostia, and we know that in later days XVII urbana guarded the Lugdunum mint, see above 64. 16 n.

6. armamentario. On any hypothesis the rest of this chapter describes a scene at the praetorian camp in Rome. The arsenal there was perhaps the only permanent one in Italy.

8. temulentos. Cf. 26. 6. Hohl, cit, 317, comments that 'es steht für Tacitus fest, dass der Soldat sich allabendlich betrinkt.'

9. tribunos centurionesque. Hohl, 315, suggests that they exonerated their *praefecti* from guilt because (I. 46) they themselves had chosen them. But it is possible that the *praefecti* were at Otho's party.

10. familiae senatorum, 'the senators' household slaves': cf. III. 64. 4, where the *primores civitatis* offer their slaves to Flavius Sabinus to support their proposed *coup d'état*. Heubner is surely right in rejecting the view of Hohl, 311 (first propounded by Durry, 372 n. 8) that this is a sarcastic reference to the urban cohorts.

13. nox abstulerat. i.e. darkness had prevented them from showing their loyalty, for darkness intensifies both confusion and nervousness.

14. severissimos centurionum, two of them, according to Plut. The tribune is presumably Crispinus himself.

15. insidentes equis. With ninety cavalrymen to each of twelve praetorian cohorts, this means over 1,000 men, Durry, 99.

81. 1. celebre, attended by eighty senators, Plut., *O.* 3.

6. cum ... timebatur, famous as a Tacitean epigram, but not one for which T. can claim originality, Plut., *O.* 4.

8. praefectos ... miserat, from the party to the camp, where the bulk of the guard were awaiting the results of the cavalry's attack, see 80. 9 n. above.

10. magistratus ... insignibus. The broad-striped toga was the most obvious thing to jettison, cf. Suet. *Iul.* 16. 1, *dimissis lictoribus abiectaque praetexta domum clam refugit,* also Hor. *Sat.* II. 7. 53.

82. 1. Palatii. above, 17. 8 n.

3. Iulio Martiale. See I. 28 for his ambiguous behaviour during Otho's coup. The order of events here is probably wrong. Martialis and Saturninus, Suet. *O.* 8. 2, were attacked when the soldiers first broke in, and it was only later that the prefects were sent back to the camp.

4. praefecto legionis. In a confused passage, which mixes up functions belonging to various periods of the empire, Vegetius II. 9 speaks of a *praefectus legionis* as one who *absente legato tamquam vicarius ipsius potestatem maximam retinebat.* But apart from the *praefecti legionum* in Egypt (so called because they were *equites* and not senatorial *legati*) the only other mention of this title in the early Empire is on *ILS* 887, where a *praefectus* of two legions had a special appointment to distribute land. Saturninus was surely *praefectus castrorum* (cf. III. 7. 3, with Wellesley's n., and Dom. Dob. 11d, for their duties). His legion must have been I Adiutrix, then in temporary quarters in Rome; but we have no means of telling why he was at the Palatium at this moment. There is no ground for supposing that the legate of the legion (?Orfidius Benignus, II. 47.3) was away from his command.

13. manipulatim, for every part of the guard, not only the cavalry who had carried out the assault, had been responsible.

Licinius... Plotius. I. 46. 2 ff. The origins, and the accounts of the two men in Book II, make it clear that there is no chiasmus here, and that it was Licinius who spoke *mitius.*

15. quina milia nummum. Plut. *O.* 3. 6 (1,250 drachmae) agrees. If there were twelve praetorian and four urban cohorts, each (at least on paper) 1,000 men strong, this would cost 80 m. HS. But the sum is only one-sixth of what Nymphidius promised the praetorians, and one-third of what both Claudius and Nero had actually paid them, above 5. 3 n. This is remarkable, for Otho had won power (perhaps six weeks earlier) on a programme of giving the guard their due; and T. or Plut. would surely have recorded any earlier donative had there been one. No doubt Otho had been able to ask for a little time, to repair the alleged venality of Galba's court, and to collect the property of Vinius, I. 49. 21; and his promise to pay *vacationes* could have won him quick popularity without any immediately heavy outlay. But there must have been apprehension that the guard would feel themselves cheated. The donative here, forced on Otho by the riot, was presumably represented by him as an instalment only, the balance to come once he had won the war. See also Drexler, 157 n. 1.

18. militiae insignibus, the gold ring and the *tunica* with narrow stripe would be worn by praetorian tribunes (for they were *equites*); the centurions would have their *vites*. Some in both groups may have also possessed special decorations.

    otium, 'discharge', the officers refusing to continue with men so disreputable.

83. 3. ambitioso imperio, 'a regime dependent on popularity'; the adjective was applied to Marius' activities by Sall. *BI* 64. 5. See also II. 12. 7, and GG on *ambitus* and related words.

5. simul reputans. In fact everything from the beginning of the chapter, and especially the last part of the *cum* clause (*vulgus . . . impellerentur*), though in form a description of the objective circumstances, is a part of Otho's thoughts in the preparation of his speech.

8. disseruit. Of all the speeches in Book I T. has adapted this one most brilliantly to the motives and problems of the speaker. It contains some surprising passages, especially at the end, but they have complete appropriateness to the occasion. Despite what he has said in 71. 1 and 77. 3 about Otho's newly found energy and moderation, T. is still determined to emphasize his servile dependence on the troops, the predicament forecast in Piso's speech, 30. 10. Yet the emperor must, especially in view of the coming war, recall the soldiers to the very thing his own rise to power had challenged—discipline, and the established constitution. For both were important, the constitution for its propaganda value, both at home and in the provinces, 76. 12. So at the end of 84 Otho's positive policy emerges again—to broaden the nature of his support and to play down the idea that he was a creature of the guard. As Alford says, one might there be reading Cicero on the Senate of the Republic. Perhaps, rather, T.'s own views on the Senate of his own time, as it should have been; but his main point here is that such views fit Otho's needs.

17. imus ad bellum. See end of argument (c) in 80. 1 n. above.

18. ratio rerum, 'a careful assessment of the situation'.

24. illic, 'in the field' (Wellesley).

84. 8. imperia ducum sciscitando. Again it is clear that the operation, whatever it was, which caused the riot, was one which required secrecy, 80. 1 n. above.

14. decora omnium provinciarum. In fact it is unlikely that in 69 there was more than a mere sprinkling of senators from provinces outside Gaul (mainly Narbonensis), Spain, and Sicily; in particular there are at that time few senators from the eastern provinces who can be confidently identified. For a summary of evidence see M. Hammond, *JRS* 1957, 74 ff., *AM* 249 ff. T. may have underestimated the effect of the generation which preceded his writing. There is similar exaggeration, but with it more rhetorical purpose, in Cerialis' speech to the Gauls, IV. 74. 6 ff.

16. Germani, Othonian language for what T. normally calls 'Germanicus exercitus'. In fact none of Vitellius' legionary troops were *Germani* and by no means all of his *auxilia* (though see I. 61. 9). Forni, cap. V with Tab. 3, and Introd. above, pp. 20 ff.

17. Italiae ... iuventus. Common opinion, perhaps in T.'s day as well as in 69, differentiated the social standing of the guard from that of that of the legionaries, see Durry, 239 ff. There were a few provincials in the guard, it is true, including some outlandish ones, not only the Anauni, etc. of *ILS* 206, but see (e.g.) *ILS* 2030. But Passerini, *coorti* 148 f., provides statistics (unfortunately not broken down into shorter periods) showing that seven-eighths of all praetorians in the first two centuries A.D. were Italian. Of these at least half came from Cisalpine Italy, which was at the same time an important recruiting area for the Rhine legions; but their companions were seldom provincials, and came mainly from Latium, Umbria, Etruria, etc. (as in *A*. IV. 5).

25. rerum, 'of our power', *A*. XV. 50 etc.; cf. Syme, 208 n. 1.

27. auspicato. Cf. III. 72. 2 on the Capitol.

29. ex vobis senatores, for they came from the better ranks of Italian society, much more markedly than the legionaries. The latter were by 69 increasingly recruited from the provinces, and not by any means from the upper classes: cf. Forni, cap. IV.

ex senatoribus principes, for at least in T.'s view (if not also in Otho's) the existence of the Senate is not only consistent with, but essential to, the imperial system.

85. 1. oratio ... animos. In support of this reading Nipperdey-Andresen cited *A*. XII. 56, *spatium amplexus ad vim remigii,* and XIII. 38, *pars in planitiem porrigebatur ad explicandas equitum turmas;* but in each of those passages there is a verb with more bearing on the action of the *ad* clause than *accepta* has here. Many editors have thought that the additional letters in M. (see app. crit.) were corrupted from some adjective or participle, and H. read *parata*. But *oratio... parata* (or *apta* etc.) ... *accepta* makes an unattractive sentence, and on the whole we should probably agree with Heubner that the reading printed in the O.C.T. is to be preferred. It involves an anacoluthon: T. starts by intending to provide a participle to govern the *ad* clause, but his thought passes from Otho's intentions to the reactions of the audience, and he writes *accepta*. In that case the passage is no real parallel to the 'hanging prepositional clause' discussed on 11. 6 above.

6. occulto habitu, 'in disguise', i. e. as civilians. Epictetus IV. 13. 5, writing in the next generation, tells of soldiers ἐν σχήματι ἰδιωτικῷ acting as spies.

9. studia partium. Heubner draws attention to the plural *studia*, found only here in T. as against four instances (e.g. I. 76. 11) of *studium partium*, 'support for the party', cf. Cic. *Quinct.* 70, *Rosc. Am.* 137, *II Verr.* II. 25. He suggests that the plural reflects the usage of Sallust (*BI* 42. 5, 73. 4), in which more than one party is meant and the genitive is subjective not objective. He thinks therefore that the Vitellians were investigating the general state of party feeling in Rome, rather than the degree of support for their own cause. I am not entirely convinced.

11. secreta domuum, 'the privacy of home', as contrasted immediately with *in publico*.

14. arduus ... modus, 'it was difficult in any matter to strike the right attitude'.

19. vulgaribus conviciis, 'commonplace insults'.

20. in clamore ... obstrepentes, referring to those who said things about Vitellius which were true. Irvine for *tumultu ... obstrepentes* has 'drowning their own meaning in a torrent of words'.

86. 1. prodigia ... vulgata. For T.'s attitude to such things see Syme, 521 ff. Plut. *O.* 4. 4 says that the authority for most of them was unknown or disputed, but that everyone saw the Victory drop its reins and the statue of Julius turn east.

2. bigae. A gold chariot containing Victoria was given by Hiero of Syracuse in 216 B.C., Livy 22. 37, and was replaced after after the fire of 83. It had always stood in the approach to the Capitoline temple.

3. cella Iunonis, the right-hand *cella* of the same temple, Ov. *Fasti*, IV. 129–30.

4. statuam conversam. Plut. *O.* 4. 5, while agreeing with T. that this happened just before Otho left Rome, records a report (φασι) that this was the moment at which the party of Vespasian were by now openly (ἐμφανῶς ἤδη) trying to seize power. Suet. *Vesp.* 5. 7 lists it among the portents which forecast Vespasian's rule, but it occurred *non multo post comitia secundi consulatus ineunte Galba*, i.e. (though the precise date is unknown to us) some time before the end of 68. Heubner takes that account to be derived from Flavian propaganda of the claim that Vespasian from the first had been marked out as the ultimate successor to the chaos left by Nero's fall. This could be right, but Suet.'s mark of time is so precise and surprising that it carries some degree of conviction. Perhaps the 'common source' of T. and Plut. found the portent in a list of those recorded for the winter of 68–9 and wrongly placed it in the reign of Otho.

But what can be made of Plut.'s reference to the Flavian rising? Is it simply that the 'common source' recorded that the Flavians made use of the portent when they declared themselves openly, in the summer, and that Plut. carelessly took this statement as giving a date for the portent itself? It is tempting to pose a different explanation, namely that the source, or even Plut. himself, knew not only that the Flavians used this portent but that they were actively issuing propaganda in early March; for this might account for the attention T. gives to their activities at the beginning of Book II. But this is a hazardous view.

9. etiam futuri pavor, for this prodigy evoked realistic fear about its economic consequences.

inundatione. See also Plut. *O.* 8. 3, for the horrors of this flood. The destruction of grain was particularly serious after the shortages of the previous winter, above 73. 5 n.; and the new Egyptian corn crop would not be harvested before April.

10. ponte sublicio, the oldest bridge in Rome, which ran from the Forum Boarium to the slopes of the Janiculum north of the Porta Trigemina; see Platner–Ashby s.v., agreeing with Lugli's map. For semi-religious reasons (perhaps because of the tradition about Horatius Cocles) it was always built of wood.

13. quaestus inopia. Unemployment would last until the floods subsided and rebuilding could begin, and meanwhile there were acute food-shortages. T. has omitted to mention that the grain-market was flooded, Plut. *O.* 4. 5.

16. paranti ... obstructum. Suet. *O.* 8. 3 says that the ruined buildings blocked the Via Flaminia up to the twentieth milestone.

18. a fortuitis ... vertebatur. For this contempt for the common people's credulity cf. II. 1. 12.

87. 1. lustrata urbe. The purification after the portents would consist of an *amburbiale sacrificium*, before which the victims would be led round the *pomerium*; cf. *A.* XIII. 24, Livy 21. 62, etc.

2. Poeninae ... aditus. Caecina had either crossed the Great St. Bernard or was in process of crossing it, see I. 70 and 89. 18 n., but it is most unlikely that Valens had yet reached the Cottian Alps, I. 63. 1 n. It would however have been an obvious move for Caecina's advance guard (70. 14), to post detachments at all the western Alpine crossings: it is not impossible that the Illyrican commanders had similarly protected the crossings over the Julian Alps.

This assumes that *Vitellianis exercitibus* is ablative, cf. *A.* XII. 68, *aditus custodiis clauserat.* But Wellesley, *JRS* 1971, 47 n. 56, suggests that the words could be dative; and syntactically they certainly could be, cf. Cic. *II Verr.* V. 6, *aditus omnis hominibus ... clausus,* Caes. *BC* II. 19, *conventus portus Varroni clausit.* This would mean that the Vitellians were thought to be blocked by snow, and that Otho could afford this expedition, given that a confrontation in North Italy could not yet be a demand on his resources.

But that this was what T. meant is unlikely, for

(a) *Galliarum aditus* (for *Galliae* see above, 8. 3 n.) cannot surely mean approaches *out of* the Tres Galliae;

(b) the Alps Poeninae were not in fact blocked to the Vitellians, for Caecina sent his advanced guard over at a time certainly not much later, and probably two or three weeks earlier, than the despatch of Otho's expedition (the exact chronology cannot be recovered, I. 89. 18 n.);

(c) there is no other indication that the Othonians, or anyone else in Rome, believed that the Vitellians were blocked in this way;

(d) the diversion of Othonian troops to Narbonensis is never defended on the ground that *at that moment* they were not needed elsewhere; nor, when the engagement on the coast had ended, did the Othonian command summon them to what was now, on any view, an impending confrontation in the Po valley.

It would of course be absurd to suppose that any sober Othonian general contemplated a crossing of the Alps at this moment, even had the passes been open. But it might have been good propaganda to suggest that this would have been done, had it been possible, and that instead Otho was at least attacking Gaul by sea. The real objectives of the expedition were, I take it, limited: maintenance of naval supremacy against the base at Forum Iulii, and control of the Riviera road from

Italy to Gaul. See Appendix, pp. 265 ff. These objectives, which were on the whole achieved, could have been part of an overall plan which was prepared to divert a fairly small body of regular troops despite the immediate threat of conflict in N. Italy. Further discussion belongs to II. 12 ff.

4. classe . . . fida. V. took this to be the Forum Iulii fleet, but that base was held by the Vitellians, II. 14. 5; the *quod* clause here, if the analysis in 6. 7 n. above be anything like valid, makes it certain that Otho is using the fleet from Misenum. They are loyal because their sailors hope that even more of their number will be rewarded with *honorata militia*. That the fleet should still be *valida* after the numbers drafted away from it is impressive testimony to the availability of recruits for this type of service.

7. honoratae . . . militiae. Cf. Livy 32. 23. 9, *navales socii relictis nuper classibus ad spem honoratioris militiae transgressi.*

urbanas, all those (probably four) which were stationed in Rome, and also the cohort at Ostia. There are no urbans in the forces which went to the Po valley.

8. plerosque, 'a substantial number'. In II. 11 we are told that five praetorian cohorts went north with Gallus and Spurinna, and that Otho himself was accompanied by *ceteris . . . cohortibus.* It may be then that the main bodies of all twelve cohorts were still available for the North Italian campaign and that only *vexillationes* were sent to Narbonensis. It certainly seems, from the account of the battle in II. 14–15, that no praetorian cavalry were included; so the *equitum vexilla* in Gallus' force, II. 11. 11, may have been the full complement of this corps. The numbers needed to act as *consilium et custodes* to the naval expedition were not large: *viris et robur* (cf. II. 11.8) implies quality rather than quantity.

10. Suedio Clementi. An inscription from Pompeii records him as a tribune in Vespasian's time, and he became *praefectus castrorum* in Egypt in 79, *ILS* 5942, MW 339 iii. 33.

primipilaribus. Above, 31. 6 n. The use of such men to command a relatively small expedition is not peculiar, but the divided command, which led to trouble (II. 12), is characteristic of Otho's regime.

11. Aemilio Pacensi. Above, 20. 14 n.

12. Moschus libertus. Freedmen commanded the Misenum fleet in the immediately preceding period, Ti. Iulius Optatus Ponticus in 52, *CIL* XVI. 1, and Anicetus in 59–61, *A.* XIV. 3 ff. Later in 69 the command, as also at Ravenna, has passed to *equites*, II. 100, III. 57, and this was the regular practice afterwards. See Starr, 33.

13. honestiorum, a judgement only on their standing, for T. thought nothing of their worth, II. 12. 5 ff.

immutatus. Many variants have been suggested (there is a lacuna in M.), but the word is wholly appropriate. In the equestrian *cursus* the *praefectura classis* was a very senior post; and although the present holder was not an *eques* but a freedman, it might have been felt that he should not sail on an expedition commanded by two *primipilares* and a tribune. But, whether or not for the reason suggested by T., Otho retained him.

14. Suetonius Paulinus won his reputation as praetorian commander in Mauretania in 42, was consul at an unknown date (but *vetustissimus consularium* in II. 32. 7 suggests a year not later than the '40s, cf. above, 8. 3 n.), and is best known for his exploits in Britain in 60. He was *cos. II ord.* in 66, an unusual feature in Nero's reign.

Marius Celsus. Above 14. 4 n.

Annius Gallus, consul between 62 and 68, *PIR*[2] s.v. See numerous references in the account of the coming war, and again in Book IV after he had been appointed to Upper Germany.

15. rectores destinati. Wellesley, *JRS* 1971, n. 58, is right in saying that we are not told when these appointments were made. But since Gallus, who proceeded north with the advanced guard (II. 11), is mentioned here along with Paulinus and Celsus, it seems reasonable to suppose that the decision about all three (and about Proculus) was made at the moment when the whole Othonian strategy was decided, i.e. to occupy Placentia and the Venetian area quickly, to send an expedition to Narbonensis, to follow both with the *profectio* of the emperor, and to relate the other movements with what could be reasonably hoped from the Danubian armies. Paulinus and Celsus, then, would be part of the supreme command when Gallus left Rome, and I agree with Wellesley that, since they conducted and possibly planned the battle *ad Castores*, and for other reasons given in his note, they must have gone north (on horseback?) well in advance of the troops who accompanied Otho. See Appendix pp. 264 ff.

88. 1. Cornelius Dolabella, probably (see *PIR*[2]) the grandson of the consul of A.D. 10 and the father of the consul of 86. He had given ground for suspicion to Galba, Suet. *G.* 12. 2, but later was suggested as a candidate for the adoption, cf. 13. 7 n. above. T. said nothing about that, but now tells us that he was related to Galba (he appears to have been his great-nephew, *PIR*[2]). Plut.'s version of the incident here is that the praetorians accused Dolabella and that (as with Celsus earlier) Otho put him out of harm's way. Ultimately he was executed by Vitellius, II. 63–4.

coloniam Aquinatem. Aquinum in the Volscian country (the birthplace of Juvenal) was not a colony in Cicero's time (*Phil.* II. 106), and may have been settled by the triumvirs.

4. multos . . . comitum specie. On 14 Mar., *ILS* 241 line 80 = MW 2, it seems that only one Arval brother had been left behind.

6. Lucium Vitellium. Vitellius' younger brother, who played an important part in the war with the Flavians, had been suffect consul in 48, the year in which Aulus was *cos. ord.* Plut. *O.* 5. 2 adds that Otho took special measures for the security of Vitellius' children and mother: cf. I. 75. 8. But he cannot be right in placing here the appointment of Flavius Sabinus as prefect of the city, see I. 46. 5: in fact Sabinus' position, given him directly after Galba's murder, was now diluted by Otho's commission to Titianus, I. 90. 19. For T.'s independent approach in this chapter see Syme, 184.

8. nullus ordo, 'none of the higher orders', i.e. the various grades of senator, and the *ordo equester.* The *populus* and *plebs* are dealt with in the next chapter.

13. luxuriosos . . . conviviorum. Cf. Caes. *BC* III. 96. 1 on the silver plate left behind by the nobles in Pompey's army at Pharsalus.

89. 1. magnitudine . . . populus. See app. crit. (there is still a lacuna in M.). If the text be kept, *expers* must, as always, govern the genitive, and the ablative *magnitudine nimia* must be causal. Alford therefore, followed by J. Delz, *Gnomon*, 1954, 409, suggests that the *magnitudo* is that of the *populus* itself: it was too numerous to have a (collective) view about political anxieties: cf. *in tanta multitudine*, I. 8. 1. Preferable is Heubner's interpretation: politics of this kind are beyond the comprehension of the *populus*, cf. Dio 53. 19. 4, 'they have no part in public affairs because such problems are too formidable'.

2. sentire paulatim . . . What follows is a telling summary of civil war in the period; and it also contains something rare in the *Histories,* a judgement (other than about the final fall of Nero) on the Julio-Claudian period, cf. IV. 42. 32 and Paratore, 467 n. 191. On the economic situation in Rome at this time see R. F. Newbold, *Historia,* 1972, 311 ff.

5. inter legiones Galliasque, but troops were also deployed in North Italy, II. 27. 14 (cf. I. 70. 6).

7. procul et in unius . . . chiastic contrast with *secura tum urbe et provinciali bello.*

9. Scriboniani. The rising of L. Arruntius Camillus Scribonianus, against Claudius in 42, was suppressed within five days, Suet. *Cl.* 13, Dio 60. 15.

12. quod raro alias, almost certainly true of the urbans. The praetorians had at least taken part in the Claudian invasion of Britain, and by T.'s day had suffered a notorious disaster against the Dacians.

14. si ducibus aliis ... Wellesley tr. 'if further commanders were to enter the lists'. But surely the past tense *bellatum foret* requires 'had the war been fought under different leaders', i.e. under leaders who could obtain more general active support.

15. religionemque ... ancilium. So also Suet. *O.* 8. 3, censuring Otho for marching *praepropere* against a religious objection. The twelve shields were moved by the Salii from the *sacrarium Martis* on the Palatine at the beginning of March, were taken in processions round the shrines, and returned to the *sacrarium* on 23 Mar. See J. G. Frazer *ad* Ov. *Fast.* III. 61–4, 92–3, 145, W. Warde Fowler, *The Religious Experience of the Roman People*, (1911), 39, 96 f.

18. Caecina ... transgressus. T.'s words clearly mean, although he may have been mistaken, the crossing by Caecina's main army rather than that by the *auxilia* sent over as an advanced guard (I. 70. 14, II. 17. 7). Nor is it inconceivable that his crossing could have been reported in Rome by mid-March. But if this be thought improbable, then it is surely preferable to think that T. was wrong rather than to emend *transgressurus*. See Appendix, pp. 264 ff.

90. 1. pridie Idus Martias, the first precise date in T. since Galba's murder, and a correct one. On 14 Mar. the Arvals sacrificed *pro salute et reditu* of the emperor (characteristically they later substituted Vitellius' name for Otho's and still later erased Vitellius too) *ILS* 76 ff. = MW 2 14. Suet. *O.* 8. 3 puts the departure on the day *quo cultores deum Matris lamentari et plangere incipiunt,* and it was long believed that this meant 24 Mar.: some scholars (e.g. Momigliano, 132) thought that this was the right date and that T. was wrong. But Hohl, *Klio*, 1939, 322 n. 5, showed fairly convincingly that Suet. referred to an earlier stage in Cybele's festival; and in any case 24 Mar. is too late, since the journey north with an army would have taken about three weeks (Wellesley, *JRS* 1971, 48 puts it at twenty-three days) and one must allow a week or more for Otho's activities in the north before Bedriacum was fought on 14 Apr. The actual *profectio* occurred on 15 Mar., the day after Otho commended the Republic to the Senate.

2. reliquias ... conversas. Some commentators have related this to the activities of Galba's commission (I. 20); and it is true that the proceeds of property recovered from Nero's beneficiaries might in equity have been awarded to the returning exiles. But why only if *nondum in fiscum conversas?* The *sectiones* of Nero are surely his own sales of confiscated goods, from which he had wanted quick returns, *festinata iam pridem exactione* (the proceedings of the Galbian commission had been slow and uncertain). Otho was simply distributing to the exiles what had remained unsold at Nero's death.

11. Galeri Trachali. P. Galerius Trachalus had been *cos. ord.* in 68 with Silius Italicus. He was patron of Mediolanum, and later proconsul of Africa, *CIL* V. 5812 = MW 255. For his oratory see Quintilian X. 1. 119 (also XII. 55), *vocis, quantam in nullo cognovi, felicitas et pronuntiatio vel scaenis suffectura.* He was probably related to Vitellius' wife Galeria, but it is curious that it is not from T. that we get any explanation of his mildness towards Vitellius.

ingenio Othonem uti, as Nero had used Seneca, *A.* XIII. 3, and as Domitian, Suet. *Dom.* 20, found he needed others to compose his speeches.

12. genus ipsum orandi, 'the actual style'.

18. sed ... servitii. A heavy stop must surely come before and not after these words, see Heubner's n.

19. quietem urbis ... permisit, in despite of Flavius Sabinus, his own appointment as *praefectus urbi*, cf. above, 88. 6 n. But Titianus remained in Rome for only a few days longer, for by the time of the council which preceded Bedriacum he had arrived to take supreme command in the north.

BOOK II

1–9. Digression on the East

T. ends this with the story of the false Nero (8–9), which leads us back to Italy and the Otho–Vitellius war. The digression was foreshadowed at I. 10. 15, and its artistry has been variously explained. To Courbaud, 147, it consisted in the way T. sustains the drama by an entr'acte: two actors have come to grips with one another, and we are asked to pause and look at a third actor who will dominate the stage later in the play. That such an effect was intended is likely, and it is certainly achieved, but it remains a question what impression this third actor was meant to make at his first appearance. Fuhrmann, 267, maintains that the essential purpose of the chapters was to underline the worthlessness of Otho and Vitellius and to portend the fall of whichever was the victor, at the hands of the worthier and more powerful Flavians: the end of I. 50 has in his view already propounded the theme.

Yet although that is a theme of which T. was probably conscious here (certainly the *fortuna* of the opening words is intended as a beneficent force), the parallel with I. 50 is not close. We are told there that Vespasian eventually changed for the better; but as an afterthought, and he is not introduced as a potential saviour. It was a chapter of gloom; and the gloom was deepened by its last sentence, in which men shudder at the prospect of yet a third contending army, led by a commander whose reputation was still suspect. More important, however, Fuhrmann seems to have underestimated the anti-Flavian features in our present chapters, which both by direct statement (see esp. 7, *ad fin.*), and by implication, say things which Flavian propagandists would have left unsaid.

For despite Fuhrmann's criticisms of him the confrontation made by Briessmann, 3 ff., with the parallel account in Josephus is surely significant. In the short passage (*BI.* IV. 498–502) which Josephus devotes to the aftermath of Galba's death (his definitive account of the Flavian rising is deferred to IV. 585 ff., when Vitellius is supposed to have entered Rome) we are told only of Titus being sent to Galba, of his return (through fear and not through policy) when he learned of the murder, and of the suspense into which the murder threw the Flavian leaders (μετέωροι περὶ τῶν ὅλων—the fate of the empire), who now postponed serious action over the Jewish War. Nothing about Titus' calculations (least of all *sin Vespasianus rem publicam susciperet*, 1. 20), nor about the consultation of the priest at Paphos, nor about the encouragement which the provinces and armies derived from Titus' return. T.'s cap. 6 on the feelings of the armies, their grievances and sense of power, does find almost direct echo in Josephus, but not in the same context: it comes in the preliminaries to Vespasian's actual proclamation, IV. 592. Finally it is T. alone who tells us that Vespasian and Mucianus composed their differences on the death of Nero, and thereby takes some form of Flavian planning back to the middle of A.D. 68.

It seems, then, that the cruder Flavian propaganda represented their rising as prompted simply by the iniquities of Vitellius after his victory. T.'s chapters here do much to cast doubts on that version, and it is tempting to think that this was one of their main purposes; moreover, if Titus' visit to the Paphian priest (confirmed by Suet.) is not a fiction, there was good evidence for the view that events in the East in the weeks following Galba's death compelled attention. The digression therefore primarily discharges a historical duty; but it was the historian's genius which added the artistic achievements described by Courbaud and Fuhrmann. (For further development of this view, but with reservations about some of Briessmann's conclusions, see the notes which follow.)

1.2. varia sorte. Paratore, 430 n. 143, believes the antecedent of *quod* to be, not *imperium*, but 'una maniera di riassumere le vicissitudini della fortuna', and consequently favours keeping *varie ortum* as read by the *recentiores* (M. is missing). It would have been almost impossible for T. to write like that. It is surely *imperium* ('the dynasty') which is in his mind when he goes on to *laetum rei publicae vel atrox*, and he could hardly have joined *ortum laetum*.

laetum rei publicae, words which make one the more keenly regret the loss of T.'s account of the principates of Vespasian and Titus.

4. missus a patre, but it was Titus himself who was said to have advertised the reasons, cf. Heubner, 19.

5. maturam ... iuventam. Titus was born on 30 Dec. 39 (PIR^2 F 399). He seems, Suet. *Tit.* 1, to have held no magistracy since his quaestorship, an office he reached *suo anno* in 65, after serving with distinction as military tribune in Germany and Britain, Suet. *Tit.* 4 and 77. 5 below. He became legionary legate of XV Apollinaris under his father, perhaps at the outset of the war in December 66, before he had had time to stand for the tribunate. He was never praetor, and probably it was that office he was seeking from Galba.

7. accitum in adoptionem. Suet. *Tit.* 5. 1 says this rumour was current wherever Titus went, but from T.'s silence in Book I it seems unlikely that Galba seriously entertained the idea.

10. decor ... maiestate. Though not tall, Titus had his father's powerful build and with it an impressive presence: *forma egregia et cui non minus auctoritatis inesset quam gratiae*, Suet. *Tit.* 3. 1. In the extant parts of the *Histories* T. is remarkably indulgent to him, cf V.1, and below 2. 2 n.; and it is sad that fuller analysis of his personality is largely lost, for he is unlike most Tacitean heroes.

fortunae capax, of imperial rule, to which the *fortuna* both of himself and of his father (I. 10. 17) was to bring him.

11. praesaga responsa, presumably the omens to which T. refers in ironical terms (so also *fortuita* here) at I. 10. 16 (cf. II. 78. 5), and which Suet. enumerates in some detail, *Vesp.* 5, *Tit.* 2.

13. Corinthi, Achaiae urbe. This piece of helpfulness is paralleled at V. 10. 3, *Euboeam, Aegaei maris insulam.* Josephus speaks simply of Achaia, proof (if one were needed) that he was not T.'s source.

certos nuntios ... All this news had got back to Judaea before his return: that it should have made him think carefully is natural, but the precise chronology is unclear. Probably we are now in early February.

15. cuncta utrimque perlustrat. It cannot but be highly significant that this survey includes the possibility that Vespasian himself will make a bid for empire. Jos. *BI.* IV. 500 knows nothing of this: so far from recording any hesitations by Titus, he emphasizes the speed (κατὰ δαιμόνιον ὁρμήν ... κατὰ τάχος) with which he returned to Caesarea. Meanwhile King Agrippa, presumably in contrast to Titus, was not alarmed by the political situation, and proceeded on to Rome.

19. incerta... The uncertainties of the text do not affect the sense. See Heubner's n.

20. excusatum. Most editors suppose the omission of *iri* from a normal future infinitive. For this there seems to be no parallel; if T. thought about the matter at all, he probably regarded *excusatum* as a participle balancing *offensam*, and with both words supplied *fore* from line 18. Again the sense is the same on either view, and it is interesting how naturally the sentence runs.

2.2. Berenices reginae. Iulia Berenice was daughter of Herod Agrippa I, and had married (1) Marcus, son of the alabarch at Alexandria and nephew to Philo (she was thus sister-in-law to Tib. Iulius Alexander, now prefect of Egypt), (2) her uncle Herod, tetrarch of Chalcis, (3) Polemo II of Pontus and Cilicia. But she had now left Polemo and was living with her brother Herod Agrippa II. Though still *florens aetate formaque*, II. 81. 7, she was eleven years older than Titus, (Jos. *Ant.* XIX. 354): for him, at the age of twenty-nine, T.'s *iuvenilis* *animus* and *laetam voluptatibus adulescentiam* are marvellously gentle treatment, contrast I. 13. 12, IV. 2. 1. For the story of the future relations between Titus and Berenice see *PIR*² s. v. *T. Flavius Vespasianus* (F 399); J. Crook, *AJP* 1951, 162 ff., has some attractive, but hazardous, conjectures about the effect on the unity of the Flavian party.

Berenice is repeatedly called 'queen' by Josephus, and also on *IG* III. 556, *CRAI* 1927, 243–4. G. H. Macurdy, *AJP* 1935, 246 ff., is at pains to refute the story, found in Jos. *Ant.* (but not in *BI*) and in Juvenal VI. 156 ff., that she lived in incest with her brother. It is rash to be so confident about Hellenistic 'sisters': agreed, however, that the main point about Agrippa and Berenice is that they were joint rulers, a fact important in the story of their relations with Rome and with the Jews.

5. suo ... moderatior. For a fuller version of this story (not one drawn from official Flavian writers) see Suet. *Tit.* 6–7.

6. laeva maris. He kept the coast on his left (for many parallels to the usage see Heubner's n.), but after reaching both Rhodes and Cyprus his voyages were more enterprising. Heubner argues that these more daring voyages began at Rhodes, but his case is not convincing. T.'s sentence does not demand that the ablatives accompanying *patebat* relate to the voyage to the islands as well as to Syria; and it would be curious for someone who had hugged the coast all round the Aegean to save time by taking the open sea from Rhodes to Cyprus rather than proceeding along Pamphylia.

T.'s description of Titus' voyage does not easily lend itself to conclusions of a political kind, e.g. that his decision to visit the oracle was more than a sight-seeing jaunt, or (more commonly among commentators) that the priest's response inspired him to *audentiora spatia* on his return home. T. himself does not draw such conclusions, and the obscurity of his account makes it hard for us to draw them. See however K. Büchner, *Die Reise des Titus, Stud. z. röm. Lit.* IV. (1964), 86 ff., and Wellesley's criticisms in *Gnomon*, 1965, 701 ff.; also Heubner's introd., 20 ff.

7. Syriam. Here too (see previous n.) there is no adequate ground for supposing that Titus was seeking a meeting with Mucianus before proceeding south to his father at Caesarea.

9. templum Paphiae Veneris, a temple still not revealed by excavation, though many features of the cult are shown on coins and gems. See esp. G. F. Hill, *History of Cyprus* (1940), 67 ff., T. Mitford and B. Iliffe, *Ant. Journ.* 1951, 25 ff. T.'s account is clearly based on literary borrowings rather than from knowledge of the site.

3. 1. conditorem templi. The shrine is already mentioned in Hom. *Od.* VIII. 362 (see also Schol. ad loc.). T. ignores the story found in Pausanias VIII. 5. 2, 53. 7, that it was founded by Agapenor on his return from Troy; and he thus says nothing of the connection between Cyprus and Arcadia, which is familiar to modern linguistic scholars and is also attested by the temple of Aphrodite Paphia at Tegea, dedicated by Agapenor's daughter Laodice (so Pausanias, cit., but Apollodorus 3. 102 says she was daughter of Cinyras). Both T.'s versions favour a still earlier date for the foundation at Paphos. Cinyras was beloved of Apollo (Pindar, *Pyth.* II. 15, *Nem.* VIII. 18) and father of Adonis (Apollodorus III. 14. 3); he is also called the inventor of tiles and of bronze instruments (Plin. *NH* VII. 195), and would thus be of an older generation than Agapenor, even though Homer (*Il.* XI. 20) says he gave Agamemnon a cuirass (and perhaps also, see Schol. ad loc., forty-nine clay ships and one real one). He was also the son of Amathusa, and that name connects with T.'s 'older' story, for at *A.* III. 62. 4 (perhaps drawing on a different source) he says Aerias was father of Amathus. Another version (Hdt. I. 105) made Paphian Venus come from Phoenicia, but this too T. ignores.

2. ipsius deae nomen. Hesychius s.v. Ἡερία, says the island too was called by this name (but other versions say Aeria was Crete). In Cypriot texts the goddess is simply called ἄνασσα.

3. conceptam. T. presumably accepts the view that the conception and birth of Venus were simultaneous, cf. Varro, *LL* 5. 63, *semen igneum cecidisse . . . in mare ac natam e spumis Venerem.*

4. accitam. Cic. *Div.* I. 2 gives the Cilicians the chief credit for developing divination from the flight and cry of birds.

5. Tamiram, a name known from Accadian inscriptions of Amathus as that of a Palestinian fertility goddess. Perhaps the original name of the Paphian deity, but certainly taken by T. as representing the foreign influence.

9. hostiae, for divination, not for sacrifice in the strict sense. Hill's suggestion, that T.'s assertion is 'inconsistent with itself' seems unnecessary. That care was taken to prevent blood reaching the altars is not disproved by the discovery at Old Paphos (Kouklia) of 'a small altar, suitable for small victims'.

11. igne puro. i.e. no blood.

12. nec ullis imbribus. Cf. Plin. *NH* II. 210, *celebre fanum habet Veneria Paphos, in cuius quandam aream non impluit.* Fabia, 247, insists that T., here as elsewhere, was drawing on Pliny (though not *NH*); but this cannot possibly be proved, and the earlier arguments in the opposite sense by Nissen, 535 ff., are telling. The undying fire at Paphos was selected by Augustine, *Civ. Dei* 21. 6, as an example of devilish magical practices, see Heubner's n.

14. metae modo. Cf. Serv. *ad Aen.* I. 720, *apud Cyprios Venus in modum umbilici vel metae colitur.* Cones appear on gems and coins which show a Greek temple, and many stones of this shape have been found on the island. A large black one in the Nicosia museum, illustrated by Hill, cit., Pl. I b, is particularly impressive. Strictly speaking, *tenuem in ambitum*, the shape is that of a truncated cone.

4. 2. laetum ... genus. Cf. Plin. *NH* III. 42, *Graii, genus in gloriam sui effusissimum.* For T.'s growing antipathy to things Greek, displayed in the *Annals*, see Syme, 512–13.

3. de navigatione primum. So also Suet. *Tit.* 5. 1, the question being whether to attempt the *audentiora spatia*, see II. 2. 6 n.

8. secreto. Cf. below, 100. 13 n.

10. ingens rerum fiducia. The view of Lipsius that *fiducia* is ablative has been rightly abandoned by all recent editors. For the nominative H. compares Ov. *Trist.* V. 6. 1, *tu quoque, nostrarum quondam fiducia rerum*; cf. also II. 5. 12, *praecipua concordiae fides Titus.*

The sentence corresponds closely with Josephus' account, *BI.* IV. 501, Τίτος ... ἀφικνεῖται πρὸς τὸν πατέρα, καὶ οἱ μὲν μετέωροι περὶ τῶν ὅλων ὄντες ... ὑπερεώρων τὴν ἐπὶ Ἰουδαίους στρατίαν. But Jos. ascribes the indecision to the Flavian leaders, whereas T. speaks of the feelings of the provinces (i.e. the leading men of the Eastern cities, cf. I. 4. 3) and armies. Briessmann, 3 ff., maintains that T. deliberately altered the version of his Flavian source, because he knew that the Flavian leaders had already been plotting; but that he then fell into inconsistency, since in II. 6 he shows that the provinces and armies were no less lacking in *fiducia*. This, however, may be over-subtle. Below in II. 74 ff. T. is perfectly prepared to admit that Vespasian hesitated long before taking the final plunge: what he will never allow is that the Eastern commanders were innocent observers until the nature of Vitellius' rule was revealed.

11. profligaverat. The Flavio–Vitellian war was considered *profligatum* after Antonius' victory at Cremona, III. 50. 5, and Cerialis claimed *profligatum bellum* against Civilis when he had entered Trier, IV. 73. 6. But a *profligatum bellum* was not necessarily over: cf. Cic. *Fam.* XII. 30. 2, *vehementius laboramus, qui profligato bello ac paene sublato bellum gerere conamur.* In Judaea it could be claimed that all had been subdued except

Jerusalem, V. 10. ff.; but three fortresses, Herodium, Machaerus, and Masada were still holding out, and the last of these (not mentioned by T. in his extant books) was captured only in 73.

13. ingenium montis, but Jerusalem is built on many hills, and T. knows of the two main ones at V. 11. 13. He is the first known writer to use *ingenium* of an inanimate object, cf. I. 51. 6.

  superstitionis. T. gives his analysis of this at V. 2. ff.

15. ut supra memoravimus. I. 10. 1 n. T. again forgets that the Syrian legions had now been reduced to three, since III Gallica must by now have been in Moesia. Similarly at II. 6. 15, but contrast 74. 6.

19. labor, an obvious dittography from the previous line. There can be no certainty what T. wrote, but *rubor* or *pudor* would introduce an unnecessary complication, for there was no reason for the Syrian legions to feel guilt about a war they had never been asked to join. Wellesley, *Gnomon*, 1965, 702, argues well for *ardor*—used with *pugnandi* in Livy and T (II. 23. 7, 42. 5). With this or with Orelli's *amor* the thought goes back to γλυκὺ δ' ἀπείροισι πόλεμος, Pindar, fr. 110, quoted by the scholiast on Thuc. II. 8. 1.

20. classes. The fleets at the eastern commanders' disposal included the Pontic, II. 83, III. 47, the Syrian (at Seleuceia), and the Alexandrian, possibly also the squadrons on the Danube; see Starr, 109 ff. 125 ff. Yet until the Ravenna fleet defected (were negotiations with Lucilius Bassus begun as early as this?), naval strength was hardly one of Vespasian's greater assets; cf. III. 1.

  reges. Cf. II. 6. 15 n., 81. 2. n, V. 1.

21. dispari fama, illustrated at once in the following chapter, before which T. probably intended no break.

5. 1. acer militiae etc. Despite the stock phraseology (for similar descriptions of the *vir militaris* cf. *Agr.* 20, *A.* XIII. 35), there is no reason to doubt that Vespasian in fact possessed these qualities; and *cibo fortuito*, which conforms to Suetonius' picture of the man, is perhaps an original point. *Die noctuque* is Sallustian (*BI* 38. 3, 44. 5, etc.), *diu* not being found between Sall. and T.; and for *consilio ac . . . manu* see the passages cited by G. B. A. Fletcher, *Annotations on Tacitus* (1944), 67. The reminiscences are natural in a description of one who was *antiquis ducibus par.*

4. prorsus, si avaritia abesset. Cf. II. 62. 3 (of Vitellius), *prorsus, si luxuriae temperasset, avaritiam non timeres* for the Sallustian echo see Martin, *Tacitus* (ed. Dorey), 129. 'Avarice' is the vice attributed relentlessly to Vespasian: cf. *Vesp.* 16, 23, Dio (=Xiph.) 66. 8, 14. Yet these writers give no actual examples before Vespasian moved to Alexandria, and at II. 84 T. admits that his behaviour was not unduly harsh until he learned evil ways from bad counsellors (see n. ad loc.). It would be interesting to know the origin of the tradition, and also whether Flavian writers were allowed to use it under the rule of Vespasian's sons. Clearly the collection of money for the civil war brought great unpopularity, see esp. Dio, cit., though at II. 84 T. gives the chief blame to Mucianus; and the economy drive after Vespasian's victory brought more, this time in Italy. But in addition unkind things were probably said in the army about a leader who was *egregie firmus adversus militarem largitionem*, II. 83. 12: compare the unlucky Trebellius Maximus, I. 60 n. Vespasian's record as proconsul of Africa may also have been remembered, cf. 97. 11 n. below.

5. Mucianus. Cf. I. 10.

dispositu...peritus. The genitive *civilium rerum* is surely governed by the ablatives rather than (as Heubner) by *peritus*. The last is a word which can easily stand alone; so can *provisu*, III. 22. 5, A. XII. 22. 2, though it is more normally followed by a genitive; but *dispositu* (first known use in Latin) seems to demand further definition. On either view, however, the meaning 'a discerning and far-sighted statesman' is clear; see Wellesley's excellent version.

7. egregium ... temperamentum. Briessmann, 5, supposes a common source behind this combination and that imagined between the virtues of Vespasian and Titus in Jos. *BI* IV. 597.

11. exitu demum Neronis. There had naturally been negotiations, friendly or otherwise, between the two commanders before this, e.g. the visit of Titus to Mucianus during the siege of Gamala in October, 67, Jos. *BI* IV. 32: the grounds for their discord are unknown—it was surely not an automatic outcome of *vicinae provinciarum administrationes*.

That they now agreed to concert their actions, in a situation which was likely to require rapid decisions, is not in itself sinister: the Danubian legates probably did the same, I. 76. 1 n., for who, in provinces far from Rome, could be sure of Galba's accession? But it is interesting that T. should be the only extant writer to give us this date for the reconciliation, cf. Briessmann, 9 f: Suet. *Vesp.* 5, and Dio (= Xiph.) 66. 8. 3, make the aftermath of Galba's death the first moment at which the leaders considered the situation; and Josephus does not allow anything significant to happen before the victory of Vitellius. What matters most, however, is that by taking us back to this starting-point T. provides a rational background for his own picture of Flavian planning. First, there was a deliberate halt in the prosecution of the Jewish War, a halt not in 69 (when fighting was temporarily resumed) but in the summer of 68. Josephus admits this, but explains it by the absence of fresh instructions from Galba, *BI*. IV. 498, and after Galba's death by Vespasian's concern for the safety of Rome, ibid. 502. T. baldly states *proximus annus civili bello intentus*, V. 10. 7, not the sort of words he uses of virtuous commanders who got on with their job and forgot politics (like the British armies, I. 9. 8). And secondly, we can understand how the East was able already to regard itself as a single united unit, 6. 12 ff. poised for attack whenever the political situation looked most favourable, and waiting only for the encouragement provided by Titus' reports to gain the resolution which removed all remaining misgivings. We must remember, too, that Titus' journey to Galba was somewhat tardy.

6. 1. antequam ... Despite tempting pointers, the chronology is elusive. Titus' return, which began at Corinth when the news of Galba's death reached him, can hardly have been completed before mid-February, leaving a period of some weeks during which the oath might have been taken, I. 76, with nn. Any news from a new claimant would go with maximum speed (*ut adsolet*), and in winter it would have gone mainly by land, over the imperial post: a month (cf. I. 12 n.) would probably have been more than enough. Anyway the Vitellians would not have got their messages through before those of Otho.

2. praecipitibus. For M.'s *precibus* I agree with Heubner in preferring Jacob's *pernicibus* to the 'breathless haste' implied by the conjecture of the *recentiores* (GG and 44. 1 below).

3. tarda ... belli. *moles belli* is a common phrase in T.; for the usage here see GG s.v. *moles*, A (b), 'the assembly of forces for a civil war'. Here we have the most explicit statement by T. that the East was already not only watching but preparing, though one of their difficulties was lack of precise knowledge about the course of events in the West.

    longa ... Oriens. Cf. *Oriens adhuc immotus*, I. 10. 1. T.'s thought concentrates first on the remarkable concord which had been achieved between East and West since Actium, and even goes on to claim, in very un-Augustan terms, that the civil wars at the end of the Republic started in Italy and Gaul. Moreover, if people remembered those wars, they would hesitate to begin one in the East, for the Westerners had always won. So they had played no part in the struggles of recent months, but the *scelesta arma* of Otho and Vitellius put other considerations into the background, especially as they were reminded of their own power.

5. Galliave. H. noted 'sc. Cisalpina', but T. was hardly being as precise as this. He thought above all of Caesar coming 'from Gaul', and possibly also of the forces from Gaul as well as Italy which supported the triumvirs and Octavian.

8. Caesares . . . inspecti. Down to Tiberius' mission of Germanicus, who died at Antioch in A.D. 19, members of the imperial house had been sent to the East at fairly regular intervals, especially Gaius Caesar, the grandson of Augustus, in A.D. 1. Since then there had been none; nor had there been any between the return of Titus to Italy in A.D. 71 and the time at which T. was writing.

9. adversus Parthos minae. *Minae* is a curious expression for the affairs (*vario eventu*) of Nero's reign; there had been actual fighting as little ago as A.D. 63.

11. mox . . . circumspicere. T. passes to a purely Flavian version of the Eastern rising, but one of which the implications are refuted by his chronology (including *tum primum* in 4 above) and by other features in his account.

10. proximo civili bello, the *bellum Neronis.*

15. septem legiones. II. 4. 15 n. Here again the revelation of Eastern solidarity finds no echo in Josephus, who speaks only of the three legions of Judaea, *BI.* IV. 598. See Briessmann, 11.

ingentibus auxiliis. At the outset of their campaign in Judaea Vespasian and Titus had twenty-three cohorts, of which ten were *milliariae*, and five *alae*, together with 15,000 men contributed by client kings. Jos. *BI.* III. 69, computes the size of this force, including the three legions, at 60,000 men, but he almost certainly exaggerates the size of the individual units. Some of the auxiliary regiments came from Syria: how many were left in that province we cannot tell. (A diploma of A.D. 88, *CIL* XVI. 35, lists seventeen cohorts in Syria).

17. Pontusque. This is Pontus Polemoniacus, the eastern part of the old Mithradatic kingdom, contiguous with Cappadocia. For modifications in its boundaries since the time M. Antonius gave it to Polemo see A. H. M. Jones, *Cities of the Eastern Roman Provinces²* (1971), 169 ff. with n. 45, D. Magie, *Roman Rule in Asia Minor* (1950), 177 ff. The kingdom had been annexed by Rome in A.D. 64 (*CAH* X. 740), and the new province had its capital at Neo-Caesarea (previously Cabeira–Diospolis). See note to map 1.

quicquid . . . praetenditur. Roman dispositions against Armenia are for this period exceptionally obscure. In Nero's reign there had at times been a large force, at one moment including three legions, in the united province Cappadocia–Galatia; for the vicissitudes see R. Sherk, *The Roman legates of Galatia from Augustus to Diocletian* (1951), 32 ff. But, mainly because of the Jewish War, no steps had yet been taken to regularize the defences of the Upper Euphrates since Corbulo's settlement with Parthia; and not only were there no actual legions there at this time, but T. calls the provinces of the area *inermes*, II. 81. 10. Yet this need not preclude significant numbers of *auxilia* (as, e.g., in Raetia and Noricum): there had of course been some garrison in Cappadocia throughout the Julio–Claudian period, cf. *A.* XI. 49. In Flavian times Cappadocia had at least 10,000 auxiliary troops, though this is no guide to 69.

18. nec virorum inopes. On the Asiatic provinces as a source of legionaries in this period see Forni, 53 ff., with discussion of the two most relevant literary texts, *A.* XIII. 13 and 35.

19. quantum ... cingitur. This superfluous definition of islands is puzzling. Heubner cites Livy XXX. 30. 25, *quidquid insularum toto inter Africam Italiamque continetur mari*, which in its context is natural: it may have been in T.'s mind.

20. secundum ... mare. For the inadequacy of Flavian naval strength as one of their actual assets see II. 4. 20 n. Yet their fleets did have defensive value. They could protect the mobilization of Asiatic forces, and we are many months away from the period (July onwards, 98. 2 n. below) when the etesian winds would best favour a naval attack from the west.

7. 2. bello civili. See app. crit. Some editors (V. especially) would omit the words, placing *bellum* at the end of the previous sentence: but the judgement which follows surely needs to be limited to civil war. Here and in line 5 the text in M. is hard to decipher. An attractive suggestion is made by D. C. A. Shotter, *Cl. Phil.* 1968, 287, who reads 'discordiam his ignaviam luxuriem; and otherwise as O. C. T. See also Wellesley's tr. which supposes a comma after *insolescere* and a heavier stop after *militis* (acc. plural).

8. ceteri olim. The statement that others of the army, presumably officers, had taken their decisions earlier (for *olim* cf. I. 60. 3) is tantalizing, but no further light is thrown by T. or any other source.

9. amore rei publicae. Cf. I. 12. 10 n. Jos. *BI.* IV. 602, speaking of the weeks before the actual proclamation, ascribes φροντὶς περὶ τῶν ὅλων to Vespasian himself: Briessmann, 7, could be right in thinking that this is another instance of the way T. tampered with his Flavian source.

10. ambiguae domi res. Cf. I. 88. 17.

8. 1. sub idem tempus. We should now be in March, possibly the later part of the month after Otho has left Rome. See n. at beginning of cap. 10 below.

falso. i.e. their alarm was 'misguided': cf. *Germ.* 36. 1, *quia inter impotentes et validos falso quiescas*; but T. is also of course quite clear that the rumour was untrue. On other false Neros, and the evidence concerning Nero's death see I. 2. 8 n. This particular one, despite *similitudinem oris*, was not strikingly like Nero (9. 11 n. below), but probably few of those who accepted him, e.g. the soldiers coming home from the East on leave, knew the emperor's appearance at the time of his death.

4. servus e Ponto sive ... libertinus ex Italia, rather different sorts of person, one might think. Could the former version be due to confusion with the *barbarum mancipium* from Pontus who gave trouble later in the year, III. 47?

10. dextras, concordiae insignia. I. 54. 2 n.

9. 1. Galatiam ac Pamphyliam provincias. Syme, seeing the significance of the plural *provincias*, showed that the union of these two provinces was due to Galba himself when he appointed Asprenas: see his account of the early imperial administration of Pamphylia, *Klio*, 1937, 227 ff. The position as Galba found it was that Lycia, previously united with Pamphylia, had been 'liberated' by Nero, and that the consular command in Cappadocia/Galatia had ceased to exist, cf. II. 6. 17 n. By the side of the *inermis legatus* in Cappadocia (II. 81. 10) Galba now provided another post for a praetorian senator in Galatia/Pamphylia, a post which had existed in Augustus' day.

The arrangement was shortlived. Whatever permanent system Nero (or Galba) may have contemplated had to be postponed till the Jewish War was over. But in A.D. 72 legions were stationed in Cappadocia, and to their consular commander was assigned a large group of provinces, among which Galatia was included, Sherk, cit., 32 ff. Meanwhile Vespasian took away the freedom of Lycia, Suet. *Vesp.* 84, and reunited it with Pamphylia.

Galba had also united the two Mauretanian provinces 58. 1 n. below. For this there were sound military and political reasons: the suggestion by Barbagallo, 53, that reduction in the number of governors was a measure of economy is not really plausible.

Calpurnio Asprenati. Clearly a member of the distinguished family of Nonii Calpurnii Asprenates, and probably the man who was proconsul of Africa in 83 (*IRT* 346 = MW 303); his consulate is not securely dated, but must belong to the early years of Vespasian (so Degrassi). He was undoubtedly related, *ILS* 927, to the Calpurnii

Pisones, and therefore to Galba's adopted son, Piso Licinianus. See the stemma in *PIR*[2] II. 54, followed in essentials by Syme, *RR*, Table 5.

3. prosequendum, 'to escort him'. Whether most provincial governors received such consideration is not known.

4. tenuit, 'entered the harbour of'.

trierarchos. See Starr, 43 ff., showing that the post, which implied the command of any naval vessel (trireme or smaller) was held at times by freedmen, and at other times by *peregrini* who received the citizenship on discharge.

10. corpus. The emendation to *caput*, accepted by K. and Heubner, rests on the ground that executed persons were usually decapitated and that the features described by T. are all facial. Yet *pervectum* is more appropriate to the body. For a delightfully dry complaint against unnecessary alteration see V.'s n.

11. oculis . . . vultus. Nero's face was handsome (*pulcher*) rather than beautiful (*venustus*), his eyes blue but rather weak, his hair reddish and arranged in bands of curls, Suet. *Nero.* 51. How the pretender resembled him is not made clear, and *torvitas* is above all surprising. It was that quality which enabled Nymphidius to claim to be Caligula's son, *A.* XV. 72, but no one ascribes it to Nero.

inde Romam. So, with a splendid piece of artistry, we return from the East. See Heubner, 45-6, on the three chapters II. 8-10.

II. 10. *The Senate in Otho's absence*

The political item which follows is unrelated either to the war or to any other part of T.'s account of Otho's principate. But it is of intrinsic interest (much more on such topics is given in Book IV esp. 4-10, 41-45), and Vibius Crispus was going to be a key figure in Flavian history. Otho is not mentioned, and the incident surely occurred after he left Rome; as usual, T. adheres closely to chronological sequence.

3. Vibius Crispus, a North Italian from Vercellae, who became one of Vespasian's chief advisers: he and Eprius Marcellus (53. 1 n. below) are described as *principes in Caesaris amicitia, Dial.* 8. He had held three consulates before A.D. 83 (Statius *ap.* Juv. IV. 94), and the second can now be confidently dated to March 74, *Epigraphica*, 1968, 11-17. An impressive revision of all earlier studies of his career, by A. B. Bosworth, *Athenaeum*, 1973, 70 ff., suggests that his first consulate was early in Nero's reign (he was already a man of some influence by 60, *A.* XIV. 28), that his African proconsulate (Plin. *NH* XIX. 4) was before Nero's death, and that quickly after his *cura aquarum* (certainly 68-71,

Frontinus, *Aq.* 102) he governed Tarraconensis, there conducting a census as part of Vespasian's policies for increasing taxation. He reached the age of eighty, Juv. cit., but had died before Quintilian published, *Inst.* V. 48 etc.

To T. he is a typical *delator*, cf. IV. 42–3, though we are not told of any individual victim. In contrast Juvenal, without any obvious sarcasm, speaks of *Crispi iucunda senectus, | cuius erant mores qualis facundia, mite | ingenium,* IV. 81–3: unlike Eprius Marcellus he 'survived', for *numquam derexit bracchia contra | torrentem,* ibid. 89–90.

4. ingenio. His oratory is often mentioned by Quintilian; for other examples of his wit see Suet. *Dom.* 3, Dio 65. 2. 3.

quam inter bonos. T. is well aware that some writer, assumed that *clari* would be *boni*, Cic., *Att. VIII.* 2. 3, Hor., *Epp. II.* I. 1.

Annium Faustum, presumably an ancestor of the wife of the Emperor Pius.

6. cognitio senatus. Mommsen, *Staatsrecht* I. 118. For the doubts, still existing in T.'s time, about the procedure in such cases see Plin. *Epp.* II. 11. 4.

7. censuerant patres. It is hard to see what the Senate decided: was anyone who had laid a charge to be investigated, or those who had laid certain types of charge, or those who had made money out of accusations? Barbagallo, 52, saw the recovery of money as Galba's main motive, perhaps rightly (contrast II. 9. 1 n.). For further instances of attacks on Neronian prosecutors see IV. 6 (Eprius Marcellus), 42 (Regulus): there too the Galbian *s.c.* may have been invoked.

10. retinebat ... terroris. See app. crit. V. defended the text (without *aliquid*) on the ground that a genitive after *retinebat* was a legitimate extension of its frequent use after the participle *retinens.* Heubner also keeps the text, adducing *Germ.* 15. 1 as a parallel.

11. fratris sui, Vibius Secundus, procurator of Mauretania in 60, who was exiled and only saved from a severer penalty by Crispus' resources, *A.* XIV. 28.

12. indefensum et inauditum. Cf. I. 6. 6. That a substantial body of the senate should have agreed to this proposal certainly suggests that the decree of A.D. 68 had been widely drawn.

14. dari tempus . . ., as in the case described in Plin. *Epp.* III. 9. 32.

11–50. *The Vitellio-Othonian war, contd.*

The major problems, above all the strengths of the two sides and the final Vitellian plan, are discussed in the Appendix.

11. 2. e Dalmatia Pannoniaque. No mention yet of movements from Moesia: these first appear in Paulinus' speech, II. 32. 25.

3. bina millia. These words could mean '2,000 in all', but every commentator has rightly assumed that they here mean '2,000 from each'. This was a recognized number of men to be sent as a vexillation from a legion which did not send its eagle: see Cestius Gallus' force in Judaea in 66 (Jos. *BI* II. 500), and for a further possible example below, 57. 5 n. One thing is certain, namely that the men from legion XIV who fought in the final battle were more than 500 strong, II. 43. 10, 66. 4.

6. rebellione Britanniae compressa. Cf. *domitores Britanniae*, V. 16. 14. XIV was the only legion which was present entire at Paulinus' victory over Boudicca, *A*. XIV. 34, thereby acquiring its title 'Martia Victrix'. So *magna ipsam fama*, II. 32. 85.

7. eligendo ut potissimos. i.e. for Nero's proposed Caucasian expedition, cf. I. 6. 12 with n., Ritterling, *RE*, s.v. *Legio*, 1731. It has sometimes been supposed that it was brought over only later, to meet the threat of Vindex; but in that case it would surely have been used in Gaul, whereas it clearly operated in Italy—27. 13 below, where the Batavian cohorts boast *coercitos a se quartadecimanos, ablatam Neroni Italiam*. Where it was placed in the period between the abandonment of the Caucasian expedition and Nero's death we do not know, nor where in Illyricum it was stationed at the beginning of 69 (Introd., p. 10).

8. virium ac roboris. Fabia, *RÉA*, 1941, 196, following Gerstenecker, maintained that *virium* meant numbers as distinct from quality, and that therefore T. could not have been speaking of the single legion XIV (for all legions would be equal in numbers of men), but was referring to the manpower of all four Illyrican legions. But the phrase is probably used as imprecisely as in I. 87. 8. The present sentence should carry on the previous one, showing why the men chosen as *potissimi* (legion XIV) were so slow in coming. Wellesley, *RLM* 273, argues for the contrary view, but not at *JRS* 1971, 43.

11. equitum vexilla. It is generally agreed, mainly on the evidence of Hyginus, *de mun. castr.* 30, that there were ninety horse to each praetorian cohort, Dom. Dob. 24, Durry, 99, Passerini, *coorti*, 69–70. They were apparently enrolled in the individual centuries, but often used as a single praetorian unit. For other references in T. see

A. I. 24. 3, XII. 56. 3. At the Castores battle these praetorian cavalry were probably an important element in the Othonian strength (why does T. mention them separately if they were only the normal adjuncts to the infantry cohorts?), but by then there would doubtless have also been legionary and auxiliary cavalry arriving from the Danube provinces.

13. etiam severis ducibus. e.g. D. Brutus, App. *BC* III. 49.

14. Annius Gallus. I. 87. 14 n. As a consular, he was the main commander of this expeditionary force.

Vestricio Spurinna. This senator was still alive when the Younger Pliny, who greatly respected him, wrote Book V of his Letters, i.e. about A.D. 105. He is treated very kindly by T., and may have been a significant source of information about this war; for a cautious summary of the evidence see Syme, 176–7.

Spurinna was about forty-five when he was Otho's general (he is seventy-seven in Plin. *Epp.* III. 1. 10). He was presumably consul under Vespasian; for the problems of his later career see Syme, App. 6.

16. transgresso … Caecina. See Appendix, pp. 264 ff. The crossing was probably that of his advanced guard, I. 70.

18. speculatorum. I. 24. 9 n. The phrase *cum ceteris praetoriis cohortibus* does not imply that the *speculatores* were regarded as a cohort: it only reminds us that five praetorian cohorts were with Gallus and Spurinna, and perhaps others in Liguria.

19. veterani e praetorio. All or some of the corps of *evocati*, whose numbers were unknown even to Cassius Dio (55. 24. 8, cf. Passerini, *coorti*, 76–8). They were a separate unit, σύστημα ἴδιον ὥσπερ οἱ ἑκατόνταρχοι.

classicorum … numerus. I. 6. 7. n.

21. lorica ferrea. The development of cuirasses in various sections of the Roman army during the first century A.D. is a complicated matter (P. Couissin, *Les Armes romaines* (1926), 439 ff.), but the point here is a simple one, namely that Otho was dressed as a soldier rather than in the full-dress uniform of a *princeps*. The ceremonial cuirass of the *princeps* was a most elaborate affair, such as Augustus wears on the Prima Porta statue: of bronze at least, or silver, or gilded, perhaps a combination of all three; in fact an armourer's finest piece. No doubt Vitellius wore some such breastplate after he had been fitted out by Iunius Blaesus (II. 59, cf. 89. 1), and his other accoutrements—camp furniture, silver plate, etc.—will have been on a similar scale. Otho may have worn the simple iron breastplate of a legionary, or more probably the moulded piece characteristic of a centurion (e.g. Favonius Facilis at Colchester).

22. famae, which produced the picture of Otho going to the war with his looking-glass, Juv. II. 99 ff.

12. 1. possessa . . . Alpium. What Otho held *per mare et navis* was not just 'the greater part' of the Italian coast, but the whole of it up to the beginning of the Maritime Alps and even beyond. He also held 'the greater part' of Italy, but not on account of his naval strength.

2. ad initium . . . Alpium. In imperial times the eastern boundary of Narbonensis remained what it had been in Caesar's day (*BC* I. 8), namely the river Varus (the Var, immediately west of Nice), Strabo IV p. 173, Plin. *NH* III. 31. The change was that the Province was divided from Italy by Augustus' creation of the small Alpine provinces, of which the most southerly was the Alpes Maritimae: for their boundaries and functions see *Cisalpine Gaul*, 25 ff. But Strabo IV p. 203 says that, although an equestrian governor administered the tribes in the mountain country, the coastal towns remained Italian. T. in line 9, *non Italia adiri* etc., implies the same: at any rate he means that Albintimilium (Ventimiglia), where the Othonians landed, was Italian, and the same is probably true of places further west, such as Nicaea (Nice) and Portus Herculis Monoeci (Monaco, just below the great trophy of Augustus at La Turbie). The words *maritimarum Alpium* are therefore used here only in a geographical sense: the procurator whose headquarters were probably at Cemenelum (Cimiez, north of Nice), was moving outside the strict bounds of his province when he came down to the coast.

7. ambitioso imperio. I. 83. 3 n.

adversus, 'when confronted by', as in the converse quality credited to Galba, *adversus blandientes incorruptus,* I. 35. 13.

9. patriae. The urbans and praetorians were almost wholly Italians, Introd., p. 20.

10. urere, vastare, etc. T. knew about this affair because the Othonians had killed the mother of his father-in-law Agricola in a raid on her estates near Albintilium, *Agr.* 7. In keeping with his reticence about himself, he refrains from recounting that incident here.

11. pleni agri, apertae domus. Not an impossible description of the Ligurian valleys and hillsides in early March, but also an obvious reminiscence of Sall. *Hist.* fr. 74, *apertae portae, repleta arva cultoribus,* and of *BI* 46. 5, where Africa is in high summer.

12. domini, 'estate owners': cf. II. 56. 6, *A.* III. 54.

13. securitate ... circumveniebantur. Those who delete *et* take *securitate pacis* as an ablative of 'circumstance' and *belli malo* as instrumental. But *et* can easily be retained if we recognize that *circumvenire* commonly means (as in the title of the Gracchan law *ne quis iudicio circumveniatur*) 'betrayed into ruin'; for Tacitean examples see GG s.v., B b).

14. procurator Marius Maturus, a keen Vitellian sympathizer, III. 42. 3. As late as Claudius' day the governor of the Maritime Alps was called *praefectus civitatium, ILS* 1349, but it may be that by A.D. 69 the title *procurator* had come into general use for these appointments.

15. gente. This should mean, not just 'people' (French 'gens'), but 'the tribe', in which case the Intemelii, Strabo IV p. 202, are presumably intended. But there were many tribes in the Maritime Alps (Plin. *NH* III. 47), and T. may be writing carelessly.

  nec deest iuventus. I. 68. 3 n.

17. non castra, non ducem. I. 68. 3 n. But in the present passage *castra* could be taken literally, 'they knew nothing of camp construction or of discipline'.

13. 1. Albintimilium. Both here and at *Agr.* 7 (*in templo*, codd.) scribes found difficulty in transcribing the name of this place, the modern Ventimiglia. Strabo, cit., calls it "Αλβιον 'Ιντεμέλιον, and T. also perhaps wrote it as two words.

8. latere. She replied 'latet', and although those who have wondered whether T. did not intend the second syllable of *latere* to be short complain that she would not by this one word be answering the question 'ubi latet?', the answer is most adequately completed by *uterum ostendens*.

14. 1. in verba Vitellii adactae. I. 76. 8.

2. Fabio Valenti. For the chronological and geographical background to this affair see Appendix, pp. 266 ff., where it is tentatively suggested that Valens got the news of the invasion when he was near Lucus at the end of February, and the news of the fighting when he was at Augusta Taurinorum at the end of March, II. 28. 1 ff.

3. legati coloniarum. Besides Forum Iulii, the nearest Narbonese colonies of any importance were Aquae Sextiae and Arelate. Although these places are some distance away from the Othonian landing, their nervousness is understandable, for the Othonians' plans were obscure, and their ruthlessness gave no comfort to any undefended area. It is also possible that Cemenelum was a colony (*CIL* V. 2, p. 916); and T., whose use of the term *colonia* is by no means reliable (e.g. III. 8. 3), may include places nearer the coast such as Vintium (Vence) or Pedo (Borgo San Dalmazzo), or even Albintimilium itself.

4. Tungrorum cohortes. A soldier of 'coh. pr(ima) T . . .' was buried at Vence, *CIL* XII. 16. The Tungrian cohorts were *milliariae*, if they are identical with the two which have left records from the following century in Britain (but *CIL* XVI. 81 also records a *cohors* IV Tungrorum of unknown size in Mauretania in A.D. 157). One of these may be the cohort which deserted to Civilis in an early battle next autumn, IV. 16. 12.

5. Trevirorum alam. This unit, under Iulius Classicus, had returned to the Rhine by the time of Civilis' rebellion, IV. 18. 10, 55. 3. It is not known from inscriptions, and may have been disbanded by Vespasian. It could be the same *Trevirorum ala* which had given trouble under Tiberius, *A.* III. 42.

in colonia Foroiuliensi retenta. It is hard to understand why the naval base needed a larger garrison, and why any advance eastwards by the reinforcements should result in an undefended position (*vacuo mari*). Starr, 11–13, maintains that after an initial phase under Augustus, when Forum Iulii was strongly fortified and harboured a large proportion of the navy (Strabo IV, p. 184), most of the ships had been transferred to Misenum. He admits, however, that T. classes it as a base comparable with Misenum and Ravenna in his description of the empire's forces in A.D. 23 (*A.* IV. 5. 1); and the impressive works there, including two camps and a *praetorium* north of the harbour, do not seem to have fallen into early decay. At III. 43. 5 T. calls the place *claustra maris*, and from the fact that the Othonians did not assault it by sea we can guess that they regarded its naval resources with respect.

A dedication at Fréjus by a *vexillatio Germanicianorum* was presumably set up by the Vitellian force now placed there, *ILS* 9121.

7. duodecim equitum turmae. An *ala* contained sixteen *turmae* if *quingenaria* and twenty-four if *milliaria*. So the force sent by Valens included at least twenty *turmae*, and at most three-fifths of them were sent into battle.

9. Ligurum cohors ... auxilium. The cohort is known from inscriptions of Cemenelum, *CIL* V. 7889 ff. H. and V. took *vetus loci* to mean 'familiar with the country, (cf. *vetus militiae*, IV. 20. 11), but it more probably means 'which had for long been garrisoning the area'.

10. quingenti Pannonii ... nondum sub signis. Pannonians undoubtedly served on the Rhine in the mid-first century A.D.: see Kraft, 22–4, and the evidence about *cohors I Pannoniorum* in his Appendix. But that their route should have taken them down to the

Riviera would be surprising, even in mid-winter; and it would be even more curious if Otho's government, which controlled not only Pannonia, but (at least) the southern part of the Po valley, should have allowed a movement of that kind, by potentially hostile troops, in recent weeks. Has not T., then, put this body of men into the wrong army? His next sentence, passing to the Othonians, is almost intolerably abrupt, and he may have been too cavalier about the order of battle reported by his source. We know that there was a Pannonian cohort, loyal to Otho, in North Italy before the main Othonian forces arrived, II. 17. 8, and it would have been easy for Annius Gallus to send 500 unbrigaded soldiers to join the Riviera expedition.

11. acies ita instructa. I cannot follow Heubner's argument that the structure of the chapter, from its opening words onwards, makes it clear that this is the Othonian battle order. Yet it certainly is so: as H. emphasized, the mention of *classici* is decisive. Some editors would insert *Othonianorum*, but probably T. was once again being careless. Similar carelessness makes him omit the urban cohorts on the Othonian side.

14. conversa. i.e. with prows facing land.

15. Vitelliani. Their order is less precisely described; and Köster, 44, is probably right in deriving the whole account of the battle from an Othonian source.

16. Alpini proximis iugis, the mountaineers on their own terrain. The exact site is impossible to determine, but must have been east of Antipolis, II. 15. 10, and west of Albintimilium, perhaps near Menton.

22. undique clausi. Why no attack by Vitellian infantry, Köster, 53? Heubner suggests that the Vitellians (*in equite robur,* 14. 6) staked all on their cavalry charge, and despaired when the Othonian fleet joined in repulsing them. That the outcome of the battle was an Othonian victory is attested by Suet. *O.* 9. 2.

15. 8. velut pactis indutiis. The two places are about 75 miles apart, but had the retreats given reason to suspect treachery T. would no doubt have said so.

10. Antipolim ... municipium, Antibes about 7 miles west of the Varus river. This town, detached from its mother-city Massilia by Caesar, had Latin rights, Plin. *NH* III. 35. There is no confirmation of T.'s *municipium*, but the word may be used loosely, II. 14. 3 n.

11. Albingaunum, modern Albenga. This was fairly certainly a *municipium*, *CIL* V. 2, p. 892.

The extent of the Othonian retreat was presumably not realized by the Vitellians, whose message to Valens stated *Narbonensem Galliam circumiri*, 28. 2 (unless Valens deliberately exaggerated, see II. 14. 2 n.).

interioris. Not 'inland', but either 'away from the frontier', or (more probably) 'nearer Rome' (IV. 2. 10, *intra Bovillas stetit*).

16. 1. Corsicam ac Sardiniam. The two islands had been made into a single senatorial province in 27 B.C., Strabo XVII p. 840 (Dio 53. 12. 4 mentions Sardinia only); but in A.D. 6 Sardinia was put under an equestrian governor, Dio 55. 28. 1, and (see below) Corsica was perhaps detached from it. In A.D. 66 Nero transferred Sardinia to the Senate in compensation for the liberation of Achaia, Paus. 7. 17. 3; the first proconsul was in office, in succession to a procurator, by 1 July 67; and his successor was L. Helvius Agrippa, who made a pronouncement about a boundary dispute in March 69 (*ILS* 5947 = MW 455). Vespasian, when he revoked the liberation of Achaia, removed the island from senatorial control, for in A.D. 74 Sex. Subrius Dexter is recorded as *procurator et praeses*, *CIL* X. 8023–4 = MW 337. See P. Meloni, *L'amministrazione della Sardegna da Augusto all' invasione Vandalica* (1958), 22 ff.

About Corsica the evidence is thin, but one inscription, *CIL* XII. 2455, mentions a *prae(fectus) Corsicae* who seems to be an independent officer, and there seems little doubt that this is a text of the Julio–Claudian period, Meloni, cit., 17. The Decimus Picarius here could be a subordinate of the proconsul of Sardinia, for procurators of this period hold very independent positions in senatorial provinces (see the activities of Antonius Naso in Bithynia in A.D. 77, without mention of his proconsul's existence, *ILS* 253 = MW 421). Yet the Othonian proconsul of Sardinia, *ILS* 5947, had at least two senators among his large staff, and one would have expected one of them to be in Corsica if that island was under the proconsul's command; there is no senator mentioned among the *principes insulae* of line 6 below. Probably therefore Corsica was still detached from Sardinia; and it surely remained so when Vespasian resumed control of Sardinia, for the procurator Otacilius Sagitta in A.D. 77 is described as being in charge, *CIL* X. 8038 = MW 460.

3. Pacarii. The name was probably Picarius, A. Stein, *RE* XXI, col. 1186.

6. principibus, 'the leading personalities' (Wellesley), Roman officials but probably also some provincials.

8. Liburnicarum. Strictly speaking, these were light, fast ships, modelled on those of the Illyrian pirates, long and narrow with triangular sails. But T. may use the word (found often in Book III) for any type of ship, Starr, 54. On trierarchs, II. 9. 4 n.

11. dilectum. Cf. IV. 14. 3.

18. balineis, presumably a locative, though the parallels cited by Heubner (e.g. Suet. *Nero.* 35. 5, where there is an ablative absolute) are not convincing.

17. 2. supra. I. 70.
   nullo ... favore etc. The rest of the sentence refers to the Transpadanes of this region, not (as Drexler, 163 f.) to the *ala Siliana* and other parts of Caecina's army, whose loyalty to Vitellius has been explained at I. 70.

4. melioribus, for the dative, *A.* XIV. 38. 3, *serendis frugibus incuriosos.*

5. quantum... Alpisque. Courbaud, 86, noted this as a characteristic instance of T.'s inexactitude when he wants to heighten the drama. The Vitellian conquest extended east only as far as Cremona.

7. capta ... Ticinumque. Two problems arise, (a) when and how did the Vitellians occupy Cremona? (b) where did these Othonian troops come from?
   (a) Plut. *O.* 7. 1 thought Cremona was still in Othonian hands when Caecina withdrew from Placentia, yet he never (nor does T.) records its subsequent capture. He probably (Passerini, 197, Momigliano, 132) misunderstood the source which T. (22. 15, 23. 6) rendered as *Cremonam petere, pergere Cremonam*: these verbs need not imply an attack on a city held by the enemy. For Cremona was surely occupied by the Vitellians in the operations reported in the present passage. The few Othonian troops in North Italy tried to retain the key fortresses, but only Placentia (south of the Po) was successfully held, and most of their men were intercepted in open country. The Flavian army, rightly or wrongly, believed that the people of Cremona received the invaders willingly, III. 32. 6.
   Fabia, 55 f., and Henderson, 338, were surely wrong in calling the Othonians here 'the garrison of Cremona', for a garrison, under orders as such, ought never to have left the town: *apud* means 'near'.
   (b) Passerini, 191 ff., thought these Othonians were part of the expeditionary force from Rome. But if Otho only left Rome on 14 Mar. (and Passerini said 24 Mar., I. 90. 1 n.), he could not conceivably have arrived by the time of these preliminary movements, or indeed much before the final battle (a highly confused passage of Plut., *O.* 5. 3—see below, 18. 6 n.—may be disregarded). The *classici* of this chapter are surely marines from Ravenna; the *Pannoniorum cohors* could be troops

left in Italy since Nero's mobilization in 68, I. 70. 3 n. Two soldiers of *coh. I. Pannoniorum equitata* (Heubner, 75) have left records at Aquileia.

11. Batavos, no part of the famous eight Batavian cohorts, which were with Valens, I. 61. 7 etc. They are presumably Batavian *alae*, for whose swimming skill see IV. 12. 14, and later Dio 69. 9 (with *ILS* 2558).

18. 1. certum erat, used in different senses with the two verbs. Fyfe tr. 'he had made up his mind'.

2. necdum venisse Caecinam. For chronology see Appendix, pp. 264.

3. tris praetorias cohortis. The remaining two (II. 11. 11) were with Gallus east of Cremona.

mille ... equitum. Passerini, 192, identified these with the *classici* and cavalry who later deserted to Caecina, 22. 16. This is not certain. Mommsen, *Gesammelte Schriften* (1905–13), IV. 355 n. 2 (see also V.) was surely wrong in regarding the *vexillarii* as legionaries who had already arrived from Illyricum.

5. indomitus ... ignarus. This picture of the praetorians, which T. consistently draws, is surely more responsible than Plutarch's μαλακοί (in the parallel passage *O.* 5. 8), cf. 44. 1 n. below.

signis vexillisque. On the correct usage of these words see I. 36. 4 n. but T. so often brackets them together to describe the standards of any kind of unit that it is unlikely that he thought of the *signa* here as belonging exclusively to the praetorians and the *vexilla* exclusively to the *vexillarii*; cf. II. 43. 8 (a legion), III. 63. 2 (Vitellian praetorians), IV. 15. 9, 34. 11 (auxiliary cohorts). See again 85. 6 n. below.

6. retinenti duci ... About the context of this affair T. is much clearer than Plut. *O.* 5. 5–6. Plut. adds (see Fabia, 51) that the mutineers came drunk one night to Spurinna's tent and asked for journey money to go and accuse him before Otho, and this has led some commentators to agree with Plut. that Otho was already in North Italy. But not only is this almost inconceivable chronologically, II. 17. 7 n., but it spoils the idea of a long journey which Plut. found in his source.

8. fit ... comes. Wellesley rightly avoids a translation which would make T. critical of Spurinna, a commander so favourably treated in the rest of the narrative and one who may have been a source for T. (II. 11. 14 n.). In *RhM* 1960, 276 he suggests 'accompanied a march dictated by the rashness of others'.

19. 1. postquam in conspectu Padus. One would see the Po from the walls of Placentia, and the sight of it given to the Othonians only after some marching has led to much attempt at emendation (see e.g. V.'s app. crit.) and to a variety of interpretations of the MS. reading. The answer to all difficulties has surely been provided by Passerini, 194 ff. The road taken by the garrison was not that which crossed the Po immediately and which led to Laus Pompeia and Mediolanum, but the road to Ticinum, which appears in the Peutinger Table and in the Ravennate geographer to have had no station in common with the Mediolanum road. Instead it crossed the Po at 'Ad Padum', which K. Miller, *Itineraria Romana* (1916), 227, identifies with Pievetta, 20 miles west of Piacenza; and between the two places the Po has made a large bend to the north. Hence the Othonians leave the river soon after their march begins, initially to the west, but come in sight of it again when they have made about a day's journey. Moreover it was along this road from Ticinum that Caecina eventually advanced; for he crossed the river before attacking Placentia (II. 20. 9), an attack most hazardous in face of the Othonians had his bridge or ford been on the Mediolanum road immediately outside the town.

Whether T. understood this geography may be doubted, but if Passerini's explanation be right he was following a reliable source, perhaps Spurinna himself (II. 11. 14 n.). In comparison Plut.'s sections (*O*. 5–6) are worthless—if indeed Plut. was writing about the same events. See also Wellesley, *RhM* 1960, 276, Heubner, 78, P. Tozzi, *Athenaeum*, 1970, 123.

5. patentibus campis. This, on the above interpretation, would correctly describe their present position south of the Ad Padum crossing, and also the country they would reach if they crossed to the left bank.

8. coloniam. Placentia was originally a Latin colony founded in 219 B.C. Asconius *in Pis.* 2, criticized Cicero for calling it a *municipium*; but the criticism was misplaced, since all the Latin colonies of Cisalpine Gaul became Roman *municipia* after the Social War. Yet T.'s *coloniam* may be right for his period, since the place was probably colonized once more by Augustus, like Parma, Bononia, and Ariminum. See *Cisalpine Gaul*, 18.

10. exploratoribus. Hardly necessary if they were close to the city, but natural if they were to watch a crossing 20 miles away.

11. solidati muri etc. For the timing of Spurinna's arrival in the Po valley see Appendix, p. 265. He evidently had time to organize quite elaborate fortifications before Caecina's main army appeared.

12. propugnacula. H. thought that this was T.'s equivalent for the technical word *pinnae* ('merlons' or 'battlements'), V. that there were external fortifications designed to cut off the retreat of a force trying to enter the city during a sortie. At V. 12. 3 and *A.* XII. 56. 3 the word does seem to describe works outside the main walls; but at III. 84. 13, *A.* IV. 51. 1 H.'s meaning is more probable.

20. 2. modesto agmine, 'with his army under control', as contrasted with their behaviour among the Helvetii (I. 67 ff.), but his personal conduct and that of his wife evoked criticism. There is no inconsistency here, as supposed by Drexler, 163: see Heubner's acute description of the skilful way T. introduces Caecina and his forces to the coming struggle.

The picture of Caecina in this chapter and in Plut. *O.* 6. 3–4 has seemed to some scholars (e.g. Syme, App. 29) to derive from a source which could not have been published in Caecina's lifetime, i.e. before *c.* A.D. 79. Plut. is certainly hostile without reserve, but T. gives friendly touches, *in superbiam trahebant* (i.e. unfairly), *in nullius iniuriam, tamquam laesi,* followed by reflections on the way any success must lead to jealousy. Anyway, do we know enough of the politics of Vespasian's reign to be sure that Caecina was immune from criticism, especially by his North Italian compatriots? See Townend, *AJP* 1964, 338.

4. bracas [barbarum tecgmen]. Apart from reading *tegumen,* K. keeps the bracketed words. Yet it seems almost incredible (though *Corinthi, Achaiae urbe,* II. 1. 13, makes one pause) that T., in his day, should have felt it necessary to explain *bracae*: the garment was well known, and its barbarity proverbial, e.g. Cic. *Fam.* IX. 15. 2, Suet. *Caes.* 80. But it could be (J. P. Postgate, *CR* 1926, 122) that *bracas* rather than *barbarum tecgmen* is the gloss, cf. Verg., *Aen.* XI. 777, *barbara tegmina crurum.*

5. uxorem ... Saloninam. Caecina was born at Vicetia, III. 8. 6, where a woman called Salonia was mother to a young senator of Claudian date, *ILS* 968. See Syme, *CQ* 1937, 45.

10. Padum transgressus, coming south from Ticinum (Pavia) and Ad Lambrum (S. Colombano) to the western crossing, II. 19. 1 n. A record of Caecina's army on the right bank of the Po is perhaps to be found in a dedication by *vexillarii* of the three Upper German legions to a soldier of IV Macedonica who died in his second year of service, *ILS* 2284, though how the stone got to Veleia, high up in the Appennines, remains a mystery.

21. 3 pulcherrimum amphitheatri opus. No trace of this has survived, and on the assumption that it completely perished in this fire it has often been assumed that it was made of wood, like the one at Fidenae which collapsed in Tiberius' reign, *A.* IV. 62, or those which were built so rapidly at Bononia and Cremona by the Othonian legionaries, II. 67. 7: see (e.g.) S. Aurigemma, *Historia* (Rome, 1932), 558. But a stone amphitheatre could suffer badly if the wooden portions of its seating caught fire; and the Placentines' dismay at their loss, and their suspicion of the jealousy of their neighbours, surely mean that their building was one in the prevailing fashion. That fashion, though the extant examples at Verona and Ariminum probably date from later in the century, was certainly for building in stone. See G. Mansuelli, *Urbanistica e architettura della Cisalpina romana (Coll. Latomus,* 1971), 143 H.

5. missilem ignem, presumably distinct from *faces* or *glandes.* The technical terms, as usual avoided by T., for wooden darts coated with pitch, were *phalaricae,* Livy XXI. 8. 10, and *malleoli, Bell. Alex.* 14, Amm. Marc. XXIII. 4.

14. pluteos ... vineas. On the various forms of construction for the protection of besiegers see H. Olck, *RE* IV. 2 (1901), coll. 1682 ff. *Crates* (Veget. V. 14 ff.) are probably not a specialized type, but T.'s generalized word for the wicker coverings used in most other forms. *Vineae* (see also T. Rice Holmes, *Caesar's Conquest of Gaul*[2] (1911), 602) resembled a pergola of vines, being shelters with sloping roofs supported by poles. *Plutei* were sheds with arched roofs, and were supported on rollers.

21. peregrinum et externum. Not of course to be taken as serious evidence about the actual origins of the Rhine legionaries (as distinct from the *auxilia*), nor even about T.'s view of the matter. In fact many of them were North Italians, see II. 56. 6 and n.

22. 2. legionum, although XXI Rapax was the only complete legion, cf. I. 11. 6 n.

4. neglecta ... fluxa, because of the *longa pax,* II. 17. 3. But the outcome of this battle shows that Spurinna had repaired the major gaps in the defences, II. 19. 11 n.

6. cantu ... corporibus. The chant (*Germ.* 3, *nec tam vocis ille quam virtutis concentus videtur*) is often introduced by T. when describing Germans in battle, e.g. IV. 18. 7, *A.* I. 65. 1; the naked bodies were remarked by Caesar, *BG* IV. 1. 10, VI. 21, and to T. are characteristic of the Germans in peace as well as in war, *Germ.* 6, 20, 24. There were certainly Germans in Caecina's army who had been recently recruited, I. 61. 9: yet this description of their habits may be purely conventional, as seems often to be the case in Book IV.

15. traiecto rursus Pado. This time he probably crossed immediately opposite Placentia, and proceeded east to Cremona along the Via Postumia, cf. II. 19. 1 n.

Cremonam petere. II. 17. 8 n. For the Vitellian march see I. 19. 1 n.

17. compluribus ... equitum. II. 18. 3 n.

Iulius Briganticus, nephew and enemy of Iulius Civilis, the rebel of Book IV, cf. I. 59. 1. He died fighting for Petillius Cerialis next year, IV. 70. 11, V. 21. 3. Since it is his nationality rather than his affinity with Caecina's army which is given as the ground for his desertion, his *ala* had probably seen service elsewhere than on the Rhine (possibly in Illyricum). It would have come to Italy for Nero's operations in A.D. 68, not for the present war.

23. 2. Annium Gallum. Clearly Gallus' main task was the protection of Othonian communications with Illyricum, and this he eventually discharged by taking his position at Bedriacum, the meeting-place of the two main roads to the east. But if Cremona, on the left bank of the Po, was now in enemy hands (as argued at II. 17. 7 n.), his march to relieve Spurinna must have been made on the right (south) bank of the river, presumably up the Via Aemilia, which approaches Placentia from the south-east. This would be natural if he had only just arrived from Rome and had not yet crossed the river. But since there is no good reason for thinking he was so far behind Spurinna, it is more likely that he had already advanced beyond the Po to Mantua or even Verona, and had now to make a southward crossing, perhaps at Brixellum. In that case he crossed back northwards when he found Spurinna no longer needed him (though whether Plut. implied a river crossing by the verb μετήγαγεν is uncertain—his account here, as we have seen, is quite unreliable).

Passerini, 198–9, though recognizing that Cremona was already held by the Vitellians, thought that Gallus operated on the left (northern) bank throughout, attempting to press on Caecina's rear, and perhaps cut his communications with Ticinum. But this would have entailed most difficult manoeuvres with a relatively small force, and Passerini inevitably had to regard the soldiers' eagerness for actual battle as the wildest piece of rashness ever shown by Otho's enthusiastic army. If Gallus was on the right bank, any battle could have been fought in co-operation with the troops at Placentia. It is just arguable that Gallus, though on the right bank, missed his chance of crossing quickly to recover Cremona before Caecina entered it, but we have too little evidence about the position of his legion when he got Spurinna's message. On the whole it seems likely that he never got as far as the point opposite Cremona from which Martius Macer (see below) attempted his crossing.

8. Bedriaci. This spelling is consistent in T.'s MSS. and in Plin. *NH* IX. 135; the MSS. of Suet. and Plut. give *Betriacum*; Juvenal, II. 106, and his Scholiast wrote *Bebriacum*. The gentile name 'Betrius' seems to be found on an inscription (*AE* 1928, 61, *Fl. Victor mil. cho. VIII pre 7 Betri*—not of early date), but Passerini's conviction that this confirmed Mommsen's acceptance of *Betriacum* (180, cf. *coorti*, 148) is puzzling.

inter Veronam Cremonamque. The case, previously accepted by many scholars who hold differing views about the subsequent campaign, for placing Bedriacum at the village of Calvatone, is well argued by Passerini, 188 f.: Wellesley, App. II. 2 to his edn. of Book III, and *JRS* 1971, 29, makes a powerful case for the more southerly village Tornata. On either view there is no good reason to question T.'s reference to Verona, as Mommsen did in *CIL* V. 411. By this time there was naturally another road running due east to Mantua, Hostilia, and Atria, but it is not in the least unlikely (our present passage is the only evidence on the point) that Postumius in 148 B.C. carried his road to Verona rather than Atria. For the whole course of the road from Genua to Aquileia, and for the connections with the other important highways of North Italy see *Cisalpine Gaul*, 33 f.

9. duabus ... infaustusque. It is a curiosity that Bedriacum, in popular usage (see Suet. and Juvenal in n. to line 8), gave its name to two battles which were fought much nearer to the large city of Cremona. In Books III and IV, however, *Cremonense proelium* is T.'s normal designation of the second battle.

11. isdem diebus. Passerini, 197 n. 4, is surely right in thinking that this action took place while Caecina was on his way rather than after he reached Cremona. Otherwise Macer's attack would have been most hazardous.

Martio Macro. A man of that name was consul-designate, I. 77 with n., but was deprived of the office by Vitellius, II. 71. 9, and is not heard of again. Dessau, *PIR*[1] M 258, identified him with a Claudian legate of Moesia who was subsequently proconsul of Achaia, *ILS* 969; but that man would have been too old for a subordinate command in 69, since his praetorian office in Moesia must have preceded the separation of the province from Macedonia and Achaia in A.D. 44.

What Macer was here trying to do is not clear. Momigliano, 137, thought he was frustrating a Vitellian attempt to bridge the Po, but whether or not that was Caecina's eventual plan the Vitellians hardly had sufficient strength near Cremona to put it in hand as yet. Passerini, 197, argued that Macer was trying to push over a force to surprise Cremona before Caecina arrived, but felt bound to withdraw, to the disappointment of his troops, when the surprise failed. This (though not Passerini's accompanying conclusions about Gallus, see on line 2 above) seems an attractive view.

13. navibus, presumably from Ravenna.

20. nam . . . praefecerat. See app. crit., but no suggested emendation really makes the parenthesis less puzzling. Probably Fisher was right to keep the MS., the meaning being that Otho had appointed the two last named, Paulinus and Celsus, as well as Gallus who has been exercising command already. For the threefold command see I. 87. 14. T. never tells us when Paulinus and Celsus arrived in North Italy, and Plut. *O.* 7. 1 says only that they gradually came to Gallus' help.

22. interfectores Galbae . . . Klingner, 3 ff., shows brilliantly how these words bring back into focus the Othonian party, with its emperor bound helplessly to his accomplices in crime and unable, despite his attempts at conciliation, to resist their suspicion of respectable elements in the Senate. But it is not clear why Klingner thinks this shows T. to have departed from the 'common source' about the timing of Titianus' appointment (see next n.).

26. Titianum praeposuit. Plut. *O.* 7. 4 makes this appointment the result of the battle at Castores, but he surely misunderstood the 'common source'. Titianus had to be summoned from Rome, I. 90. 19, and if the order was sent to him after Castores he could not possibly have arrived before the final Othonian offensive. T.'s *interea* at the beginning of the next chapter marks the interval between appointment and arrival: Plut. confused the two. Moreover T.'s context for the appointment is quite reasonable: Macer's restraint of his men was a comparatively minor affair, but when combined with Gallus' caution it was viewed with extreme suspicion by the soldiers.

Where Otho himself was at this moment is uncertain, 33. 12 n. below, but there is every ground for rejecting the view of Fabia, 58, that Titianus was anywhere than in Rome.

24–6. *The battle at Ad Castores*

For the moment, the Othonians have some measure of superiority. Though Otho and his bodyguard may not yet have arrived, Paulinus and Celsus probably brought with them more troops from Rome, e.g. there are three praetorian cohorts at 24. 15 rather than the two Gallus had originally (II. 18. 2 n.). More certainly, the *vexillum* of XIII Gemina has now arrived from Pannonia, and with it would have come some auxiliaries, including some of the cavalry mentioned in the battle. Possibly some other contingents from the Danube. When Caecina's army later complained to Valens' force *expositos se tanto pauciores integris hostium viribus*, II. 30. 6, they were undoubtedly comparing their strength with that of the enemy they had had to face, rather than with that of the army which later reinforced them, cf. Passerini, 210–11. In patrolling skirmishes the Vitellians had the worst of it, 24. 4, and Caecina tried to redeem his reputation, after his failure at Placentia, by planning an ambush against the Othonian advance.

T. gives a fairly close attention to the dispositions in the battle which followed. The Othonians had been warned of the ambush, and organized their advance in the order described at 24. 14 ff. Their wings pushed ahead of the heavy infantry in their centre, and their cavalry, appearing to pursue the Vitellian horse, induced the Vitellian ambushers to leave their cover too quickly and to come forward into a trap. In front of them were the Othonian heavy infantry, on the wings the Othonian *auxilia*, and meanwhile Othonian cavalry had come round them on the Cremona side, see 25. 4 ff. From this pocket some of the Vitellians, supposedly because Paulinus was too slow with his infantry, escaped into a vineyard and a wood, and did some damage to the Othonian cavalry who attacked them. Meanwhile Caecina sent out further cohorts, not *en masse* but one after another, and gradually his army, much discontented, was pursued back to his camp.

Various problems remain:

(a) The Vitellians had to confront *legionum adversa frons*, 25. 5; where were the praetorians? Probably, though carelessly, T. included them with the *legiones*, who somewhat outnumbered them. There is no reason to think they had been moved to the rear.

(b) *subito discursu terga cinxerant equites*, 25. 5, has caused doubts, but I take it for certain that the *terga* are Vitellian and the *equites* Othonian. But are these Othonian cavalry men led by Celsus from the wings, or the reserve of 1,000 described at 24. 18? It was that reserve which included praetorian cavalry, and it was praetorian cavalry who attacked the men who escaped into the wood. Yet I suspect, without confidence, that the trap was closed by more forward horsemen, under Celsus' direct control.

(c) Why did Caecina send out his relieving cohorts one by one, thus causing anger in his camp and chaos in the field? Hanslik, 116 f., explains this in terms of the difficulty of any march, other than *in aggere viae*, until the nearby ditches had been filled up—the operation which Paulinus on the other side had been facing. Heubner, 104, emphasizes the reluctance of both sides to reach a decisive conflict at this moment:

the circumstances of the battle had taken both by surprise. So Caecina sent out the minimum of men whom he thought could extricate his entrapped troops; and he gradually got many of them back, because Paulinus, 26. 13 ff., was afraid of an unknown body of fresh Vitellians from the camp.

(d) On the whole, Heubner's view seems right, especially as Paulinus was *cunctator natura*, 25. 7. What the Othonians had planned was simply a heavy rebuff, which they achieved, to the Vitellian ambush, and they were hoping for rapid reinforcements from Rome as well as from the Danube. Moreover the idea that Caecina's whole army could have been destroyed, 26. 11, is not really likely.

24. 1. Paulini et Celsi. Gallus may already have met with the accident reported at II. 33. 2.

7. ad duodecimum. Passerini, 214–15, puts this point 2 km west of the right incline which the Via Postumia made in joining the *decumanus* of Cremona. On this view the bend in the road made it easier for the Othonians to make their preparations unobserved.

8. Castorum. Not 'it is called Locus Castorum', but 'the place gets its name from the Castores'. Suet. *O.* 9 has *Castoris, quod loco nomen est,* and Orosius VII. 8. 6 says simply that it was called 'Castores'. The shrine which must have existed here may have been the 'ancient temple' which Plut. (*O.* 14) saw, with corpses piled up to its roof, when he visited the battlefields with Mestrius Florus; and it is tempting to think that 'Virgil' (*Catal.* 10) had it in mind when his Transpadane muleteer dedicated himself 'to twin Castor and to Castor's twin'. The *luci* of the next line were presumably also dedicated to the brothers.

12. curam . . . sumpsere. Not a permanent division of command (as Drexler, 171, seems to think), but one made simply for the purposes of the engagement now planned, Heubner, 100.

14. auxiliorum cohortes. All *auxilia*, including the cavalry on the flanks, are troops which accompanied the vexillum of XIII Gemina from Illyricum, Gerstenecker, 20.

15. altis ordinibus, 'in column' on the narrow *agger* of the road, raised above the canals and ditches at the sides: cf. II. 42. 12.

17. ex praetorio. The praetorian cavalry are used as a single unit, cf. *A.* I. 24. 3, Passerini, *coorti*, 69.

25. 7. cunctator natura, so also of Tampius Flavianus, III. 4. 3. The phrase echoes Livy XXX. 26. 9, *ingenio cunctator,* but the Paulinus of *A.* XIV. 33. f., e.g. *mira constantia Londinium perrexit,* is hard to recognize.

8. fossas, irrigation canals, essential in this region.

9. iubebat. Imperfect tense important: he had been engaged on this business before the ambush was sprung, for it was essential that the infantry should deploy for some distance on each side of the road.

11. vineas... impeditas. In Italy, and above all in the Po valley, the vines are commonly planted among elms or fruit trees, and are looped from tree to tree. *Traduces* are branches of the vines themselves: the word is elsewhere found only in the agricultural writers.

14. rex Epiphanes, 'the prince Epiphanes', son of Antiochus IV of Commagene. His father was an early supporter of Vespasian, II. 81 with n., and it is interesting that at this point he had been sent to support Otho. When Antiochus was deposed in A.D. 72 he first fled to Parthia, but he was pardoned by Vespasian and brought to Rome, Jos. *BI.* VII. 219 ff., *ILS* 9200 (= MW 372). His son was C. Iulius Antiochus Philopappus, whose tomb was the famous monument in Athens, *ILS* 845 (=Sm. 2, 207), *PIR²* J 151, C. P. Jones, *Plutarch and Rome* (1971), 59.

26. 1. Othonianus pedes, i.e. praetorians as well as legionaries, see point (a) in Introd. to these three chapters.

6. praefectus castrorum. This was a high-ranking officer, who had normally served as *primus pilus* and sometimes also as tribune or *praefectus equitum,* cf. *ILS* 6285, Suet. *Vesp.* 1. 3, etc. His duties were administrative, including of course responsibility for the construction of camps, but also disciplinary: in the latter he often incurred unpopularity, III. 7. 4, *A.* I. 20.

Since even under the early Empire most winter-quarters contained only one legion (with *auxilia* attached) it was common for that legion to be mentioned in the prefect's title, e.g. *ILS* 6285, *A.* XIV. 37. 6. But each camp or expeditionary group had a single *praefectus,* whatever units it contained: for detachments smaller than a single legion see *A.* I. 38, Vell. II. 120. 4, and for larger groups *A.* I. 16 and 20. So there seems to be only one *praefectus* in Caecina's force here, in Valens' force at II. 29. 7, in the large Vitellian army on the Tartarus at III. 14. 4, and in the two-legion camp at Mogontiacum at IV. 59. 15. For the special case of the praefectus of VII Galbiana in the Flavian invasion see Wellesley's n. to III. 7. 3.

13. ferebat, 'used to say'. Paulinus wrote memoirs about his Mauretanian campaign in A.D. 42, but it is most unlikely that he left written records about A.D. 69.

27. 4. Fabii quoque Valentis. The transition from Caecina to Valens is artistically achieved, and the chronology presents no difficulty. Valens was at Augusta Taurinorum in the very last days of March, I. 63. 1 n., and is now at Ticinum; for his route see P. Tozzi, *Athenaeum*, 1970, 119. But we are told nothing about his crossing of the Alps.

5. reciperandi decoris. Where had they been discredited? Heubner suggests the Narbonese defeat, but this involved a small number of cavalry regiments and in any case was not decisive. T. surely implies confidence in his own account of the disreputable march through Gaul.

6. aequalius. 'with more equanimity' or 'more consistently' would both conform with the few other Tacitean usages of *aequalis* and its derivatives, but the former seems here more probable; cf. *A.* I. 32. 7, *tanta aequalitate et constantia ut regi crederes.*

7. alioquin. In Livy and other authors (LS have a useful entry) the word commonly meant 'in other respects', e.g. Livy VII. 19. 2, *triumphatum de Tiburtibus: alioqui mitis triumphus fuit*; and *TLL.*I, col. 1593, appears to be satisfied with that meaning here, the sense being presumably 'Valens' troops were behaving properly, but in other respects mutiny had continued to be rife'. But the contrast is unreal (indeed *TLL*'s underlining of *cohortes Batavorum* shows misunderstanding of the context) and with that meaning *alioquin* should have started the sentence.

By T.'s day the word was used as follows: (1) 'at other times', with the implication either (i) GG (b) 'and all the more now' (III. 32. 13, *tempus quoque mercatus ditem alioqui coloniam maiore opum specie complebat*, cf. *A.* IV. 37. 2), or (ii) GG (a) 'but now the reverse' (*A.* III. 8. 4, XIII. 20. 1); (2) GG (c) 'besides' or 'in any case' (*A.* XIV. 61. 5, *quod alioquin suum delictum?*, cf. *A.* IV. 11. 4); (3) GG (d) 'otherwise' (common esp. in Pliny's *Letters*, e.g. VIII. 8. 1), *A.* II. 38, XI 6.

Wellesley with 'anyway', following GG 'ohnehin', opts for (2) above. Goelzer has 'du reste', and Irvine defends 'besides' by suggesting that T. gives the failure of the earlier mutiny as a reason for the present discipline. But the end of II. 29 by no means makes this clear, and once again *alioquin* with this sense would come more appropriately at the beginning of the sentence.

To me T.'s usage (1), as in III. 32. 13, seems a more likely parallel. 'The mutiny would have been serious at any time, but was all the more so at a critical period of the war'. Certainly this was a characteristic Tacitean thought, especially in this part of his work.

8. ordinem interrumpi. From II. 28. 8, *postquam in conspectu sit hostis,* we must infer that the mutiny occurred after Valens had crossed the Alps.

Walser, 86 f., claimed this incident, and Valens' suspicion of *perfidia* (line 17) as support for his view that in 68 the Batavians had been 'Galbiani' and were still disloyal to Vitellius' party. But this view (see Brunt, *Latomus*, 1960, 501) is almost impossible to reconcile with II. 66. 15 (*ut fidos*) and with IV. 17. 15. Note too that the mutiny here was not one by the cohorts but by the legions: though they had been irritated by the cohorts' silly arrogance, they were now protesting against the detachment of their bravest allies away from the main seat of war, II. 28. 6 ff., Heubner p. 110.

9. bello Neronis. For the phrase cf. I. 70. 3, Syme, *AJP* 1937, 10 ff. On the events see Introd., pp. 7, 14.

12. rettulimus. I. 59. 4.

14. ablatam Neroni Italiam. Brunt, *Latomus*, 1959, 541, is clearly right to relate this claim, whether exaggerated or not, to events before Nero's death. For the subsequent events, particularly the behaviour of XIV Gemina, see Introd., p. 10.

28. 1. pulsam Trevirorum alam ... See II. 14–15, and, on the timing of the message, Appendix, p. 267. Either Valens deliberately magnified the Othonian success to give himself an excuse for getting rid of the Batavian cohorts, or the first reports reaching him were too pessimistic.

3. socios, 'allied communities', though the same word is used to mean 'auxiliary troops' only three lines later.

7. tot bellorum victores, presumably in Britain, nine years before.

10. columen. The bracketed words come from a gloss reported by Placidus, *CGL* V. 11. 10, *columen, vel sanitas vel sustentaculum, quia e columna fit.* Hence presumably cornerstone, cf. IV. 84. 22, *Memphim ... Aegypti columen, A.* VI. 37. 5, *columen partium Abdagaeses.* For *verteretur* cf. Cic. *Verr.* I. 20, *omnia in unius potestate ac moderatione vertentur,* and other passages cited by Heubner, but the reading is uncertain, quite apart from the gloss.

29. 3. spolia Galliarum. I. 64 ff., and esp. I. 66. 10.

7. decurionem. I. 70. 7 n.

Alfenus Varus. This *praefectus castrorum* (II. 26. 6 n.) became prefect of the guard after Caecina's disgrace, III. 36. 14, and shared the command of Vitellius' praetorians in the Appennine campaign, *PIR*²

A522. He may be the man who is described as *trecenarius Aug. n.* on a Pompeian tablet of A.D. 53, *CIL* IX, Suppl. 1. XLV: see Passerini, *coorti* 94, for the post of *trecenarius*, though it may have been held in a legion rather than in the guard, I. 24. 9 n.

9. omisso tubae sono. For this part of Roman army routine cf. Jos. *BI* III. 86 ff.

30. 1. Munientibus ... Ticinum. The arrival at Ticinum, some 95 miles from Augusta Taurinorum, is dated by Köster, 17, to 6 Apr., which seems reasonable. The battle at Castores was perhaps on the previous day.

2. prope renovata seditio. There is no inconsistency here with the claim at II. 27. 6 that the troops of Valens had begun to show greater discipline, for on this occasion no *seditio* in fact broke out. See Heubner, 110, against Drexler's article.

5. rapido agmine, covering rather over 50 miles.

7. tanto pauciores. See n. to II. 24–6.

10. prope duplicatus ... i.e. on T.'s showing about 54,000 against rather under 30,000, but perhaps both figures are too high, I. 61. 2 n. Clearly any computation must take account of losses to date. Valens had parted with two cohorts, one *ala*, and four *turmae*, II. 14. 3: Caecina's battle losses may have been significantly larger than this, but he had acquired some more *auxilia* in North Italy.

13. quodam inani favore, 'a kind of unreasoning popularity'.

14. foedum ac maculosum, the precise words used of Fonteius Capito, I. 7. 7 (cf. *A*. XIII. 33. 3). For T.'s choicer language about Valens see III. 62: for Valens' view of Caecina Wellesley's 'pompous ass' comes near the mark.

31. 1. sane. Yet it was perhaps less an assessment of merits than thought for the future (*respectus veniae*) which made some of the Othonian leaders hold back from attacks on Vitellius.

utriusque exitum. Of Vitellius' death T. says *deformitas exitus misericordiam abstulerat*, III. 85. 28, but his account of Vitellius' reign, heavily influenced by Flavian propaganda, hardly suggests that the world only fully appreciated his viciousness after his death. It is the change in Otho's reputation of which T. was mainly thinking.

3. flagrantissimae libidines. I. 50. 1, 71. 1. Yet for ten years he governed Lusitania *non ex priore infamia*, *A*. XIII. 46. 5; see I. 13. 18 n.

5. nemo imputabat. Unclear whether T. means that people had forgotten that Vitellius was a rebel against Galba, or that they blamed Caecina and Valens (and the army) rather than Vitellius himself.

9. consultavit. Plut. *O.* 8 says the conference was held at Bedriacum.

32. 1. Suetonius Paulinus. I. 87. 14 n. But, as Fabia, 61, pointed out, Plut. is more likely to be right in making Titianus, as supreme commander, speak first. T.'s failure to give him any serious arguments (II. 33. 5 is not serious) is not a creditable proceeding, especially as the arguments developed by Paulinus are vulnerable at many points (see below). Nor does he even speculate, as Plut. (*O.* 9) does, about the reasons for Otho's impatience.

3. toto genere belli, 'the general military situation'.

4. exercitum advenisse. Plut. gives the argument which Paulinus was countering, 'not to sit still waiting for Vitellius himself to arrive from Gaul'. Probably both sides were exaggerating. Vitellius was still to come with *tota mole belli*, I. 61. 10, but Paulinus gave his reasons for thinking this would amount to little, and in the sequel these reasons were shown to have had weight, see Hordeonius' attitude to Vitellius' appeal in September, II. 97. 3. Yet there was a persistent belief at that later date (admittedly after some Vitellian troops had been sent back) that manpower from the Rhineland was almost inexhaustible, III. 2. 9, 15. 6, 35. 10.

7. Britannicum militem. It is true that there was trouble with the Brigantes (III. 45), but Paulinus was wrong to claim that no troops would come from Britain, see II. 57. 6.

8. Hispanias. There were two legions there at this time.

10. transpadanam ... vastam. If, as seems certain, *vastam* means 'ravaged' (so *vastatam*, recc.), Paulinus is again only specious. The army had no reason to ravage the early corn through carelessness or in order to deny it to the enemy, and at this season they could not harvest the corn for their own use.

11. non frumentum usque. It certainly looks as if it could plausibly be denied that there was any surplus from the previous harvest, see *Cisalpine Gaul*, 136.

14. in aestatem. In another month the weather in the Transpadana might be continuously hot by the Germans' standards (and all Danubian reinforcements would have arrived). There was also a danger of malaria anywhere in the eastern half of the Po valley. Paulinus is not necessarily contemplating waiting till July.

fluxis, 'weak'. The change of climate, and perhaps also malaria, did certainly cause widespread sickness among the Germans in Trastevere later, II. 93. 5 ff.

17. Pannoniam ... cum integris exercitibus. This is a highly misleading flourish, since (a) almost all the troops from Pannonia and Dalmatia had arrived already (see Appendix), and some of them were in no sense *integri*, having taken part in the battle at Castores, (b) there is no evidence that anyone ever contemplated the transfer of troops from 'the East', i.e. Syria or Judaea. The real argument emerges (though even there exaggerated—*paucis diebus*) in line 25: what can be expected are troops from Moesia, and the legion XIV Gemina. Plut. puts Paulinus' case with much greater precision.

19. numquam obscura nomina. I. 76. 12 n.

22. obiacere flumen Padum. Earlier commentators (e.g. Sp., who observed 'this would have been easy') thought Paulinus was advising retreat south of the Po. But the loss of communications with Illyricum, to which he has just attached such importance, would have been fatal. He was thinking (see V.'s excellent n.) of the Placentia–Cremona stretch, along which the two armies faced one another, Cremona on the north bank, Placentia on the south. Here the Vitellians may have hoped to cross, but Paulinus thought little of their chances, see Wellesley, *RhM* 1960, 279.

24. paucis diebus. But the most reliable evidence about the Moesian legions, Suet. *Vesp.* 6, is that even their advanced guard had not reached Aquileia, more than 180 miles from Bedriacum, when they heard of the Vitellian victory.

25. magna ipsam fama. II. 11. 6 n.

33. 6. numen. Not a phrase of significance in the history of ruler-cult. 'Protecting genius' is a fair translation, cf. *A.* II. 17. 2, *aves, propria legionum numina*.

8. concesserant. The pluperfect probably implies that Otho *had been* flattered by Titianus and Proculus from the outset of the council, and that they now repeated their flattery and carried the day.

7. neu = *et ne*, a usage found often in verse, but also *A.* II. 83. 2.

12. Brixellum, on the right bank of the Po, in a direct line from Verona and Mantua to Parma. If Mommsen (see map in *CIL* V, followed by Kiepert) was right in thinking that a road crossed the Po there, it was a place of strategic importance. If Bedriacum was at

Calvatone, II. 23. 8 n., Brixellum was about 15 miles to the south; from Tornata a little less.

Plut. *O.* 5. 3 makes Otho take his headquarters there immediately he arrived in the north. This may be right (and Fabia, 50, was entitled to use the discrepancy to confirm Plut.'s independence of T.), but we do not know when the arrival took place. Plut. seems to put it before the Placentia siege, which is certainly too early. One might infer from Suet. *O.* 9. 1, *nec ulli pugnae adfuit*, that he had the opportunity of being present at the Castores battle; but in T. his first appearance is at the council of war, and he had probably only recently arrived.

13. summae rerum et imperii, 'general charge of affairs', cf. Plin. *Pan.* 56. 3.

13. is primus ... adflixit. The reasons given show that T. was thinking primarily not of the decision to fight, but of Otho's withdrawal. Certainly the loss of these praetorians with their cavalry was a serious matter for the Othonians, especially as many of them were picked troops. But the other reasons (not found in Plut.) give support to Courbaud's view, 88–9, that T. was here sacrificing history to drama. For the unfortunate Paulinus *imperia ducum in incerto* is the reverse of the truth, II. 40. 7. And *remanentium fractus animus* accords little with the subsequent behaviour of the troops, e.g. II. 39. 6: indeed T. allows *fractus animus* to recur at II. 44. 16, but *after* the defeat, and even there the praetorians are clamouring to resume the fight.

15. speculatorum. I. 24. 9 n.

34. 1. Vitellianos. As in II. 27 T. finds a neat transition to the Vitellian side, with the word *transfugiis.*

5. transitum Padi simulantes, a fundamental problem of the whole campaign. Momigliano, 136 ff., maintained that the Vitellian attempt to cross the Po was genuine (so also Henderson, 93–4, but with absurdities), and that the consequent threat to Othonian communications with Rome was the main cause of Otho's haste. K., *Riv. class. e med.* 1961, 23, agrees and thinks the need to watch both banks of the Po was the main reason of Otho's withdrawal to Brixellum. Wellesley, *JRS* 1971, 38 ff., argues that the coming Othonian attack was directly pointed at the bridge-building. For the position, south-east of Cremona, of the intended pontoon, following a presumed destruction of the regular bridge by the Othonians, see his p. 33.

There are two questions, (i) was Caecina only bluffing (but Plut. *O.* 10. 2, says categorically ζευγνύντος τὴν διάβασιν)?, (ii) did his activity, whether bluff or not, influence the main Othonian plans?

(i) To build an adequate bridge near Cremona, against determined opposition from the south bank, would have been extremely difficult. Caecina had temporary successes against Macer's gladiators, but these were then reinforced from Placentia (chapters 34–6). But (see Wellesley, *RhM* 1960, 279) only knowledgeable Vitellian sources could have told us confidently whether Caecina was bluffing, and neither T. nor Plut. used them. As to Caecina himself, he probably preferred, after his later treachery, to be silent about his services to Vitellius.

(ii) A successful Vitellian penetration to the south bank would have been devastating to Othonian plans. But the startling thing is that the threat of a bridge is nowhere mentioned as a factor in the calculations of Otho or his commanders. This argument, however, is not decisive. T.'s (and Plut.'s) source goes back to Paulinus and his friends, who would have argued that Caecina's activity, if not just a feint, could lead to nothing serious (see II. 32. 22 n.); and they may have been right. The trouble is that T. has made no attempt to give us the arguments, misguided or not, put forward by Titianus and Proculus, II. 32. 1 n.

9. super. Despite Heubner's very learned n., I think this means simply 'besides' (= *insuper*), as Goelzer and other translators.

11. augescente. In spring the current here can be very strong.

13. educta, 'moved out to whichever ship was at the near end'.

14. Othoniani ... iaculabantur. Plut. *O.* 10 adds one detail, that they sent empty fire-ships and burned the bridge of boats. In other respects he omits everything which makes sense of this engagement or of the general strategical situation, Fabia, 66.

35. 1. insula. There are many islands in this part of the Po, but the land visible above water need not have been in the same positions in antiquity: for discussion of Cisalpine hydrography see Brunt, *Italian Manpower* 176 f. Those who think that the final Othonian advance aimed at the confluence of the Po and Arda (II. 40. 1) have favoured a round island about 4 miles south of (and downstream from) Cremona; but the approaches to a crossing here would, today at least, be difficult from both sides. Similar arguments apply to an island about 6 miles west of the city, immediately east of the Adda confluence, favoured by Sp. and others. Perhaps the best existing candidate is a long thin island the eastern end of which is about two miles west of (and upstream from) the city walls; it lies nearer to the left bank, and would have been easily approachable from the Cremona–Ticinum road (which ran through modern Pizzighetone). Probably, however, any point west of Cremona is too far to explain Caecina's swift return from the bridge to the camp (II. 41, see Wellesley, *RhM* 1960, 279), and it is better to assume that the island was south-east of the city but has not survived.

2. praelabebantur. The sentence has been interpreted in many ways (and has led to at least one emendation—*perlabebantur*, Halm). Heubner, *Gymnasium*, 1955, 105 ff. argued that the essential mistake had been to assume that a verb compounded with *prae* involved anticipation; he claimed that *praelabebantur* is governed by both subjects, and translates 'were carried towards', comparing the use of *praevehi* at II. 2. 7, 23. 12, and of *praelabi* in Cic. *Nat. deor.* II. 211, Apul. *Socr.* 4. More probable seems one of the views put forward by V., keeping the full sense of *prae-*: Othonians and Vitellians alike were anticipating one another in landing (the Vitellians, skilled in amphibious warfare, swimming downstream, the Othonians rowing against the current), and at one moment more Batavians (*forte pluris*) attained their objective.

It is of course improbable that the only objective on the Vitellian side was the relief of *segne otium*, II. 34. 7. Their purpose was to achieve, or to pretend they were achieving, a crossing, and some, if not all, Othonian movements were designed to prevent them, II. 34. 5 n.

3. Liburnicis. II. 16. 8 n. Again use of the Ravenna fleet. The *remiges* are their marines.

11. auctorem cladis. Macer, not Otho. It is only later that we begin to be told of *fastidium utriusque principis*, II. 37. 2, and on the Othonian side this attitude was not that of the common soldier.

36. 9. Flavium Sabinum. I. 77. 10 n. If the view taken there be right, he was the son of the prefect of the city, and had just entered upon his consulate.

The reorganization shows that Caecina's operations were taken seriously by the Othonians, but does not prove that they were the prime motive for the coming offensive.

37. 1. invenio apud quosdam auctores. Comparison between these two chapters and Plut. *O.* 9. may help little over source–criticism or over the political and military situation preceding Otho's defeat, but it tells us much about T.'s attitude to the history of A.D. 69.

Plut. introduces the rumour of a possible agreement between the armies in a chapter immediately following the Othonian council of war. Many reasons are given, he says, for the decision to fight at once, and he instances three: first the impatience of the praetorians, who expected a quick victory and were anxious to get home; secondly (and for this Otho's secretary Secundus is cited as authority) Otho's unstable character, which made the suspense intolerable to him; and thirdly, ἑτέρων δ' ἦν ἀκούειν, the rumour found here in T., which made the

Othonian generals counsel delay but terrified Otho into action. The first two versions are found also in Suet. *O.* 9. 1.

T., as we have seen, gives no counter-arguments to those of Paulinus at the council, contenting himself with *Otho pronus ad decertandum*, but he seems to have believed in Plut.'s second reason, e.g. *aeger mora et spei impatiens*, II. 40. 10; of the first reason he says nothing explicitly, though he of course recognized the praetorians' enthusiasm and confidence. But the third reason he has placed in this quite different context, separated from the council of war, and arising from his picture of Othonian soldiers who were not so much enthusiastic as exasperated: he does return to Plut.'s context when he says the rumour was regarded as a reason for Paulinus and his friends to urge delay, but he says nothing of Otho's reaction.

Still more important, Plut. thought the story quite probable (καὶ οὐκ ἀπεικός ἐστι), but T. introduces it only to refute it; and to do so he uses the very argument which Plut. believed to be in its support. Reflection on the horrors of earlier civil wars would in Plut.'s view have made the soldiers long to end a struggle between two so unworthy leaders. T. knows this theme well, I. 50, II. 31, in relation to other parts of Roman society, but he has not applied it to the attitude of the common solider. Here, by brilliant paradox, he argues in the opposite direction: if *civium legiones* were prepared to fight at Pharsalus and Philippi, how much more would savagery and criminal outlook prevent the armies of 69—either soldiers or their generals—from stopping short of their goal or from being content with any *princeps* who was not ever afterwards in their relentless debt? Moreover, not only does this paradox show close reflection: it may even reveal the truth, Syme, 187.

It can hardly be doubted (though Mommsen, *Gesammelte Schriften* VII. 236, did strenuously deny it) that among T.'s *quidam auctores* and Plut.'s ἕτεροι there was at least one common source. In the actual story, as distinct from its context and interpretation, the discrepancies between the two authors are trivial, indeed almost limited to the fact that Plut., omitting the name of Paulinus, calls the peacemakers τοὺς περὶ τὸν Κέλσον. Both mention the same alternatives, either that the armies select a new emperor, or that they refer the choice to the Senate. And both (though with very divergent results) found a lead from the story into earlier Roman history, with Marius, Sulla, and Pompey (to whom Plut. adds Caesar) as their examples; that this should be pure coincidence between the individual reflections of T. and Plut. is incredible.

There are good grounds for supposing that in Plut.'s case the rival versions were not collected from different sources by his own efforts but were found in the main source he was using. ἑτέρων δ᾽ ἦν ἀκούειν (Mommsen's translation 'one could hear other soldiers say' is surely impossible in the context) is neither ἕτεροι δ᾽ ἔγραψαν nor ἑτέρων δ᾽ ἔστιν ἀκούειν: it implies that his source stated that such things were heard. Similarly Secundus (διηγεῖτο not ἐμοί . . . διηγεῖτο like Mestrius Florus in cap 14) neither met Plut., nor (as far as is known) produced a written account), but was the oral informant of Plut.'s source. Whether T. too by *invenio apud quosdam auctores* meant (or should have meant, had he been candid) 'I find in my source that some authorities said', as Fabia, 65, supposed, is unproven. But we must surely believe that at least one of his sources for the rumour, direct or indirect, was identical with one of Plut.'s sources.

Moreover Fabia was right not only in taking the divergence over context as proof that Plut. did not use T., but in claiming that the common source recorded the rumour where Plut. puts it. For Plut. to find it, with the accompanying digression into past history, in T.'s context and transfer it to become a rival version of the reasons for the Othonian offensive would have required a type of ingenuity he did not normally show. It was T. who altered the context, and in doing so he made his defence of Paulinus easier than if he had made the rumour explain the views expressed at the council. But this was not his main motive. The story of the rumour led him to a theme about which he cared more deeply than about the motives of individual senators, namely the causes of civil wars in general and of this one in particular, and the part contributed by the behaviour of the armies. Opportunity for discussing this theme did not easily arise from the debate on Othonian strategy, but it came admirably at the one moment before the final battle when some Othonian troops showed signs of discouragement. On the passage as an instance of T.'s rejection of accepted causal connections, see Klingner, 14 ff.

About the truth behind the rumour we have no adequate clue. Was Paulinus intending treachery, and if so was he moved by love of peace, by detestation of the rival leaders, by despair or resentment at the rejection of his strategy, or by pure ambition? That there were traitors among the Othonian officers is fairly clear, below, 41. 2 n. But against Paulinus, a man towards whom T. (as towards Verginius, or, in the *Annals*, Seneca) is strikingly ambivalent, the only evidence may have been his own grovelling 'confession' to Vitellius, II. 60. 7; but if he, like his companion Proculus, was lying, this is no evidence at all. The praetorians, who remembered the rumour of an armistice with which the Vitellians deceived their enemies just before the battle, II. 42. 1, Suet. *O.* 9. 2, could never believe that their defeat was due to anything but treachery; and when a culprit actually presented himself the concoction of the story was easy. But that is not to say that it did not happen to be true. Paulinus, in the circumstances of early 69, was *capax imperii* in comparison with most conceivable rivals.

5. senatui ... imperatorem. I. 12. 3 n.

7. vetustissimus consularium. I. 87. 14 n. (also I. 8. 3). The only near competitor among those on active service was Titianus, *cos.* 52.

14. linguis moribusque dissonos, an exaggeration of which T. is fond, especially when he is talking about the army of Germany, II. 21. 21, I. 75. 6. Foreign speech might be found among the *auxilia*, but it was not they who were taking the decisions here.

38. 1. vetus ac iam pridem ... As one would expect, this chapter is closely modelled on Sallust, in style, language, and thought, Syme, 198. See esp. *BC* 10–11, *Hist.* I. 7 and 12.

3. aequalitas, 'equality' (*A.* III. 74. 7, *nec super ceterorum aequalitatem*), but here the essential sense is *concordia*, cf. II. 27. 6 n. and V.'s n. to the present passage. The contrast is to the supremacy of individuals.

   subacto ... excisis, after, say, 146 B.C. Anyway the *prima ... certamina* are not the early Republic's 'struggle of the Orders', but the struggles, commonly called those between *optimates* and *populares*, from the time of the Gracchi.

6. consules praevalidi. Commentators instance L. Opimius (*cos.* 121 B.C.), Scaurus (115), or Caepio (106). Probably all that mattered to T. was that, for the most part, the consuls were regarded as the guardians of the *res publica* against certain tribunes.

7. temptamenta, 'a foretaste' (Wellesley).

8. e plebe infima, another piece of schoolroom history, which suited T.'s version of the struggle as one between *patres* and *plebs*. Plut. *Marius* 3. 1. has the same story, but it had been fashionable to ascribe humble origins to 'new men' of the late Republic (e.g. Cic. *II in Verr.* V. 181, on the first consular ancestor of Pompey, *humili atque obscuro loco natus*). But there is in fact little doubt that Marius' father was an *eques*, e.g. E. Badian, *Historia*, 1961, 214.

10. Cn. Pompeius ... For T. on Pompey see *A.* III. 28. 1. It is not clear whether he is supposed to be working for the *patres* or the *plebs*. Among many Ciceronian passages about his double-talk the wittiest is Caelius in *Fam.* VIII. 1. 3, *solet enim aliud sentire et loqui neque tantum valere ingenio ut non appareat quid cupiat.*

12. civium legiones. Yet Caesar and his enemies recruited an exceptional number of non-citizens into their legions and gave them citizenship on enlistment. Is T.'s real distinction, then, one between Italian and provincial legionaries, for it can be shown that the majority of legionaries in 69 were non-Italian (Introd., p. 20)? But it is out of character for T. to disparage non-Italian citizens. He is opposing the soldiers of the earlier civil wars to the *exercitus ... dissonos* of 69, for (II. 21–2 nn.) he likes to 'barbarize' the Rhine armies by implying that the behaviour of the legionaries was similar to that of the auxiliaries.

14. deum ira. I. 3. 9 n.

15. singulis velut ictibus. I. 89. 14, *si ducibus aliis bellatum foret, longo bello materia.*

18. venio. Heubner's n., supporting Andresen, shows how *venio* rather than *redeo* gives T.'s thought at this point—he is reaching the crisis.

39–44. On these chapters I have not included notes on the main crux, i.e. the distance and direction of the Othonian march. See Appendix.

39. 4. tribuni centurionesque. T. is inclined to group them together, and always as a force for respectability as against the common soldiers, I. 80. 9, 82. 17, II. 18. 7.

8. adeo imperite. Plut. *O.* 11. 1 describes the waterless site in similar terms (although with many more words). At this point at least the two were using a common source.

9. tot circum amnibus. In particular the many small streams (Plut., cit., πολλὰ νάματα καὶ ποταμοὺς ἀεννάους), above which the road was banked, II. 24. 15.

12. copias ... acciri. If this suggestion was a responsible one, it was a call for the troops at Brixellum, not for the force under Flavius Sabinus near Cremona. The latter were heavily engaged; moreover it was probably hoped by Titianus and Proculus that they would co-operate in the eventual battle, either having crossed the Po or at least by tying down Caecina's Batavians, see Passerini, 218 n. 98.

40. 1. non ad pugnam sed ad bellandum. i.e. with their baggage trains; contrast the Vitellians after their victory, *expeditis et tantum ad proelium egressis*, II. 45. 3. Cf. *Germ.* 30. 3, *robur in pedite, quem super arma ferramentis quoque et copiis onerant: alios ad proelium ire videas, Chattos ad bellum.*

3. Celso et Paulino abnuentibus. It seems that the argument in the last chapter was about whether to offer battle at all: here it is about the direction of the advance. Paulinus and Celsus are maintaining their objections to the last, and it could be that the absurdly short march of 4 miles on the first day was a compromise, based on their plea that more news about the situation might yet come in. Whatever the reason, it was strongly disapproved by Otho, *increpita ducum segnitia*, line 9.

Syme, 678, suggests that the two councils, and the two messages from Otho, represent a 'doublet' resulting from T.'s conflation of two sources. But he is careful to emphasize that this cannot be proved, and it would still leave unsolved the main difficulties about strategy and topography. See also Heubner's powerful objections (150).

9. Numida. This seems to have become a technical term for a fast rider, Sen. *Epp.* 87. 9, *cursores et Numidas*, Suet. *Nero* 30, *cum Mazacum turba atque cursorum*, Plut. *O.* 11. 2.

10. aeger . . . impatiens. T.'s version of Plut. *O.* 9. 2, see II. 37. 1 n.

41. 2. praetoriarum cohortium tribuni. For the movement of some of Spurinna's praetorians to join Macer's gladiators see II. 36. 5. Yet nothing is heard of them in the narrative of the battle: the force defeated by the Batavians, before the latter joined the main Vitellian line with decisive effect, is still called *gladiatorum manus*, II. 43. 13.

3. audire . . . ac reddere, possibly reminiscent of Verg. *Aen.* I. 409, *audire et reddere voces*. Courbaud, 115 n. 3, finds similar poetical echoes in all the battle narrative.

5. incertum . . . coeptaverint. The perfect subjunctive, cf. III. 84. 31, IV. 86. 5, should imply that the doubt persisted when T. wrote.

insidias . . . consilium. By *insidias* he must mean a trap directed against the Vitellians. For the variation *an . . . vel* cf. *A.* XIV. 3. 2, *veneno an ferro vel qua alia vi*, where V. argues that *an* is the stronger particle: the sense will then be 'some design to trap the enemy or a genuine parley (whether treacherous to the Othonian cause or no)'.

As Passerini, 230, says, it is hard to see what *consilium* which was *honestum* to Otho could have justified a conference with Caecina at this juncture, but it could be that T. by *honestum* implied some proposal to end the war of the kind which caused the rumours of II. 37. As to *insidiae*, the opportunities to the Othonian side were limited, but perhaps they offered peace disingenuously, to add surprise to their intended attack (if so, a ruse which boomeranged, 42. 2 n. below). But if actual *proditio* is the answer, it is worth remembering that the commander of the Othonian force on the south bank was now the younger Flavius Sabinus, who was allowed by Vitellius to hold his consulship for April and May, I. 77. 12 n.

7. revectus. Wellesley, *JRS* 1971, 33, convincingly sustains his view (*RhM* 1960, 103) that this return to the camp may have been accomplished in under fifteen minutes.

9. equites prorupere. The Vitellian cavalry; their repulse by a smaller Othonian force was recalled later by Antonius Primus,

III. 2. 20, *duae tunc Pannonicae ac Moesicae alae perrupere hostem*, a detail which it is surprising T. did not give us here.

14. aspectus armorum. But in fact their confidence must have resulted not from their inability to see the enemy but from his inability to see them.

19. vocantium. K. in his 1969 edition gives good ground for reading *volitantium*, cf. *A.* II. 21. 2.

20. prorumpebant . . . relabebantur. For the 'double zeugma' see I. 6. 1 n.

42. 2. in languorem vertit. The apparent inconsistency with *proelium . . . acriter sumpsere* (line 10) has been exaggerated, e.g. by V. Had it not been for the rumour the Othonians would have charged first, but when the enemy fell upon them they did show determined resistance.

4. seu dolo seu forte. Whether the doubt arises from a conflict between T.'s sources (cf. III. 28), or from two versions suggested by a single source (as probably at III. 71. 16), or from his own perplexity, we cannot tell. Suet. *O.* 9 makes the rumour the reason for Otho's defeat, *fraude superatus est*, for his men were brought out in hope of an armistice and then suddenly attacked. That would mean that the rumour started among the Vitellians, and it is probably with deliberate emphasis that T. records a contrary view to that of Suet.'s source, namely that it began *in ipsa Othonis parte*. Plut. *O.* 12. 1 seems to support the latter version, though it is doubtful whether he had any more precise knowledge, e.g. when he says that it was the Othonian front line who were taken in.

It may be that the rumour was connected with the colloquy at the bridge, II. 41. 2 n., but Suet.'s casual words are scarcely proof of this.

10. arboribus ac vineis impeditos. II. 25. 11 n., 41. 14. Plut. *O.* 12. 2 speaks of ditches and pits. The main obstacles, especially for cavalry, were probably the irrigation canals of the region, even though to the south of the Via the armies met *patenti campo*, II. 43. 1.

12. catervis cuneisque. *Caterva* (see GG) means any relatively disorganized body of soldiers, e.g. II. 88. 19 (of the Vitellian entry to Rome). *Cunei* are closely packed troops, III. 29. 8 (formed by VII Gemina attacking Cremona), *A.* I. 51. 1 (Germanicus divides his army into four *cunei*), cf. Livy 7. 24. 7, Frontin. *Strat.* II. 3. 20. Walser 95, is mistaken in making T. 'barbarize' the Batavians when he uses this word about their formation in Book IV.

14. noscentes inter se. V. (also Momigliano, 142) must be wrong in arguing that the troops in the centre, both Vitellians and Othonians, are supposed to come from the same areas, and that therefore the Othonian centre were not praetorians. All T. means is that both sides knew to which side the other troops belonged. As Passerini shows, 235, the praetorians must have been in the Othonian centre, because they are not mentioned elsewhere, 44. 1 n. below.

43. 4. non ante ... deducta. So Plut. *O.* 12. 3 about the Othonians generally. But I. Adiutrix had fought at Castores.

5. principiis. This could mean 'their headquarters', but from Plut. *O.* 2. 2, τοὺς προμάχους, it seems likely that this means 'the first ranks', cf. Livy II. 65. 2, Sall. *BI* 56. 2.

8. signa vexillaque. II. 18. 3 n.

a parte alia, probably on the Othonian right wing. The legion XIII is clearly now in full strength, as contrasted with the detachment from XIV which is overcome by superior numbers, Passerini, 206.

10. ducibus ... profugis. All of them? Probably so, from what is said in the next chapter, though Plut. omits this point.

12. Varus Alfenus, Valens' *praefectus castrorum*, II. 29. 7.

13. gladiatorum manu. II. 41. 2 n. Plut. *O.* 12. 4–5 shows that many Othonians had crossed the Po but were routed before they landed. The Batavians, having fought a separate engagement with the gladiators, presumably on the river bank, then came north to join the battle round the Via Postumia.

44. 1. media acie perrupta. The centre gives way, and the centre was formed mainly by the praetorians, Passerini, 234. Plut., in a sentence which follows on his account of the Batavian defeat of the gladiators, alleges that the praetorians put up the worst fight of all, and that they fled through the ranks of their unbeaten comrades. He cannot be right. T. would never have missed the opportunity of recording the praetorians' disgrace had they shown exceptional cowardice: what he does is to report (without comment) their claim that they were defeated by treachery, not by superior valour.

Could Plut.'s source have referred, not to the main praetorian body, but to the cohorts under Flavius Sabinus, many of whom had been treacherously persuaded to give up the fight, II. 41. 2 n.?

fugere passim Othoniani. T.'s account of this decisive part of the battle is thin. Plut. *O.* 12. 6 says that many of the Othonians had to fight their way back through troops who had surrounded them. Cf. 70. 12, *circumfusas auxiliorum manus.*

2. Bedriacum. Plut. says they regained their camp, and this must mean, not the waterless site 4 miles from their first base, but Bedriacum itself, where Annius Gallus received the fugitives, ἐν τῇ πόλει, Plut. *O.* 13. 1. The main Othonian camp was just outside the village, just as the Vitellian camp (Wellesley, *JRS* 1971, 31 ff.) was just outside Cremona.

immensum id spatium, possibly as much as 18 miles.

3. neque enim civilibus ... For the general point cf. III. 34. 9 ff. Plut. *O.* 14. 2 says that the pile of bodies shown him outside a temple (II. 24. 8 n.) was of a size which surprised both him and his consular friend Mestrius Florus. Dio (= Xiph.) 64. 10. 3 says that the casualties on the two sides together totalled 40,000, but that figure is incredible.

6. Vedium Aquilam, still in command of that legion in the autumn, III. 7. 2.

13. Annius Gallus, left behind because of his accident, II. 33. 2.

18. ne Vitellianis ... perituros. The first part of these arguments is put by Plut. *O.* 13. 1 into the mouth of the praetorians but of Annius Gallus. So V. transposed all these words to follow *levamentum*, suggesting also that some further words had fallen out between *ceteris ... fremebat* and the last sentence of the chapter. He claimed that *ne Vitellianis ... perituros* embraced arguments appropriate to a general trying to calm his troops rather than to enraged praetorians complaining of treachery.

But some of the detail (*pulso equite, rapta legionis aquila*) would be inept in a speech by the one general who had not been at the battle. Moreover the chapter of Plut. is a tissue of inconsequential items. Gallus is first made to encourage the officers, surely to further action. Then Celsus, introduced by δέ, argues that Otho will no longer want to squander the lives of his men. This wins over the officers, and then the troops too are found to be anxious for peace. So Gallus and Celsus, although they had championed opposing views, go to confer with the Vitellian commanders.

As against this, T.'s chapter, ordered as in M., makes perfectly good sense. Gallus restrains the men from mutiny, claiming that they must maintain *consensus* whether they mean to make peace or to resume the fight. Then comes the response of the troops to the two alternatives: *ceteris fractus animus*; but the praetorians believe they have been betrayed, not necessarily by the generals, but by the rumour spread at the beginning of the battle, and perhaps by Flavius Sabinus at the bridge, II. 41. 2 n. So they are anxious to demonstrate their courage once more, and survey all the factors which could be still favourable to the Othonian cause. They did not need anyone to tell them that they had nearly won.

See also Fabia, 76, who thought Plut.'s distaste for the praetorians, see n. to line 1 above, prevented him from allowing them warlike sentiments.

20. militum quod trans Padum fuerit. The praetorians at Brixellum, II. 39. 12 n.

21. magnam exercitus partem. Probably greatly exaggerated. Obviously any army would leave a reserve at its main camp, but it is unlikely to have been of a size which could resist assault by the victorious Vitellians (and they too will have had some reserve at Cremona).

23. his cogitationibus . . . *Pavidi* refers back to *ceteris fractus animus*, though the reflections T. has set out are all such as would inspire anger rather than fear.

45. 1. quintum. On Wellesley' reconstruction, *JRS* 1971, 29 ff., this would be near San Pietro di Mendicate, at about the beginning of the last stretch of the road after the left incline towards Bedriacum. It is only a mile from the waterless camp of II. 39, but we have seen that the Othonians were not there but at Bedriacum.

2. non ausis. Cf. Antonius Primus' reflections before Cremona, III. 18–20.

3. expeditis. II. 40. 1 n.

5. postera die. On all of what follows, as on the events of the preceding chapter, Plut. is much fuller. After the council addressed by Gallus and Celsus, II. 44. 16 n., the two generals are sent to negotiate with Caecina and Valens; on the way they met some Vitellian centurions, also sent to negotiate, and the whole party turned back to confer with Caecina. Celsus narrowly escaped death at the hands of some cavalry he had ambushed at Castores, but Caecina received him well, and both Vitellian and Othonian generals then went to Bedriacum. Meanwhile Titianus had repented of the decision to surrender, but when the soldiers saw Caecina riding forward with outstretched hand they refused to offer further resistance. Then comes the story of Plut.'s tour with Mestrius Florus, and only then the death of Otho, which T. reaches immediately our present short chapter is over.

There is no reason to think (see Fabia, 76 ff.) that Plut. obtained these details from a separate source: they were available for T. to use, but he chose to ignore them. His interest was first in describing yet another instance of military indiscipline (II. 44), and then in drawing his splendid picture of the fraternization between the two armies, see Courbaud, 65.

Klingner, 22, rightly claims parts of these chapters as an example of the way T. can desert the causal connections given by the 'common source', cf. II. 23. 22, 37. 1. The movements of Paulinus and Proculus have no point for him except to show the temper of the soldiers, whereas for Plut. (doubtless following the source) they explain why those two generals were not present at the council. But Klingner's main contention is that T.'s purpose was less an artistic one than an assertion of his independent judgement about the reasons for Otho's suicide, which was a sacrifice for the general good, II. 50. 4, and was uninfluenced by the surrender at Bedriacum, of which Otho never heard (so Plotius Firmus could speak to him of *fidissimum exercitum*, II. 46. 10). That this was T.'s theme, and one to which he devoted great skill, Syme, 205, we must of course agree. But is there good ground for supposing that he found a different chronology, or a different set of motives, in his source? Neither Plut. nor Suet. nor Dio (whatever their sources may have been), suggest that Otho was told of the surrender as distinct from the defeat: indeed Suet. *O.* 9. 3 claims that the defeated troops were to the end ready to resume the struggle.

7. missa legatio. Gallus and Celsus, according to Plut., 44. 18 n. That Celsus played a significant part we may well believe: why else should Vitellius, against some opposition, allow him to hold the consulate which Otho had promised him? For T.'s partiality to Celsus I. 14. 4 n.

9. ea res haesitationem attulit. It was doubtless at this point that Titianus had misgivings about the decision to surrender, Plut. *O.* 13. 6.

46. 1. nequaquam trepidus ..., for, although *aeger mora et spei impatiens* before the battle, II. 40. 10, he had been persuaded, rightly or wrongly, that all was lost unless an immediate battle could be fought and won.

7. instinctu. I. 57. 15 n.

16. praemissi e Moesia ... What they reported is the nearest anything in T. comes to precision about the movements of the Moesian troops, but even here he is only telling us what a prejudiced group of soldiers said. See also II. 32. 24, *paucis diebus quartam decimam legionem ... cum Moesicis copiis adfore*, 44. 20, *venire Moesicas legiones* (both from speakers who had reason to exaggerate), and 85. 5, *(legiones) Aquileiam progressae* (on which see n. about other difficulties). Suet. *Vesp.* 6. 2–3, on the other hand is quite clear, and contradicts the above passages by asserting two points: first that the Moesian movement was limited to vexillations (2,000 from each legion); secondly that these troops had still not reached Aquileia when they heard of Otho's death, which puts their movement several days behind that implied by T.'s speakers.

Suet.'s account has been widely supported (e.g. Braithwaite's edn.) on the following grounds, (a) that his father Suetonius Laetus was in 69 a tribune of XIII Gemina and in a good position to know the facts, (b) that at II. 67. 5 ff. T. in describing the removal of other Othonian legions from Italy says nothing about the dismissal of any Moesian troops to their camps, (c) that the situation on the Danube frontier, I. 79, was too precarious to allow whole legions to move to Italy.

As regards (a), tribunes were present in councils of war, but an officer of a legion which entered Italy much earlier could hardly know with confidence what was happening east of Aquileia. (b), like many of T.'s omissions, proves nothing, for if he fails to record a return of whole Moesian legions he is also silent about what happened to any vexillations; II. 67 is concerned with the dispersal of *defeated* troops, not with intact Moesian units which could have moved back of their own accord. As to (c), we know that extensive movements away from the Moesian sector of the Danube occurred in the following autumn, so much so that a barbarian attack was averted only by the arrival of Mucianus, III. 46. A movement by legions, as distinct from *vexilla*, need not mean that the camps were utterly deserted (cf. the movement of the Vitellian troops, I. 61); it could imply that 4,000 men (rather than 2,000) from each legion came to Aquileia with their eagles, accompanied by a considerable force of *auxilia*. Yet (see Appendix) I think the two Illyrican provinces were almost denuded of troops, to meet Otho's crisis, just as the frontiers had been most dangerously deserted at various moments in 49–31 B.C

Certainty is impossible, but the following conclusions seem reasonable. (i) Paulinus, II. 32 (cf. Plut. *O.* 8) believed that a large force was on its way from Moesia, and probably such had been Otho's order. (ii) Whatever force actually moved, it moved gradually (cf. II. 11 on the movements from Pannonia and Dalmatia); a few Moesian cavalry units actually fought at Bedriacum, III. 2. 27; another group of *praemissi* (probably also cavalry) arrived at Brixellum (our present passage); but the force still to come was still divided into an advanced party known as *vexilla* and the main body (with the eagles). (iii) Since the speeches about the matter in T. are all optimistic, Suet. was probably right in believing that even the *vexilla* were short of Aquileia when they heard of Otho's death. (iv) the troops who pushed on to Aquileia and rioted there were the *vexilla*, not the main bodies, see also 85. 5 n. below.

Against Wellesley's view, *RhM* 1960, 276 ff., that the *legiones* are XI from Burnum and VII Galbiana from (?) Carnuntum, whom the Moesian cavalry had passed on their way, see Appendix, p. 270.

18. nemo dubitet. The present tense emphasizes the voluntary act of Otho's suicide. The war could have been resumed, but T. does not say it could have been won.

47. 1. inquit. Historiographical tradition allowed speeches to be freely composed, so there is no close resemblance between the one which follows and those given to Otho by Plut. *O.* 15 and Dio (= Xiph.) 64. 13. T. introduces no theme peculiar to himself, but this version is immeasurably superior to the others in rhetoric.

4. experti in vicem. What fortune had done for Otho is obvious. What he himself had done is shown by *temperare felicitati* in the next sentence, for he is able (despite, e.g., I. 77. 4, *pleraque contra decus . . .*) to claim that he had shown restraint. For the thought cf. I. 15. 19, 29. 14.

5. nec tempus computaveris. Sp. missed the point completely with 'it is a short reign which gives the surest test'. Otho is answering an objection that restraint in a short reign proves little, with the reply that it proves more in a reign which had been challenged from the start.

10. fratre, coniuge, liberis. I. 75. 9, 88. 6 and nn.

12. Romanae pubis, echoing his address to the praetorians, *Romana vere iuventus,* I. 84. 17.

14. animus, tamquam, 'the thought that'. For *tamquam* cf. I. 8. 10, *metus tamquam alias partis fovissent.*

18. de nemine. i.e. about none of his generals.

48. 7. pecunias distribuit, to his servants (Plut. *O.* 17. 1, Suet. *O.* 10. 2), rather than to his friends.

8. Salvium Cocceianum, called Κοκκήιος by Plut., but T. (confirmed by Suet.) is clearly right. Son of Titianus, and of a mother who may have been the future emperor Nerva's sister (Syme, 628), he was executed by Domitian for celebrating Otho's birthday, Suet. *Dom.* 10. 3.

The advice given him not to forget his uncle nor to remember him too well is recorded also by Plut. *O.* 16. 2, and several writers have maintained that this advice would only have been remembered (or invented) after Cocceianus had disregarded the last part of it. But if we knew nothing about Cocceianus' future, we would surely not be surprised at a writer contemporary with Otho's death recording these words to his nephew. All the less so if (as Plut. says) Otho told Cocceianus that he had intended to adopt him: the nephew's notoriety would then have been inescapable, and the advice most salutary. (The

intended adoption has been doubted because of Suet.'s story that Otho
hoped to marry Nero's widow Messalina and wrote to her just before
his death, *O.* 10. 2, but the two things are not inconsistent.)

16. Servios. So too Plut. *G.* 3. 1 speaks of τὸν Σερουίων οἶκον (and
includes the Servii among the great patrician *gentes, Romulus* 12). But
Galba's gentile name was Sulpicius: Servius was his *praenomen*, and one
which he had officially discarded in favour of Lucius until he became
emperor, Suet. *G.* 4. 1. It is true that by the end of the Republic Servius
as a *praenomen* had gone out of fashion with every *gens* but the Sulpicii,
and that that *gens* used it very frequently indeed, see F. Münzer, *RE* II
A, col. 1832. Perhaps, like M. Brutus (Q. Caepio Brutus) he was still
commonly known by his original name, and even called 'Servius' (as
Cicero speaks of 'Appius'), especially as that would mark his ancient
lineage in contrast with newer families like Sulpicii Quirinii. Yet to
treat 'Servius' as a gentile name is still a curious bit of carelessness on
the part of T.'s source.

in familiam novam. Otho's father was consular, his grandfather
praetorian, so that on the strict definition of *nobilitas* he was *nobilis* and
not *novus*, I. 30. 1 n. But T. was well aware of the facts (II. 50. 1, and
familia consulari, A. XIII. 12. 1), and it was natural to feel a sharp
distinction between three great patrician *gentes* and one ennobled by
Augustus. It is unwise to take this passage as evidence that the concept
of *nobilitas* had changed, except that T. is clearly able, cf. I. 30. 1 n., to
regard one man as more *nobilis* than another.

49. 2. supremas iam curas. Cf. *suprema mandata*, II. 53. 10. His will,
and the letters to his sister and to Statilia Messalina, Suet. *O.* 10. 2.

4. abeuntibus. They threatened departing senators with death unless
they stayed with their emperor, Plut. *O.* 16. 3, but Plut. says nothing of
Verginius. The point with him was that he was a possible alternative
princeps, acceptable to other armies, if the praetorians lost Otho.

8. duobus, inserted because of the parallel passages in Plut. and Suet.
But K. (1969 edn.) may be right in thinking that T. felt the point was
adequately made by *utrumque*. For the provision of two daggers cf. Suet.
Nero. 49. 2.

14. ambitiosis, commonly translated 'earnest'. But the entry in GG
gives good support for their 'ehrsüchtig', i.e. to avoid *ludibrium*. Perhaps
'with prayers designed to save his dignity and prevent ...'.

17. non noxa, 'not from consciousness of wrong done to Otho'; but
what possible wrong could they have done him? Plut. has οὐδὲν ...

πεπονθότες χρηστὸν, which could be the real point, but was there perhaps something in the common source which puzzled both writers?

21. modicum et mansurum. Plut. saw it, with an inscription, Δαίμοσι (a certain emendation for Δηλώσει) Μάρκου ᾽Οθωνος = Dis Manibus M. Othonis, O. 18. 1. Vitellius commented that this was dignum eo Mausoleo, a remark which Suet. Vit. 10. 3 found to have been in characteristically bad taste, but which may have been intended innocently.

septimo et tricensimo. The date is now 16 Apr., twelve days after Otho's thirty-seventh birthday, Suet. O. 2. 1 (though at II. 11. 2 he gets the age wrong). For a minute, and acceptable, chronology see Hölzapfel, Klio, 1913, 289 ff.

50. 1. Ferentio. Cf. Suet. O. 1. 1: Ferento near Viterbo in Etruria, not Ferentinum in northern Campania. At Ferento was found a dedication to Otho, NS 1911, 22.

pater consularis. L. Salvius Otho was suffect A.D. 33, the year in which Galba was ordinarius, Suet. G. 6. 1. He governed Dalmatia after Scribonianus' rebellion, and was subsequently raised to the patriciate by Claudius and given the proconsulate of Africa. His wife Albia Terentia is called splendida femina by Suet. O. 1. 3, which probably means that she was the daughter of a knight, hence maternum genus impar.

2. avus praetorius. M. Salvius Otho, son of a knight and of a woman of lowly (perhaps servile) origin. Suet., cit., attests the influence of Livia Augusta in his advancement.

3. monstravimus. I. 13. 12 ff.

8. avem invisitata specie. So also Dio (= Xiph.) 63. 10. 3, and a more complicated battle of eagles at Suet. Vesp. 5. 7. Plin. NH X. 135, has venerunt in Italiam Bedriacensibus bellis civilibus trans Padum et novae aves—ita enim vocantur—turdorum specie, paulum infra columbas magnitudine. Was T.'s story drawn from a variant version in Pliny's a fine Aufidi Bassi, or from a secondary source? No means of telling, nor is it certain that Pliny, despite his reference to Bedriacum, was in the NH talking about the same birds as the present passage. Note that Regium is not north of the Po: it lies (Reggio Emilia) about midway between Parma and Mutina, 24 miles south of Brixellum.

14. cum Othonis exitu. Unless this can mean the whole period between the battle and Otho's death, i.e. about thirty-six hours, it is tempting (see app. crit.) to assume some lacuna in the text.

51. 1. seditio. Presumably this corresponds with Plut. *O.* 18, where we hear of an attack on 'Pollio' the praetorian prefect, followed by a story about Verginius which almost exactly coincides with T.'s.

4. Verginius. Plut. gives his reasons for refusing, namely that he thought it madness to accept from a beaten army what he had refused from a victorious one, and because (an important statement) he could not negotiate with the German army which he had often resisted forcefully in the past. This is the effective end of Verginius' career; and though in A.D. 97 T. spoke his obituary, it is with some contempt, here and at 68, that T. leaves him. Cf. D. C. A. Shotter, *CQ* 1967, 376–9.

6. Rubrius Gallus, Nero's commander in 68, Dio 63. 27, intermediary between Flavius Sabinus and Caecina in the autumn, II. 99. 13, and governor of Moesia after the death of Fonteius Agrippa in 70, Jos. *BI* VII. 92. He is assumed by Degrassi to have been a Neronian consul.

8. per Flavium Sabinum. It looks as if this force came over to Vitellius with suspicious ease, cf. II. 41. 1 n.

52. 1. extremum discrimen adiit. T. makes clear that the plight of this group of senators was real, and I do not think Wellesley, *RhM* 1960, 286, is right in interpreting this chapter to mean that their behaviour was 'discreditably craven'. T.'s attitude is not so much contempt for their fears and indecision, as indignation that the ending of a civil war should place senators in so humiliating a position.

4. infensum ... arbitrabatur. This, not wholly fairly, was the persistent view of the praetorians, not wholly eradicated by Otho's attempts at reconciliation, I. 83–4.

5. custodire sermones, 'kept watch on their conversation'.

10. inter multos ... tutior, 'and all (understood from *nemo* in the previous words) saw more safety if they shared the blame'.

13. intempestivo honore, for if they were the Roman senate they might be expected to evolve a policy, and either recognize Vitellius as *princeps* or not.

53. 1. Licinius Caecina. A man of this name is called vir *praetorius* by Pliny, *NH* XX. 199, but nothing is known of his politics.

Marcellum Epirum. T. Clodius Eprius Marcellus (*PIR*² E 84, cf. *AE* 1956, 186, K. R. Bradley, *Symbolae Osloenses*, 1978, 171) was born at Capua *sordide et abiecte* (Dial. 8), praetor for one day in 48 (*A.* XII 4), legate of Lycia and corruptly acquitted of extortion (*A.* XIII. 33), proconsul of Asia for three years (R. McElderry, *JRS* 1913, 116 ff.), and *cos.* II in May 74, having held the office for the first time in 62. His delations under Nero (IV. 7), especially of Thrasea Paetus (*A.* XVI. 22 ff.), earned him the hatred of Thrasea's son-in-law Helvidius Priscus (IV. 6–9) and T.'s disapproval, but he rose high in Vespasian's favour, according to T. (*Dial.* cit.) because of his eloquence (see 10 nn. on Vibius Crispus). Besides his second consulship and his exceptional tenure in Asia he held three priesthoods (*ILS* 992 = MW 271), though in the end he was mysteriously inculpated with Caecina in a "conspiracy" and put to death, Dio (= Xiph) 65. 16. 3.

6. ut novus ... claresceret, just as Pliny, *Epp.* IX. 13. 2, regards revenge for the younger Helvidius as an opportunity *se proferendi.*

7. Bononiam, 24 miles south-east on the Via Aemilia, connecting also with the Via Cassia to Rome.

10. suprema eius mandata. II. 49. 2 n. Wellesley, *RhM* 1960, 282, shows that this freedman could easily have reached Bononia, 55 miles from Brixellum, on the evening of 16 Apr., just as the news of the battle (II. 52. 3, *de proelio adlatum*) could have travelled over the slightly shorter distance from Bedriacum to Mutina by the afternoon of the day before.

13. hinc ... inclinavere, one of T.'s masterpieces.

54. 1. L. Vitellius. I. 88. 6 n.

4. quartam decimam. Another argument for Passerini's view that this had been the only Illyrican legion whose main body had missed the battle, Appendix, pp. 269ff.

6. diplomata. Two tablets fastened together, which bore the emperor's name and seal, and were warrants authorizing use of the imperial post, Plut *G.* 8. 4, *O.* 3. 2. For discussion of the authority by which they could be issued in various parts of the empire see 65. 6 n. below.

8. iussu Vitellii. Obviously the order could not have come from Vitellius 'within a few days', but emendation is quite unjustified. Probably the order came from Valens.

10. publici consilii facie, 'to all appearances acting officially'.

14. quo laudabilior eo velocius audita. Wellesley, *RhM*, 1960, protests that the news of suicide would not be sent more speedily because the act was noble, and that in any case the arrival of this news at Bononia was not particularly quick. What was quick was the carriage of news to Rome—necessarily so, because the capital had to learn without delay of the death of a *princeps*, especially during a civil war. In his view T. has misrepresented the facts because his mind 'has already moved south to Rome' and to the events of the next chapter.

About the speed of the official messages Wellesley is surely right: the senators at Bononia eventually but not rapidly got one from Valens. But what T. is thinking of in the sentence before us (see Heubner, 205–6) is the rapid spread of *unofficial* news about Otho's death. The reason for that was the utter surprise caused by the patriotic suicide of a man like Otho.

55. 1. at Romae. All through this chapter T. is concerned to point the contrast which civil war produced, between the horror of the battle area, and the carelessness, or callousness, which affected people in Rome. Wellesley, *RHM* 1960, is right about this, see also Heubner's nn., esp. on II. 56.1

Ceriales ludi. These were held over the eight days 12–19 Apr., Ov. *Fast.* IV. 389, but the celebrations on the last day were in the circus, not the theatre, *CIL* I². 315, *A.* XV. 53 (with Furneaux's n.). So though it may have been on the 19th (line 8 n.) that Vitellius was given his *imperium*, the news must have reached Rome on the previous afternoon, which means that the 344 m.p. from Brixellum were covered in about sixty hours, presumably by means of relays. This is a record for all postal news in this period, see also I. 76. 1 n.

Wellesley brings out this point clearly, but it is hard to agree with him that mention of the games, begun before the battle of Bedriacum was fought, is a *suggestio falsi*. T.'s imperfect *spectabantur* is carefully chosen, and his readers would have been well aware of the dates of the games. Yet the celebration of the games does remain part of his contrast between the routine of Rome and the impending climax in the north.

2. Flavio Sabino. I. 46. 5 n.

5. Galbae imagines. The posthumous popularity of Galba was something with which all his immediate successors had to reckon. For the Flavians it was relatively easy (III. 7. 7, IV. 40. 4, and the coinage, *RIC* I 197), though Vespasian ultimately put a stop to this propaganda, Suet. *G.* 23. But the people in Rome may have remembered little about the date and circumstances of Vitellius' rebellion. What they had actually witnessed was the horror of Galba's murder, and many of them were ready to revive his memory once his murderer had been overthrown. If Vitellius and his supporters had any view about such celebrations, they perhaps found comfort in the doctrine expressed at I. 44. 14.

8. cuncta ... decernuntur. This action, presumably (*statim*) taken on the 19th, was confirmed by *comitia trib. pot.* on 30 Apr. and by a *dies* *imperii* (whatever that may imply) on 1 May, *AFA (Henzen) XCII*=*ILS* 241. 82, 85=MW, 14. (For further discussion of the Lex de Imperio see 79. 3 n.) Wellesley claims (*RhM* 1960, cit.,) that *statim* is inserted by T. out of deliberate hostility to Vitellius; but I. 47 shows that T. was almost equally emphatic about the Senate's craven behaviour over Otho, and implies a similarly rapid change of sides towards Vespasian, IV. 3. 11.

Vitellius' answer is presumably the edict of II. 62. 9. What T. fails, oddly, to tell us is that in July Vitellius became consul for life, *ILS* 242–3=MW 81, a move which seems to have been heavily criticised by Flavian propagandists, Suet. *Vit.* 11. 2.

10. quae gaudio fungeretur. Irvine's 'to offer their formal congratulations' brings out the use of *fungor* to express an action taken officially and not spontaneously.

12 quod non scripsisset. On this point the constitutional theory is not quite clear, but probably a letter to the Senate or consuls should come only from a magistrate or a pro-magistrate with *imperium :* Valens and Caecina were only *legati*. In practice it was unusual by this time for anyone but the *princeps* himself to write, at any rate on matters such as those covered by Valens' despatch. This point is emphasised more strongly in relation to Mucianus, IV. 4. 2, *si privatus esset, cur publice loqueretur? potuisse eadem paucos post dies loco sententiae dici.*

56. 1. ceterum, returning to the other side of the contrast between Rome and the battlefields.

3. fas nefasque. See Heubner's parallels, but I see no difficulty about people being either *avidi* or *venales* for *fas* as well as *nefas*.

4. venales. They hired themselves out as criminals. This does not, as V. maintained, involve a repetition of what we are told in the next sentence, where T. says certain Vitellians in disguise indulged their own vendettas.

5. specie militum. The murderers were civilians, disguised as, or pretending to be, soldiers: contrast *ipsique milites* which follows.

6. regionum gnari. This conforms with what we know from epigraphy about the high proportion of North Italian legionaries at this time, Forni, App. B 2. After A.D. 69 the numbers declined, but not because of any political decision taken as a result of the civil wars, see *Cisalpine Gaul*, 122. The legionaries wanted booty from whatever social class they had been derived, and the *dites domini* of North Italy were obvious victims.

8. obnoxiis ducibus. The generals were 'subservient' to their men (for the absolute use of *obnoxius* see I. 1. 10), and it is otiose to ask whether the cause uppermost in T.'s mind was the breakdown in discipline or the indebtedness created by the generals' ambition or greed. The question attracted other writers. e.g. Nepos, *Eumenes* 8. 2, App., *BC v.* 17.

10. attritis Italiae rebus. This passage stands out in Roman writing as an assertion of the economic decline of Italy as a whole in the first century A.D., as distinct from that of particular districts in Latium and the south (on which see Strabo and other earlier writers). It is remarkable in that it is directed immediately at conditions in the Po valley, which were probably more prosperous than those in some other districts cf. II. 17. 5.

57. 1. interim Vitellius ... The chapters dealing with Vitellius' journey to Rome and his activities there (II. 57–73, 89–101) show bias, influenced in part by flagrant Flavian propaganda, which surpasses almost anything of that kind in T.'s works. See nn. below, and Wellesley, *RhM* 1960, 287–8.

2. reliquas ... viris. As at I. 61. 10, *tota mole belli secuturus*, T. is convinced that the army accompanying Vitellius was very large. That the words which follow, *pauci veterum militum in hibernis relicti*, are reasonable we need not doubt: yet the depletion of the camps (probably less than that of the Danube camps during the Flavian invasion) can be exaggerated. Vitellius' own force can hardly have been as large as either one of his advanced guards. He had the eagle of only one legion, XXII Primigenia, II. 89. 5, 100. 4; and from the others (and from XXII itself) substantial vexillations had gone with Valens and Caecina. Vitellius had his British troops (line 6 below), perhaps 1,000 men from each of five Rhine legions, together with *auxilia*. Add to these the *per Galliam dilectus* for auxiliaries, men later sent home (II. 69. 7), but available for renewed recruitment in the autumn, IV. 19. 12, 26. 2. 31. 5. Yet it is difficult to allow him more than 25,000 men in all.

4. nomina. Cf. IV. 14. 20, 15. 20, where *nomen* (=paper strength) is opposed to *robur* (=actual fighting power), also Cic., *Att.* V. 15. 1, *me nomen habere duarum legionum exilium.* At II. 69. 10 the same concept is expressed by the word *numeri* (read by Acidalius here).

6. octo milia. 2,000 men from each legion (cf. II. 11. 3), or 1,000 with equivalent auxiliaries, would have been a natural draft. But although there had been four legions in Britain until Nero withdrew XIV Gemina, II. 11. 7 n., and there were to be four again under Vespasian, yet in A.D. 69 there were only three; and 8 is not a multiple of 3.

Elsewhere T. is aware of the size of the British garrison, II. 100. 6, III. 22. 8, but for our present passage either he or his source may have been told that *bina milia* were withdrawn from the legions, and then used the wrong multiplier. 8,000 men, even if *auxilia* were included, would have meant a very serious diversion of men from a province which could ill spare them at this time; cf. 97. 5.

9. Asiaticum. Suet. *Vit.* 12 relates the same episode, saying it occurred on the first day of Vitellius' *imperium*, i.e. 1 May (55. 8 n.), but did he really know?

On *equestris dignitas* and the rings, I. 13. 3 n. Nutting (there cit.) defends the MS. *oneravit* in line 12, suggesting that Vitellius' action was made peculiarly repellent by the pile of rings he bestowed. He was bemused by T.'s distaste for Vitellius.

58. 1. utramque Mauretaniam. In A.D. 40 Caligula executed king Ptolemy, son of Juba II and Cleopatra Selene, and annexed his kingdom: Claudius, *CAH* X. 675 with reff., created the two provinces Tingitana and Caesariensis, each under an equestrian procurator: in Tingitana, the westerly province menaced by Moors, the governor was called *procurator pro legato*, *AÉ* 1924, 66, *ILS* 1352, B. E. Thomasson, *Die Staathalter der römischen Provinzen Nordafrikas* (1960), I. 102. Why Galba unified the two provinces we are not told (see II. 9. 1 n. on his similar measure over Galatia and Pamphylia): perhaps he thought a firm control was needed in the area west of Africa after Clodius Macer's rising. Unification again took place, probably for reasons of security, at later dates, see (e.g.) *SHA Hadr.* 5. 8: indeed in A.D. 75 the two provinces were governed by a senator with the title *leg. Aug. pro pr. (ordinandae) utriusque Mauretaniae*, MW 277–8. For Mauretania during this period and its relation to Africa see P. Romanelli, *Storia delle province romane dell'Africa* (1959), 296 ff.; he connects the appointment just mentioned with the disturbed conditions reported in our present chapter.

2. Lucceius Albinus, previously, in A.D. 62–4, procurator of Judaea, where his rapacity shocked Josephus, *PIR*[1] L 500. He may be the father of the senator of that name who was twice briefed with Pliny in extortion trials, *Epp.* III. 8. 7, IV. 9. 13, but there is no sign of especial sympathy towards him for T.

3. haud spernendis viribus. The size of the combined garrison is not dissimilar from that attested for the two provinces in T.'s day. *CIL* XVI. 56 (A.D. 107) gives ten cohorts and four *alae* in Caesariensis; *ibid.* 73 (A.D. 128) eight cohorts and three *alae* in Tingitana.

6. ingens Maurprum iuventus. Cf. I. 68. 6 n.

9. Cluvio Rufo. The account of this incident has struck source critics in different ways. Seeck, *RhM* 1901, 231, thought the whole affair was exaggerated because Cluvius reported it; Fabia 175–6, suspected that more would have been known had Cluvius' own evidence been available. If Romanelli (n. to line 1 above) was right in thinking repercussions were still felt in A.D. 75, then T. has been somewhat reticent; but that may have been the result of his own judgment (and desire not to interrupt his main narrative), rather than that of his source.

   decimam legionem. So this legion, which in later Julio-Claudian times was in Pannonia, had now been sent back to Spain, presumably by Galba. It had therefore played no part in the North Italian campaign.

14. Iubae nomen. Juba II, son of Pompey's ally the king of Numidia, was given the kingdom of Mauretania by Augustus in 25 B.C., and retained it until his death in A.D. 23, *A.* IV. 5, 23. He was a remarkable scholar, and also did much for the civilization of Mauretania.

59. 3. dum e Tingitana. Despite the frequent unification of the two provinces, there seems to have been no recognized land-route from one to the other, Syme, *CAH* XI. 149.

7. impar curis gravioribus. It is not obvious how Vitellius from Gaul could give personal attention to an affair requiring immediate attention the other side of Spain, nor what he was expected to do other than take note when he heard that Cluvius had, for the moment at least, made the rising collapse. When disagreeable events occurred in Africa early next year, IV. 48–50, Vespasian's participation in them (rightly or wrongly) is not even mentioned, and no one blamed him for carelessness.

8. Arare flumine. The road, that taken by Valens earlier, runs along the Saône to Lyon, but Vitellius apparently went by boat, *delicatissimis et variarum coronarum genere*, Suet. *Vit.* 10. 2.

9. vetere egestate. The squalor of his arrival in Germany in 68 is recounted with details in Suet. *Vit.* 7.

10. Iunius Blaesus. I. 59. 10 n.

18. Germanicum. Vitellius had already taken the name, I. 62. 11. The boy, aged six, had been brought from Italy. He was executed by Mucianus next year, IV. 80. 1.

19. nimius honos, yet the precedents for *Germanicus* and *Britannicus* in past years, though *breves et infausti, A.* II. 41, may not have been considered all that monstrous at this time.

20. in solacium cessit. Wantonly to insert a negative (app. crit.) produces banality unworthy of T. Yet he has not made it clear who was consoled (see V.'s n.), and the sentence is not one of his best efforts. The thought, presumably, is that used more fully, and more appositely, about Julia and Agrippina at *A.* XIV. 63, *praesentem saevitiam melioris olim fortunae recordatione adlevabant.*

60. 1. Tum interfecti centuriones . . ., for it was almost wholly in the armies that Otho had determined partisans. Vitellius' clemency to the senatorial commanders, including Otho's brother, is very marked.

2. Illyricos exercitus. V. and others have taken this to mean the Moesian legions, making *ceterae legiones* the armies of Syria and Judaea. But surely *contactu* refers to direct contact between such Danubian legions as fought at Bedriacum (whichever these were, see introd.) and the Moesian legions. Considerable parts of the latter must by now have entered Aquileia. 85. 5. n. below.

5. squalidos. Perhaps actually *sordidatos,* i.e. in the garb of accused men.

7. proditionem ultro imputabant. T. has no doubt, *magis . . . quam honestis,* that none of this can be taken to throw doubt on the actual plans or movements of the Othonians before the battle. For the possibility (no more) that there was *proditio* see 37. 1 n.

10. fidem absolvit. Not 'pardoned their loyalty' (GG, H., V., etc.), which misses the epigram; and *absolvere* does not mean 'pardon', nor had Vitellius any need to pardon if *credidit de perfidia* is true. Wellesley and other translators are right with 'acquitted them of loyalty'. With the accusative *absolvit* means something like 'disposed of': so *TLL* I, col. 173, though even there the wrong rendering is given for this passage.

12. Mario Celso consulatus. For previous dispositions of the consulates see I. 77. 5 n. For Vitellius' changes, and for Caecilius Simplex, II. 71. 5 n.

14. restitit. Did Vitellius decline Simplex' bribe, or refuse to listen to the charges against him? The former is in T.'s present compressed manner, leading on to the paradox that Simplex got his consulate none the less.

16. Trachalum, a Galerius, I. 90. 11 n.
Galeria, daughter of a praetorian senator, Suet., *Vit.* 6.

61. 2. Mariccus quidam. Even if Mariccus called himself *adsertor Galliarum* and thus recalled the propaganda of the Vindex rebellion, his rising had no real affinity with what had occurred in Gaul in A.D. 68 nor with what was to follow in 70. He was of the people, hostile to the aristocracy, and of a different stamp from either Vindex or Classicus. The account given of him by C. Jullian, *Histoire de la Gaule* (1908–26), IV. 192, is therefore misleading: Rostovtzeff, *SEHR*[2] 301, puts the affair more securely into its context.

How the rising developed depends on the translation of 5–6, *pagos . . . trahebat . . . civitas.* There is certainly an opposition between town and country: Mariccus won over the outlying villages, but was overcome by the people of Augustodunum, the Aeduan state capital. Yet for *pagos* the translation 'villages' is wrong. T. invariably uses the word, as did Roman writers from Caesar onwards, to mean 'cantons', extensive subdivisions of tribes (usually Gallic or Germanic) which included the villages (*vici*), but also the cultivated fields and pasture-land, *Germ.* 6. 17, 12. 10, and in *Hist.* IV. 15. 22, 26. 15 (GG did not explain why *A.* IV. 45. 7, *ducto per proximos pagos equo,* should be considered an exception to this usage). See also J. G. C. Anderson's edn. of *Germania* (1938), lvii ff.

That *civitas* in T. can mean either the state or its capital city we have already seen, I. 54. 1 n. Here the former meaning is indicated by the epithet *gravissima.* The authorities of this powerful (or highly respected) state dispersed a *fanatica multitudo.* No doubt the initiative came from the city aristocracy, but there is no necessary opposition between the *civitas* and its *pagi.*

Finally *trahebat.* In support of the meaning 'winning over' V. cites 86. 12, *exercitus Delmaticum militem traxere,* and III. 44. 4, (*prima Adiutrix*) *decimam quoque ac sextam traxit.* This is unconvincing. Here the translation 'was engaged in ravaging', which suits the imperfect tense better, is paralleled by *A.* III. 74. 3, *ne Cirtensium pagi impune traherentur* (cf. *A.* III. 45. 2, *vastat Sequanorum pagos*), with a meaning often found in Sallust (e.g. *BI* 41. 3). If this be right, we need not deny that Mariccus was leading a 'peasant' revolt, but there is no ground for crediting him with organized support in the 'villages'. His method of attacking society was purely destructive, without much plan.

Were such risings common in the Roman provinces under the early Empire? On the one hand we can be fairly sure that T. records this one (*pudendum dictu*) only because Vitellius happened to be in Gaul at the time. On the other hand the evidence for parallels does not exist before the second century, Rostovtzeff, *SEHR*[2], and our knowledge of social conflicts in early imperial Gaul is thin. Florus and Sacrovir in A.D. 21 had drawn ready support from the vulgus, *A.* III. 42, but it was the client–patron relationship which won them this rather than the acute distress of the clients.

e plebe Boiorum. The Boii had been settled, at the request of the Aedui, between the Loire and the Allier, Caes. *BG* I. 28. 5.

inserere sese fortunae, 'pushed himself into prominence'.

6. electa iuventutute. For the young nobles at Augustodunum cf. *A.* III. 43. 1, *nobilissimam Galliae subolem.*

8. feris obiectus *Dig.* 48. 19. 38. 2 (Paul), *auctores seditionis et tumultus, populo concitato, pro qualitate dignitatis, aut in furcam tolluntur, aut bestiis obiiciuntur, aut in insulam deportantur.*

62. 1. in defectores. These, carrying on from the previous chapter, must be the followers of Mariccus, since nowhere else are the Othonians called *defectores*. But these peasants can hardly have had property worth confiscating, and the latter part of the sentence (see the words which follow) comes back to the Othonians. Heubner ad loc. sees the combination of the two enemies of Vitellius as T.'s sarcasm: I think it more probably due to his reluctance to spend much time or care over this part of his narrative.

saevitum, yet to Suet., *Vit.* 14, *saevitia* was one of Vitellius' most notable vices. For T. the vices are *luxuria* and *socordia*: the deaths of Dolabella, II. 63–4, and Blaesus, III. 38–9, are activated by Vitellius' brother.

3. prorsus ... timeres. The contrast with Vespasian is deliberate, II. 5. 4, and is emphasized by the use of *prorsus* in both passages.

4. epularum ... libido. About this vice T. is persistent, cf. I. 62 etc., and is developed with greater detail by Suet., *Vit.* 13. But whether anything lies behind the present than that a large army was moving from the Rhine camps to Rome is doubtful; cf. II. 88. 4 ff.

6. utroque mari, for sea-transport greatly reduced the cost of moving food north from Rome and other parts of Italy. Vitellius seems to be still at Lugdunum, II. 65. 1, but movement up the Adriatic would still be valuable when he reached the Po valley.

7. degenerabat. Though much of T.'s account of Vitellius may be derived from his own judgement or from general senatorial tradition, this picture of the Vitellian army was one drawn from pure Flavian propaganda, cf. Jos. *BI* IV. 585 ff. It bears no relation to the determination with which the leaderless Vitellians fought at Cremona in October.

9. edictum, II. 55. 8 n. For Vitellius' policy about his titles see I. 62. 11 n., III. 58. 17, Hammond, *AM* 61, 112.

11. mathematici, I. 22. 6 n. Suet. *Vit.* 14. 4 says they were made to leave Rome and Italy by 1 Oct., and that they replied with a poster with the wish that by that date Vitellius would have ceased to exist.

12. priores id principes. As often (e.g. *A.* XV. 18. 8) this essentially means one recent *princeps*, in this case Nero, *A.* XIV. 14. The dictator Caesar had put pressure on a Roman knight to go on the stage, Suet. *Iul.* 39. 2, Cic. *Fam.* XII. 18. 2, and had allowed some senators to fight as gladiators; but Augustus had prohibited performances by knights, as had Tiberius and Claudius, Suet., *Aug.* 43. 3, *Tib.* 35. 2, Dio 59. 10. 4, 13. 2. Vitellius' measure may have disappointed the Roman *plebs*, R. F. Newbold, *Historia*, 1972, 308.

63. 2. Dolabellam. I. 88. 1 n.

5. Plancium Varum. The career and connections of M. Plancius Varus, whose son was probably adopted by Pliny's friend and colleague Cornutus Tertullus (*cos.* 100), have been convincingly reconstructed by Shelagh Jameson, *JRS* 1965, 54, and by Stephen Mitchell, *JRS* 1974, 27. He belonged to an Italian family established at Perge in Pamphylia, and possessed great estates much further north, in Galatia and southern Pisidia. Under Vespasian he became a legate (to the proconsuls) in Achaia and Asia, and then, probably in the late 70s proconsul of Bithynia. It seems that he never reached the consulate.

6. apud praefectum urbis. For the origin and extent of the urban prefect's jurisdiction see G. Vitucci, *Ricerche sulla praefectura urbi in età imperiale* (1956), cap. II, with T. J. Cadoux's discussion *JRS* 1959, 156 ff. From the first the prefect could use summary powers in the city to suppress disorder, *A.* VI. 11, but by Nero's reign he is also found dealing, though not without challenge, with criminal cases which did not lead to any riot, *A.* XIV. 41: later see Stat. *Silv.* I. 4. 47. Vitucci holds that Dolabella's case was brought before him because it involved a charge of tampering with the urban cohort at Ostia, the urbans being under the prefect's command. But T. implies that it would have been natural for Flavius Sabinus to take the case anyway, even had that additional charge not been made. It was natural that the prefect's position should acquire greater significance when the princeps was out of Rome. Otho had given *quietem urbis curasque imperii* to his brother, I. 90. 19, but that arrangement was now ended, and to whom but the regular prefect would one turn with a charge of this political importance?

8. cohortem quae Ostiae ageret. I. 80. 2n.

10. seram ... quaerebat. Not clear. The *scelus* is certainly not (as H.) the murder of Dolabella, but Plancius' disgraceful behaviour. But does he seek pardon for himself from Dolabella, for himself from the world (Wellesley's tr., rightly, I think), or for Dolabella from the court (Heubner)? There is no indication of misgivings by the court, *impulit ruentem*, line 15.

13. ingenio mitis. For fuller description of his character see III. 75; in recounting his behaviour T. frees himself from any purely Flavian bias.

64. 1. Petroniam. Vitellius' first wife was daughter to a consular, Suet. *Vit.* 6, probably P. Petronius, *cos.* 19, legate of Syria under Caligula. For earlier connections between the two families see Syme, 386 (in n. 5 read 'Vitellia'). Petronia may have been the sister of Nero's general Petronius Turpilianus, whom Galba had executed, I. 6. 5. T.'s story of Vitellius' fear and hatred of her second husband is closely paralleled by what he claims Tiberius felt towards Asinius Gallus, *A.* I. 12. 6.

3. vitata ... celebritate. The modern Via Flaminia runs from Narni through Terni (Interamna), and then goes north through Spoleto and Foligno. This was the line of ancient road too, but then the Flaminia proper took the shorter line Narnia–Carsulae–Mevania–Forum Flaminii. See R. Fell and T. Ashby, *JRS* 1921, 166 ff. On the populous towns of this stretch of road, Strabo, V p. 227.

4. Interamnium. The more normal spelling Interamna is found at III. 61. 5, 63. 7. This is the modern Terni.

iussit. This governs the intransitive *devertere* and the passive *interfici* so easily that it almost passes notice. Where Vitellius gave his order remains obscure.

8. Galeria. II. 60. 16 n.

9. Sextilia, *probatissima nec ignobilis femina*, III. 67. 1, Suet. *Vit.* 3.

10. primas ... epistulas. The name Germanicus presumably occurred in a letter to Sextilia, who then recalled the deaths of earlier Caesars who had borne it.

65. 1. Cluvius Rufus, even less likely to be a source here than in previous passages, e.g. II. 58. 9.

4. Caesaris libertus. Though he refused the name Caesar, Vitellius not only had freedmen of his own, but acquired many when he became *princeps*.

6. diplomatibus. II. 54. 6 n. In Trajan's time the emperor used to issue batches of these tickets, with the governor's name and the period of validity: the governor then used his discretion, reporting doubtful cases to Rome after the event and seeking indemnity if he had allowed travel for private needs, Plin. *Epp.* X. 45–6, 64, 120–1. Since Galba's death Cluvius had evidently manufactured his own tickets, for during a civil war every provincial governor ought to have declared for one side or to remain neutral, even though he had not to make any military move (for the ambiguity of all Cluvius' actions, I. 76. 3). Vitellius would have been faced with grave problems had he wanted to punish neutrality: he was even prepared to continue in office the openly Othonian legates of the Danubian provinces. What Cluvius had said in his speeches we have no means of telling, but it is most unlikely that he could have felt himself to be *capax imperii*.

11. exemplo L. Arruntii. This allusion to a notorious puzzle in the history of provincial administration under Tiberius helps in no way towards its solution. At *A.* I. 80 T. speaks of men who received provinces from Tiberius, but were then retained in Rome because the emperor could not trust them. At *A.* VI. 27 he mentions the only two cases known to us (yet he does not connect them with one another), namely L. Aelius Lamia, *cos.* A.D. 3., who was *administrandae imagine tandem exsolutus* in A.D. 32 and died as city prefect next year, and L. Arruntius, *cos.* A.D. 6, who in A.D. 33 had for nine or ten years been prevented from going to Spain. Suet. *Tib.* 63. 2 alludes to these affairs without mentioning names, but suggests that Tiberius was experimenting in some form of delegation while keeping the senior officers in Rome, so M. P. Charlesworth, *CAH* X. 649. Yet with Arruntius we must surely (R. S. Rogers, *CP* 1931, 31) connect the story in Dio 58. 8. 3, that in 31 Tiberius quashed an indictment against one of Sejanus' enemies, chosen ten years earlier to govern Spain, but still under charge (κρινομένου ἐπί τισιν); and that henceforth any person selected for public office was to be immune from similar suits during the period before he took up his duties. It remains strange that even then, after Sejanus' fall, Arruntius stayed in Rome (and *ob metum* is puzzling too), but perhaps Tiberius was by now exhausted with the matter. Anyway it seems more likely that these cases are related to politics than to administrative experiments. For further discussion see Syme, 442–3, K.'s n. on *A.* VI. 27, and B. Levick, *Tiberius the Politician* (1976), 128 f.

As to Cluvius, it is improbable that Vitellius at this moment had any complicated plans. He perhaps had no other obvious person to appoint, and therefore temporized. Tarraconensis was regarded as vacant early next year, IV. 39. 19.

13. Trebellio Maximo. I. 60. 10 n.

15. Vettius Bolanus. *cos. suff. c.* 66 and previously a legate under Corbulo, is addressed by Statius, *Silv.* V. 2. In T.'s view he governed Britain *placidius quam feroci provincia dignum est, Agr.* 8, but see E. Birley, *Roman Britain and the Roman Army* (1953), 12 ff. For his subsequent activities in the civil war see 97. 4 n. below.

66. 1. Angebat. The chronology of Vitellius' journey cannot be precisely determined. Suet. *Vit.* 10. 1 puts the dismissal of the praetorians, which in T. follows the action taken about XIV Gemina, immediately after Vitellius got the news of Bedriacum, and this may be right: according to him, Vitellius was still in Gaul. But he must have been nearing the Cottian crossing to Augusta Taurinorum: the next we hear of him, he was at Ticinum (Pavia). And if T.'s account here is to make sense, the order to XIV Gemina must have been his first move.

legionum. This chapter and the next show that there were now five complete ex-Othonian legions in North Italy, four from Illyricum, and I Adiutrix. They are all described as *victae*, but XIV Gemina distinguishes itself from the others by its claim that its main body had not been present at the battle. See Appendix, p. 270.

6. unde a Nerone ... II. 11. 6 n.

7. tendere, 'to share camp with': cf. I 31. 5.

veterem ... discordiam. I. 59. 12 n., II. 27. 9.

15. agmini ... fidos. Unclear whether he was already at Turin or was ordering the cohorts to await his arrival. At any rate, II. 69. 4, they did not march far with him.

The passage shows that at this point Vitellius regarded the cohorts as friendly to him, and that it is therefore wrong, with Walser, 89 ff., to suppose them a recognizable 'Galbian' body which could be expected to join any hostile party, in the way they later pretended to join the Flavians on Hordeonius Flaccus' bidding, IV. 15 ff. Vitellius took a risk in sending them back through eastern Gaul, but it was a risk for Rome rather than for his own party. See Brunt, *Latomus*, 1960, 501 n. 3.

16. quo Viennam vitarent. Yet the legion's threat to Vienna, line 21, shows that they came near to it, so they probably went to Lugdunum. But the Itineraries show no road to Chambéry and over the Mont du Chat to Bourg-en-Bresse. The legion probably went to Geneva and thence down the Rhône.

17. timebantur. Vienna had been a Vindician stronghold, whereas
XIV had been obstinately loyal to Nero, II. 7. But at this moment any
rational fears would not be for the legion but for the town, which had
been heavily punished and disarmed during Valens' march, I. 66.

67. 2. separati. Despite the masculine gender T. need not imply that
the cohorts were broken up before the discharges began. In this chapter
(contrast 93) he is not thinking of *ordo militiae*, but of individuals who
later entered the Flavian army. The exact process is not clear, but
probably all that is meant is that each unit was isolated in different
parts of North Italy (cf. *sparsae per Italiam*, 66. 2, and the appearance of
two cohorts at Augusta Taurinorum, 66. 13.).

Fabia, *Rev. Phil.* 1914, 34, criticizes Suet. *Vit.* 10. 1, for saying that
Vitellius pretended his treatment of the praetorians was a punishment
for their desertion of Galba. Certainly Vitellius' real motives are more
adequately given by T., but Suet. may be right about what he said, cf.
II. 55. 5 n.

honestae missionis, presumably with gratuity, though they were
not time-expired. The risk taken in allowing these men to be at large,
with resources, in North Italy, was of course enormous.

3. arma ... deferebant. So Antonius III. 24. 13 says to the soldiers
who have re-enlisted *illic* (i.e. among the Vitellian enemy) *signa armaque
vestra sunt.*

4. robur Flavianorum partium, surely greatly exaggerated:
contrast *praetorianum vexillum*, III. 21. 13.

5. prima ... in Hispaniam, giving Spain a third legion (with VI
Victrix and X Gemina) for the first time since A.D. 43. Both VI and I
Adiutrix were sent to the Rhineland next year, IV. 68. 22.

7. suis hibernis. VII (Galbiana) clearly in Pannonia, with Antonius
Primus as its legate, II. 86. 1, XI in Dalmatia, III. 50. 5.

tertiadecimani. They are back in Pannonia by August, II. 86. 1.

68. 3. Vitellio, possibly an unnecessary emendation of M.'s *bello*,
though the whole passage is corrupt, and the addition of *ni* in the
previous line is essential, cf. Wellesley, *Rh M* 1960.

5. tempestivis conviviis. Cf. *A.* XI. 37. 2. An early meal (for the
adjective cf. Cic., *Att.* IX. 1. 3, 13. 6) seems to have been one which
began before the ninth hour; so Juv. I. 49, *ab octava Marius bibit*, and
Martial's description of the hours in IV. 8.

7. pervigiliis. The only other use of the word by T. is at *A.* XV. 44,
where after the fire *sellisternia ac pervigilia celebravere feminae*. It seems to

mean 'nocturnal ceremonies', but V. points out that there is no instance of its use in a bad sense ('orgies'), and suggests that here *pervigiliis ac bacchanalibus* is a hendiadys, balanced by the more obvious hendiadys *disciplinae et castris*.

9. Galli, a misprint in OCT. for *Gallis*.

16. agminis coactores, 'the rearguard'. The noun is not found in this sense elsewhere, but *agmen cogere* (*TLL* s. v. 'agmen') is the standard phrase for 'to bring up the rear'.

20. ad omnis suspiciones pavidus, hardly borne out by what we know of him. Was he not rather too easy-going—cf. (e.g.) II. 67. 2 n.?

22. quondam ducis. This would apply to troops from the Lower, as well as the Upper, German army, I. 51. 11, *contractae legiones*.

24. ut fastiditi. Irvine is surely wrong in doubting that this refers to Verginius' refusal of the empire in 68 (and not, as Heubner ad loc., in 69, for the offer then came from the Othonian troops).

69. 1. senatus legatione, appointed about 19 Apr., II. 55. 10.

5. remissae, not to Britain, as was originally planned, II. 66. 7, but to the Rhineland, where they are next heard of at IV. 15. 5.

6. principium interno simul externoque bello. In Book IV T. does not conceal the part the Flavians played in promoting the rebellion of Civilis, though he never goes into the question closely, see Wellesley's n. on III. 35. 7. But he certainly saw the affair (and rightly, *pace* Walser) as in essence a *bellum externum*.

7. Gallorum auxilia. This is the first we have heard of abnormal recruitment in Gaul, except for the legions which remained on the Rhine, II. 57. 3. Since T. here speaks of auxiliaries recruited at the outset of Vitellius' revolt, they may be identical with the *Germanorum auxilia* of I. 61. 9.

8. inter inania belli, 'as a form of military window-dressing' (Wellesley).

10. numeros, 'units' (I. 6. 11 n.), of which the paper strengths, and nominal identity, remained unaltered, but the effectives were considerably reduced.

11. exitiabile id rei publicae. That Vitellius in the outcome did harm to his own cause by these actions is true, but it is hard to see what harm he was doing to the Empire as a whole. His troops were on Italian soil, and their numbers were greatly inflated.

13. vires luxu corrumpebantur. Cf. II. 93. But this is a quite different point, nothing to do with the reduction in numbers.

70. 1. flexit, from Ticinum, instead of joining the Via Aemilia at Placentia.

munere Caecinae. II. 67. 8. Here and at Bononia, II. 71. 1, the building operations of legion XIII have been remarkably speedy.

Gladiatorial shows, which Rome borrowed from Etruria, were originally part of the cult of the dead, and one may suspect that Vitellius' visit to Cremona, which ended with a *sacrum* to the local divinities, was intended as an act of piety rather than of sadism. Yet had he disdained to look upon the *foedum atque atrox spectaculum* some other means of attacking his inhumanity would no doubt have been found.

intra quadragesimum pugnae diem, the first note of time in the story of Vitellius' movements. We are now therefore in the fourth week of May, little more than a month away from the official proclamation of Vespasian, and presumably very close to the time when Mucianus is supposed to have made the speech of II. 76–7.

8. regium in morem, 'in the manner of oriental kings'. But there is a close parallel in the honours paid to Gaius Caligula on his way from Misenum to Rome immediately after his accession (Suet. *Cal.* 13), when his religious policy had not yet taken any extreme turn.

12. circumfusas auxiliorum manus. II. 44. 1 n.

15. aggerem armorum, presumably a trophy, cf. *A.* II. 18, *struxitque aggerem et in modum tropaeorum arma . . . imposuit.*

18. tot milia. II. 44. 3 n.

71. 2. propinquabat. We now begin the journey down to Rome, with no further precise indication of time until 18 July, II. 91. 3.

4. ingenio, 'characteristic figures'. There seems to be no close parallel for the usage.

5. Neronem . . . celebrabat. If the story of the sacrifices told in II. 97 be true, Vitellius did find it politic to revive the memory of Nero; and it may be that Pedanius Costa's consulship, line 12, was cancelled for that reason. But we can easily see the Flavian source of the story that Vitellius used to enjoy Nero's singing *non necessitate, qua honestissimus quisque*: a decent man went to sleep, Suet. *Vesp.* 4. 4.

8. coartati . . . consulatus. See the general discussion of the consulates of 69, I. 77 n.

10. Valerium Marinum. Despite his mild nature, he seems to have rapidly joined Vespasian at Alexandria, Plin. *NH* XIX. 3.

14. actaeque ... gratiae, by the defeated candidates; cf. *Agr.* 43. 2: Seneca's policy for getting on at court was *iniurias accipiendo et grates agendo, de Ira* II. 33. 2. T. could hardly, in Trajan's reign, have sneered at Vitellius for accepting thanks from the successful candidates.

72. 2. Scribonianum Camerinum. Two men named Sulpicius Camerinus, father (*cos.* 46) and son, were executed in 67 after a charge brought by M. Regulus, Dio 63. 18. 2; earlier commentators thought one of these was meant, and that he had acquired the name Scribonianus from a mother who was related to the wife of M Crassus Frugi, *cos.* 27 (I. 14. 7 n.). But we surely need here someone who was actually of the family of the Crassi, and Dessau, *PIR*[1] S 205, had some ground for suggesting a son of M. Crassus Frugi, *cos.* 64, who also perished on Regulus' accusation in 67 (cf. IV. 42). His name Camerinus would derive from a marriage alliance with the Sulpicii, whom Regulus attacked simultaneously. He was also the nephew of Piso Caesar, Galba's adopted son, which fact, together with the eminence of his father, could have made his supposed reappearance highly embarrassing to Vitellius.

4. occultatum. Is this what the impostor said, or what T.'s source believed to be the case? The indicative *manebat* in the *quod* clause implies the latter, but what then happened to the real Scribonianus?

illic ... manebat. No confirmation has emerged from epigraphy, but for great estates in Histria see Rostovtzeff, *SEHR*[2] 551–2, A. Degrassi, *Il confine nord-orientale dell'Italia Romana* (1954), 78 ff. A large imperial estate also existed there from Augustan times, and Nero would doubtless have been glad to add to it by confiscation.

For the Crassi of early imperial times see Syme, *JRS* 1960 13 ff.

6. in argumentum fabulae, 'to play parts in his play'.

73. 2. speculatores. Not here the *speculatores* attached to the legions, I. 24. 9 n., but ordinary spies, or possibly imperial couriers (Suet. *Cal.* 44).

3. nuntiavere. When? If after Vespasian's proclamation on 1 July, and if T. knew that this was so, he could hardly have forborne to point out the irony. But probably he had no accurate knowledge. The next known date is the edict of 18 July (II. 9.), which probably came directly after Vitellius' entry into Rome.

7. externos mores. Cf. *regium in morem*, 70. 8. T. gives no detail whatever until we reach the massacre of civilians outside Rome in II.

88. Moreover that was an act of indiscipline by the soldiers, and T. does not elsewhere suggest that only foreign troops were capable of *saevitia*, *libido*, or *raptus*, cf. I Kojanto, *Latomus*, 1970, 714.

74–86. *The Flavian Proclamation*

74. 2. miles ipsi adeo paratus. Jos. *BI* IV. 603, says that when Vespasian was actually proclaimed (II. 80) the officers were insistent, and the men drew their swords to threaten him with death unless he was ready ζῆν ἀξίως (i.e. to grasp his *fortuna*). That story, see Townend, *Latomus*, 1961, 339, would make Vespasian into a Verginius without his virtues. But it does not fit T.'s much more plausible account of Flavian planning, see nn. to II. 1–7.

3. fausta omnia precantem. Cf. IV. 49. 18. The formula for wishing success is a common one (e.g. Livy XXIV. 16. 10), and Lipsius was certainly wrong in reading *omina*.

5. in Titum pronior. II. 5. 14.
 Ti. Alexander. I. 11. 6 n. For T., Alexander is already Vespasian's ally: contrast Jos. *BI* IV. 616 ff. (Briessmann, 12). Moreover his negotiations are not with Mucianus, but with Vespasian himself, whose personal calculations are the subject of this chapter. For speculation about the method of negotiation see 78. 16 n. below.

6. tertiam ... suam numerabat. Indeed T. at I. 10. 1, II. 6. 15 had included it among the legions of Syria. It had been moved to Moesia just before Nero's death, Suet. *Vesp.* 6, when the Jewish War was well advanced and the need for troops in the East less pressing.

7. ceterae ... sperabantur. That the Flavians at this stage had hopes of Danubian support is the most that T. will allow: there was no certainty, and consequently, II. 83. 7, Mucianus was doubtful whether he should march through the frontier provinces or go straight to Dyrrachium. But Suet. *Vit.* 8. 1, *Vesp.* 6. 2, supports the view that the Danubian army was essential to Flavian success and was a determining factor in Vespasian's calculations.

8. omnis exercitus flammaverat. At IV. 23. 15, its only other use in T. (*A.* XV. 44. 6 must surely be emended) *flammare* is transitive, as it commonly is in Silver Latin. So *adrogantia* is the subject.

9. truces corpore, horridi sermone, characteristic exaggeration about the outlandish nature of the Rhine legionaries. *Horridi* implies rudeness and foul-mouthed talk, Cic. *Brut.* 28, *qui horride inculteque dicat*, rather than inability to speak Latin.

12. quis ille dies . . ., 'what a day that would be when . . .'. It is hard to see why Vespasian should reckon his own age (fifty-nine) or that of his elder son (twenty-nine) among the *adversa*. What better ages would one choose (see indeed Jos. *BI.* IV. 597)?

13. sexaginta . . . iuvenes. Vespasian was born on 17 Nov. A.D. 9, Titus 30 Dec. 39, Domitian 24 Oct. 51.

14. esse . . . progressum, 'in private problems one could make one's own running'. Although the possibility of retreat, as well as of slow advance, is present, the addition of *esse regressum* (see app. crit.) does not seem necessary.

75. 2. viro militari, a phrase especially characteristic of T.'s thinking about the senators of his day (see GG), e.g. in relation to the career of his father-in-law, *Agr.* 9. 2, 40. 4 (*militare nomen*). In several parts of his writing (e.g. *JRS* 1957, 133 ff.) Syme has shown how men who merited this epithet enjoyed favoured careers. Some reservations have been entered by B. Campbell, *JRS* 1975, 11 ff., but I do not understand him when he says of our present passage (my italics) 'Tacitus means only that Vespasian had the *limited* experience and knowledge available to one who had commanded armies.'

6. praesenti facinore, 'the act of a moment'.
   ex diverso, 'from the other side': cf. III. 5. 7, 13. 14.

7. Scribonianum, I. 89. 2 n. The mention of an individual murderer is confined to T., though it is supported by the word *occiso* in Plin. *Epp. III. 16. 7*.

8. summa militiae, perhaps to the rank of *primus pilus*.

76. 3. coram, an actual meeting, as distinct from negotiations, *secretos sermones*, through intermediaries of the kind recorded at II. 5. 12, 79. 6. But it was also an open meeting. T. was not averse from composing a speech made at a private talk, I. 15–16, but here he claims that Mucianus spoke before many witnesses, and was deliberate in so doing. Yet not only the words, but the arguments are surely his own, *qui deliberant desciverunt* (II. 77. 18) comes from the 'common source', used by it in a different context, and *ultionis cupiditas* (77. 13) is wisdom after the event. Nor would Mucianus have counted nine legions (76. 31).

   But the rhetoric is carefully and appropriately conceived, each later section picking up not only Mucianus' initial questions (*quod incohatur rei publicae . . . simul ipse qui suadet . . .*) but also Vespasian's doubts in II. 74–5. See Heubner, 249 ff., especially for his emphasis on the escape Mucianus is allowed to make from such impressive phrases as *iuxta deos in tua manu positum est*.

The speech should also be read as an antistrophe to Galba's adoption speech, I. 15–16, but Paratore's view, 463, that 'adoption' is a prime theme here has little force. ·

omnes, qui ... suscipiunt. This opening is closely modelled on Sall. *H. IV. 69.* For the Sallustian rhythm and rhetoric of the whole speech see A. Salvatore, *Stile e ritmo in Tacito* (1950), 152–4.

14. aut Claudii vel Neronis, I. 50. 11 n. (GG 1744, s.v. *vel*, I. 3) b)). 'or even Nero' is a reasonable translation here, for against him rebellion was not inconceivable, though still rash for an upstart such as Vespasian.

19. non cupisse. M. *concupisse.* Those who emend (e.g. H.) suppose that *con-* has appeared by dittography from *concupiendum.* But the decision is a close one. If *non cupisse* stood in the MS., no one could object to the sense: Mucianus says first, that the success of Vitellius makes any man of Vespasian's distinction an obvious claimant; secondly, and more important, Vespasian's behaviour in recent months has been too blatant for people not to suspect him (*qui deliberant, desciverunt*, II. 77. 18). But with *concupisse* (retained by K.) there is also good sense. *videri* should then be taken as the emphatic word: 'under Nero or Galba you might safely have *seemed* to want the Empire, because they would never have thought a man of your standing had a chance; and during the Othonian-Vitellian war neither contestant was in a position to deal with you; but unless you now take action, Vitellius can make you suffer the fate of Corbulo'. V., followed by Heubner, has a valuable n. on the passage in the latter sense.

20. an excidit trucidatus Corbulo? It seems inescapable that this is an echo of Plin., *Pan.* 53. 4, *an excidit dolori nostro modo vindicatus Nero?* unless both authors had a common model. See Durry's edn. of the *Panegyric*, and discussion by K. Büchner, *RhM* 1955, 309. For Corbulo's enforced suicide in late 66 see Dio 63. 17.

21. quam nos. Corbulo was more noble than us, but Nero more noble than Vitellius; so (possibly) we are men whom Vitellius might execute. *Nos* avoids the offensiveness of attributing lowly origins to Vespasian alone, and also underlines the unity of the Flavian party.

nobilitate. H. Hill *Historia*, 1969, 235, rightly takes this as an ablative of respect (as is more common after *anteire* in T.), rather than as causal. Hence the sentence does not deny *nobilitas* to Vitellius, whose father actually held a third consulate (A.D. 47) but was the first consul of his *gens*. See II. 48. 16 n.

23. posse ab exercitu principem fieri. I. 4. 9 n.

24. nullis stipendiis ... This seems to have been essentially true. Suet. does not record even a military tribunate, and Vitellius, through his father's reputation, became consul in 48 at the age of thirty-three. His only known provincial appointment is the proconsulate of Africa, in 59–60, before he went to Lower Germany in November 68.

25. ne Othonem ... vi. See Appendix, p. 270.

28. spargit ... cohortis 66–7; the cohorts are praetorians. 'Scattering the legions' apparently means sending I Adiutrix to Spain and XIV back to Britain, neither of them irresponsible moves: one could more reasonably criticise Vitellius' rashness in relation to his own cause, when he allowed the Moesian legions to go unpunished and three of the defeated Othonian legions to return to Illyricum. But it is unlikely that Mucianus had in fact received news about any of Vitellius' military measures: even T. does not credit him with knowledge of the revision in the size of units, II. 69.

31. novem legiones, again forgetting the transfer of III Gallica to Moesia, II. 74. 6 n.

33. classium. II. 4. 20 n.

77. 1. nobis. Here we reach Mucianus' second point, 76. 5, *simul ipse qui suadet considerandus est.*

4. triumphale nomen. Vespasian lacked *nobilitas* (the point has not been explicitly made, yet Mucianus counters it). What he had were *triumphalia ornamenta* for the British expedition, Suet. *Vesp.* 4, an honour shared by several senators (he himself when emperor was sparing with this honour, and seems to have given it only to consulars).

capax iam imperii alter ... For Titus' career, II. 1. 5 n. His German tribunate, probably that on which the Elder Pliny served with him, *NH praef.* 3, may have been as early as 58, Syme, 61, and he was probably military tribune for longer than most *laticlavii.* But we are not told what exploit brought him this renown at a time when the Rhine frontier was abnormally peaceful.

9. vincimus. The present tense implies that Mucianus regards the issue between peace and war as already effectively decided, cf. Sall. *BC* 58. 9, *si vincimus, omnia nobis tuta erunt.*

11. tu tuos exercitus rege. *Tu* is needed (see app. crit.) to balance *mihi.* V., who is almost alone in refusing to insert it, seems wrong in his n. by assuming that *tuos exercitus rege* means 'you be emperor', for (on that interpretation) what mattered to a *princeps* would simply have been his control of the armies. Mucianus is speaking only of the immediate military situation: the main armies in question are those of the East, and he means 'you hold our position here, and I (with only a portion of the troops, II. 82. 17) will fight Vitellius'.

14. aperiet et recludet. But the two verbs are synonyms, as had been *discrimen ac pericula* in line 10. There is no redress.

16. parsimonia. *Vigilantia* has its converse in *torpor*, and *sapientia* in *inscitia*. Vespasian's best-known quality, II. 5. 4, with n., is a virtue in Mucianus' eyes (so also *A*. III. 55. 4), and it balances *saevitia*. The last was to Suet. 13–14 one of Vitellius' two worst vices, but less so in T., and there is little concrete evidence.

18. qui deliberant, desciverunt, IV. 49. 9, *in pace suspecto tutius bellum*, *Agr*. 15. 5, and (not dissimilar) *Hist*. I. 81. 3. As often with T.'s more famous sentiments it has an earlier origin, presumably in the speech Plut. gives to Vinius addressing Galba (*G*. 4), from the 'common source'.

78. 2. responsa ... motus. T.'s contemptuous attitude to these has already been made plain at I. 10. 15, and it is sustained in this chapter. Here he presumably refers to fresh reports, as distinct from the *vetera omina* of line 5. No doubt all of them were given publicity for the first time at this moment (*aperiebat*, line 20), for it would have been dangerous for them to be advertised about a mere subject.

3. nec erat intactus. That Vespasian himself believed the prophecies is accepted also by Suet. *Vesp*. 5. 1. How did anyone know?

4. Seleucum. Suet., almost certainly wrongly, gives this as the name of Otho's astrologer, *O*. 4 and 6. See I. 22. 6 n.

5. vetera omina. Of these Suet. *Vesp*. 5 enumerates no less than ten (or eleven, if the prophecy of Jos. *BI* III. 400 ff. be counted—a surprising omission by T.), and other authors (esp. Dio, 66. 1) confirm all but two of them. T. confines himself to one (though perhaps the story in V. 13. 8 should be added), and the story of the cypress is a curiously insignificant one to choose. Yet that story has interest in that it casts doubt on the view, Fabia, 158, that Pliny was the common source for all these omens; for at *NH* XVI. 131 he tells several anecdotes about revivified trees and is silent about Vespasian's case.

6. in agris eius. Suet. *Vesp*. 5. 4 has *in agro avito*, i.e. on the estate of Vespasian's grandmother Tertulla at Cosa.

7. latior. Height rather than breadth is what one would expect from a growing cypress, so H. accepted the emendation *laetior*; cf. Curtius VI 5. 14, *ex alia radice laetiores virent*, Plin. *NH* XV. 121, *mystus exuberans ac* *laeta.* Irvine, keeping *latior*, translates 'thicker', but is this a possible meaning of the word? If the MS. reading be kept, the most attractive defence is Heubner's, that T. is thinking of what Plin. *NH* XVI. 141 oddly calls the 'male cypress', *mas spargi extra se ramos.* Suet. *Vesp.* 5. 4, *viridior ac firmior resurrexit,* gives no help.

9. iuveni admodum. In T. the critical instance of this phrase is the reference to himself at *Dial.* 1. 2. Syme, 671, shows that there and elsewhere T. means a man of 'young pre-quaestorian' age. Hence the incident here occurred about A.D. 27, and it is not surprising that it was thought to portend a successful senatorial career for the young *novus homo.* Less credible is the story in Suet. *Vesp.* 5. 2, that the behaviour of an oak at the time of Vespasian's birth was believed by his father to indicate that he had begotten a 'Caesar'.

10. triumphalia, 77. 4 n.

12. Iudaeam inter Syriamque, or more precisely between Phoenicia and Galilee. Carmel is a spur of the Anti-Libanus, projecting north-westwards, with the mountain standing up sheer from the sea.

13. Carmelus. Suet. *Vesp.* 5. 6 agrees that this was the god's name: there is no evidence from any other source.

nec simulacrum . . . In the ninth century B.C. the worshippers of Jehovah seem to have regarded Mount Carmel as a home of 'Baal', I Kings 18. 18 ff. The development of the cult over the ensuing centuries has been much discussed among Semitic scholars, see bibliography in Heubner's n. Neither T. nor Suet. throws any serious light on the problem.

16. Basilides sacerdos. The same name is given at IV. 82. 4 to the Egyptian nobleman (Suet. *Vesp.* 7 calls him a freedman) who appeared in the temple of Serapis at Alexandria though Vespasian knew he had left him sick several days' journey away, IV. 82. 4. K. Scott, *JRS* 1934, 138, argued that the two were identical, and that Basilides was an emissary sent by Tib. Alexander from Egypt to take part in the planning which led to Vespasian's proclamation. This is just possible, for in Suet.'s account of the later incident Basilides seems to be a priest: yet here T. surely took him to be a resident priest on Carmel. For the almost certain identification of the Basilides at Alexandria with a man who was procurator in Egypt in A.D. 49 see *PIR*² s.v.

20 aperiebat, 'proceeded to unravel'.

22. sperantibus plura dicuntur, 'for hope is eloquent' (Wellesley).

24. caput, i.e. the seat of the Roman governor. The residence of the Judaean procurator at Caesarea (formerly Turris Stratonis) is well known from the Acts of the Apostles.

79. 1. initium. About 1 July Suet. *Vesp.* 6. 3 agrees, but is careless at *Vit.* 15. 1 in saying that the first move came from the Danube legions in August. Jos., *BI* IV. 601, says it came from the army in Judaea, Vespasian then writing to Tib. Alexander that he needed his help because he had had to bow to the wishes of his army. That (see Briessmann, 12 ff.) was a later Flavian version, some of which T. (79.7 and 81) has allowed to stand, but the essential parts of which he discards in favour of the view that the Flavian leaders had a carefully laid plan. Alexander's letter preceded, rather than followed, the proclamation, and the first committal action was taken, as with Vitellius, I. 55 ff., outside of the province of the destined emperor.

3. isque ... dies. That Vespasian's *trib. pot.* dated from 1 July 69 is consistently shown by coins and inscriptions, Hammond, *AM* 72–3. Suet. *Vesp.* 6. 3 confirms that he opted for that day.

This looks like a departure from the policy of his immediate predecessors. See I. 47. 3 n. on Otho and Vitellius: both proceeded by stages, and neither formally related his powers to action by the troops. Admittedly the nature of our evidence about Vespasian is different: for him we possess no *AFA* of the relevant dates, and it is just possible that they might have revealed some ingenious constitutional tricks. But this is unlikely. Nor does Hammond's suggestion, cit., that Vespasian chose 1 July because it had been Augustus' 'day' take one far, since 1 July 70 (not 69) would have the right answer had Vespasian been feeling extreme respect for proprieties. Perhaps he remembered that 1 July had Augustan precedent and therefore told Alexander to acclaim him on that day. But that is not what Hammond meant.

Retrospective sanction for all action taken by him between 1 July and the Senate's approval of him on 21 Dec., IV. 2, was achieved by the last clause of the *Lex de imperio Vespasiani*, MW 364, Brunt, *JRS* 1977, 106. That 'law', as Brunt shows beyond reasonable doubt, was passed simultaneously with, or very soon after, the Senate's action (though whether it was drafted on explicit instructions from the East or by prudent men in Rome, we do not know). Vespasian's biographer, Suet. *Vesp.* 12, was thus able to claim that it was only 'late' that he accepted *trib. pot.* (though actions in virtue of that particular power were not needed before he got back to Rome). It is clear that in taking the day of his acclamation, rather than that of his confirmation as his *dies imperii*, he initially behaved differently from Vitellius. I think both T. and Suet. mean to emphasize that point, for it set a clear precedent for the doctrine that acclamation by the troops had constitutional force. Yet even Hadrian in 118 apologized for not awaiting action by the Senate, *SHA Hadr.* 6. 2, *salutatus scilicet praepropere a militibus imperator.*

5. nonas Iulias. Suet. *Vesp.* 6. 3 says *Idus*, and some commentators have thought him right on the ground that the news from Alexandria could not have reached Caesarea in two days. But if the whole operation was, as I think, planned in advance of the dramatic day 1 July, there is no difficulty in accepting T. Nor is there any evidence that Titus had been intended to come back before the acclamation by his father's army.

7. cuncta impetu militum. T. returns to the official Flavian version, Jos. *BI* IV. 603. No doubt the Flavian leaders in fact performed the pretence of a *recusatio* before Vespasian accepted.

80. 1. dum quaeritur ... Although the decisive step has already been taken at Alexandria, T. returns to the Flavian source which pretended that subsequent moves in Judaea were forced on Vespasian by the soldiers.

4. solito ... salutaturi. There is no other evidence for regular salutation of a provincial governor.

5. Caesarem et Augustum. Unlike Vitellius, I. 62. 12 n., Vespasian had no hesitation about taking the familiar titles from the start: see the coins attributed to the period before the Senate confirmed him, 82. 3 n. below, and early documents carrying Σέβαστος. *RE* VI, col. 2635.

6. mens ... transierat. Many translators (including Wellesley) take this to refer to Vespasian's adherents, in contrast to *in ipso.* ... But *metus* previously has been ascribed only to Vespasian himself, and *fortuna* is the regular term for 'acquisition of the Principate', I. 10. 17 n. He now has the supreme position, but there is no arrogance, etc. For Vespasian's *civilitas* as *princeps* cf. IV. 3. 18, Suet. *Vesp.* 12, Dio 66. 10.

8. altitudinis. Triller's correction of *multitudinis* is irresistible in view of Livy XXVI. 45. 3, *cum altitudo caliginem oculis offudisset.* T. has characteristically adapted Livy's words to a psychological situation.

9. laeta omnia, 'congratulations', for which *laeta omnia precari* is the standard phrase.

12. ubi ... mos est, a fact about Greek cities which impressed itself on Roman writers, Cic. *Flacc.* 16, Livy XXIV. 39. 1, Frontin. *Strat.* III. 2. 6. But for the governor to make his speech in eloquent Greek was surely unusual.

14. omniumque ... ostentator. Once more T. is at his best on Mucianus, cf I. 10. 2, II. 5. 5 with nn. Here he perfects Livy XXVI. 19. 3, *arte ... quadam ab iuventa in ostentationem* [sc. *virtutum*] *compositus.*

16. adseverabat Mucianus. The imperfect tense (and, see Heubner, 258, repetition of the subject *Mucianus*) imply that Mucianus was constantly saying this, in the theatre and previously. So Suet. *Vesp.* 6. 4, *dissipatus rumor.*

20. sueto ... contubernio. Of the six legions now in Syria and Judaea three, VI Ferrata, X Fretensis, and XII Fulminata, had been in the East since Augustus' day. The remaining three, IV Scythica, V Macedonica, and XV Apollinaris, had arrived during Nero's reign (IV Scythica as early as 58). Vespasian, as emperor, retained the first three and IV Scythica in the eastern provinces (which now included Cappadocia) and also recalled the former Syrian legion III Gallica, which in 68–70 was temporarily in Moesia, II. 74. 6.

21. necessitudinibus ... mixti. Forni, 84, concludes from evidence which is mainly epigraphical (and also A. XIII. 35) that T.'s picture here is right, i.e. that the eastern provinces were by now the recruiting ground for all Rome's eastern units. From III. 24. 15 it seems that some legionaries had Eastern habits; more important is the fact that their *contubernium* in Syria involved urban life which made them notoriously indisciplined and effete, *A.* XIII. 12. 2, XII. 35 (and a century later Fronto, *ad Verum* II. 1. 19. *Princ. Hist.* 12).

On the relations between legionaries and provincials elsewhere see I. 53. 11 ff., though with the Rhine troops we are not told explicitly that the neighbouring civilians had blood relationships: the ties between soldiers and civilians (descendants of veterans) at Colonia Agrippinensis, IV 65. 10, are a special case. Yet many Rhine legionaries, IV. 17. 14, and even their officers, IV. 61. 14, were born in Gaul.

81. 2. Sohaemus, son of Sampsigeramus, had succeeded his brother as king of Emesa on the upper Orontes in 54. Described as 'rex magnus, Philocaesar, Philoromaeus', *ILS* 8958, he helped Rome during the Jewish war, Jos. *BI* II. 501, III. 68, participated in the Commagene campaign of 72, *ibid.* VII. 226, and received consular ornaments. His dynasty came to an end in Domitian's reign, but one of its descendants was Septimius Severus' wife Iulia Domna.

It was probably a different Sohaemus to whom Nero, also in 54, gave the kingdom of Sophene, *A.* XIII. 7. Stein, *RE* III A, col. 797 points out that Sophene, east of the extreme upper Euphrates, is far away from Emesa.

haud spernendis viribus. In 66–7, Jos. llc., he had supplied up to 4,000 men, of whom 1,000 were cavalry, the rest archers.

3. Antiochus. Epiphanes IV (for his son see 24. 15 n.) was a Seleucid, restored to his father's kingdom of Commagene first by Gaius, and then again by Claudius in 41, Dio 59. 8, 60. 8: his wealth was increased by the assignment to him of certain Cilician districts. His contribution of troops for the Jewish War had been even greater than that of Sohaemus, Jos., llc. But in 72 he was accused by Caesennius Paetus, governor of Syria, of planning an alliance with Parthia, and was deposed after a short campaign, Jos. *BI* VII. 226, *ILS* 9198 (=MW 49), 9200 (=MW 372).

5. Agrippa. For the career of Herod Agrippa II see *PIR*² VI. 132, and for his policies A. H. M. Jones, *The Herods of Judaea* (1938), 217 ff. At this time he was ruling a large but scattered kingdom, principally the non-Jewish districts beyond Jordan, but also four Jewish toparchies in Galilee and Peraea; and he was recognized as controller of the temple at Jerusalem, with the right to nominate the high priests. He was the first of his house to use the Roman names to which they were entitled, *ILS* 8957, and had given vital service to Vespasian in the war against his countrymen. In early 69 he had accompanied Titus on his voyage to congratulate Galba, Jos. *BI* IV. 498, and continued on to Rome when Titus turned back.

Heubner, like other recent editors, follows Andresen, *Wochenschr. cl. phil.* 1915, 957, in punctuating with a comma after *ditissimus* and a colon after *Agrippa*, thus making Agrippa a further subject of *accessere*. This seems a probable reconstruction of the various sentences, and it would mean that Agrippa's recall (*excitus*) took place before the proclamation, another example of careful Flavian planning. *Celeri navigatione* might mean not much more than a fortnight: Pliny, *NH* XIX. 3. gives an example of a voyage from Puteoli to Alexandria of nine days and this was the season when the winds were favourable.

6. Berenice. 2. 2 n.

10. inermes. At I. 1. 11 the *inermes provinciae* are those which contained no troops. Here they include such areas as Cappadocia, where there were significant numbers of auxiliaries and local levies.

11. nondum ... legionibus. II. 9. 1 n. Until he wrote the *Annals* T. was perhaps unaware that there had been a consular commander on the upper Euphrates during several years of Nero's reign. Admittedly there were no legions there in 66–70, but this may have been a temporary expedient caused by the needs of the Jewish War. On the plural *legionibus* (one legion was at Melitene, but the camp of the second is still not known) see Syme, *CAH* XI. 141.

12. Beryti, a natural meeting place, about half-way between Antioch and Caesarea. The council or war, preceded by magnificent gifts and crowns from the client states, is given more prominence by Jos. *BI* IV. 620.

13. splendidissimo ... militum. For attendance of men below centurion rank at councils of war cf. III. 3. 2, 13. 2. In the main they may have been those who had received military decorations.

82. 1. revocare veteranos. For a period, nominally five years, discharged soldiers were retained *sub vexillo*: they lived away from the camps, often under a *curator veteranorum. Revocare* (surprisingly for T.) happens to be the technical term for recalling them to camp when needed, *ILS* 2034, 2312.

2. exercendis armorum officinis. Only here and at II. 84. 1 is there any mention in the *Histories* of the manufacture of arms.

3. aurum argentumque, again a vital preparation for war about which T. is silent elsewhere; and even here he says nothing about the coin legends which in modern times are regarded as so vital a part of civil-war propaganda. For the earliest Vespasianic issues at Antioch see *RIC* II. 4 and 56.

6. vitia ... dissimulans. What is held to be virtue in Vespasian comes close to what was vice in Galba, I. 49. 11 etc.

7. praefecturis et procurationibus. No one of these equestrian appointments can be confidently identified, but a probable example is C. Velius Rufus, *ILS* 9200 = MW 372, whose brilliant military career under the Flavians began with the primipilate of XII Fulminata.

8. plerosque ... percoluit. Here too Vespasian's action was remarkably high-handed. He was not in Rome, and no parallel action is recorded of Vitellius when he was on the Rhine. Secondly, although the *princeps* could qualify men for the Senate by granting the *latus clavus* and could apply unofficial pressure to secure that a man did, or did not, become a senator, yet it had hitherto been usual to acquire censorial powers to give men a formal introduction to the body. This was especially the case if they were to be brought in at a rank above the lowest, e.g. *inter praetorios* (Claudius in 42 had made some knights tribunes, but they may not thereby have become senators, Dio 60. 11. 8).

For men adlected to the Senate by Vespasian, either now or in his censorship of 73–4 see W. Eck, *Kölner Jhrb. für Frühgeschichte*, 1972/73, 102. Among those adlected in 69 were Ti. Iulius Celsus Polemaeanus of Ephesus (*cos.* 92), who started his career as (equestrian) tribune of III Cyrenaica in Egypt, surely at the time of the proclamation (*ILS* 8971 = MW 316); and L. Plotius Grypus, who was made legate of one of the legions which invaded Italy, III. 52. 11, with Wellesley's n.

12. quam alii in pace. Claudius and Nero had each given 15,000 HS to each praetorian, but of accession donatives to the legionaries in the Julio-Claudian period we are not told. Mucianus paid 100 HS a head after he entered Rome, Dio 65. 22, surely perhaps a payment on account. Vespasian gave some reward to the troops who remained in the East. The contrast may be with the enormities of Nymphidius Sabinus, I. 5. 3 n.

13. missi ad Parthum ... Suet. *Vesp.* 6. 4.

14. provisumque ... nudarentur. Similar measures were taken by the Flavian leaders in Illyricum, III. 5.

16. claustra Aegypti. For his action, III. 48. 13. The same phrase is used by Suet. *Vesp.* 7. 1 and by T. at *A.* II. 59. It is defined at *Bell. Alex.* 26. 2, *tota Aegyptus maritimo accessu Pharo, pedestri Pelusio, velut claustris munita existimatur.*

18. ac nihil arduum fatis, 'destiny, to whom all things are possible' (Irvine).

omnis exercitus legatosque, above all to the Danubian legates, to whom the credit went for re-enlisting some of the praetorians, III. 21. 13. etc.

20. militiae praemio, not a donative, but the prospect of more rewarding service.

83. 1. expedita manu, i.e. without a baggage train, II. 40. 1 n. Mucianus went ahead with an advanced guard, followed gradually (*sequebantur*) by the *ingens agmen*, which could not have crossed Asia Minor and the Danube lands without supplies. By October VI Ferrata was with him, III. 46, but even then there may have been more troops to come up.

5. tredecim vexillariorum milia. There must surely have been *auxilia* in the force. Either T., contrary to his normal practice (I. 61. 6, II. 11. 9), has failed to take account of them; or, more probably, they are included in the 13,000 (for *auxilia* described as *vexilla* or *vexillarii*, I. 31, 17, 70. 5, III. 6. 1). If the latter, H. and other editors had no good

ground for estimating the number of men drawn from the other five
eastern legions; cf. II. 57. 6 n.

6. classem e Ponto. Starr, 125 ff. King Agrippa is reported by
Josephus, *BI* II. 367, to have assessed it at forty ships, but whether his
source was contemporary is doubtful.

7. ambiguus consilii. Once he was assured of Danubian support he
can hardly have remained in serious doubt. Indeed the arguments
given for the alternative policy of proceeding to Dyrrachium seem to
be part of the later Flavian myth, e.g. III. 8. 10 ff., that Vespasian's
victory could have been *incruenta* had Antonius Primus not invaded
Italy. For as long as Vitellius could count on the Ravenna fleet (and its
possible defection is not mentioned before 100 below), the idea that
Mucianus' small naval forces could close the Adriatic and make
Vitellius uncertain which part of Italy to protect is not even wishful
thinking.

12. sibi, Vitellio, a dative of '(dis)advantage', see Heubner's n.

84. 2. pecuniarum conquisitio. Although Vespasian's reputation
for *avaritia* may have been consolidated at this time, II. 5. 4 n., it is
interesting that T. makes Mucianus the main author of policy.

7. etiam in pace. For a summary of Vespasian's later tight hold over
finance see Suet. *Vesp.* 16. He may have been the *princeps* whom Pliny
had chiefly in mind when he composed *Pan.* 41.

8. ad obtinendas iniquitates, 'to maintain unjust decisions': cf.
Livy XXIX. 1. 17, *pertinax ad obtinendam iniuriam*; *ius suum obtinere* is to
'hold on to one's legal rights'.

9. haud perinde obstinante. Not so much as Mucianus? Or not so
much as later: cf. I. 89. 4, *quae motu Vindicis haud perinde plebem attriverat*
(though there too the meaning is not certain)? Or 'not so very . . .' (IV.
62. 10, *deformitas haud perinde notabilis*, cf. *Agr.* 10. 6, *Germ.* 5. 3, 34. 1)? It
seems to me impossible to decide.

For Flavian exactions in the provinces see also Dio 66. 2. 5, 8. 2–4,
Jos. *BI* VII. 446. They clearly continued for some years, cf. Dio Chrys.
XLVI. 8.

pravis magistris. Mucianus and Marcellus, II. 97. 17?

didicit aususque est. Yet for T. Vespasian, in other respects, *in
melius mutatus est*, I. 50. 21.

11. quod avidius . . . sumeret. See app. crit. But *quod* is relative,
with antecedent *eo*, and the subjunctive is natural, see V.'s n.

Like so much that is alleged about the leaders of this period, the accusation against Mucianus receives no detailed justification.

85. 1. Illyrici. I. 2. 5 n. Here Moesia is expressly included.

2. tertia legio. I. 74. 6 n.

5. Aquileiam progressae ... T. here differs from Suet. *Vesp.* 6. 2–3 on two points, one minor, the other of some importance. The first is whether the Moesian troops which rioted were whole legions, as T. appears to say, or only detachments: this, with the related question whether they had entered Aquileia or were still a few days away when they heard of Otho's death, is discussed in n. to II. 46. 16. The other question is whether they then and there proclaimed Vespasian emperor. Suet. (though at *Vit.* 15. 1. he dates the Danubian revolt to Vitellius' eighth month, i.e. August), thought they did, in which case the Flavian leaders by 1 July could have planned their campaign with fair confidence that they would be able to use the Danubian armies. T. however is no doubt deliberate in placing the legions' declaration for Vespasian after the proclamations in the East: the Moesian troops rioted, see also II. 60. 4, but had no candidate of their own as yet. Fabia, 155, claimed that this account was illogical, since their attempt to find justification for their misbehaviour in April must have been made well before 1 July. But that argument is unconvincing, given the confused conditions of 69: Vitellius may have felt able to consider the misconduct of these men only after his arrival in Rome. None the less the Danubian armies, or at least their legionary legates, may have been Vespasian's accomplices before his proclamation, *JRS* 1957, 34.

6. vexillis, the flags, which carried the name of the accepted emperor, Rostovtzeff, *JRS* 1942, 92 ff. In the previous year the name of Verginius had been erased when he made his refusal, Dio 63. 25. 1.

8. posse imputari Vespasiano, 'that they could get credit from Vespasian', I. 38. 11 n.

10. adliciebant Pannonicum exercitum. As at II. 96. 1, T. is clear that the first open defection of Danubian troops occurred in Moesia, with III Gallica taking the lead. There is no inconsistency, see Fabia, 346, with III. 53. 6, where Antonius Primus (legate of VII Galbiana in Pannonia) claims *suis stimulis excitos Moesiae duces*, for there Antonius refers not to the rebellion but to the decision to invade Italy, for which he was certainly responsible. That Jos. *BI* IV. 633 should make Antonius a commander in Moesia, and Dio 65. 9. 3, should say that he was chosen as supreme commander, are blunders.

11. Aponius Saturninus ... Tettium Iulianum. I. 79. 24–5 nn.
Of their quarrel we have no other knowledge, but it is characteristic of
Flavian diplomacy that Tettius retained his praetorship, but that no
vindictiveness was shown to Aponius. Yet the last words of the chapter
show how uncertain initially were the relations between the Danube
officers and those in the East.

16. montem Haemum, the Balkan range.

86. 1. septima Galbiana. Again it is strange (see Appendix) that
historians should maintain that neither the bulk of this legion, nor its
legate, had been present at the battle.

3. Primi Antonii. For the career of M. Antonius Primus, 'the hero of
Book III', see Wellesley's edn. of that Book, pp. 3–5, 15 ff. In *c.* 95 he
was still living at his birth-place Tolosa, having retired there after his
cold reception by Vespasian at the end of the war. For the present
chapter T. uses a violently hostile source, probably Pliny, whereas in
III he is usually ready to supply a more favourable version of Antonius'
actions than that suggested by his enemies (above all Mucianus),
especially in the early chapters when he used the memoirs of the young
Vipstanus Messalla, temporarily legate of the legion VII Claudia.

7. in nullo ... usu, a passage commonly taken to show that his legion
(apart from a *vexillum*) did not fight for the Othonians, but by Passerini,
209, to support the opposite conclusion, that a legate of a legion which
had arrived too late for the campaign could not reasonably have argued
that no use of him was made in the councils of war.

9. strenuus manu ... T. shows reminiscences of three authors: Verg.
Aen. XI. 340, *seditione potens*; Livy VI. 31. 10, *tractandi animos artifex*; Vell.
II. 11. 1, C. Marius ... *quantum bello optimus, tantum pace pessimus*; and
both *raptor* and *largitor*, though not found in extant prose before the
Silver Age, are surely Sallustian (for the thought, *BC* 5. 4). Yet
(Courbaud, 183) T. has chosen his borrowings with faithful attention
to the character he now supposes Antonius to be.

14. divites senes. Despite their apparent uselessness during the war,
these two consulars were highly honoured in the early years of
Vespasian's principate. Silvanus was made loan commisioner in 70, IV.
47. 3, and became *curator aquarum*. Flavianus succeeded him in the latter
post in 73, Frontinus, *Aq.* 102, and the two held second consulates
together, possibly in 75 (Syme, *RÉA* 1956 239), possibly in the very last
months of 74.

M. Pompeius Silvanus Staberius Flavinus had been consul in 45, and
proconsul of Africa in 53 (*IRT* 338 = Sm. 1, 320). L. Tampius Flavianus

was perhaps slightly younger, but his proconsulate of Africa, in which he had an encounter with a dolphin (Plin. *Epp.* IX. 26, *intra hos annos*) was almost certainly held before Nero's death, for there is no room for him in the years after 69, A. B. Bosworth, *Athenaeum*, 1974, 78 f. The operations beyond the frontier of Pannonia, for which he received triumphal ornaments (*ILS* 985 = MW 274) cannot be confidently dated. Townend, *JRS* 1961, 60, suggested a victory 'over a body of men crossing the Danube on the news of the incipient civil war'. If so, the civil war would be the Flavio-Vitellian war, for there was not time before 1st Bedriacum: for measures taken by the Flavians to secure their rear in Pannonia see III. 5. But it remains possible, and perhaps even likely, that Flavianus was rewarded, like Plautius Silvanus Aelianus (*ILS* 986 = MW 261), for operations conducted under Nero.

Who appointed the two elderly legates? Not Vitellius surely (though Flavianus was related to him, III. 4. 5, 10. 9) for T. would then have told us this, e.g. at II. 66. Possibly Galba in 68. But most probably Nero in his last years, when he wanted safe commanders, *JRS* 1957, 32.

16. Cornelius Fuscus, Domitian's prefect of the guard, killed in fighting the Dacians in 86 or 87, Syme, App. 33. Since Syme's article in *AJP* 1937, 7 ff., editors have been rightly satisfied that M.'s *quietis cupidine* should be retained, for *quies* is 'a technical term of political life ... and denotes a reluctance to bear the dignity, the burdens, and the dangers of the senatorial life', cf Plin. *Epp.* I. 14. 5, though Fuscus, when he came out in Galba's support, evidently changed his mind: under a new *princeps* life might be different. As to his birth-place, the colony which he brought over to Galba, there has been less unanimity with Syme. Since Cichorius in 1904 published his studies of the altar to fallen soldiers at Adam-klissi in Bulgaria, it has always been tempting to believe that the prae [fectus] at the head of the inscription, *ILS* 9107, *col. Pomp. domicil. Neapol. Ital.*, i.e. a man from Pompeii who was accepted by Neapolis after the destruction of his birth-place in 79, was the supreme commander of Domitian's force, the prefect of the guard. Domaszewski dissented vigorously, on the ground that Pompeii was too insignificant to play a part in the politics of A.D. 68, and Syme agreed with him; 'Vienna, Corduba, or Aquileia, anywhere but Pompeii'. Cornelius Fuscus (as in his opinion Cornelius Tacitus also) could have been one of the Cornelii from Forum Iulii in Narbonensis.

Yet Aquileia is not very likely, given the absence of Cornelii on inscriptions found there, A. Degrassi, *Scritti vari dell' antichita* (1962), 89 ff. And does *claris natalibus* adequately befit the son of a senator from Narbonensis or Spain? Moreover J. Colin, *Latomus*, 1956, 52, in identifying the name Cornelius Fuscus on Pompeian inscriptions, again called attention to the possible significance of Pompeii in these years, for its proximity to the Misenum fleet (in 69 a senator who happened to be at the nearby Minturnae played a role, III. 57), as the birth-place of the Poppaei, and as a colony rebuilt by Nero after the eruption of 63, *ILS* 6444, *Puteolos, Antium, Tegeano, Pompeios, hae sunt verae coloniae.* There is no confirmation of support for Galba in Italy but we know too little of the events in mid-68.

20. non tam praemiis ... Again Sallustian, *BC* 5. 5, 17. 6. Syme, App. 33, may be too sanguine in thinking that T. was giving Fuscus a 'favourable' presentation, if what he most recalled was Catiline.

24. quartadecimanos ... primanos. For their dispatch to these provinces, II. 66–7 with nn. That happened in late May at earliest, so the events here described can hardly be earlier than July: if Suet. *Vit.* 15. 1 be right about the 'eighth month', the messages must come later, for otherwise they would have been intercepted.

26. per Gallias. i.e. to the Gallic states, for all Roman armies in Gaul and the Rhineland were now Vitellian. Presumably Hordeonius also received an appeal, IV. 13. 13 etc.

87–101. *Vitellius' attempted plans*

87. 1. dum haec ... geruntur. The last temporal indication about Italian affairs took us to the later days of May, 70. 4 n. Vitellius now continues his southward march with the harvest not yet in (line 15), but the first dated event after his entry to Rome is on 18 July, 91. 4. Yet Josephus, *BI* IV. 585 ff. (see nn. to II. 1–9 above) implies that the events of the following chapters, and a report on them to the East, had happened before Vespasian was proclaimed.

  ducibusque partium, a phrase used frequently of the Flavian command in Book III.

2. contemptior ... segniorque. T. returns to generalities about Vitellius' luxury and his disreputable followers, and again succeeds in drawing a convincing picture without providing evidence for its authenticity. Even *segnior* of the march has little justification, since from Cologne to Rome Vitellius' army covered 1,200 miles in eighty-six days, Wellesley, *RhM* 1960, 287.

4. sexaginta milia. Even if the numbers brought by Valens and Caecina to Italy have been exaggerated by T., I. 61. 5 n., they can hardly have totalled less than 60,000, and we have also to reckon with the numbers brought later by Vitellius himself, II. 57. 2 n. But the 60,000 here are those which remained after battle losses, and more particularly after significant quantities of men had been sent back to

their homes or allowed to retire, II. 69. 7 ff. What should be noticed
here is that the forty-six auxiliary regiments in the force entering
Rome, II. 89. 6, would, if one reckons one in four for regiments to be
milliariae rather than *quingenariae*, be less than half the total force. The
legionaries could have comprised (but subject again to battle losses) the
whole of I Italica and XXI Rapax, the greater part (but not the whole,
IV. 22) of V Alaudae and also of XXII Primigenia (II. 100. 4), and
vexillations, about 2,000 from each legion, from the other four
Rhineland legions and from the legions of Britain, II. 57. 5. n. That
should total more than 30,000.

6. etiam inter servos, 'even in comparison with the slaves': cf. V.
17. 12. *Calones* and *lixae* are often grouped together, III. 20. 22, 33. 1.
But *calones* were slaves, Festus 62 M: *lixae* (bakers, tradesmen, actors,
etc.) seem to have been normally free (for a clear example see *A*. II. 62.
3).

V.'s view that the genitive *lixarum* depends on *numerus* to be
understood from the previous clause seems intolerably harsh.

8. modestia, 'discipline'.

11. flagitiosa per obsequia . . . II. 71. 4, with n., but with again no
example.

88. 1. seditionem Ticini. II. 68.

88. 3. paganos, 'civilians'. I. 53. 14 n.

4. singulis . . . dividebat. Why was it so improper to issue the troops
with food? The emphasis is, presumably, on *paratos cibos*, for normally
the men would have got their needs, against payment, from the
common store. But in preparation for the entry to Rome each man, not
unreasonably, was served with a prepared meal, which gives T. the
opportunity for saying they were being fed up like gladiators.

7. vernacula utebantur urbanitate. The 'fun' of the Roman
populace was a commonplace, e.g. *Dial.* 28, *ego de urbe et huius propriis ac
vernaculis vitiis loquar*.

14. in quo Galba iacuisset, II. 55. 7 n.

nec minus saevum. Here T., see Walser, 83, is undoubtedly
'barbarizing' the German army. But in ascribing the behaviour of even
the legionaries to their unfamiliarity with the streets and people of
Rome he is surely nearer to the truth than Jos. *BI* IV. 566, who talks of
their greed at the sight of Rome's riches.

89. 1. ponte Mulvio, 2 miles north of Rome, where the Via Flaminia crosses the Tiber. Here Galba, before his entry to the city, met the luckless marines, I. 6. 7. n.

paludatus. The *paludamentum* is the dress, normally white or purple, (Val. Max., I. 6. 11) of the *imperator* in the field. In Republican times it was issued to a departing general, Varro *LL* VII. 37, Livy XLI. 10. 5, for himself and his lictors, and before he re-entered the city he laid it down (a triumphal robe is a different thing). Before Caracalla's time it was rarely, if ever (see I. 7. 6 n. on Galba), that such uniform was worn by a *princeps* inside the *pomerium*, Hammond, *AM* 35–8, 54–6. So when Suet. *Vit.* 11, says *urbem denique ad classicum introiit paludatus ferroque succinctus*, he is unlikely to be right against T. Possibly Vitellius entered the Porta Flaminia in uniform, and did not lay it down till he crossed the *pomerium* through the Porta Fontinalis, where the Via Lata met the Servian wall near the Capitol, Platner–Ashby, 502.

3. ut captam . . . deterritus. Incredible, from what T. tells us in the rest of this Book about Vitellius' conduct.

4. praetexta, the purple-bordered civil dress of a magistrate.

incessit. See Courbaud, 127 ff., on the aorist–imperfect–aorist structure of the chapter, which he shows to be characteristic of T.'s portrait-painting.

5. quattuor legionum aquilae, I. Italica, V Alaudae, XXI Rapax, XXII Primigenia.

totidemque, but in fact not only from the four German legions which did not send eagles, but from the three British legions too. They are again explicitly mentioned at II. 100. 6.

8. nomina gentium, presumably the national titles of the regiments, though these were seldom a clue to their actual composition.

9. praefecti castrorum. II. 26. 6 n.

primi centurionum, probably the *primi ordines*, on whom see Wellesley's ed. to Book III, App. VII. 5.

11. phalerae torquesque, the decorations appropriate to rankers. The description by P. Steiner, *Bonn. Jahrb.* 1906, 1 ff., is still valuable.

14. Augustae nomine. The precedents for the name Augusta are Livia after Augustus' death, *A.* I. 8. 1, Antonia under Gaius (Suet. *Cal.* 15—but she refused it and received it posthumously from Claudius, Suet. *Cl.* 11), Agrippina under Claudius, *A.* XII. 26. 2, and most recently Poppaea, *A.* XV. 23. 1.

90. 1. alterius. Heubner, following GG s.v. *alter*, b), cites *Agr.* 5. 3, 17. 2 (but in both passages *alterius* relates to one definite person), and *A.*

XV. 25. 2 (but there *cuius* before *alterius* clarifies the sense). Moreover GG's classification of this usage as *minus acriter facto opposito* does not fit the present passage, where the contrast could hardly be more acute (Wellesley 'a foreign state'), cf. I. 45. 1, *alium crederes senatum, alium populum*. But whether T's choice of *alterius* was, as H. thought, caused by avoidance of the archaic genitive *alīus* we cannot be sure.

7. nomen Augusti. Vitellius had postponed the title, not refused it, 62. 9. For coins carrying the title see *RIC* I. 221.

8. tam frustra. For the construction see V., *Riv. Fil.* 1908, 380. The sense certainly is 'their success in making him take it was as futile (for he had so little time to live) as his earlier refusal (which he had to reverse so soon)'.

91. 2. maximum pontificatum adeptus, not as part of the *cuncta* of II. 55. 8. Otho had proceeded by gradual stages from his assumption of *imperium* on 16 Jan., and only became *pont. max.* on 9 Mar., *ILS* 241 = MW 2: Vitellius, closely attentive to 'constitutional' niceties, was probably as cautious about this title as about the name Augustus. So Suet. *Vit.* 11, though the chapter is a careless one, may be right in making 18 July, the day on which T. says he issued the edict, the one on which he had assumed the office.

4. antiquitus infausto die. For 18 July for the date both of the massacre of the Fabii on the Cremera (477 B.C.) and the defeat by the Gauls on the Allia (? 389 B.C.) see Livy VI. 1. 11; for the Cremera also Ovid, *Fasti* II. 195 ff.

7. comitia ... celebrans, 'canvassing with his candidates like a common citizen' (Fyfe). Why T. thought this incident warranted his remarkable piece of alliteration is not clear. But Vitellius was undoubtedly engaging in an abnormal kind of flourish, and G. Tibiletti, *Principe e magistrati repubblicani* (1953), 202–3, was wise to discourage the use of this passage to illustrate electoral procedure in the first century A.D. (Plin. *Pan.* 77, *comitia consulum obibat ipse* etc., does not imply the 'throng' of *celebrans*).

Vitellius here is not concerned only with elections for the remaining months of 69, for which he had already rearranged the consulates, II. 71. 8 with n. Helvidius Priscus, line 12, becomes praetor designate for 70; and since Nero before his death in June 68 had already designated consuls for 69, I. 77. 10, it was high time to do the same for 70, at least for the early months. Vitellius took action again in November, III. 55. 8, but at that point he was designating consuls for several years ahead (Suet. *Vit.* 11 says ten years, but wrongly refers the action to July), going far beyond what the present passage records.

Suet., cit., also dates to this time Vitellius' assumption of a perpetual consulship, a move which Momigliano, 123–4, thinks was made to please the constitutionalists. On that Suet. may be right, though the title *cos. perp.* appears for certain on only one inscription (*ILS* 242 = MW 81, but see also *ILS* 243). If so, Vitellius cannot have intended to be one of the regular pair of consuls, since he was simultaneously designating two consuls for each remaining period of 69.

12. Priscus Helvidius, introduced with some formality at IV. 5. For his praetorship in January 70, IV. 53. 10.

14. tribunos plebis ... potestatis. Though action by the ordinary tribunes is known during the Julio-Claudian period (M. Hammond, *The Augustan Principate* (1933), 138–9, 310–11), the only recent instance of a *princeps* using his own tribunician power is Nero's veto on a condemnation in A.D. 62, *A.* XIV. 48. 3. Here Vitellius pretends that he is only one tribune among many.

18. Thraseae, Helvidius' father-in-law, the celebrated 'Stoic' senator who was forced to suicide in 66, *PIR*² C 1187. For an instance of disagreement between him and Vitellius see *A.* XIV. 49.

21. gloriae, the goal at which Thrasea, Helvidius, and some of their friends aimed, IV. 4. 19, and *A.* XIV. 49, with other instances in GG, and for which they were criticized, probably by more orthodox Stoics, IV. 6. 1.

92. 1. praeposuerat praetorianis ... Nothing is known of either man outside the *Histories*. Priscus was presumably a legionary centurion, for Vitellius would hardly have appointed an officer from Otho's guard. These are much less distinguished appointments than those made by Otho, I. 46; indeed such promotions are unparalleled. But Vitellius was not in a good position to use the existing holders of high equestrian posts.

4. auctoritas, a misprint in OCT.[1] for *auctoritatis.*

7. ambitu, 'the numbers who courted their favour, attended them when they went out, and crowded their morning levees ...'.

8. variis ... inclinationibus. Given what we know of the abilities of the two, should we think that Vitellius would have been more successful, or more reputable, had he favoured one or the other more consistently? Should not a good ruler (T. shows no awareness of the question) weigh the advice he gets from different sides? But for him *numquam satis fida* paves the way for Caecina's treachery.

10. Vitellium ... metuebantque. D. Mervyn Jones, *CQ* 1945, 12, commenting on K. Brink's article cited at I. 79. 12, establishes this as a 'double zeugma' complicated by chiasmus. They feared Vitellius for his readiness to take offence, and despised him for his susceptibility to flattery.

13. egens nobilium turba, for neither the Galbian commission, I. 20, nor Otho's distribution of unsold Neronian confiscations, I. 90, had achieved much for them.

16. iura libertorum, 'rights over their freedmen', *Dig.* XXV. 3. 5. 19 ff., XXXVII. 14. 4. What mattered most financially would have been (a) the right of a patron to be maintained if he fell into poverty, (b) the right of succession to a proportion of the property of a freedman who died childless or without many heirs, *Cod. Iust.* VI. 3, (c) succession to the property of all Latini Iuniani, Gaius III. 56.

17. corrumpebant. Besides the possibility of denying that they were freedmen, or that they had relations to the nobles in question, one way of making Vitellius' provision ineffective would have been to prove that they had insufficient means, *Dig.* XXIII. 3. 5. 25.

18. per ... sinus. *Sinus* are the folds of the toga, which when pushed back over the other shoulder would form a pocket; so a place for safe-keeping, III. 19. 10, IV. 14. 16; moreover Lipsius pointed out that the word is used of a person by Plin. *NH* 36. 15, *M. Scaurus Mariani sodalicii rapinarumque provincialium sinus.* So here *occultos* means obscure persons, whom nobody would think of probing; and *ambitiosos* influential ones, whom no one wanted to approach, but with whom the freedmen had acquired favour.

93. 1. plenis castris, the praetorian camp. In Galba's time too there had been overflowing into porticoes or temples, because regiments from outside had entered Rome, I. 31.

2. non principia noscere, 'they did not know where to parade'. The parade ground was outside the commander's headquarters, the *principia*, see App. VII. 4 (by the late I. A. Richmond) to Wellesley's edn. of Book III.

6. infamibus Vaticani locis. Trastevere is still known for 'cattiva aria'. For *infamis* ('unhealthy', perhaps malarial, see Brunt, *Italian Manpower*, 623) cf. Frontin. *Aq.* 88.

8. fluminis aviditas, 'their passion for taking to the water'.

9. confusus ... militiae etc. I. 31. 14 n. for *ordo militiae* as 'military propriety'; here perhaps 'accepted military organization'. Under

Tiberius, *A.* IV. 5. 7, the guard was recruited from the older districts of Italy, and throughout the Julio-Claudian period it was rare to bring in provincials, Durry, 240, Passerini, *coorti,* 141 ff. Admittedly three known examples of Vitellian praetorians are ex-legionaries, *ILS* 2034–6 = MW 375, 381–2, and two of these were certainly Italian. But the Vitellian enrolment also involved auxiliaries, i.e. men who were not yet even citizens: see *alaris,* 94. 4, and the soldier from an auxiliary cohort on *AE* 1932, 30 (Passerini, cit., 167).

On the other problems raised by *confusus . . . militiae* see Introd., pp. 16ff. But a more difficult question about the urbans remains.

If the new urbans were all Vitellius' men, as seems to be implied by *viginti milibus* at II. 94. 7, why did they constitute a force on which Flavius Sabinus could rely against the Vitellians in December, III. 64. 3, 69. 5? Many views have been expressed. Fabia, *Rev. Phil.* 1914, 42, thought T. simply wrong in stating that the urbans were reconstituted at all; but T. is not given to imprecision about troops in the city, e.g. II. 55. 3, and his reference to urbans should mean that he found them in his source. Momigliano, 146, observed that if Caecina could betray Vitellius, so could his ex-legionaries in the urban troops: G. Vitucci, *Ricerche sulla praefectura urbi in età imperiale* (1956), 96 ff., agreed with him, and argued that the rallying of any soldiers to Sabinus was not unnatural once it was believed that Vitellius had abdicated. Wellesley, ed. to III, cit., thinks (rightly) that the urbans who first rallied to Sabinus were officers (for the cohorts could not possibly have crowded into Sabinus' house, III. 69. 5), and that the advice given to Sabinus to rely on the urbans is part of 'T.'s practice of (putting) into the mouths of his characters arguments which are plausible without necessarily being sound'. Yet it is unmistakable that many rankers joined Sabinus on the Capitol. The question is one on which T. has given too little evidence, but it seems likely that the process of reconstituting all the cohorts (*scribebantur*) was a gradual one, and that attention to the urbans was not given high priority, especially as the prefect of the city (Flavius Sabinus) would have been in charge. By the time the main Vitellian forces left for the front in September, these units had perhaps suffered little change.

94. 3. urbanae militiae. I. 4. 8 n.

6. robora . . . subtracta. The subsequent campaign shows this to be almost absurd exaggeration.

7. convulsum castrorum decus, 'the dignity of the praetorian camp was destroyed'. T. is thinking of the actual camp, and it is wrong, with V., to take the phrase as equivalent simply to *corrupta disciplina.*

This would lose the force of *decus*, and make T. repeat what he has said in the last chapter.

viginti milibus. This should mean that all the praetorians and urbans were reconstituted, one way or another, but see above.

10. duces Galliarum, otherwise unknown. From their names one would think they were Roman citizens, perhaps members of the οἱ δυνατοὶ τῶν ἐπιχωρίων from Vienna, Jos. *BI* IV. 440.

13. liberti principum, the freedmen of Vitellius' predecessors, who had passed to him with other imperial property. Cf. Millar, *JRS* 1963, 41, Brunt, *JRS* 1966, 79.

15. stabula ... opplere. The concrete evidence against Vitellius' government begins to thicken here and in the next chapter. But suppose one wrote 'Shortage of funds now made Vitellius postpone the essential donative to his troops. Only by a special levy on the freedmen who had made their wealth in past reigns was he able to keep up the regular shows in the circus: building in this summer had to be confined to the provision of some stables in the circus wings.' What has T. added or modified?

95. 1. natalem Vitellii diem. Suet. *Vit.* 3 provides 7 and 24 Sept. as alternative days for the birthday.

2. vicatim. The *vici* were subdivisions of the 14 Augustan *Regiones* of Rome. In Pliny's day, *NH* III. 66, there were 265 of them each under four *vicomagistri*. Where and how these gladiators combated is not clear.

5. inferias Neroni, also emphasized by Suet. *Vit.* 11, Dio 65. 7. For Neronian sympathies of Vitellius cf. 71. 13, but in contrast II. 62. 12.

6. Augustales. This brotherhood was founded by Tiberius at the end of A.D. 14, and was originally composed of twenty-one *primores civitatis* selected by lot, together with four members of the imperial house. Its task was the cult not only of Augustus but of the *gens* Iulia, *A*. I. 54 (with Furneaux's n.), III. 64.

7. Romulus Tatio regi. i.e. had founded the *sodales Titii*, on the origin of which ancient writers were perplexed. T. corrects himself at *A*. I. 54, where he calls Tatius himself the founder, the purpose being to preserve the rites of the Sabines. Varro, *LL* V. 85 (Müller) writes *sodales Titii dicti ab Titiis avibus, quas in auguriis certis observare solent.*

8. nondum quartus ... mensis. But here we go back to early August (from Bedriacum on 14 Apr.), at least some weeks before Vitellius' birthday (line 1). T. presumably follows up some incident in which Asiaticus had been involved.

9. Polyclitos ... Patrobios, freedmen of Nero, I. 37. 23 (with n.), 49. 5.

13. noviens miliens. T. is more precise than Suet., but since accounts were now not published how did he know? Anyway one may wonder what comparable sum was expended by the Flavians between their rising and the end of the year.

17. Marcellus. II. 53. 2 n.

96. 1. prima ... nuntiatur. If this letter reached Vitellius before the official news of the proclamations in Egypt and Judaea, Suet., *Vit.* 15. 1, can hardly be right in dating the Danubian revolt as late as August: probably his source said the news of all the proclamations reached Rome in August.

T. does not explain how much Aponius, a governor later probably pardoned by Vespasian, III. 11, suppressed in his letter: did he, in particular, mention that the legion had not only revolted, but had declared for Vespasian? Anyway Vitellius, given the earlier behaviour of the Moesian legions (II. 85 with nn.), and also perhaps given secret news of the Eastern commanders' plots, probably already suspected the worst: hence the measures recorded in the following chapters. T. never tells us when the news from the East came in, nor when Vitellius allowed it to be released. It seems likely that (apart from a very secret message to Agrippa, II. 81. 5), the Eastern commanders had been rigorous in suppressing news to Italy, although (II. 82. 18) they were getting communications through to the Danubian and Western armies. So Aponius' message may have reached Rome as early as the first week of August or alternatively almost a month later: the disturbance of T.'s chronology in the previous chapter makes any guess the more hazardous.

6. constare fidem. FIDES EXERCITUUM and CONCORDIA EXERCITUUM are legends on Vitellian coins struck in Rome, Gaul, and Spain, *RIC* I. 224 ff. (an example in MW 36).

97. 3. suspectis iam Batavis. Their natural militancy had already doubtless found encouragement from the messages sent by the Flavian commanders to Gaul, II. 86. 23. But Hordeonius' own attitude was indeed *ambiguus*: at IV. 13. 13 it is alleged that he was a Flavian sympathizer and withheld reinforcements from Vitellius to prevent any resumption of civil war.

4. Vettius Bolanus, the newly appointed governor, II. 65. 15 n. The trouble in Brigantia, briefly described at III. 35, was enough to prevent him depleting his army still further, cf. II. 57. 5. But the Flavians had sent their emissaries to his province too, II. 86. 23.

6. nullo ... consulari, for Cluvius Rufus had departed, 65. The three legions are now VI Victrix, X Gemina, and (II. 67. 5) I Adiutrix.

7. certaturi, 'who would have been rivals in their loyalty': cf. III. 54. 7, *si liceret, vere narraturi.*

9. Africa, potentially of vital importance in this war: cf. III. 48. 15. **legio ... Clodio Macro.** I. 11 6 n. The present passage is the only evidence that Macer was able to raise *auxilia.* The phrase *militiam capere* appears to be used only here in extant Latin, but there is no good reason to doubt the natural meaning of T., namely that a second legion was reconstituted in Africa, presumably with a new name. There is no numismatic or other contemporary evidence for it: it was of course disbanded by the Flavians.

10. dabat impigre nomina. *nomen dare* is a technical term for submitting one's name for military enrolment, III. 58. 8 and *TLL* s.v. *do,* col. 1675. 5 ff. The enthusiasm of the provincials, to which T. gives his explanation in the next sentence, perhaps owes its origin to the harsh treatment parts of Africa had received in Nero's reign.

11. integrum ... Vitellius. Suet. *Vit.* 5 agrees, *singularem innocentiam praestitit,* and says Vitellius continued in the province for a second year as legate to his brother. Aulus was in Rome in 62, *A.* XIV. 49, but he had been highly favoured in his career (*cos.* 48), and his proconsulate was more probably before 62 than after.

12. famosum ... Vespasianus. Here, however, Suet. *Vesp.* 4 says *Africam integerrime nec sine magna dignatione administravit.* Fabia, 160, thought this was a blunder: the 'common source' compared Vitellius with Vespasian, and Suet. reported of the latter what had been said of the former (forgetting, presumably, that he had attributed those qualities to Vitellius in the other biography). More likely, Vespasian showed in Africa the qualities for which he was later famous (or infamous), namely strictness (sufferers called it *avaritia*) but personal integrity. Hence the other facts recorded by Suet.: there was a riot at Hadrumetum, in which he was pelted with turnips, but he returned in poverty. So P. Romanelli, *Storia delle province romane dell'Africa* (1959), 275: similarly Braithwaite ad loc., who also gives grounds for dating Vespasian's proconsulate about 62/3.

98. 1. Valerius Festus. The career of C. Calpetanus Rantius Valerius Festus is given on *ILS* 989 = MW 266 (found at Trieste, though Festus' tribe, Pomptina, is not known in that part of Italy). Like Tampius

Flavianus, II. 86. 14n., III. 4. 5, he was a relation of Vitellius who crossed to Vespasian, for whom his services, followed by a successful war against the Garamantes, are recorded at IV. 49–50. He was rewarded by military decorations appropriate to a consular, became (though still *adulescens*, IV. 49. 2) consul in 71, curator of the Tiber in 72–3 (MW 443), then governor of Pannonia, and of Tarraconensis before Vespasian's death, see W. Eck, *Senatoren von Vespasian bis Hadrian* (1970), 119 f. A Festus who died early in Domitian's reign is called *amicus Caesaris* by Martial, I. 78, and it was perhaps that position which earned him the hostility of T. and of Pliny, *Epp.* III. 7. 12, and which made them so certain that Piso the proconsul (IV. 49–50) had been an innocent victim.

Note the absence of reference to any proconsul in the present passage, though Piso had presumably taken up office.

7. Vitellii paratus noscebantur. T. does not explain how. And is he thinking of information passing to Vespasian himself (who seems to have made little use of it) or to the commanders in the Danubian provinces?

9. Pannonicae Alpes, the Julian Alps: cf. III. 1. 4. with Wellesley's n. The military road from Italy through Aquileia crossed the Adelsburger pass to Emona (Laibach) and so on to the Pannonian headquarters at Poetovio (Pettau).

10. etesiarum flatu. These seasonal winds blow from the north-west for more than a month from mid-July, Plin. *NH* V. 55, Caes. *BC* III. 107, and are most unfavourable for navigation westward. They had received their name as early as Herodotus' time, II. 20. 2, and were recognized as far east as the Caspian, *A.* VI. 33.

99. 1. inruptione ... exterritus. H. took *atrocibus ... nuntiis* as ablative of 'circumstance', and is followed by Heubner. It seems more likely that V. was right in thinking that it was the *nuntii* who frightened, and that *inruptione* is temporal (see I. 2. 2. for numerous parallels). In either case emendation is unnecessary.

4. longe alia. Dio 65. 10. 2 gives a similar description of the Vitellian army, and makes its weakness the cause of Caecina's treachery (similarly Jos. *BI* IV. 635, says Caecina became terrified of the Flavian power). Briessmann, 31 f., suggests that Dio's account figured in a source used also by T., but that T., who had other views about Caecina, transferred it to an account of the army as it left Rome. This is possible, but the main point is that T. believed he had other evidence (II. 100–1) about Caecina's treachery.

6. fluxa arma. Whether T. means that the arms were in bad condition or were being carried loosely is not quite certain. Probably the former, since there seems to be reminiscence of Livy XXI. 40. 9, *quassata fractaque arma, claudi ac debiles equi.*

12. credidere plerique. T. does not mean this explanation to be inconsistent with his fuller analysis in II. 101.

13. Rubrio Gallo. II. 51. 6 n.

15. admonebatur, governing both the preceding genitives and the *ut* clause, cf. III. 24. 15.

100. 3. primae ... sextae decimae. The restoration may be regarded as certain. The four legions can be identified from other sources as those of the Rhine legions which had not sent their eagles to Italy, and all are mentioned as present at the Cremona battle, III. 22.

4. quinta et duoetvicensima. V Alaudae had come with Valens, I. 61. 6, XXII Primigenia probably with Vitellius in the force recorded at II. 57. 1.

5. postremo agmine. XXI Rapax had been with Caecina, I. 61. 8 etc. I Italica had been picked up by Valens at Lugdunum, I. 64. 15.

6. vexillariis trium Britannicarum legionum. These too are present at the Cremona battle. Wellesley, in his n. to III. 21. 3, claims that they, together with two full legions and the vexillations of the four mentioned in line 3 above, are included in T.'s computation of 'six' Vitellian legions on the Tartarus.

7. quem ipse ductaverat. i.e. all the troops which had come from Lower Germany, plus I Italica. When Valens eventually left Rome, his escort was not a military one, III. 40, and he had to send for some praetorian cohorts.

10. mutatum id consilium. Caecina was presumably lying: it suited his plan of treachery to keep the whole Vitellian force together. But it would have been arguable that the right course was to place the whole Vitellian force on or near the Po, even had his intentions been honourable.

11. legiones Cremonam, pars Hostiliam. Two full legions, I Italica and V Alaudae, went to Cremona, III. 18. 2, the rest of the force to a camp on the Tartarus, a stream running parallel to the Po north of Hostilia. For the geography see Wellesley's n. to III. 9. 4. Hostilia is on the left bank of the Po, S.E. of Mantua, in the territory of Verona; for its status as a *vicus*, not an independent town, Plin. *NH* XXI. 73. The

Itineraries show a road from it west to Bedriacum and Cremona, a road from Verona to Mutina passing through it, and communications (by road or water) with Ravenna *per Padum*.

12. Ravennam devertit. Once again, a loyal commander could make an excellent case for consulting with the fleet, so suspicion did not immediately arise.

13. Patavii secretum. R. H. Martin, *Eranos*, 1951, 174, argued (a) that GG rightly translated *secretum* as 'a secret interview' rather than 'a secret place' (see II. 4. 8, IV. 49. 5, and the other passages they cite), and (b) that *patuit* is a much more probable correction of M.'s *patui*, since the sentence would then conform with a type common in T. whereby a pretence is shown up in its true colours, e.g. II. 77. 7 ff. Anyway, why did Caecina and Bassus go to Patavium, over 100 miles north of Ravenna and on the line of the invading Flavians, to hold their meeting? On (a) he is undoubtedly right. As to (b) there were as yet no Flavian troops at Patavium, and Flavian emissaries might have been helpful to the conference. But it is sufficiently out of the way for an interview between the two men to have caused surprise, and I feel sure that Martin is right. K. gives no reason for not adopting the suggestion in his last edition.

14. Lucilius Bassus. The earlier career of Sex. Lucilius Bassus, and the circumstances in which he betrayed Galba (plural *videntur* at II. 101. 6) are unknown: presumably his *praefectura alae* was held on the Rhine. Vespasian's grants of citizenship to men from both the Ravenna and the Misenum fleet who had served under him, *CIL* XVI. 12–15 (13 = MW 398) have been held to imply that Vespasian reinstated him in the combined command; but there is no sign of this in T., and these documents concern men who had previously served under Bassus but were now settled in colonies (see Nesselhauf on *CIL* XVI. 12). Bassus was sent to pacify Campania soon after the Flavians entered Rome, IV. 3, and his main reward came when he was adlected to the Senate and made governor of Judaea during 71, Jos. *BI* VII. 163. There he successfully reduced Herodium and Machaerus, but died in 73 before the last Jewish fortress at Masada had fallen, ibid. 252.

14. post praefecturam cohortis. For the men actually appointed to the guard, whom Bassus could reasonably regard as his juniors, see II. 92. 1.

15. Ravennati ... praepositus. V. has no adequate ground for taking this to be a temporary appointment: *praeponere* is T.'s normal word, I. 46. 3, II. 92. 1. But there is no known parallel for a combined command of the two fleets, and it is hard to see how it was intended to

work, though see D. Kienast, *Untersuchungen zu den Kriegsflotten der röm*
... *Kaiserzeit* (1966), 29, 34.

18. nec sciri potest... Unless Bassus, who had a genuine grievance
against Vitellius, was peculiarly persuasive, the first explanation is
inadequate; for defection of the Ravenna fleet was not enough to
destroy confidence that the Flavian invasion could be defeated. T., to
judge from the following chapter, thought the second explanation was
right, thereby to some extent deserting what at II. 99. 12 he has
recorded that *plerique* believed.

What was the truth? Momigliano, 156 ff., linked the problem with
another, namely the extreme rashness with which Antonius Primus
exposed his Pannonian legions to Vitellian attack in the early stages of
his invasion, see esp. III. 9. 5. Should we not infer that he was already
aware of Caecina's defection, and may this not imply that he and
Caecina were already in league? On this view their plan was to end the
war quickly, and to put themselves in control of Rome and Italy before
Mucianus arrived, thus becoming the chief *amici principis* of Vespasian's
regime. The plan miscarried because Caecina proved unable to deliver
the desertion of his army, and he therefore incurred the contempt of
Antonius, IV. 80. 12. Moreover the delay in North Italy prevented
Antonius from a rapid march southwards, and he entered Rome only
a few days before Mucianus. Antonius' reputation in the Flavian party
was then destroyed by various charges of disobedience, ruthlessness,
and incompetence, see Wellesley, ed. to III, pp. 15–19; and Caecina,
sent to Vespasian because Antonius had no further use for him, was
granted honour (Jos. *BI* IV. 644), but no particular post so far as we
know.

This is an ingenious theory, and one by no means inconsistent with
the politics of the time. Yet is it credible against the complete silence of
out sources about the behaviour attributed to the two main characters
involved? I prefer to believe, with T.'s *plerique*, in the persuasiveness of
Vespasian's agents, and above all of Flavius Sabinus himself. But on
any view the *naïveté* of Caecina, in thinking he could gain significant
power in the over-crowded Flavian party, is extreme, JRS. 1957. 34.

101. 1. scriptores temporum, see Introd. 26ff. These are likely to
have been writers of Vespasian's reign, since shortly before Vespasian's
death in 79, Dio, 66. 16, Caecina was put to death for 'conspiracy'.
They surely included the Elder Pliny, who (apart from Vipstanus
Messalla, who probably concerned himself with military rather than
political matters) is the only writer cited by T. in the *Histories*: he was
an admirer of Vespasian, and his Histories were composed before 77
(though not published till after Vespasian's death, *NH. praef.* 20). Yet

not all Vespasianic historians took this friendly view of Caecina: Josephus, who says he submitted his *Bellum* for the approval of Vespasian and Titus (*Vita* 359, 361, 363, *c. Apion.* I. 50) simply calls him a traitor, cf. I. 99. 4 above. See my review of Briessmann, *JRS.* 1956. 204, and Townend, *AJP.* 1964. 339.

4. prodito Galba, III. 86. 12.

6. anteirentur ... videntur. The singular verb in the *recc.* is surely wrong. T. includes Bassus, and therefore starts the next sentence with the name Caecina.

9. lubrica ... classe, 23. 13, etc. Men from this fleet were later put into the new legion II Adiutrix, III. 50. 13.

This last chapter, followed by *meliore fato fideque* of the Flavians at the beginning of Book III, is a splendid piece of composition.

APPENDIX: THE OTHO–VITELLIUS CAMPAIGNS

(A) THE CHRONOLOGY OF THE EARLIEST MOVES

THAT the Vitellian forces moved off from the Rhine camps very quickly is clear from Valens' presence in the capital of the Leuci (Toul) when he heard of Otho's accession, I. 64. 1 n. From that point his march has been carefully studied by Köster, I. 63. 1 n., who concluded that Valens' army crossed the Cottian Alps about 25 March, a date which, given the time needed for the stages on the journey and the relationship of Valens' arrival at Ticinum to the final battle, is unlikely to be far wrong. But what of Caecina with his force from the Upper army? Without doubt he would have moved with at least equal speed, and he had no more than a week's journey with his contingents from Mainz to reach the Helvetian country. When he arrived there and attacked the Helvetii, the tribe had not yet heard of Galba's death, I. 67. 3. His campaign against them was a set-piece operation, requiring not more than a week or two; then, after waiting a few days, say ten, to get instructions from Cologne, he was ready to plan his descent into Italy, I. 70. 2. But about this time he heard of the *coup* achieved by the *ala Siliana*, so he sent some auxiliary units over into the Po valley. So far, it looks as if we are talking about mid-February, not earlier than the end of the first week of that month, nor later than the end of the third.

To say this calls immediate attention to the extraordinary background to all these early operations, namely that a sizeable force (T. says 30,000 men, but possibly rather too high a figure, I. 61. 5 n.) crossed the Great St. Bernard by mid-March at the very latest, and that a not insignificant number of auxiliary troops was sent over distinctly earlier. Caecina's feat here is impressive, whatever the weather, cf. I. 70. 22 n.; but one must surely also conclude that it was an abnormally mild winter, for in most years the pass would not be open to waggons before end-March. These two factors, the weather and Caecina's resolution, make it the more impossible to be confident about absolute timing.

The operations conducted by the reinforcements sent by Caecina to the *ala* Siliana met with no effective resistance north of the Po. Units left there from the *bellum Neronis*[1] of 68 were overwhelmed, and the Vitellians gained possession of Cremona, II. 17, 22–3. But the same was

---

[1] Introd., pp. 11ff. II. 17. 7 n.

not true of the area south of the river. Vestricius Spurinna had been able to occupy Placentia on the right bank well before Caecina's main army had arrived, II. 18. 1, and evidently also before his advanced guard had found it possible to attack it.

The conclusion so far must be that the Othonian force sent north from Rome under the consular Annius Gallus, of whom Spurinna was a subordinate legate, had arrived in the Po valley before the Vitellian invaders, though they crossed with unexpected suddenness, had been able to mop up all the pro-government forces in the area. It seems therefore that, at whatever date Caecina sent over his detachments, Otho must have dispatched his advanced guard from Rome even earlier. And since it would have taken them over three weeks to arrive in the north and deploy,[2] he must have begun to execute his plans to fight in the Po valley before any clear news had reached him about the surprising speed of the Vitellian crossing. If that be so, then it seems likely that he gave his orders to Gallus directly he believed he could count on support from the Danubian armies, I. 76. 1 n.

The next move came from the Vitellian side. Caecina took his whole army down the Val d'Aosta into the Transpadana and moved against Placentia. When Spurinna's three cohorts, with a small number of auxiliaries, put up an effective resistance, he turned eastward and formed a front at Cremona against Gallus and the troops advancing from Illyricum. At this time Otho's main body had certainly not arrived from Rome; indeed they were at best many days away. Had they even started? Or, to put the question the other way round, can T. be right in saying that a reason for Otho's hasty *profectio* on 15 March, I. 90. 1 n., was Caecina's crossing, and have meant by that a crossing by Caecina's whole army?

That question cannot be answered with real confidence, see I. 89. 17 n. Tacitus' words should mean that Caecina himself had crossed; and it is not absolutely inconceivable both that that was so and that the news had reached Rome, i.e. that Caecina was down by Augusta Praetoria by, say, 8 March. But Tacitus or his source may have been wrong. On the whole it seems likely that, from the moment Caecina began to send troops over, people in Rome started to talk about 'Caecina's crossing', and to put greater urgency into plans already formed for an Othonian front on the Po.

(B) OTHO'S NARBONESE EXPEDITION

What remains in these early stages of the war is the Othonian expedition to Narbonensis. From the Roman end, even if the chapters

[2] See Wellesley, *JRS* 1971, 47 n. 58.

of *Histories* I are chronologically arranged, we can say little more than that it was launched before Otho left Rome on 15 March. Can we get more precision from the Vitellian side? Valens heard quickly of the impending threat, and dispatched an expeditionary force to the coast during his march into Italy, II. 14. Köster, see I. 63. 1 n., considered where Valens could have been at that moment, and concluded that he would have been at or near Lucus, which on Köster's view he entered on 28 February. But Köster adhered rigidly to the doctrine that the expedition could not have started before the day defined by Vegetius (I. 4. 39) as that of the opening of navigation, namely 10 March; and he therefore became involved in the absurd conclusion (unique in his otherwise careful analysis) that Valens heard of the expedition's imminence before it even left Rome. Furthermore, Vegetius' 'day' conflicts with the evidence of Pliny, *NH* II. 122, who gives 8 February as the first day for sailing; and Caes. *BC* III. 25 (cited by Heubner) shows how the calendar could be made to surrender to wartime needs. One should also remember the clemency of the late winter in 69.

If we can really make use of our slender evidence, then the argument could be as follows. The Othonian fleet would reach a Riviera port from Rome in three or four days; and the news of its arrival would be conveyed by fast messenger to Valens in another four days (possibly more if he had already started on the Alpine ascent from Gap to Briançon).[3] But the later the landing, and therefore the farther Valens had advanced, the longer the journey of his reinforcements to the coast; for there was no military road before they returned to the Rhône valley and then marched eastward through Aquae Sextiae (Aix). Now take what seems, from the Roman end, to be the latest extreme, i.e. a departure of the expedition about 10 March.[4] Then Valens, nearing Briançon, would have got the news about 18 March; and his reinforcements, which Köster calculated would have reached the coast in seventeen days from Lucus, would have needed at least twenty days from Briançon and would have arrived at earliest in the first week of April. Then it had to fight its two battles. But this is impossibly late, both in relation to the decisive battle of 'Bedriacum' on 15 April, and to the fact that Valens had heard of the Riviera battles when he was at Ticinum, II. 28.[5]

It is therefore obvious that the expedition must have set out at least two or three weeks earlier. Let us choose an arbitrary date, 20 February,

[3] T. in II. 14 records the message to Valens after he describes the early activities of the Othonians in Liguria. I assume, however, that the procurator Marius Maturus would have alerted Valens directly the Othonians landed. Their atrocities would have occurred in the interval before Valens' detachment reached the coast.

[4] This happens to be Köster's date, but on his impossible assumption about the way news was conveyed to Valens before the expedition started.

[5] Probably before he got there, for *exarserat*, with the following sentence, could mean many days earlier.

remembering at the same time that every earlier day for the embarkation shortens the time which Valens' reinforcements needed to get back to the Rhône valley on their journey to Forum Iulii (Fréjus). Then Valens might have got the news on 28 February and have been near Lucus (as Köster supposed). His detachment reaches Forum Iulii in seventeen days, i.e. about 17 March, fights its two battles on 21 and 24 March, and Valens has the news of them at Augusta Taurinorum, which he may be supposed to have reached (see I. 63. 1 n.) at the turn of the month.[6]

If that chronology makes sense, then the Narbonese expedition left at much the same time as the departure for North Italy of Gallus' force. It was part of a coherent plan once the Danubian legions had declared for Otho.

From modern scholars the conception behind the expedition has received occasional support,[7] but more commonly contempt;[8] for its execution contempt (shared by Tacitus) has been almost unanimous. The commanders may, of course, have been as futile or as irresponsible as Tacitus suggests, though one may wonder whether he was not unduly suspicious when an enterprise was put under the command of people under senatorial rank. If, however, we can discard Henderson's idea that this small force was supposed to stand, like Horatius Cocles, in the way of Valens' men attempting to cross the Mt. Genèvre,[9] we must try to see what they were in fact supposed to achieve. Three targets are intelligible, (a) to see whether the naval base at Forum Iulii could be captured, (b) to assert Othonian naval supremacy in the western Mediterranean, (c) to win control over the coast road into Italy, which might have been of great importance later, in the event that Othonian operations in the Po valley were reasonably successful. Of these objectives the first was certainly not met; the second was met abundantly, II. 16; the third seems to have been attained as well, though the disaster at 'First Bedriacum' made the achievement unimportant and unremembered.

The force which Otho diverted for these purposes was not very large: that which the Vitellians diverted to combat it was almost as numerous. It is therefore hard to regard the affair as one which signally contributed to Otho's ultimate defeat. As to the withdrawal to Albingaunum after the battles, it is fairly clear that an assault on

---

[6] Heubner, while emphasizing that our evidence is inadequate, comes to the same approximate conclusion, citing B. Hallerman, *Diss. Würzburg* 1963 (which I have not seen). Wellesley too, *JRS.* 1971, 47, favours 'late February'; yet I cannot agree with him (see I. 87. 2 n.) about the expedition's context.

[7] Henderson, 77, maintaining that if the Othonians had moved up to Briançon after their victory they could have prevented Valens from joining Caecina in time.

[8] Hardy, 127 f., Syme, 676 f.

[9] The main point against Henderson (see Syme, cit.) is, however, that there was no military road from the Riviera to Briançon.

Forum Iulii was not immediately possible. What else could the Othonian commanders do?

(c) OPERATIONS IN NORTH ITALY

So at some date in March Caecina crossed into Italy. He was repulsed from Placentia by Spurinna, retreated east to Cremona, and was defeated in the early days of April at the battle ad Castores by the force which Annius Gallus, and his new colleagues Suetonius Paulinus and Marius Celsus, had assembled at Bedriacum as a front to be joined gradually by troops from the Danubian provinces, and by additional troops from Rome. The details of these operations are discussed in notes to II. 21–2, 24–6. But on the morrow of the Castores battle Valens arrived at Ticinum (Pavia), and despite troubles with his soldiers was able to join Caecina at Cremona. The assembly of the Vitellian expeditionary forces was now complete: the Othonians had to decide what to do (II. 31. 8). The decision they took led to the battle near Cremona which in modern times has been called the 'First battle of Bedriacum'.

The strategy of that battle is an inexhaustible subject, and I do not propose to contribute anything to its topographical aspects: these now seem to me drawn, almost conclusively, by Wellesley's excellent discussion in *JRS* 1971, 28 ff. He seems to me right on all essentials: the Cremona fortifications, the Vitellian camp, the road from Cremona eastwards, and (approximately, as he concedes), the point at which the Vitellians started a bridge across the Po. The exact site of Bedriacum (Tornara, as he suggests, or Calvatone, as has generally been thought) matters little to his main thesis, namely that the pressing argument for haste, in the minds of Otho and of the advisers Otho favoured, was the fear that a crossing of the Po would be achieved by the enemy.

It is true that the only arguments given us from the Othonian side are those in Paulinus' speech at II. 32, and that these never mention the bridge. But that the Othonians, probably those supporting Paulinus as well as his opponents, were concerned with this possible threat is shown by their movement of Spurinna's cohorts to the possible bridge-point on the south bank (II. 36. 6).

Yet there was still great room for doubt within Otho's Council. It could be argued that the threat of a bridge was a bluff; and that even if the Vitellians were genuinely attempting a crossing, the bridgehead to the south could not quickly be established in sufficient strength to ruin Othonian communications with Rome. Which side was right in the council is discussed at II. 34. 5 n., and we cannot be sure about the actual facts: all that seems certain is that T. and his sources believed that the threat could be discounted. The Vitellians were only pretending, *transitum Padi simulantes*; and Wellesley's proposed emendation of the last word to *simul copulantes* contradicts the rhetoric of the whole sentence, which describes Caecina and Valens as *quieti intentique . . . quando hostis imprudentia rueret*. But of course T., using a source which certainly reflects the opinions of Paulinus, may have been wrong.

Yet even if the threat of the bridge was something serious, suppressed or overlooked by Tacitus but the vital consideration in the minds of Proculus and Titianus, it is not obvious that it was irrelevant to describe Otho as *pronus ad decertandum*, II. 33. 4. For Otho himself had other motives for haste, above all the impetuosity of his praetorians, to whom he owed his elevation and on whom his future safety depended. About this Tacitus is insistent, and there is no adequate reason for disbelieving him. Moreover, though it is sad that Tacitus has not given us the arguments on the other side, Paulinus and his allies in the council of war still had a strong case. They could claim not only that the bridge was unbuilt, and that if it were built its crossing could be slow and could be challenged; but also that further troops from the Danubian provinces could very soon arrive and help in the challenge, and that any such reinforcements would arrive much sooner than those of the Vitellians.

(IV) THE OTHONIAN MOBILIZATION

All of that they could say, and much of it T. tells us they did say. But if the movement of troops from the Danube was as incomplete as Wellesley claims, then their argument for delay, if only for delay of a week or ten days, would have been even more powerful; and after the events, phrases like *pronus ad decertandum*, or *praepropera desperatione* (II. 76. 26), could seem even closer to the mark. The speed of that movement is the main subject of the present note.

All commentators have inevitably agreed (II. 43. 9) that the main body of one legion, XIII Gemina from Poetovio, was present at the final battle, and that the main body of XIV Gemina (camp unknown) was not. The other two legions from Illyricum, VII Galbiana from (presumably) Carnuntum on the Danube, and XI Claudia from Burnum in Dalmatia, are not mentioned in Tacitus' account of the battle, and Wellesley maintains that their main bodies were not there. On 15 April, the morrow of the battle, he places VII at Ateste, little over 80 miles from Bedriacum, and XI perhaps near Aquileia.

The case for that view he constructs as follows: (i) at the battle of Castores (Köster's date, *c* 5 April, which seems acceptable, I. 63. 1 n., II. 24.) a detachment of XIII was present, but the main body is mentioned only in the Cremona battle, 43. 9; (ii) a legion's daily march may be assumed as 15 miles, and the daily speed of a courier as 100 miles; (iii) VII from Carnuntum had about 180 more miles to march to Bedriacum than had XIII from Poetovio, and the main body of the latter had only arrived after 5 April; (iv) XI needed fewer miles than XIII, but it does not appear in the account of the battle, and its governor was sluggish (III. 50. 5). Consequently, if we take the movement of XIII as our base, the summons to all Danube legions was sent from Rome about 3 March, and they started to move about 15 March.[10] The main bodies of all but XIII were too late for a battle on 14 April.

The first reason for doubting this reconstruction is that Tacitus records the oaths taken to Otho by the three Danube provinces at I. 76. 1, before he mentions the consular elections on 26 January. I return to this point later, since it would not appear compelling but for the numerous passages in T. which were assembled by Passerini to prove the participation in the battle of all the Illyrian armies except the main body of XIV. These passages may be classified as follows (see also nn. above):

(a) *Reinforcements still to arrive.* Paulinus says, II. 32. 24, *paucis diebus quartam decimam legionem, magna ipsam fama, cum Moesicis copiis adfore.*[11] Why would he fail to mention a legion (VII Galbiana) well past Aquileia, and another which had surely already entered Italy from Dalmatia? Add to that passage II. 44. 20 (*venire Moesicas legiones*, but not others), 46. 16 (can Wellesley really be right in thinking that these *praemissi e Moesia* referred in part to legions coming, not from Moesia, but from Pannonia and Dalmatia?), 54. 3 (Why did the liar Coenus not expand further by speaking of VII and XI?).

(b) *The aftermath of the battle.* In II. 66–7 Vitellius is concerned with the 'defeated legions' (*victarum legionum*). They include VII and XI (67. 6), but at 66. 3 XIV is distinguished from the others, *praecipua . . . ferocia*, on the explicit ground that its *vires* had not been present at the battle. It was sent to Britain, whereas VII and XI were returned to their former camps. For those two cf. II. 86. 2, *dolorem iramque Bedriacensis pugnae retinentes*, III. 2. 15, *Pannonicae legiones deceptae magis quam victae*, and Antonius' challenge to them at III. 24. 3.

(c) The general statement by Mucianus at II. 76. 25, that Otho was not defeated *exercitus vi.*

To take the last point first, it must at once be admitted that in total number of effectives the Vitellian army, after Valens' arrival, was significantly the larger; and that the addition of the main bodies of VII

---

[10] What Wellesley, 41, says about the measures to be taken when a summons arrived, enabling a detachment to start quickly but not the whole body, seems convincing.

[11] On the Moesian legions see II. 46. 16 n.

Galbiana and XI to the Othonian strength[12] would have affected the disparity but little. T. says the initial expeditionary forces of the Vitellians totalled 70,000 men, and that Valens later picked up the whole of I Italica and the eight Batavian cohorts.[13] Even if these figures be exaggerated, and even if we allow for battle losses, the Vitellians at the time of the final battle must have disposed of well over 55,000 men, which is the most we can allow to the Othonians.[14]

But what must count in a full-dress civil-war battle is the weight of heavy armour, i.e. the legionaries and the praetorians. The Vitellians had brought two whole legions, I Italica and XXI Rapax, the majority (but not the whole) of V Alaudae, and vexillations, which we can assume to have been 2,000 strong, from each of the other five Rhine legions: say 25,000 men in all. The Othonians too, on any view, had two whole legions, I Adiutrix and XIII Gemina, detachments from each of three more legions, and perhaps nine praetorian cohorts. That could mean, if we rate the effective strength of a praetorian cohort at 800 men, a total very near to that of the Vitellians. But the praetorians were by no means in full strength at the Bedriacum camp: some, presumably three cohorts, were with Flavius Sabinus south of Cremona, and many others were with Otho at Brixellum.[15] In this element of the armies, then, the Othonians would have been outnumbered by something like 4 to 3, if only the units listed so far be counted: the addition of 7,000 legionaries could have made a very great difference indeed. Even with parity in this arm, the attackers needed surprise, and surprise was not achieved:[16] so there had been *praepropera desperatio*.[17] But if these 7,000 men had been a week or so away from Bedriacum, it seems incredible that no one in the council of war is made to point out the case for a brief delay in those terms.

So we must ask whether a 'movement order' to the Danubian legions as late as 3 March is likely from what else we know, or can guess, about Otho's planning. Here we must consider first the chronology of his other movements, and secondly the speed with which he might have been able to establish an understanding with the Danubian commanders.

The Narbonese expedition, if the arguments at pp. 265ff. above be accepted, started in mid-February. The dispatch of Gallus and Spurinna

[12] Wellesley leaves the advanced guards of VII and XI at the foot of p. 41, and does not refer to them again. But I assume that he allows that these, and the *auxilia* of all four legions, had arrived.

[13] I. 61, with n., 64. 9 and 15.

[14] 11,000 legionaries, 7,200 praetorians, detachments (6,000) from three other legions, *auxilia* from four legions (say 16,500), 2,000 gladiators, and miscellaneous other troops (especially marines).

[15] II. 33, *is primus dies Othonianas partis adflixit*, with n.

[16] Wellesley, 50.

[17] II. 76. 26.

to North Italy occurred (as Wellesley, 47, says, and I agree) 'by the latter part of February'. Otho's own *profectio* was not until 14 March, I. 90, but there was no need for his presence in the North until the bulk of his available forces had been concentrated there; and there were good reasons for his appearing to discharge the functions of a *princeps* in Rome, I. 77 ff. But once he had set in hand the operation of defending North Italy, what reason was there for delaying the movements from Illyricum and Moesia? We must remember that he had originally hoped to prevent Caecina from entering Italy at all, I. 89, and even in a normal winter this would have meant meeting a serious challenge, by both Vitellian armies, by the second week of April.

Was the delay then due to the time needed to secure the full collaboration of the three Danubian provinces? If Otho could count on their loyalty only after Galba's death, a case might be established on those lines. Couriers could be quick, but there might be deliberations and misunderstandings at the other end. How far was Otho in a position to cut any deliberations short?

His *coup* against Galba succeeded only five days after Piso's adoption, and it is obvious that he had acquired almost commanding support within the praetorian guard before the decision about adoption was taken. But he would have needed support even had he won the adoption, for then Galba's choice would have been widely unpopular, I. 13. And whichever way the choice had gone, it would have been wise for him to seek allies among one or more groups of the provincial armies, since the troops in the city might not be able to sustain the new situation alone.

This he was in a good position to do. Cluvius Rufus in Spain looked a likely friend, and was so at first, but that complicated person, for reasons unknown to us, went over to a not entirely welcoming Vitellius, I. 76. 3, II. 65. 1. But in Pannonia there were more far-reaching possibilities. Otho had, directly after Galba's acclamation, begun working on any troops with whom he came in contact, and especially during the march from Spain, *iam pridem . . . in itinere, in agmine*, I. 28. 2 (see n. and *JRS* 1957 33) *Suet. O.* 4. Now the core of the army on that march was Galba's new legion VII, sent off to Carnuntum before 1 January under its new legate Antonius Primus, who later went out of his way to offer Otho his services.[18]

The events of 68–9 can hardly be understood unless intrigues fairly constantly took place between the more ambitious senators in Rome and those in the provinces, and between those in one province and those in another. Otho could have reached an understanding with

---

[18] *ducem se partibus offerens*, II. 86. 7, i.e. asking at least to be taken into the main council of war. But Otho by then had many senior counsellors. Antonius' later complaint need not mean that he did not reach Bedriacum in time, see n. ad loc.

Antonius well before 15 January. But there is a possibility of much
more. It was on the news of Nero's death, II. 5. 11, that Mucianus and
Vespasian composed their differences, and began to construct the unity
among the eastern governors and client kings of which we have signs
early in this Book. Similarly Vitellius' proclamation was the product of
both Rhine armies, and also of Britain and Raetia, I. 59. 12 with n. It
is surely not improbable that the same pattern of solidarity had been
established between the Danubian commanders, and that the direction
of their policy (as later in 69) was heavily influenced by the energetic
legate of legion VII. Support Galba, if he adopts Otho; support Otho,
if he does not.

If this was the situation when Otho came to power (the case for it of
course rests on speculation about the later months of 68, on which our
sources are notoriously lacking in detail), then a message to Poetovio,
despatched from Rome in the evening of 15 January could have been
confident and effective. Otho could indeed have received a declaration
of support involving all three Danubian provinces by 26 January, I. 76.
1, and his 'movement orders' could have been sent at any time
thereafter. Moreover we could feel sure that the movement of VII from
Carnuntum would have been as rapid as possible, following XIII with
very *modica intervalla*. As to legion XI from Burnum, there is no
compelling reason to think that it was as hesitant on this occasion as it
turned out to be for the Flavian war, and it had no greater distance to
cover than had XIII from Poetovio.

There remains the point from which Wellesley starts, namely that
T.'s very full description of the Othonian deployment at the Castores
battle includes no Danubian legionary troops other than the *vexillum* of
XIII, and that Paulinus at that battle could count on *nullum retro
subsidium*, II. 26. 15. But in the interval of at least a week between
Castores and the advance from Bedriacum there was time for the
arrival of the *vexilla* of VII, XI, and XIV, and of the main bodies of
XIII, VII, and XI. That all those forces had arrived by 14 April is what
the passages classified on p. 270f. above seem to prove was Tacitus' view
of the matter.[19] The later part of this note is designed to show that he
was very likely right.

[19] Add II. 11. 6 ff., on which Wellesley, 43, agrees that *tarditas* is ascribed only to XIV.

INDEX

(Personal names, except for those of emperors and of Greek and Latin writers, are so far as possible listed under the *gentilicium*. All dates are A.D.)